Examining Deviance Experimentally

Selected Readings

examining deviance experimentally

Selected Readings

Edited by
DARRELL J. STEFFENSMEIER
North Carolina State University
and
ROBERT M. TERRY
University of Akron

ALFRED PUBLISHING CO., INC.

Library of Congress Catalog Card Number: 74-32334
ISBN: 0-88284-021-5

Printed in the United States of America

Library of Congress Cataloging in Publication Data
Steffensmeier, Darrell J   1942-   Comp.
    Examining deviance experimentally.
    Includes bibliographical references.
    1. Deviant behavior—Addresses, essays, lectures.
I.   Terry, Robert M., 1936-   joint comp. II. Title.
[DNLM: 1. Social behavior disorders—Collected works.
WM600 S817e]
HM291.S817   301.6'2   74-32334
ISBN 0-88284-021-5

Alfred Publishing Co., Inc.
75 Channel Drive, Port Washington, N.Y., 11050

Preface

The inherently interesting nature of deviance has been both a blessing and a curse to behavioral scientists. The blessings have been bestowed indirectly through the attraction of large numbers of students to our courses and more directly through the power and prestige we have attained because we have been able to convince many that we really do know quite a bit about persons who are different or who do different things. The curses have been accorded because we have been unable to deliver on many of the claims that we have made and because we have often even succeeded in making our inherently interesting subject matter boring and distasteful to those who were potentially eager to learn. The latter is probably more due to the complexity of the subject matter and our attempts to be intellectually honest than to our style of presentation, our use of films and other materials to illustrate what we are interested in or our failure to maintain contact with what is currently taking place within our society.

In this book we hope to select, organize and present materials in such a way that we can add to our blessings and at the same time eliminate some of our curses. We recognize that deviance is a complex phenomenon, but we think that just makes it more interesting. We wish to maintain intellectual integrity, but in doing so we argue that this is best maintained by the careful application of rigorous scientific methods. We think that we really do know something about deviance and that we know how to accumulate significantly more knowledge. We also think that in this volume we have reproduced materials that will convince the student of deviance that rigorous research and critical thinking are not boring and distasteful.

The guiding framework that we have used in order to accomplish the foregoing is that of the interactionist-labeling perspective on deviance. This perspective views deviance as an outgrowth of interpersonal processes and is principally concerned with the processes by which deviant identities are established and maintained. It seeks to study the processes of and responses to social differentiation, with special attention focused on the consequences of these for the person's self-attitudes and interpersonal relations. This necessitates studying not only alleged deviants, but also the reactions of others and, especially, the reactions of social control and helping agencies established to deal with deviance.

The conceptualization of deviance in an interactionist-labeling framework provides a basis for understanding not only deviance, but also behavior in general. It is a general perspective that emphasizes (a) the collective nature of human activity including the importance of symbols, language and gestures in the formation of social action; (b) the dynamics of interaction between self and others wherein personality is seen as generated through interaction and consists of "self-other" systems; and (c) the processual and emergent nature of human interaction, and the importance of seeing reality from the point of view of those engaged in action.

Within the interactionist-labeling tradition much of the direction of research and writing has moved toward description, participant-observation and analysis of behavior within the phenomenological perspective. While many superior works in sociology have been carried out using these techniques and procedures, many others have resembled low-grade journalism projects. Especially noteworthy have been attempts to do cute things and to avoid at all costs writing about and studying persons or behavior that have never been studied by anyone else before. At times these studies have broken significant new ground but frequently they have held back the accumulation of knowledge because of the tendency to avoid any kinds of verificational research.

This book, while staying in the interactionist-labeling camp, attempts to strike out in another direction—that of taking advantage of rigorous statistical and methodological procedures and developments and applying them to the study of deviance. The study of deviance is implicitly at least regarded as being more amenable to the "softer" methods of research. We regard this assumption as erroneous and attempt in this book to demonstrate the utility of experimental procedures to empirical research. This is not an attempt to negate or denigrate the softer methods, but is an attempt to restore some semblance of balance and to provide some basis of encouragement to others to use experimental strategies in conducting deviance research.

It should be noted that a fundamental weakness of nonexperimental approaches (whether "hard" or "soft") lies in the problem of specifying cause-

and-effect relationships. Our preference is for the development of research strategies that are better able to test hypotheses about casual relationships and the major value of experimental research rests in doing precisely this. This should become clearer to the student after he has gone through the readings.

Unfortunately, there is no single way of building and conducting an experiment. The studies included in this volume provide a variety of illustrations of how experimental studies might be done. The plan of the book is such that we have conveniently divided the studies into interview experiments, quasi-experiments, laboratory experiments and field experiments. Each of these constitutes a separate section in the book. Editors' notes accompany each of the studies included and attempt to interpret the reports within the interactionist-labeling perspective and to indicate their overall significance for studying deviance. Also included is a section on the nature of deviance. This precedes the experimental sections and largely serves as an introduction to the book as a whole.

A final comment has to do with additional criteria used in selecting studies to be included in this volume. We have tried to choose studies that are embedded within a theoretical framework and thereby highlight the interrelationship between good theory and sound research. We have also tried to locate studies that address themselves to a variety of substantive issues and interests. While we by no means claim to include research studies covering all topics in the deviance area, we have brought together a fairly broad spectrum of issue-related studies. We were, of course, limited by the availability of relevant published materials. Finally, and perhaps of special relevance to those offering or taking courses in deviance, social psychology or research methods, we have attempted to select materials that are both fun and interesting to read. If we have accomplished only some of our objectives we will have succeeded.

Contents

Part I

On the Nature of Deviance

DARRELL J. STEFFENSMEIER
and
ROBERT M. TERRY

On the Nature
of Deviance

Attempts to understand "deviant behavior" and "deviance" have led behav-·
ioral scientists down a variety of rather tortuous paths. Each has produced
varying increments in knowledge, but all have failed to result in the kinds of
breakthroughs or definitive answers so intensely sought after. It is apparent
that the conceptual and theoretical structure of deviance analysis requires a
major overhaul before more than tentative answers to crucial questions about
problematic behavior can be developed.

Despite the many ambiguities and confusions in theoretical statements on
deviant behavior, it should be recognized that deviance research has at least
eliminated obviously incorrect answers and cast considerable doubt on others.
Accumulating evidence has moved the study of deviance away from fixed
psychological and physiological states into the realm of the social and interpersonal. In addition, it is increasingly being recognized that traditional ways
of defining and measuring deviance have resulted in obvious shortcomings in
generating solid empirical evidence which, in turn, has contributed to what
have often been rather grossly inaccurate theoretical statements about deviant
phenomena. Consequently, it goes almost without saying that new definitions,
assumptions, methodological strategies and conceptual orientations need to
be developed to reflect the social nature of deviant phenomena and its distribution in the real world.

How we define deviance is significant in that it sets the stage for the kinds
of theoretical formulations we develop, the kinds of research questions we
ask, the empirical evidence we gather, the methodological procedures we use
and, ultimately, the kinds of interpretations and answers we provide. While

definitions are neither right nor wrong, they are more or less useful. Our objective in this section is to provide a definition of deviance which is of greater usefulness than those commonly used by behavioral scientists. Before doing so, however, it is necessary to detail several obvious deficiencies in some current conceptions of deviance.

Probably the most widely used conception of deviance is that it is norm-violating behavior. The result of this definition usually involves attempting to discover whether or not persons have violated a norm or set of norms. A major difficulty in this definition arises in connection with the concept of norm. Adherence to one norm might (and frequently does) involve violation of another norm. In a complex society much of the behavior engaged in by most people violates the norms of some other group somewhere in the same society. Thus, the definition requires that one use particular sets of norms as the standards by which to judge behavior and to treat as irrelevant other sets of norms. In practice, this results in using the norms of the politically powerful, the norms that have been codified into law (e.g., criminal law), the norms of the majority (although this is rarely defined), or, in summary, the norms of the "conventional" society as the standard. That the result is to limit the distribution of deviance and the population of deviants to particular segments of the society should be obvious. Given such a definition it is not surprising that the less powerful and most disadvantaged groups within the society should be most heavily involved in doing deviant things.

Another problem arises in traditional conceptions of norms. Norms are frequently dealt with by behavioral scientists as rules that exist "out there" and which are used as the orienting perspectives by the actor in determining his course of action. Actually, however, we know that many norms are implicit and taken-for-granted and that at times we may be unaware of their "existence" unless and until someone has engaged in a course of action or has presented certain characteristics or attributes that are regarded as different, unusual, out of the ordinary or in other ways exceptional. A more appropriate conception of norms, then, might be one that regards norms as rules that are developed in the course of interaction with others, and that are selected and applied frequently (or even usually) in a retrospective manner to behavior that has been differentiated out from other sets of behavior which may be regarded as norm-irrelevant. This perspective, of course, requires that one include social audiences in the study of deviance, as it is the audience along with the actor himself who are developing, selecting and applying norms.

Another aspect of traditional definitions of deviance is to construe as deviance only those phenomena that are "undesirable." Thus, subjects for research include prostitution, mental illness, crime and delinquency, homosexuality, suicide and the like. This is the case in spite of the fact that even in the most elementary of textbooks in the behavioral sciences we inform our students that one may deviate from norms in positive and negative directions and that one accrues positive and negative sanctions as a consequence of such deviations. Increasingly, behavioral scientists are paying lip service to the existence of positive deviance, but have had considerable difficulty in going beyond the mere statement of its existence. This is in large part due to definitions of deviance and the consequences of using these definitions in the design and development of research on deviance. Generally existing definitions of deviance place the phenomenon of positive deviance outside the realm of discourse. Conceptually, for example, we have no commonly used notions to handle "supra-conventional" behavior whereas we have numerous notions that enable us to speak intelligently about "sub-conventional" behavior.

The similarities between positively and negatively evaluated deviant phenomena are striking. The Congressional Medal of Honor winner who returned to his home in the rural midwest several years ago found that his heroism had made him into another person in the eyes of his fellow townsfolk. After a short period of time he re-entered the military because life as a hero was intolerable. Positive deviations such as becoming heavyweight champion of the world, an Olympic gold medal winner, making it into major league baseball, being a professional quarterback or even more widespread phenomena such as getting promoted on the job, becoming a college graduate or getting married are valued activities that result in the imposition of new standards for behavior, different rights, privileges and obligations and the differential response of members of the social audience to one's behavior, some of which might have gone unnoticed before. Changing expectations and obligations along with differential responses constitute some of the key things that happen to people who do desirable as well as undesirable things. A conception of deviance, then, might seem to be much more useful if it includes the possibility of including positive as well as negative deviance.

While the foregoing merely touches upon the variability and complexity of deviance, it seems appropriate to define deviance for our purposes at this time. *Deviance consists of differentially valued phenomena.* What we are including in this definition is best illustrated by dealing with each of the three elements in turn.

Differentially refers to the idea that the phenomenon must be separated out from other phenomena as something worth noticing or attending to. The usual manner in which phenomena are differentiated is in terms of naming, although there are considerable differences in the ease with which phenomena may be named. An act of theft, for example, might be readily differentiated and named whereas considerable difficulty may exist in differentiating acts of "mental illness." Acts of heroism can often be differentiated rather easily whereas considerable difficulties are likely to exist in identifying and naming numerous acts of upward mobility. Furthermore, there are difficulties in determining how and when acts become differentiated in one manner as opposed to another. The point at which one's drinking behavior is defined as symptomatic of alcoholism rather than signifying one who drinks a lot is an example. The college professor and his students might be aware of his being a "poor lecturer" but are unable to determine why this is the case until some observant student brings to their attention that the professor has used the same cliche over one hundred times in the course of each fifty-minute lecture. Or, the professor might believe that his lecture is particularly entertaining until a student indicates that the smiles on the faces of his fellow classmates are more due to the professor's open fly rather than the humor and wit of the lecture material. When such designations are made, by the actor or audience, the phenomenon is differentiated. For deviance to exist, we argue that differentiation must take place.

Valuated specifies that phenomena which are differentiated must also be appraised in hierarchically arrayed terms ranging from optimally desirable (good, worthwhile, beneficial, etc.) to optimally undesirable (bad, terrible, horrendous, etc.). While philosophical arguments may abound in terms of whether or not phenomena may even exist unless they are differentiated, most phenomena are not necessarily or usually valuated and it is this valuation that distinguishes the grist of deviance from the rest of human phenomena. Acts or attributes that are differentiated become "deviant" only when the actor or others (or both) judge them in terms of their relative desirability. Thus, watching television frequently is not usually valuated behavior, but in some contexts it may become such. Positively, watching television may become valuated favorably if children do so when their parents are entertaining adults and do not wish to be disturbed. Negatively, the child who watches television rather than completing his homework may incur the wrath of teacher and parent. Most of the time, however, watching television is simply norm-irrelevant and remains non-valuated. For deviance to exist, valuation must take place.

Phenomena is a necessary ingredient of the definition so that we may appropriately include both behavior (what persons do) as well as attributes (what persons are or have). Being black, deaf, physically handicapped or exceptionally beautiful are similar in terms of their implications for the study of deviance to stealing, cheating or performing heroic deeds. A female measuring 46-24-36 presents attributes which greatly differ from the female measuring 24-24-36, but in both instances, to the extent that each constitutes differentially valuated phenomena, these females are potential subjects in the study of deviance. In societies where concern with female breast size is non-existent these females would not be of interest to the study of deviance. We should point out, however, that the argument that behavior and attributes are similar, does not imply that they are identical. Moreover, whether phenomena are deemed volitional or non-volitional may make for significant differences in the interpretations and actions taken by audiences, as well as for the actors themselves, and thus alter the likelihood that the phenomena will be differentially valuated.

Our definition of deviance is, as most definitions are, a "sensitizing concept." And rather than prejudge the results of deviance analysis and research along the lines suggested by our definition, we regard it as advantageous to be inclusive at this stage in the study of deviance. Thus, whether or not this definition is too imperialistic or too inclusive is a matter for subsequent deviance research to decide.

The definition of deviance as differentially valuated phenomena needs to be viewed in terms of its utility. If worthwhile, it should point out the kinds of theoretical and empirical questions that will enable us to add to our knowledge of human behavior in general and, in particular, of deviance. Let's examine, then, some of the consequences that flow from this definition of deviance, in particular focusing on the kinds of questions it raises.

1. How do attributes and behaviors become differentiated? How do they become differentiated in the manner that they do? In ordinary day-to-day settings many instances of behavior are treated in a taken-for-granted context and remain unnoticed and unworthy of attention. Other instances of behavior are differentiated quickly and obviously as events of extraordinary import. Some phenomena that are differentiated become the grounds for mobilization of action on the part of large numbers of actors. Others are quickly ignored or normalized and thereby remain as passing events that are quickly forgotten. In some instances, terminology and categorization schemes exist and the behavior is quickly named and classified whereas in other instances considerable effort on the part of numerous parties may be involved in attempts to appropriately differentiate the behavior (e.g., mental illness). How this takes place, why, who is involved, and in what contexts are crucial issues in the study of deviance.

2. How are behavior and attributes valuated and what are the processes by which valuation takes place? How do people, for example, decide that murdering a president is worse than murdering an ordinary citizen and, given this, why do they do so? In American society bribing an athlete is more severely penalized than most kinds of assault and mistreatment of animals may incur more severe penalties than the mistreatment of children. What can we learn from these apparent differences in valuation? Why is the rape of a white female by a black male valuated as more undesirable than the rape of a black female by a white male? Why is murdering a man on the street more undesirable than murdering a man whom one finds in bed with his wife? How these distinctions develop through time in the course of interaction is signifi-

cant, as well as the processes by which they are negotiated and applied.

3. Who differentially valuates phenomena and how do differentiation agents differ? What audiences are involved in determining whether or not the actor's behavior or attributes constitute deviance? How do audiences differ in terms of their willingness to differentially valuate particular behaviors and attributes, and what social and personal characteristics distinguish between "highly tolerant" and "less tolerant" audiences? Some deviant phenomena are assigned to the province of formal social control agencies. Others are dealt with informally by individuals carrying out the ordinary functions of living. What are the implications of formal and informal responses to deviant phenomena—of being told, for example, to discontinue acts of theft by one's parent versus being arrested for theft by the police? What differences are there between those acts of heroism that are praised by one's spouse, and then forgotten, and those whose heroic deeds are signified by a ticker-tape parade in New York City? What are the implications for self-labeling if the actor serves as his own audience? What difference does it make if one worries about undesirable behavior that he engages in privately and secretly, or is told by a psychiatrist that he is suffering from a deep-seated mental affliction?

4. Having decided that particular behaviors and attributes constitute deviance, what are the behavioral implications of differentiation processes for both actors and audiences? How does the audience transform the actor's identity, both personal and social, from a normal to a deviant one? What differences exist between those whose deviance is deemed volitional as opposed to those for whom it is regarded as non-volitional? Many individuals (perhaps all) engage in "deviant behavior" or possess "deviant attributes," but only some become deviants. How does one move from the point of doing deviant things or having deviant attributes to being chosen or singled out as a deviant? What kinds of contingencies operate to prevent some individuals who engage in deviant activities or foster deviant attributes from becoming deviants while others do in fact become deviants? Most importantly, perhaps, what are the consequences of differentiation and labeling for self-attitudes and interpersonal relations? What actions do others take on the basis of the differentiation and public redefinition of the person? How does a person judged to be a deviant react to this differentiation? To what extent does he realign his self-conception to accord with the deviant role assigned? What effect do the social cues and responses, in contrast to more official reactions, of the deviant's immediate interactional context have on the redefinition of self? What changes in group memberships result for the individual labeled deviant? Do differentiation processes move the individual into a deviant subculture and to what extent does the deviant subculture provide opportunities for role performance consistent with the symbolic processes instigated by the labelers? How does the labeling affect potential deviant careers and what are implica-

tions for secondary deviance? Other questions raised by this difinition include: How does the person whose deviance is known only to himself control
such information and manage his relationships with others? In turn, how does
the person labeled deviant negotiate with others? How does he, for example,
present himself to audience members in such a way as to provide them with
alternative interpretations of the valuated phenomena, be it behaviors or attributes, that are the object of the differentiation? And then, how do members
of the audience deal with the deviant's attempts to counter their differentiation and labeling of him?

Answers to these and still other questions that are of paramount importance for the study of deviance are possible only if and when behavioral scientists recognize that deviance is different from what they have traditionally
thought to be the case, recognize that deviance is broader and more inclusive
than that which they have been willing to consider and recognize that deviance has more in common with ordinary, non-deviant behavior than they
have commonly believed. The complexities are so great, however, that even
reorientation of thinking is unlikely to occur for some time, a reorientation
that is drastically needed if major breakthroughs in knowledge of deviant
phenomena are likely to take place.

The student is advised to consider the foregoing questions as he proceeds
through the remainder of this book. The definition of deviance we have developed and the questions raised provide an orienting framework for the editors'
notes accompanying each of the selections as well as for many of the selections themselves. That resolution of the issues we have considered in this
section is far from achieved will be obvious. Nevertheless, the excitement of
grappling with some of these significant issues by the utilization of imagina-
tive and rigorous research designs holds considerable hope for the future.

ALEXANDER LIAZOS

The Poverty of the Sociology of Deviance: Nuts, Sluts, and Preverts*

In recent years students of deviance have tried, ostensibly at least, to get away from the difficulties and intellectual sterility of what used to be called "social problems," "social pathology" or "social disorganization." These rubrics are now considered obsolete and the contemporary study of deviance supposedly avoids the "do-goodism, muckraking and world-saving" of which C. Wright Mills once accused sociologists.

Liazos, in his analysis of recent texts produced in the area of deviance, demonstrates that these attempts to become academically respectable have been less than successful. Discrepancies exist between what students of deviance claim they are doing and the works they actually produce. This includes, despite claims to the contrary, dealing with the same kinds of behavior that occupied the attention of more traditional theorists as well as an unwillingness or inability to really regard deviants as persons who are as good, similar and so forth, as the rest of us.

Reprinted by permission of *The Society for the Study of Social Problems*. From Alexander Liazos, "The Poverty of the Sociology of Deviance: Nuts, Sluts, and Perverts," *Social Problems*, 1972, 20:103-111.

*The subtitle of this paper came from two sources. a) A Yale undergraduate once told me that the deviance course was known among Yale students as "nuts and sluts." b) A former colleague of mine at Quinnipiac College, John Bancroft, often told me that the deviance course was "all about those preverts." When I came to write this paper, I discovered that these descriptions were correct and concise summaries of my argument. I thank both of them. I also want to thank Gordon Fellman for a very careful reading of the first draft of the manuscript, and for discussing with me the general and specific issues I raise here.

Also Liazos argues that significant areas of concern remain neglected by students of deviance in that they are largely unwilling or unable to fully implement their conceptions about human behavior. In terms that we discussed earlier (On the Nature of Deviance) standards of the conventional society have been adopted and the object of study has consisted of deviants located chiefly among the less powerful segments of society. Consequently, considerable time and effort has been allocated to the study of homosexuality, drug addiction and the like. In contrast, very little attention has been given to studying deviance initiated, participated in and fostered by the large corporations, the military establishment or the government itself. It is the latter, Liazos argues, that should be the "stuff" of deviance research and writing.

Finally, Liazos points out that while students of deviance generally maintain that designations of deviance are made by powerful persons acting toward less powerful individuals and that this feature of deviance labelling processes is fundamentally significant, these same students rarely utilize the concept of power and delineate its operation in the labelling process. Thus while power is held to be a most critical variable in understanding deviance processes, it is virtually ignored in existing writings on deviant phenomena.

C. Wright Mills left a rich legacy to sociology. One of his earliest, and best, contributions was "The Professional Ideology of Social Pathologists" (1943). In it, Mills argues that the small-town, middle-class background of writers of social problems textbooks blinded them to basic problems of social structure and power, and led them to emphasize melioristic, patchwork types of solutions to America's "problems." Moreover, these "problems," "ranging from rape in rural districts to public housing," were not explored systematically and theoretically; they were not placed in some larger political, historical, and social context. They were merely listed and decried.[1]

Since Mills wrote his paper, however, the field of social problems, social disorganization, and social pathology has undergone considerable changes. Beginning in the late 1940's and the 1950's, and culminating in the 1960's, the field of "deviance" has largely replaced the social problems orientation. This new field is characterized by a number of features which distinguish it from the older approach.[2]

First, there is some theoretical framework, even though it is often absent in edited collections (the Rubington and Weinberg [1968] edited books is an outstanding exception). Second, the small-town morality is largely gone. Writers claim they will examine the phenomena at hand—prostitution, juvenile delinquency, mental illness, crime, and others—objectively, not considering them as necessarily harmful and immoral. Third, the statements and theories of the field are based on much more extensive, detailed, and theoretically-oriented research than were those of the 1920's and 1930's. Fourth, writers attempt to fit their theories to some central theories, concerns, and problems found in the general field of sociology; they try to transcend mere moralizing.

The "deviant" has been humanized; the moralistic tone is no longer ever-present (although it still lurks underneath the explicit disavowals); and theoretical perspectives have been developed. Nevertheless, all is not well with the field of "deviance." Close examination reveals that writers of this field still do not try to relate the phenomena of "deviance" to larger social, historical, political, and economic contexts. The emphasis is still on the "deviant" and the "problems" *he* presents to himself and others, not on the society within which he emerges and operates.

I examined 16 textbooks in the field of "deviance," eight of them readers, to determine the state of the field. Theoretically, eight take the labelling-interactionist approach; three more tend to lean to that approach; four others argue for other orientations (anomie, structural-functional, etc.) or, among the readers, have an "eclectic" approach; and one (McCaghy, *et al.,* 1968) is a collection of biographical and other statements by "deviants" themselves, and thus may not be said to have a theoretical approach (although, as we shall see, the selection of the types of statements and "deviants" still implies an orientation and viewpoint). A careful examination of these textbooks revealed a number of ideological biases. These biases became apparent as much from what these books leave unsaid and unexamined, as from what they do say. The field of the sociology of deviance, as exemplified in these books, contains three important theoretical and political biases.

1. All writers, especially those of the labelling school, either state explicitly or imply that one of their main concerns is to *humanize* and *normalize* the "deviant" to show that he is essentially no different from us. But by the very emphasis on the "deviant" and his identity problems and sub-culture, the opposite effect may have been achieved. The persisting use of the label "deviant" to refer to the people we are considering is an indication of the feeling that these people are indeed different.

2. By the overwhelming emphasis on the "dramatic" nature of the usual types of "deviance"—prostitution, homosexuality, juvenile delinquency, and others—we have neglected to examine other, more serious and harmful forms of "deviance." I refer to *covert institutional violence* (defined and discussed below) which leads to such things as poverty and exploitation, war, such as Vietnam, unjust tax laws, racism and sexism, and so on, which cause psychic and material suffering for many Americans, black and white, men and women.

3. Despite explicit statements by these authors of the importance of *power* in the designation of what is "deviant," in their substantive analyses they show a profound unconcern with power and its implications. The really powerful, the upper classes and the power elite, those Gouldner (1968) calls the "top dogs," are left essentially unexamined by these sociologists of deviance.

Always implicit, and frequently explicit, is the aim of the labelling school to humanize and normalize the "deviant." Two statements by Becker and Matza are representative of this sentiment.

> In the course of our work and for who knows what private reasons, we fall into deep sympathy with the people we are studying, so that while the rest of society views them as unfit in one or another respect for the deference ordinarily accorded a fellow citizen, we believe that they are at least as good as anyone else, more sinned against than sinning (Becker, 1967:100-101).

> The growth of the sociological view of deviant phenomena involved, as major phases, the replacement of a correctional stance by an *appreciation* of the deviant subject, the tacit purging of a conception of pathology by a new stress on human *diversity*, and the erosion of a simple distinction between deviant and conventional phenomena, resulting from intimate familiarity of the world as it is, which yielded a more sophisticated view stressing *complexity* (Matza, 1969:10).

For a number of reasons, however, the opposite effect may have been achieved; and "deviants" still seem different. I began to suspect this reverse effect from the many essays and papers I read while teaching the "deviance" course. The clearest example is the repeated use of the word "tolerate." Students would write that we must not persecute homosexuals, prostitutes, mental patients, and others, that we must be "tolerant" of them. But one tolerates only those one considers less than equal, morally inferior, and weak; those equal to oneself, one accepts and respects; one does not merely allow them to exist, one does not "tolerate" them.

The repeated assertion that "deviants" are "at least as good as anyone else" may raise doubts that this is in fact the case, or that we believe it. A young woman who grew up in the South in the 1940's and 1950's told Quinn (1954:146): " 'You know, I think from the fact that I was told so often that I must treat colored people with consideration, I got the feeling that I could mistreat them if I wanted to.' " Thus with "deviants;" if in fact they are as good as we are, we would not need to remind everyone of this fact; we would take it for granted and proceed from there. But our assertions that "deviants" are not different may raise the very doubts we want to dispel. Moreover, why would we create a separate field of sociology for "deviants" if there were not something different about them? May it be that even we do not believe our statements and protestations?

The continued use of the word "deviant" (and its variants), despite its invidious distinctions and connotations, also belies our explicit statements on the equality of the people under consideration. To be sure, some of the authors express uneasiness over the term. For example, we are told,

> In our use of this term for the purpose of sociological investigation, we emphasize that we do not attach any value judgement, explicitly or implicitly, either to the word "deviance" or to those describing their behavior or beliefs in this book (McCaghy, *et al.,* 1968:v).

Lofland (1969:2, 9-10) expresses even stronger reservations about the use of the term, and sees clearly the sociological, ethical, and political problems raised by its continued use. Yet, the title of his book is *Deviance and Identity.* Szasz (1970: xxv-xxvi) has urged that we abandon use of the term:

> Words have lives of their own. However much sociologists insist that the term "deviant" does not diminish the worth of the person or group so categorized, the implication of inferiority adheres to the word. Indeed, sociologists are not wholly exempt from blame: they describe addicts and homosexuals as deviants, but never Olympic champions or Nobel Prize winners. In fact, the term is rarely applied to people with admired characteristics, such as great wealth, superior skills, or fame—whereas it is often applied to those with despised characteristics, such a poverty, lack of marketable skills, or infamy.

> The term "social deviants". . . does not make sufficiently explicit—as the terms "scapegoat" or "victim" do—that majorities usually categorize persons or groups as "deviant" in order to set them apart as inferior beings and to justify their social control, oppression, persecution, or even complete destruction.

Terms like victimization, persecution, and oppression are more accurate descriptions of what is really happening. But even Gouldner (1968), in a masterful critique of the labelling school, while describing social conflict, calls civil-rights and anti-war protesters "political deviants." He points out clearly that these protesters are resisting openly, not slyly, conditions they abhor. Gouldner is discussing political struggles, opression and resistance to oppression; conflicts over values, morals, interests, and power; and victimization. Naming such protesters "deviants," even if *political* deviants, is an indication of the deep penetration within our minds of certain prejudices and orientations.

Given the use of the term, the definition and examples of "deviant" reveal underlying sentiments and views. Therefore, it is important that we redefine drastically the entire field, especially since it is a flourishing one: "Because younger sociologists have found deviance such a fertile and exciting field for their own work, and because students share these feelings, deviance promises to become an even more important area of sociological research and theory in the coming years" (Douglas, 1970a:3).

The lists and discussions of "deviant" acts and persons reveal the writers' biases and sentiments. These are acts which, "like robbery, burglary or rape [are] of a simple and dramatic predatory nature . . ." (The President's Commission on Law Enforcement and the Administration of Justice, in Dinitz, et al., 1969:105). All 16 texts, without exception, concentrate on actions and persons of a "dramatic predatory nature," on "preverts." This is true of both the labelling and other schools. The following are examples from the latter:

> Ten different types of deviant behavior are considered: juvenile delinquency, adult crime, prison sub-cultures, homosexuality, prostitution, suicide, homocide, alcoholism, drug addiction and mental illness (Rushing, 1969: preface).

> Traditionally, in American sociology the study of deviance has focused on criminals, juvenile delinquents, prostitutes, suicides, the mentally ill, drug users and drug addicts, homosexuals, and political and religious radicals (Lefton, et al., 1968:v).

> Deviant behavior is esentially violation of certain types of group norms; a deviant act is behavior which is proscribed in a certain way. [It must be] in a disapproved direction, and of sufficient degree to exceed the tolerance limit of the community. . . . [such as] delinquency and crime, prostitution, homosexual behavior, drug addiction, alcoholism, mental disorders, suicide, marital and family maladjustment, discrimination against minority groups, and, to a lesser degree, role problems of old age (Clinard, 1968:28).

Finally, we are told that these are some examples of deviance every society must deal with: ". . . mental illness, violence, theft, and sexual misconduct, as well as . . . other similarly difficult behavior" (Dintz, et al., 1969:3).

The list stays unchanged with the authors of the labelling school.

> . . . in Part I, "The Deviant Act," I draw rather heavily on certain studies of homicide, embezzlement, "naive" check forgery, suicide and a few other acts . . . in discussing the assumption of deviant identity (Part II) and the assumption of normal identity (Part III), there is heavy reference to certain studies of paranoia, "mental illness" more generally, and Alcoholics Anonymous and Synanon (Lofland, 1969:34).

> Homicide, suicide, alcoholism, mental illness, prostitution, and homosexuality are among the forms of behavior typically called deviant, and they are among the kinds of behavior that will be analyzed (Lofland, 1969:1). Included among my respondents were political radicals of the far left and the far right, homosexuals, militant blacks, convicts and mental hospital patients, mystics, narcotic addicts, LSD and Marijuana users, illicit drug dealers, delinquent boys, racially mixed couples, hippies, health-food users, and bohemian artists and village eccentrics (Simmon, 1969:10).

Simmons (1969:27, 29, 31) also informs us that in his study of stereo-types of "deviants" held by the public, these are the types he gave to people: homosexuals, beatniks, adulterers, marijuana smokers, political radicals, alcoholics, prostitutes, lesbians, ex-mental patients, atheists, ex-convicts, in-tellectuals, and gamblers. In Lemert (1967) we find that except for the three introductory (theoretical) chapters, the substantive chapters cover the fol-lowing topics: alcohol drinking, four; check forgers, three; stuttering, two; and mental illness, two. Matza (1969) offers the following list of "deviants" and their actions that "must be appreciated if one adheres to a naturalistic perspective:" paupers, robbers, motorcycle gangs, prostitutes, drug addicts, promiscuous homosexuals, thieving Gypsies, and "free love" Bohemians (1969:16). Finally, Douglas' collection (1970a) covers these forms of "deviance:" abortion, nudism, topless barmaids, prostitutes, homosexuals, violence (motorcycle and juvenile gangs), shoplifting, and drugs.

The omissions from these lists are staggering. The covert, institutional forms of "deviance" are nowhere to be found. Reading these authors, one would not know that the most destructive use of violence in the last decade has been the war in Vietnam, in which the U.S. has heaped unprecedented suffering on the people and their land; more bombs have been dropped in Vietnam than in the entire World War II. Moreover, the robbery of the cor-porate world—through tax breaks, fixed prices, low wages, pollution of the environment, shoddy goods, etc.—is passed over in our fascination with "dramatic and predatory" actions. Therefore, we are told that "while they certainly are of no greater social importance to us than such subjects as banking and accounting (or military violence), subjects such as marijuana use and motorcycle gangs are of far greater interest to most of us. While it is only a coincidence that our scientific interests correspond with the emotional inter-est in deviants, it is a happy coincidence and, I believe, one that should be encouraged" (Douglas, 1970a:5). Add Matza (1969:17), in commenting on the "appreciative sentiments" of the "naturalistic spirit," elaborates on the same theme: "We do not for a moment wish that we could rid ourselves of deviant phenomena. We are intrigued by them. They are an intrinsic, inerad-icable, and vital part of human society."

An effort is made to transcend this limited view and substantive concern with dramatic and predatory forms of "deviance." Becker (1964:3) claims that the new (labelling) deviance no longer studies only "delinquents and drug addicts, though these classical kinds of deviance are still kept under observation." It increases its knowledge "of the processes of deviance by studying physicians, people with physical handicaps, the mentally deficient, and others whose doings were formerly not included in the area." The power-ful "deviants" are still left untouched, however. This is still true with another aspect of the new deviance. Becker (1964:4) claims that in the labelling perspective "we focus attention on the other people involved in the process. We pay attention to the role of the non-deviant as well as that of the deviant." But we see that it is the ordinary non-deviants and the low-level agents of social control who receive attention, not the powerful ones (Gouldner, 1968).

In fact, the emphasis is more on the *subculture* and *identity* of the "deviants" themselves rather than on their oppressors and persecutors. To be sure, in varying degrees all authors discuss the agents of social control, but the fascination and emphasis are on the "deviant" himself. Studies of prisons and prisoners, for example, focus on prison subcultures and prisoner rehabilitation; there is little or no consideration of the social, political, economic, and power conditions which consign people to prisons. Only now are we beginning to realize that most prisoners are *political prisoners*—that their "criminal" actions (whether against individuals, such as robbery, or conscious political acts against the state) result largely from current social and political conditions, and are not the work of "disturbed" and "psychopathic" personalities. This realization came about largely because of the writings of political prisoners themselves: Malcolm X (1965), Eldridge Cleaver (1968), and George Jackson (1970), among others.[3]

In all these books, notably those of the labelling school, the concern is with the "deviant's" subculture and identity: his problems, motives, fellow victims, etc. The collection of memoirs and apologies of "deviants" in their own words (McCaghy, *et al.,* 1968) covers the lives and identities of prevert deviants:" prostitutes, nudists, abortionists, criminals, drug users, homosexuals, the mentally ill, alcoholics, and suicides. For good measure, some "militant deviants" are thrown in: Black Muslims, the SDS, and a conscientious objector. But one wonders about other types of "deviants:" how do those who perpetrate the covert institutional violence in our society view themselves? Do they have identity problems? How do they justify their actions? How did the robber barons of the late 19th century steal, fix laws, and buy politicians six days of the week and go to church on Sunday? By what process can people speak of body counts and kill ratios with cool objectivity? On these and smilar questions, this book (and all others)[4] provides no answers; indeed, the editors seem unaware that such questions should or could be raised.

Becker (1964), Rubington and Weinberg (1968), Matza (1969), and Bell (1971) also focus on the identity and subculture of "prevert deviants." Matza, in discussing the assumption of "deviant identity," uses as examples, and elaborates upon, thieves and marijuana users. In all these books, there are occasional references to and questions about the larger social and political structure, but these are not explored in any depth; and the emphasis remains on the behavior, identity, and rehabilitation of the "deviant" himself. This bias continues in the latest book which, following the fashions of the times, has chapters on hippies and militant protesters (Bell 1971).

Even the best of these books, Simons' *Deviants* (1969), is not free of the overwhelming concentration of the "deviant" and his identity. It is the most sympathetic and balanced presentation of the lives of "deviants:" their joys, sorrows, and problems with the straight world and fellow victims. Simmons demystifies the processes of becoming "deviant" and overcoming "deviance." He shows, as well as anyone does, that these victims *are* just like us; and the differences they possess and the suffering they endure are imposed upon them. Ultimately, however, Simmons too falls prey to the three biases shown in the work of others: a) the "deviants" he considers are only of the "prevert" type; b) he focuses mostly on the victim and his identity, not on the persecutors; and c) the persecutors he does discuss are of the middle-level variety, the agents of more powerful others and institutions.

Because of these biases, there is an implicit, but very clear, acceptance by these authors of the current definitions of "deviance." It comes about because they concentrate their attention on those who have been *successfully labelled as "deviant,"* and not on those who break laws, fix laws, violate ethical and moral standards, harm individuals and groups, etc., but who either are able to hide their actions, or, when known, can deflect criticism, labelling, and punishment. The following are typical statements which reveal this bias.

". . . no act committed by members of occupational groups [such as white-collar crimes], however unethical, should be considered as crime unless it is punishable by the state in some way" (Clinard, 1968:269). Thus, if some people can manipulate laws so that their unethical and destructive acts are not "crimes," we should cater to their power and agree that they are not criminals.

Furthermore, the essence of the labelling school encourages this bias, despite Becker's (1963:14) assertion that ". . . insofar as a scientist uses 'deviant' to refer to any rule-breaking behavior and takes as his subjects of study only those who have been *labelled* deviant, he will be hampered by the disparities between the two categories." But as the following statements from Becker and others show, this is in fact what the labelling school does do.

Deviance is "created by society . . . *social groups create deviance by making the rules whose infraction constitutes deviance,* and by applying those rules to particular people and labelling them as outsiders" (Becker, 1963: 8-9). Clearly, according to this view, in cases where no group has labelled another, no matter what the other group or individuals have done, there is nothing for the sociologist to study and dissect.

> Rules are not made automatically. Even though a practice may be harmful in an objective sense to the group in which it occurs, the harm needs to be discovered and pointed out. People must be made to feel that something ought to be done about it (Becker, 1963:162).

What is important for the social analyst is not what people are by his lights or by his standards, but what it is that people construe one another and themselves to be for what reasons and with what consequences (Lofland, 1969:35).

... deviance is in the eyes of the beholder. For deviance to become a social fact, somebody must perceive an act, person, situation, or event as a departure from social norms, must categorize that perception, must report the perception to others, must get them to accept this definition of the situation, and must obtain a response that conforms to this definition. Unless all these requirements are met, deviance as a social fact does not come into being (Rubington and Weinberg, 1968:v).

The implication of these statements is that the sociologist accepts current, successful definitions of what is "deviant" as the only ones worthy of his attention. To be sure, he may argue that those labelled "deviant" are not really different from the rest of us, or that there is no act intrinsically "deviant," etc. By concentrating on cases of successful labelling, however, he will not penetrate beneath the surface to look for other forms of "deviance"—undetected stealing, violence, and destruction. When people are not powerful enough to make the "deviant" label stick on others, we overlook these cases. But is it not as much a *social fact,* even though few of us pay much attention to it, that the corporate economy kills and maims more, is more violent, than any violence committed by the poor (the usual subjects of studies of violence)? By what reasoning and necessity is the "violence" of the poor in the ghettoes more worthy of our attention than the military bootcamps which numb recruits from the horrors of killing the "enemy" ("Oriental human beings," as we learned during the Calley trial)? But because these acts are not labelled "deviant," because they are covert, institutional, and normal their "deviant" qualities are overlooked and they do not become part of the province of the sociology of deviance. Despite their best liberal intentions, these sociologists seem to perpetuate the very notions they think they debunk, and others of which they are unaware.

Notes

1. Bend and Vogenfanger (1964) examined social problems textbooks of the early 1960's; they found there was little theory or emphasis on social structure in them.

2. What I say below applies to the "labelling-interactionist" school of deviance of Becker, Lemert, Erikson, Matza, and others: to a large degree, however, most of my comments also apply to the other schools.

3. The first draft of this paper was completed in July, 1971. The killing of George Jackson at San Quentin on August 21, 1971, which many people see as a political murder, and the Attica prisoner rebellion of early September, 1971, only strengthen the argument about political prisoners. Two things became clear: 1)

Not only a few "radicals," but many prisoners (if not a majority) see their fate as the outcome of political forces and decisions, and themselves as political prisoners (see Fraser, 1971). Robert Chrisman's argument (in Frazer, 1971) points to such a conclusion clearly: "To maintain that all black offenders are, by their actions, politically correct, is dangerous romanticism. Black antisocial behavior must be seen in and of its own terms and corrected for enhancement of the black community." But there is a political aspect, for black prisoners' conditions "derives from the political inequity of black people in America. A black prisoner's crime may or may not have been a political action against the state, but the state's actions against him is always political." I would stress that the same is true of most white prisoners, for they come mostly from the exploited poorer classes and groups. 2) The state authorities, the political rulers, by their deeds if not their words, see such prisoners as political men and threats. The death of George Jackson, and the brutal crushing of the Attica rebellion, attest to the authorities' realization, and fear, that here were no mere riots with prisoners letting off steam, but authentic political actions, involving groups and individuals conscious of their social position and exploitation.

4. With the exception of E. C. Hughes, in Becker (1964).

ERVING GOFFMAN

Deviations and Deviance

The following selection is taken from Erving Goffman's work *Stigma: Notes on the Management of Spoiled Identity*, a book which deals at some length with the problems imposed upon those who are undesirably different and the techniques used by these individuals to maintain some degree of self-respect by managing impressions and controlling information about themselves. The reading constitutes the final chapter of the book and begins at point when Goffman has convinced the reader that stigma management is part and parcel of ordinary everyday life and that all of us manage impressions and control information about ourselves in order to sustain favorable social and personal identities.

Of special import is that Goffman focuses on the ways in which persons, once defined as deviant, attempt to carve out enduring and self-sustaining relationships that sanction the behavior or attributes they have either voluntarily or involuntarily been cast into as a result of the labelling process. In so doing he develops four categories of deviants and discusses some of the similarities and differences of each. All are alike in that they must function as stigmatized persons and yet the adjustments they make may vary in view of relationships they maintain with others. These relationships vary with the variety and meaning that the deviations take. In-group deviants must manage their stigma in ways considerably

From Erving Goffman, *Stigma: Notes on the Management of Spoiled Identity;* © 1963, pp. 140-147. Reprinted by permission of Prentice-Hall, Inc., Englewood Cliffs, New Jersey.

different from those used by social deviants. Minority members must function as stigmatized persons in some settings where impression management and information control may be restricted by visible physical attributes that are not easily manipulated. Lower class persons, in turn, hampered by patterns of speech, dress and manners may find that such "lower class" characteristics cannot readily be manipulated with finesse. These examples illustrate a fundamental emphasis of Goffman, namely, that the management of a spoiled identity is more problematic for some than it is for others and that non-deviants differ only in that they have more going for them than do deviants. Impression management and information control are more easily pulled off by "normals" because they can more readily and convincingly represent themselves as normal persons. Finally, the Goffman selection is of particular significance in that it invites the student of deviance to extend the boundaries of what is typically taken to be deviant phenomena. Also, and perhaps most importantly, by focusing on processes of differentiation, sigmatization and strategies and devices of impression management, Goffman makes the crucial point that the study of deviance becomes the study of social interaction and the situationality of interaction.

Once the dynamics of shameful differentness are seen as a general feature of social life, one can go on to look at the relation of their study to the study of neighboring matters associated with the term "deviance"—a currently fashionable word that has been somewhat avoided here until now, in spite of the convenience of the label.[1]

Starting with the very general notion of a group of individuals who share some values and adhere to a set of social norms regarding conduct and regarding personal attributes, one can refer to any individual member who does not adhere to the norms as a deviator, and to his peculiarity as a deviation. I do not think all deviators have enough in common to warrant a special analysis; they differ in many more ways than they are similar, in part because of the thorough difference, due to size, of groups in which deviations can occur. One can, however, subdivide the area into smaller plots, some of which might be worth cultivating.

It is known that a confirmed high position in some small close-knit groups can be associated with a license to deviate and hence to be a deviator. The relation of such a deviator to the group, and the conception members have of him, are such as to withstand restructuring by virtue of the deviation. (When the group is large, however, the eminent may find they must fully conform in all visible ways.) The member who is defined as physically sick is in somewhat the same situation; if he properly handles his sick status he can deviate from performance standards without this being taken as a reflection on him or on his relation to the group. The eminent and the sick can be free, then, to be deviators precisely because their deviation can be fully discounted, leading to no re-identification; their special situation demonstrates they are anything but deviants—in the common understanding of that term.[2]

In many close-knit groups and communities there are instances of a member who deviates, whether in deed or in the attributes he possesses, or both, and in consequence comes to play a special role, becoming a symbol of the group and a performer of certain clownish functions, even while he is denied the respect accorded full-fledged members.[3] Characteristically, this individual ceases to play the social distance game, approaching and being approached at will. He is often the focus of attention that welds others into a participating circle around him, even while it strips him of some of the status of a participant. He serves as a mascot for the group although qualified in certain ways to be a normal member of it. The village idiot, the small-town drunk, and the platoon clown are traditional examples; the fraternity fat boy is another. One would expect to find only one of such persons to a group, since one is all that is needed, further instances merely adding to the burden of the community. He might be called an *in-group deviant* to remind one that he is deviant relative to a concrete group, not merely norms, and that his intensive if ambivalent inclusion in the group distinguishes him from another well-known type of deviator—the group isolate who is constantly in social situations with the group but is not one of their own. (When the in-group deviant is attacked by outsiders, the group may well rally in support; when the group isolate is attacked, he is more likely to have to do his own fighting.) Note that all the types of deviators considered here are fixed within a circle in which extensive biographical information about them—a full personal identification—is widespread.

It has been suggested that in smallish groups the in-group deviant can be distinguished from other deviators, for unlike these others he is in a skewed relation to the moral life that is sustained on the average by the members. Indeed, if one did want to consider other social roles along with the in-group deviant, it might be useful to turn to those roles whose performers are out of step with ordinary morality, although not known as deviators. As one shifts the "system of reference" from small family-like groups to ones which can support greater role specialization, two such roles become evident. One of these morally mis-aligning roles is that of minister or priest, the performer being obliged to symbolize the righteous life and live it more than is normal; the other is that of law officer, the performer having to make a daily routine out of other people's appreciable infractions.[4]

When the "system of reference" is further shifted from a face-to-face local community to the wider world of metropolitan settlements (and their affiliated areas, resort and residential), a corresponding shift is found in the variety and meaning of deviations.

One such deviation is important here, the kind presented by individuals who are seen as declining voluntarily and openly to accept the social place accorded them, and who act irregularly and somewhat rebelliously in connection with our basic institutions[5]—the family, the age-grade system, the stereotyped role-division between the sexes, legitimate full-time employment involving maintenance of a single governmentally ratified personal identity, and segregation by class and race. These are the "disaffiliates." Those who take this stand on their own and by themselves might be called eccentrics or "characters." Those whose activity is collective and focused within some building or place (and often upon a special activity) may be called cultists. Those who come together into a sub-community or milieu may be called *social deviants,* and their corporate life a deviant community.[6] They constitute a special type, but only one type, of deviator.

If there is to be a field of inquiry called "deviance," it is social deviants as here defined that would presumably constitute its core. Prostitutes, drug addicts, delinquents, criminals, jazz musicians, bohemians, gypsies, carnival workers, hobos, winos, show people, full time gamblers, beach dwellers, homosexuals,[7] and the urban unrepentant poor—these would be included. These are the folk who are considered to be engaged in some kind of collective denial of the social order. They are perceived as failing to use available opportunity for advancement in the various approved runways of society; they show open disrespect for their betters; they lack piety; they represent failures in the motivational schemes of society.

Once the core of social deviancy is established, one can proceed to peripheral instances: community-based political radicals who not only vote in a divergent way but spend more time with those of their own kind than is politically necessary; the traveling rich who are not geared into the executive's work week, and spend their time drifting from one summering place to another; expatriates, employed or not, who routinely wander at least a few steps from the PX and the American Express; the ethnic assimilation backsliders who are reared in the two worlds of the parent society and the society of their parents, and resolutely turn away from the conventional routes of mobility open to them, overlaying their public school socialization with what many normals will see as a grotesque costume of religious orthodoxy; the metropolitan unmarried and merely married who disavail themselves of an opportunity to raise a family, and instead support a vague society that is in rebellion, albeit mild and short-lived, against the family system. In almost all of these cases, some show of disaffiliation is made, as is also true of eccentrics and cultists, providing in this way a thin line that can be drawn between all of them and deviators on the other side, namely, the quietly disaffiliated— hobbyists who become so devoted to their avocation that only a husk remains for civil attachments, as in the case of some ardent stamp collectors, club tennis players, and sports car buffs.

Social deviants, as defined, flaunt their refusal to accept their place and are temporarily tolerated in this gestural rebellion, providing it is restricted within the ecological boundaries of their community. Like ethnic and racial ghettos, these communities constitute a haven of self-defense and a place where the individual deviator can openly take the line that he is at least as good as anyone else. But in addition, social deviants often feel that they are not merely equal to but better than normals, and that the life they lead is better than that lived by the persons they would otherwise be. Social deviants also provide models of being for restless normals, obtaining not only sympathy but also recruits. (Cultists acquire converts too, of couse, but the focus is on programs of action not styles of life.) The wise can become fellow-travelers.

In theory, a deviant community could come to perform for society at large something of the same functions performed by an in-group deviant for his group, but while this is thinkable, no one yet seems to have demonstrated the case. The problem is that the large area from which recruits to a deviant community are drawn is not itself as clearly a system, an entity, with needs and functions, as is a small face-to-face group.

Two kinds of deviators have been here considered: in-group deviants and social deviants. Two neighboring types of social category ought to be mentioned. First, ethnic and racial minority groups:[8] individuals who have a common history and culture (and often a common national origin), who transmit their membership along lineage lines, who are in a position to demand signs of loyalty from some of the members, and who are in a relatively disadvantaged position in society. Secondly, there are those members of the lower class who quite noticeably bear the mark of their status in their speech, appearance, and manner, and who, relative to the public institutions of our society, find they are second class citizens.

Now it is apparent that in-group deviants, social deviants, minority members, and lower class persons are all likely on occasion to find themselves functioning as stigmatized individuals, unsure of the reception awaiting them in face-to-face interaction and deeply involved in the various responses to this plight. This will be so if for no other reason than that almost all adults have to have some dealings with service organizations, both commercial and civil, where courteous, uniform treatment is supposed to prevail based on nothing more restrictive than citizenship, but where opportunity will arise for concern about invidious expressive valuations based on a virtual middle class ideal.

It should be just as apparent, however, that a full consideration of any one of these four categories leads beyond, and away from, what it is necessary to consider in the analysis of stigma. For example, there are deviant communities whose members, especially when away from their milieux, are not particularly concerned about their social acceptance, and therefore can hardly be analyzed by reference to stigma management; an instance would be certain outdoor milieux on the warm beaches of America where can be found those aging young people who are not yet ready to become contaminated by work and who voluntarily devote themselves to various forms of riding the waves. Nor should it be forgotten that apart from the four categories mentioned, there are some disadvantaged persons who are not stigmatized at all, for example, someone married to a mean and selfish mate, or someone who is not well off and must raise four children,[9] or someone whose physical handicap (for example, a mild hearing disability) has interfered with his life, even though everyone, including himself, remains unaware that he has a physical disability.[10]

I have argued that stigmatized persons have enough of their situations in life in common to warrant classifying all these persons together for purposes of analysis. An extraction has thus been made from the traditional fields of social problems, race and ethnic relations, social disorganization, criminology, social pathology, and deviancy—an extraction of something all these fields have in common. These commonalities can be organized on the basis of very few assumptions regarding human nature. What remains in each one of the traditional fields could then be re-examined for whatever is really special to it, thereby bringing analytical coherence to what is now purely historic and fortuitous unity. Knowing what fields like race relations, aging, and mental health share, one could then go on to see, analytically, how they differ. Perhaps in each case the choice would be to retain the old substantive areas, but at least it would be clear that each is merely an area to which one should apply several perspectives, and that the development of any one of these coherent analytic perspectives is not likely to come from those who restrict their interest exclusively to one substantive area.

Notes

1. It is remarkable that those who live around the social sciences have so quickly become comfortable in using the term "deviant," as if those to whom the term is applied have enough in common so that significant things can be said about them as a whole. Just as there are iatrogenic disorders caused by the work that physicians do (which then gives them more work to do), so there are categories of persons who are created by students of society, and then studied by them.

2. The complex relation of a deviator to his group has recently been reconsidered by L. Coser, "Some Functions of Deviant Behavior and Normative Flexibility," *American Journal of Sociology*, LXVIII (1962), 172-181.

3. On these and other functions of the deviant, see R. Dentler and K. Erickson, "The Functions of Deviance in Groups," *Social Problems*, VII (1959), 98-107.

4. This theme is developed in H. Becker, *Outsiders* (New York: Free Press of Glencoe, 1963), pp. 145-163.

5. A general point suggested to me by Dorothy Smith.

6. The term "deviant community" is not entirely satisfactory because it obscures two issues: whether or not the community is peculiar according to structural standards derived from an analysis of the make-up of ordinary communities; and whether or not the members of the community are social deviants. A one-sexed army post in an unpopulated territory is a deviant community in the first sense, but not necessarily a community of social deviants.

7. The term "homosexual" is generally used to refer to anyone who engages in overt sexual practices with a member of his own sex, the practice being called "homosexuality." This usage appears to be based on a medical and legal frame of reference and provides much too broad and heterogeneous a categorization for use here. I refer only to individuals who participate in a special community of understanding wherein members of one's own sex are defined as the most desirable sexual objects, and sociability is energetically organized around the pursuit and entertainment of these objects. According to this conception there are four basic varieties of homosexual life: the male and the female types found in custodial institutions; and the male and female "gay" worlds sustained in urban centers. (In this latter connection, see E. Hooker, *op. cit.*) Note that an individual can retain membership in the gay world and yet not engage in homosexual practices, just as he can exploit the gay through sale of sexual favors without participating socially and spiritually in the gay community. (In this latter connection see Reiss, *op. cit.*) If the term homosexual is used to refer to someone who engages in a particular kind of sexual act, then a term like "homosexualite" is needed to refer to someone who participates in a particular kind of deviant community.

8. For a recent analytical treatment, see R. Glass, "Insiders-Outsiders: The Position of Minorities," *New Left Review*, XVII (Winter, 1962), 34-45.

9. Toynbee, *op. cit.*, Chaps. 15 and 17.

10. An instance is to be found in Henrich and Kriegel, *op. cit.*, pp. 178-180.

ANTHONY N. DOOB

Deviance: Society's Side Show

In the following article, Anthony Doob reports on a series of experiments
conducted by himself and Jonathan Freedman in an attempt to experimentally examine the implications of deviance for the person's own patterns of action as well as the response of others to those who are deviant. In attempting to cut through the irrelevancies and difficulties of
typical deviance research (which focuses on causes and prevention of
deviance) the researchers define the deviant as one who is different from
surrounding norms, regardless of whether this difference is evaluated
positively or negatively. This conception of deviance, of course, is quite
similar to our position discussed in the section, "On the Nature of
Deviance."

The basic experiment involved the use of falisified personality tests to make
some subjects feel deviant, others non-deviant. Whether or not they succeeded in manipulating subjects in a "content-free" manner is ques-
tionable (why is differentness necessarily undesirable?), yet their efforts
to be content-free enabled the researchers to discuss deviance untram-
meled by the specifics of particular behaviors or attributions, thereby
allowing them to generalize to the commonalities of deviance.

After experimentally producing deviants (and non-deviants), a variety of experiments were conducted to determine some of the effects of being
different. It was found that deviants changed their interaction patterns,
preferring other deviants to non-deviants. Moreover, and in line with
Goffman's analysis presented earlier, deviants attempted to manage

Reprinted from *Psychology Today* Magazine, October 1971, 5:47-51, 113. Copyright ©
Ziff Davis Publishing Company.

27

information about themselves in such a way as to avoid detection and to maintain their reputations as "normal" persons. In addition, deviants were more likely to give and seek help than were non-deviants. Finally non-deviants tended to choose the deviants for unpleasant tasks and punishments.

These experiments convincingly support the interactionist-labeling position which contends that being deviant brings about changes in self-definitions and behaviors. It also demonstrates how audiences (non-deviants) differentially interact with persons who are deviants such that various conventional patterns of behavior tend to be increasingly closed off. Thus the deviant must alter his associational patterns, manage information about himself more carefully, and generally put up with many slights and rebuffs from non-deviants. Non-deviants, in turn, tend to exclude deviants from ordinary social participation or, when deviants are included, to limit the pattern of interaction and opportunities available to deviants.

Unfortunately, the experiments do not enable us to answer the crucial question of whether labeling and audience reactions serve as further determinants of deviant behavior, although they are suggestive of this. An extension of the kind of experimental design used in the Doob research seemingly would enable one to not only experimentally produce deviants, but also to determine whether or not such deviance results in even further deviation when recognized by the deviant, non-deviants, or both

When man invented the circus, he also invented the side show. A minor attraction near the main tent, the side show offered to the public such exotic specimens as the bearded lady, the strong man, the most beautiful girl in the world, the midget, the giant and the double monster. People who paid to see the freaks came away reassured of their own normality; kids learned the consequences of not eating their greens. Society too has always had a side show, featuring blacks, criminals, homosexuals, hippies, Jews, drug addicts and the halt, the blind, the maimed and the deaf. Paranoia and prejudice have replaced the townspeople's old feeling of reassurance; many adults consider the generation of disobedient kids today to be a deviant class in itself.

Freaks and social outcasts are seldom able to escape the stigma attached to their deviance. As a result they are subject to persecution and second-class citizenship. They cannot find jobs or decent housing. They receive unjust treatment from the courts and from law-enforcement agencies. Until recently there was a San Francisco city ordinance that read: "It shall be unlawful for any person who is diseased, maimed, mutilated or deformed as to be an unsightly or improper person to be allowed in or on public streets, . . . thoroughfares or public places, to expose himself/herself, or his/her injury to public view."

Although an enlightened society has tried to abolish many of its discriminatory laws, deviants still are subject to unwritten codes of prejudice and abuse. The restaurants that once refused to serve blacks now refuse to serve hippies, and if we are to believe movies like *Easy Rider* and *Joe,* long hair is a fatal disease in some parts of the country.

Virtually any characteristic can be deviant if it is not shared by the rest of the comparison group. At one time or another every person feels different from the people around him. The border between individuality and deviance is often quite arbitrary: a business executive dressed in a three-piece suit will feel completely at ease on Madison Avenue. If he wears the same outfit to a public beach or to a white-tie dinner, he will feel less comfortable. If he wears it to a nudist colony or hippie commune he will feel totally out of place. He probably would fire his secretary if she wore a bikini to the office. When a person feels out of place, it usually means that he has trespassed against someone else's sense of propriety. The penalties are notoriously severe.

Focus

Perhaps deviance is, like beauty, only in the eye of the beholder. A great deal of the research on deviance focuses on the causes and prevention of antisocial behavior rather than on the deviants' own feelings, or on other persons' reactions to deviance.

Deviance is a universal attribute. Measures of individual differences are relative. A genius is just as unusual as an idiot, a midget just as strange as a giant. Right-wing groups like the Minutemen are surprisingly similar to left-wing groups like the Weathermen. Policemen are as different from the rest of society as are the criminals they apprehend.

This sameness suggests that the important point to consider in research is that if a person is different in any way from surrounding norms, regardless of whether this difference is evaluated positively or negatively, he will consider himself deviant. It seems likely that every person who feels deviant will to some extent be affected in the same way and will have certain behavior in common with other deviants. Also, the people around him will treat him the way they ordinarily treat deviants. The feeling of deviance would be as major a factor in behavior as height, intelligence or need for achievement.

Ideas

Jonathan Freedman and I recently conducted a series of experiments on reactions to deviance per se. We tried to find out how the feeling of deviance, without regard to the particular type of deviance, influenced behavior. Although we began the research without any clear theoretical assumptions, we did have some ideas about what might be the major concerns of a deviant, and some ideas about what kinds of behavior would be affected by these concerns.

We suspected that a person who felt he was deviant would be worried about the kind of treatment he would receive at the hands of nondeviants. He would try to minimize possible mistreatment by avoiding contact with non-deviants, or, if that were not possible, try to please nondeviants in order to compensate for any prejudice. We also suspected that deviants, at least those with traits that are generally considered to be negative, would prefer to be nondeviants. The deviant would try to conceal his deviance, or to lessen his feelings of deviance, by associating with other deviants. A review of the literature on specific types of deviance supported many of these predictions, but we were eager to see if we could reproduce such reactions in a controlled laboratory setting.

Values

Our first problem was to devise a "content-free" form of deviance. Each type of deviance carries with it a large assortment of specific values and effects. Being black means one thing, having long hair another. We wanted to eliminate the negative effects of prejudice from the effects of deviance per se. To accomplish this we needed a form of deviance that subjects would consider important, but that could not be labeled good or bad. We decided upon a laboratory manipulation of personality.

Personality is a rather ambiguous concept. Everybody has one but nobody knows what it looks like. To produce a feeling of deviance in certain subjects we administered a series of personality tests, the results of which we manipulated to make people feel that they were deviants or nondeviants.

Before the tests began we showed the subjects a feedback sheet similar to the one we would give them at the end of each test. This sheet supposedly showed the scores of the previous week's group and those of a standardized population of 1,000 students. We explained that while we would show each subject at the end of each test how he stood in relation to other members of his group and to the standardized population, we could not reveal the meaning of the scores until the end of the experiment.

We accomplished our manipulation by handing back sheets that were completely unrelated to subjects' actual test performances. In fact, we had prepared the individual "results" long before we recruited any of the subjects. We gave to persons in the deviant conditions sheets that showed their scores to be at or near the end of the distribution on each of six scales. In contrast we gave to subjects in the nondeviant conditions sheets that showed their scores to be near the center of the distributions. From the point of view of the subjects, the feedback sheets looked like reasonable and legitimate results—good pictures of what they were like.

Quite often when a subject received the first feedback sheet showing that he was different from the rest of the group he would laugh a little or would ask the experimenter for more information about its meaning. When the second feedback sheet was given to him, however, the subject seemed much more concerned. As the experiment progressed, it became very clear that the subject was worried about his scores. By the time of the last test, the subject usually was able to anticipate quite accurately what his results would look like.

Although we never mentioned any particular dimensions of personality, the subjects in the deviant condition were easily convinced that they were different in some way and that other members of the group were nondeviants.

Patterns

Having produced this controlled feeling of deviance and nondeviance in the subjects, we began testing their reactions, first probing the willingness of deviants to interact with nondeviants. It seemed likely that deviants would prefer to associate with other similar deviants rather than with nondeviants and that this preference would extend to deviants who were not like themselves. Certainly this is the pattern we find in society: artists associate with artists, Jews associate with Jews, homosexuals associate with homosexuals.

To study grouping preference among deviants and nondeviants we had subjects choose three partners for an experiment in cooperative problem-solving.

The subjects made their selections from a sheet supposedly containing the scores of 25 subjects who had taken the test. The subjects in the deviant condition, whose scores were on the bottom of the scale, had a much greater tendency to choose partners from those subjects who had extreme scores than did the nondeviants (averaging 2.00 extreme choices compared to .91 by nondeviants).

In addition, the deviants showed a greater tendency to select scores that were above the median (and therefore different from their own) than did the nondeviants (1.21 and .52 respectively).

These results confirmed our expectation that deviants tend to associate with other deviants, including those dissimilar to themselves. Presumably they form these associations because they want to lessen their feelings of difference or because they expect better treatment from persons who share their condition.

Hide

In order to understand more completely the effect of deviance on a person's interactions with other persons, we decided that it was necessary to differentiate between subjects who felt that everyone knew they were deviants and subjects who felt that their deviance was not known by other subjects. In a sense, we sought to account for the difference between a person who has an obvious deviant trait—a cripple or a blind person—and one who has an easily hidden deviant trait, like genius or sexual deviance. We established these two conditions by announcing test scores publicly in one case and confidentially in the other. Our assumption was that most deviants would prefer to be nondeviant. There is a wealth of evidence to support this idea. Immigrant families Americanize their names; light-skinned blacks pass as whites. Stutterers avoid difficult words.

We expected that subjects with undisclosed deviance would try to avoid detection. To test this idea we again asked subjects to engage in an experiment in problem-solving, working alone or in groups, and asked that they indicate their preference for either on a scale from one to six, with six being the maximum preference for working alone. The effect of public knowledge of deviance was significant. Subjects with undisclosed deviance, given a choice, preferred to work alone more than either the known deviants or the nondeviants. The average preference rating of undisclosed deviants was 2.85, compared to 1.67 for known deviants and 2.15 for nondeviants. These results confirmed our expectations.

Help

The previous experiment allowed subjects to choose their working conditions and thereby avoid direct confrontation with nondeviants. We wondered if feelings of deviance would influence a subject's willingness to cooperate with a person who asked for help. It seemed likely that deviants would more readily agree to help than nondeviants would: doing another person a favor makes one feel like a nice guy, which is better than being just a deviant.

We thought the deviance of the person making the request might also affect compliance. From the point of view of a deviant, there is more to gain or lose when one confronts a nondeviant. Thus to the extent that concern about mistreatment increases compliance, the deviant would be more concerned about mistreatment from the nondeviant, and would comply more readily to his request than he would to a similar request from a fellow deviant. It also seemed possible that nondeviants might express the opposite tendency. People who are normal often feel apprehensive and uncomfortable in the presence of deviants. A deviant is different, odd and perhaps antagonistic. A nondeviant subject might comply more readily to a request from a deviant than he would to a request from a nondeviant.

After the personality tests, in which test scores were public, the experimenter left the room. A confederate got up from his booth, and asked another subject if he would be willing to write some letters about preserving the redwoods. If a subject refused to write any, the confederate returned to his seat. If the subject agreed, the confederate then said that he tried to get people to write as many as 50 letters.

The measure of compliance was the number of letters the subject agreed to write. We found that deviants agreed to write twice as many letters as nondeviants did (14.98 and 7.22 respectively). Deviants complied more to requests from nondeviants than to requests from deviants. Conversely, nondeviants complied more to requests from deviants than to requests from other nondeviants.

Eye Patch

Barbara Paye Ecker and I confirmed this tendency in research done with housewives and a person conducting a survey. The experimenter asked housewives to fill out a 79-item questionnaire and return it through the mail, or to submit to a 15- to 20-minute interview. For half of the subjects, the person making the request wore a black eye patch; for the other half the person making the request had no eye patch. We found that when the subject did not anticipate having to interact in the future with the person making the request (by filling out the questionnaire), 69.2 per cent of the housewives were willing to comply to the poll taker who wore the eye patch, while only 40 per cent complied to the normal researcher. When the request involved further interaction—the request for an interview—there was no such effect (mean-compliance rate in the eye patch condition was 33.7 per cent, no eye patch—32 per cent).

These findings can be explained by two forces—the subjects felt sorry for the experimenter because she was handicapped, yet they were uncomfortable dealing with her. As a result, the housewives tended to comply with the request to fill out questionnaires but not with the request for prolonged interviews. They avoided prolonging the encounter.

Victim

This experiment suggests that deviance does provoke certain reactions among nondeviants. It remained to be seen whether we could find support in our laboratory for the popular theory about the mistreatment of deviants. We addressed ourselves to two questions: 1) Does deviance affect the amount of punishment a victim will receive from other subjects? 2) Do attitudes about deviance affect a subject's choice of victim?

One of our initial assumptions was that subjects who were deviant believed they would receive better treatment at the hands of similar deviants than they would at the hands of nondeviants.

To test our hypothesis we planted a confederate in the group and prepared a feedback sheet that made him appear either deviant or nondeviant. After the personality test we asked the group to participate in a perception experiment involving a very elaborate piece of equipment. They would, of course, be paid for their extra time.

While the experimenter was out of the room, the confederate "accidentally" broke the equipment making it impossible for the group to earn an extra $5.00 they had thought they were going to get. Then, under the pretext of a creative free-association test, the subjects in the group got to give what they thought were electric shocks to the confederate.

When deviant subjects thought the clumsy subject was deviant, they gave her fewer shocks than nondeviants did and also fewer than when they thought she was nondeviant. The popular conception was supported. This experiment offered a preselected victim. The scapegoat theory of prejudice distinguishes between expressing aggression against a previously selected object, and selecting an object of aggression from a variety of objects. It suggests that the choice of victim is the crucial point at which mistreatment of minorities is determined.

Thus we would expect nondeviants to choose deviants for unpleasant things, but to avoid picking them for good things. If the person himself were deviant we would expect him to act quite differently—picking nondeviants for bad things and deviants for good things.

The results confirmed these expectations. After the personality test we asked one group to select someone to perform a special task that would require him to receive electric shocks. We told another group that the special task was simple and straightforward (not involving pain) and that the person doing it would receive an extra $2.50. Overwhelmingly the nondeviants picked deviants for the unpleasant task and picked nondeviants for the pleasant task. Deviants tended to pick deviants for the pleasant task and to avoid picking them for the unpleasant task. If we rank their choices from one to four, with the number one indicating that the deviant was chosen first, the average rank of deviants for punishment was 2.82 when chosen by deviants, versus 1.09 when chosen by nondeviants. When chosen for rewards the deviant was ranked 1.27 by other deviants, versus 2.18 by nondeviants.

Inside

The subjects in these experiments were all normal persons. When they came into the laboratory they were not in any sociological sense deviant. Yet while they were in the laboratory they behaved very much like sociological deviants, and other subjects treated them the way they normally treat sociological deviants.

Our research suggests that it is the deviance of the subjects per se that determines much of what we normally consider to be deviant or antisocial behavior. Most persons will act like deviants if they are made to feel different.

Our work suggests that we can explain the behavior of deviants most economically by studying the deviants' feelings of deviance. The side show is all in your mind.

Part II

Experimental Approaches

DARRELL J. STEFFENSMEIER
and
ROBERT M. TERRY

The Experimental Study of Human Behavior*

Our intent at this point is to provide a basic discussion of issues that are fundamental to the experimental study of deviance. How one studies deviance is in large part dependent upon the kinds of objectives that are sought and to a secondary degree on the circumstances and opportunities that are available to the researcher. Unfortunately, no single technique has been able to provide the kinds of answers that social scientists would like to obtain. Thus, the experimental study of deviance employs a number of strategies within the experimental framework, each giving us various kinds of evidence with differing implications for internal and external validity. Before discussing the advantages and disadvantages of various kinds of experimental designs, a few elementary issues in research methodology are dealt with.

The Goal of Scientific Research:
Assessing Causality

The aim of much scientific research is to provide evidence of cause-and-effect relationships. There are three criteria needed to demonstrate causality.

1. There must be an observed *association* between the independent and dependent variables.** That is, changes in the values of one variable must in

---

*This section was written with the joint participation of Renée Hoffman Steffensmeier.

**The independent variable refers to the variable that is assumed to be the causal factor or determining condition in the relationship being studied. The dependent variable is the presumed effect. More specifically, in terms of experimental research, the independent variable is the condition or stimulus which the experimenter manipulated or had under his control; the dependent variable is that part of the subject's behavior which changes as the independent variable changes.

38

some sense go with changes in the values of the other variable. For example, in the Steffensmeier and Terry study of reactions to shoplifting (p. 234) it was found that having a "hippie" rather than a "straight" appearance increases an individual's chances of being reported for shoplifting.

2. *Causal direction* must be established. The independent variable must occur prior to the dependent variable in the sense that a change in the value of the former is followed by a change in the latter and not the reverse. In many kinds of behavioral science research, the direction of causality is not clearly evident. In much survey research (questionnaires, interviews, etc.), decisions of causal direction must be made on theoretical or logical grounds since the research is retrospective (both the independent and dependent variables have already varied). In some instances this is fairly straightforward since one variable simply cannot change the other. Police arrest for delinquency cannot change one's sex, but a person's sex can influence the likelihood of police arrest. In other instances, however, causal direction is more problematic. Do poor interpersonal relationships produce alcoholism, for example, or does deviant drinking produce poor interpersonal relationships? In experimental research, direction of causality is less often a problem than in survey research because the investigator has manipulated the causal variable himself in order to produce changes in the dependent variable. He is thus able to observe the sequence of causation directly.

3. The final criterion, that of *non-spuriousness,* is the most difficult issue to deal with. This means that the relationship between the independent and dependent variables must not disappear when the influences of other variables causally *prior* to *both* of the original variables are removed. While one can never definitively resolve the question of spuriousness, the more evidence that can be adduced to demonstrate that no third factor is simultanously producing changes in both the independent and dependent variables, the more confidence we have that the association is valid or real. It is more difficult to rule out the possibility of non-spuriousness in non-experimental than in experimental research because most of the controls must be applied after the data have been collected. On the other hand, experimental research is generally designed so that extraneous factors that could cause spuriousness are eliminated. If the investigator himself produces changes in the independent variable, then he can be sure that some third factor cannot be simultaneously producing a change in both the independent and dependent variables. In addition if he assigns the subjects to experimental conditions at random, then the conditions can differ on the relevant variables only by chance.

Let's take some examples to illustrate this point. In Sweden there is a relationship between the number of storks in an area and the number of children born in the area. This is not a causal relationship, however, because there is a third variable, rural-urban location, that is related to both the number of storks and the number of babies. More storks are found in rural than urban areas and the rural birth rate is higher than the urban birth rate.

Let's suppose again that it is noted that an association exists between type of prison treatment received and recidivism, such that those on work-release programs are less likely to commit new crimes than those receiving more custodial treatment. This relationship may be accounted for by type of offender. Prisoners who have been convicted of committing more serious offenses are more likely to both receive custodial treatment and to reengage in criminal behavior upon release. To design an experiment that would rule out this third factor, an investigator could match the criminal histories of prisoners receiving more traditional custodial treatment with those receiving newer modes of treatment such as work-release. Thus both prisoners with more serious offenses and those with less serious offenses would be assigned to traditional and newer treatment programs. Random assignment of prisoners to the two treatment groups would be an alternative procedure for ruling out this particular source of spuriousness and would also assure that the two groups of prisoners were comparable with respect to other extraneous factors.

Advantages of Experimental Research

More than other research designs, experimental research allows us to build into the research design controls for assessing causality. If assessing causality is our objective, then the advantages of experimental research are significant indeed. Let's take an example using the classical experimental design as our model. As shown in Figure 1, there are four comparison groups in the experimental design.

FIGURE 1

	Time 1	*Time 2*	*Time 3*
Experimental group	"Pre" test	Administration of independent variable	"Pre" test
Control group	"Pre" test		"Pre" test

This design enables us to examine the difference in values on the dependent variable between the experimental as compared to the control group, and between the pre-test and post-test results. An experimental group is defined as the group which is exposed to (receives) the experimental treatment or stimuli, and the control group is the group from which the treatment is withheld.* The pre-test and post-test measure the values of the dependent variable both before and after subjects are exposed to the experimental treatment.

Suppose we hypothesize that favorable teacher expectations cause an increase in reading ability. The independent variable is teacher expectations and can be dichotomized into favorable versus unfavorable. The dependent variable is reading ability as measured by a standard reading test. The experiment might consist of administering a reading test to a group of elementary school students prior to the start of the school year. The second step would be to randomly assign students to either the experimental or control group. For the students in the experimental group, teachers would be told that unusual advances in reading ability could be expected within the upcoming school year. For students in the control group, no such "information" would be given to the teachers. At the end of the school year both groups would be retested on their reading ability and comparisons between the groups could be made.

This hypothetical study is very similar to an actual study done by Rosenthal and Jacobson and reported in this volume. Using the Rosenthal and Jacobson study as an example, let's see how evidence of causality is established with such a research design. Their experiment dealt with the effects of teacher expectations on the intellectual growth of students. The investigators were interested in whether those children of whom the teachers held especially favorable expectations would show greater intellectual growth than the remaining students in the control group. The independent variable, teachers' expectations, was operationalized (manipulated) by telling teachers that some students had an unusual potential for intellectual growth. These "unusual" students constituted the experimental group and were compared to a control group consisting of students for whom such intellectual blossoming was not expected. (Students were then randomly assigned to either the experimental or control group.) The dependent variable, intellectual growth, was defined as the difference between a student's pre-test IQ and his IQ on a post-test. The post-test was given eight months after the experimental treatment (manipulation of teachers' expectations) and one year after the pre-test.

Let's now examine in specific detail how evidence for causality is established with this research design. For simplicity and clarity's sake, approximate pre-test and post-test means scores are given only for the first-grade students in the experiment. We have used 100 as our pre-test base for making comparisons.

---

*In general, most experiments do not include a control group in the traditional sense of a group that is not given any experimental treatment whatsoever. Usually the different experimental conditions constitute different degrees of the independent variable.

	pre-test	post-test
Experimental	100	127
Control	100	112
Difference	0	15

It is evident from the difference between the mean scores of the experimental and control groups on the post-test that being defined as a potential "bloomer" or "academic spurter" is *associated* with higher test scores. Since the experimenters manipulated the independent variable, *causal direction* was determined before the research was started. The third criterion of causality is *non-spuriousness*. By manipulating the independent variable, teacher expectations, the investigators ruled out the possibility that some third factor produced the change in the independent variable. Thus a spurious interpretation is obviously not possible because there is no third variable that could be causing a change in *both* the independent and dependent variables. In addition the investigators ruled out other possible determinants of reading ability by randomly assigning students to the experimental or control groups. On the average, factors such as sex, IQ, previous knowledge, teaching skill of teacher, and so forth, are equal in the two groups. There is no reason to suspect that one group is systematically different from the other one. Processes such as randomization and/or matching ensure that the experimental and control groups are identical in all respects other than the presence or absence of the experimental variable. With such procedures we can be reasonably certain that the observed difference on the dependent variable didn't result from initial differences between groups.

A caveat is in order at this point. Lest the student get the *mis*impression that all experimental research consists of a unitary design, that of the classical experiment, it should be quickly noted that there are a large number of variations on the design we have described. Some experiments use several experimental and control groups and others include a number of tests administered over a long period of time. In others, random assignment is impossible and only separately selected control and experimental groups can be compared, and still other experiments are characterized by a multitude of additional variations. In other words, experimental designs fall along a continuum— they vary in terms of the degree of control over extraneous factors and in terms of the amount of achieved manipulation of the independent variables, the comparability of experimental and control groups and so on.

Nonetheless, in general experimental procedures have distinct advantages over non-experimental procedures because of their ability to directly cope with issues of causality as part of the research design rather than by means of the application of statistical techniques to the data after they have already been collected.

Experimental vs. Non-experimental Research

In the rubric of non-experimental research we include such things as field studies, surveys, correlational studies and so forth. While experiments have built-in controls for spuriousness and causal direction, non-experimental designs must start with observed associations and then apply statistical controls for spuriousness after the data have been collected. Thus, non-experimental research is *ex post facto* research. The distinguishing features of non-experimental research are that the independent variable is *not* manipulated and the random assignment of subjects is not possible. Non-experimental research employs statistical techniques in order to deal with the problem of causality and spuriousness, but these statistical techniques do not provide the same degree of confidence for drawing conclusions regarding cause-effect relationships as is possible with the use of experimental designs.

Non-experimental research is commonly of the survey variety in which samples are selected from some predefined population and data are collected by means of questionnaires or interviews. An important criterion in evaluating such research is assessment of the representativeness of the samples used. The scientific selection of samples from some pre-defined population constitutes a general advantage of non-experimental research over most experimental research. In such instances we have greater assurance that the results obtained are applicable to a larger group of persons and situations than we have been able to study directly. Another advantage is that many kinds of phenomena cannot be manipulated experimentally and therefore non-experimental designs must be used if we are to study the phenomenon at all.

Two Experimental Research Settings: Laboratory and Field

Experiments may be conducted in either a laboratory or a field setting. While intuitively the distinction between laboratory and field settings may seem obvious, unfortunately in practice the distinction is not always clear. This is compounded by the fact that in certain instances an experiment may contain features of both settings. Two fairly common criteria for distinguishing between the two experimental settings served as guidelines in the editing of this book.

The first criterion concerns the degree of control over the data collection situation and the resultant possibility that factors unknown to the investigator will interfere with the results. (Control here would include such matters as control over the behavior of subjects and over the influences of the environment or circumstances present in the situation.) A salient characteristic, as well as a major advantage, is the greater degree of experimental control generally possible in a laboratory setting. However, because the amount of control is always a matter of degree, this criterion does not provide an absolute means of distinguishing between a laboratory and a field setting.

A second way of distinguishing between experiments conducted in the two settings is whether or not the subjects are aware that they are participating in a social psychological study. If subjects are aware that they are in an experiment, then it is a laboratory study; if subjects are unaware, then it is a field study. This distinction, moreover, points to a major advantage of experiments carried out in a field setting. Unaware subjects don't behave as "guinea pigs" and hence a major source of possible error in the interpretation of experimental results is eliminated.

There are some notable differences between experiments carried out in these two settings which affect their validity. Fundamental here is the distinction between internal and external validity. Internal validity refers to whether or not the experimental treatment did in fact make a difference. External validity refers to the generalizability of research findings. To what populations, settings, treatment variables, and measurement variables can this effect be generalized? Both types of validity are obviously important, but sometimes increasing one may jeopardize the other. The ideal, of course, is to use experimental designs strong in both types of validity. However if an acceptable balance between the two can't be reached, it is usually internal validity that is given greater consideration.

There are many threats to internal validity and some research designs avoid more of these than others. The Ross, Campbell and Glass reading in this volume, for example, discusses six such factors. The fewer threats to internal validity that we can detect in the research the more confidence we have in the results. *

One threat to internal validity is reactivity, which means that the very procedures used to measure the dependent variable may cause changes in the phenomenon being studied. Reactivity can arise from the awareness of persons that they are subjects in a scientific study. Subject awareness has been shown to lead to unusual displays of cooperativeness, docility and so on. For example, in an attempt to play the role of a "good subject," a person may in various ways conform to the perceived expectations of the investigator and thus "fulfill" the experimental hypothesis. The point is that the behavior of subjects may have been different if subjects had been unaware of being in an experiment.

---

*It should be noted that no experiment ever proves a theory; it merely probes it by showing that there are no other available plausible hypotheses to explain the data. The general program of experimental analysis is to eliminate rival explanations of the results.

A mundane example of reactivity is the subject who continues to perform an assigned task without protest despite increasing darkness in the room. The investigator testing for optimal levels of light for work effectiveness may be baffled by the subject's performance unless he is cognizant of the possible reactivity that exists.

Reactivity is harder to avoid and more of a problem in experiments conducted in the laboratory than it is in experiments conducted in the field. Experiments which occur in a natural environment avoid many kinds of reactivity because subjects are unaware that they are under observation. Aside from reactivity, laboratory experiments are stronger in terms of internal validity than field experiments are, because greater control of extraneous factors can be achieved in a relatively isolated setting.

On the other hand, experiments conducted in field settings are generally stronger with respect to external validity. In comparison to the artificiality of the laboratory setting, the natural environment of experiments conducted in a field setting increases external validity of the results. Since the variables under study occur in a natural context and are not combined in unusual or artificial ways, generalizability is increased.

Another common difference between laboratory and field experiments that contributes to the greater generalizability of field experiments is the selection of subjects. While there is nothing inherent in either setting to determine the selection, it happens almost without exception that college students are the subjects of laboratory experiments. It is easier to obtain a sample of the general population in a field experiment and this is often done.

Comparison of Research Designs

So far we have discussed only laboratory and field experiments. There are however two other kinds of research designs: quasi-experiments and interview experiments. Both quasi-experiments and interview experiments share with their more popular kin, laboratory and field experiments, a number of common characteristics. Yet each of the four kinds of experiments has certain unique features as well as its own particular advantages and disadvantages. Before discussing in detail each of these (kinds of) experiments, let us briefly indicate the salient characteristic of each:

Laboratory Experiment: this kind of experiment involves the intervention of the experimenter in manipulating independent variables while observations are made in artificially created and controlled contexts.

Field Experiment: this kind of experiment involves the intervention of the experimenter in manipulating independent variables in an otherwise natural setting.

Quasi-experiment: in this kind of research design, manipulation of independent variables occurs only by naturally occurring events rather than by the intervention of the experimenter.

Interview Experiment: this kind of experiment involves the intervention of the experimenter in the manipulation of independent variables by a randomization procedure wherein some subjects are presented with one set of stimuli and other subjects receive a second set of stimuli.

The Laboratory Experiment

The term "experimentation" has often been taken to be syononymous with laboratory experimentation. In fact the terms "laboratory" and "experiment" are so often linked together that "laboratory study" and "experimental study" are frequently regarded as one and the same thing. This is unfortunate, however, because not all laboratory studies are experiments and, as we have already seen, experimental studies need not be conducted in a laboratory.

Usually laboratory experiments are conducted in a highly controlled, artificial situation—hence the term "laboratory"—in which the investigator is able to exercise control over the environment in the sense of altering some things and holding others constant. That is, the investigator is able to control and manipulate any and all conditions within the range of his physical ability and ethical responsibility. In the laboratory experiment the investigator is usually able to randomly assign subjects to different experimental manipulations. Random assignment controls the effect of numerous extraneous factors and thus eliminates a large source of possible error in research results.

The greater amount of control that is generally characteristic of the laboratory experiment constitutes a major advantage over other kinds of research designs. There are some serious limitations in the laboratory experiment, however, that warrant caution on using it to the exclusion of other kinds of experiments. The most notable limitation is the relatively artificial nature of the laboratory setting and the relatively limited ability to generalize from findings in the laboratory to social phenomena in real-life situations. The other major problem facing the laboratory experiment is that of reactivity, particularly that having to do with the effects associated with the subject's awareness that he is in an experiment.

The Field Experiment

The highly disproportionate use of the laboratory experiment alone may result in much information about deviant behavior and other social phenomena in the laboratory, but it may neglect the bridge from the laboratory to real-life settings. A major advantage of the field experiment is the naturalness of the environment for the subjects in the study. The refinement of laboratory control and manipulation is utilized in the study of human subjects in habitats that are familiar to them. This not only provides evidence about cause-and-effect relationships but also increases the generalizability of the findings. Field experiments are more likely to use subjects selected from a fairly heterogeneous population and who are more representative of the population as a whole. In addition, problems of reactivity are minimized since subjects are unaware that they are in an experiment and thus there is less chance that the process of measurement itself will alter the event being measured. The problems of inadequate sampling and reactivity are generally a crucial concern in laboratory experiments where subjects are aware of being in an experiment and where subjects are likely to be college students. The advantages of generalizability and non-reactivity of field experiments leads us to conclude that this is the preferred mode of experimental research. However since it is not always possible to manipulate independent variables in natural settings, either because it is beyond the experimenter's control or because of ethical reasons, field experiments, unfortunately, will continue to be too-infrequently used in the study of deviant phenomena.

Quasi-experiment

Quasi-experiments refer to research designs which do not allow the investigator a sufficient amount of manipulation of experimental stimuli to be considered full-fledged experiments. Quasi-experiments extend the logic of experimentation into situations where the investigator cannot create changes by himself. Instead, naturally occurring events produce a change in conditions which serves the purpose of a manipulated independent variable. By capitalizing on the naturally occurring event the investigator schedules the data collection procedures and determines when and to whom the measurements are administered.

The strengths and weaknesses of quasi-experiments can only be assessed in comparison to other types of research designs. In comparison to full-fledged experiments, quasi-experiments provide less clear-cut evidence of causality since the investigator enters the environment only after the occurrence of some critical change in natural conditions. In such a situation it is often difficult to rule out the effects of changes other than the critical event. For example, the approval of stronger penalties for convicted rapists, may be accompanied by a decreased willingness of rape victims to report the crime. In this way the effect of the new legislation is diminished, by an unknown and uncontrolled extraneous factor.

In comparison to field experiments, quasi-experiments allow less generalization to different situations because the manipulation of independent variables occurs only by way of a set of unique circumstances. On the other hand, quasi-experiments allow greater generalization than lab experiments since they do say something about "real-world" situations and the general population.

Lastly in comparison to *ex-post factor* research designs, quasi-experiments are better able to provide evidence of cause and effect relations since the independent variable is known to have varied prior to the dependent variable and greater controls are exercised over the data collection and measurement procedures.

The Interview Experiment

In this kind of research design, different values of the independent variable are randomly presented to subjects either in the context of an interview or self-administered questionnaire.* That is, some subjects are presented with one value of the independent variable and other subjects are presented with a different value. For example, if an investigator wishes to determine whether social reactions are harsher toward male rather than female homosexuals, subjects could be randomly assigned to one of two conditions. One set of subjects would be presented stimuli representing male homosexuality, the other set of subjects stimuli describing female homosexuality. Sex of homosexual is then experimentally manipulated by this random assignment procedure.

This type of research design contains some elements of both experimental and correlational designs. In this sense it is something of a hybrid and thus difficult to classify or to evaluate in terms of its positive and negative features. As compared to full-fledged and quasi-experiments this research design relies on self-reports rather than observations or measures of actual behavior. In comparison to other kinds of experiments the interview experiment is least likely to produce convincing evidence for interpreting cause-and-effect relationships since the time-order or causal direction of the variables is not clear cut.

Also, in terms of such characteristics as experimental control, reactivity and generalizability of findings the interview experiment generally has less research value than the other three kinds of experiments. Despite its limitations, the interview experiment does have a great deal of merit and is generally superior to correlational research in the control of extraneous factors and for assessing causality.

We have seen that laboratory, field and quasi-experiments can be classified in terms of the setting—laboratory or field—in which they are conducted. However, determining the experimental setting of the interview experiment is a troublesome issue. In which setting, laboratory or field, does it properly belong? Recalling an earlier discussion of the criteria for distinguishing between the two, it falls somewhere in between. The interview experiment lacks the experimental control of the laboratory setting; it also lacks the naturalness and non-reactivity that is characteristic of the field setting.

---

*The use of both types of data collection procedures—interview and self-administered questionnaire—makes the title somewhat of a misnomer.

Summary

Each of the four kinds of experiments we have been discussing has its advantages and disadvantages. To sum up the major comparisons that have been made, it can be noted that there are at least two criteria that characterize these four kinds of experiments:* (1) the degree of experimental control available to the investigator and (2) the naturalness of the environment for the subjects of the study. Laboratory, field, quasi- and interview experiments are characterized by a decreasing amount of control over extraneous factors and manipulation of the experimental stimuli (independent variables). Laboratory experiments generally rank high on experimental control while quasi- and interview experiments respectively are on the low end of the "control" continuum. Thus laboratory experiments, as well as many field experiments, tend to be strongest with respect to internal validity. On the other hand, with respect to naturalness of the environment, laboratory experiments are on the low end of the "naturalness" continuum, with field and quasi-experiments on the high end respectively and with interview experiments somewhere in the middle. Field experiments, in particular, tend to be especially strong in terms of external validity.

The relatively high ranking of the field experiment on the dimensions of experimental control and naturalness of environment, and in terms of internal and external validity, leads us to conclude that it is an especially advantageous kind of experiment for testing hypotheses about deviant phenomena. The laboratory and quasi-experiment having lesser merit. However the nature of the phenomenon being investigated as well as the feasibility of conducting a specific kind of experiment will often dictate which of the experiments is best suited for the investigator's purposes.

This preference for the field experiment and our conclusions regarding the overall merit of each of the experimental types is reflected in the organization of this volume. The plan is to "save the best for last." Thus the section of studies on interview experiments is first, followed by sections having quasi- and laboratory experimental studies and then a final section containing field experimental studies.

---

*A caveat is in order at this point. As noted earlier there are no hard and fast rules distinguishing these various kinds of experiments, especially since they are not exclusive of one another and each can be employed as part of the others.

A. Interview Experiments

JOHN P. CLARK
and
LARRY L. TIFFT

Polygraph and Interview Validation of Self-Reported Deviant Behavior*

In recent years it has become commonplace for students of crime and delinquency to argue that the limitations inherent in official and quasi-
official sources of data on criminal and delinquent behavior must be
overcome. In particular, self-report studies of delinquency have sought
to provide answers to such questions as the extent of "hidden" delinquency and whether hidden delinquents are beneficiaries of "discretionary" law enforcement in that their deviant acts are overlooked or ignored
because of such things as social class and family background.

Answers to these questions are of crucial importance to causal inquiries
about delinquency. The logic of much delinquency research is that
"non-delinquents," those not having contact with official control agencies, can be meaningfully compared to arrested juveniles, court cases
or other "officially recognized" delinquents. It is assumed that the two
groups are quite different in terms of deviant behavior, so that any differences in social and personal characteristics between them can be
interpreted as casually significant. However, if many of the non-delinquents are frequently involved in undetected delinquent behavior, then

Reprinted by permission of the American Sociological Association from John P. Clark
and Larry L. Tifft, "Polygraph and Interview Validation of Self-Reported Deviant Behavior," American Sociological Review, Vol. 31, 1966, pp. 516-523.

*We wish to expressly thank Professor Daniel Glaser for helpful editing of earlier
versions of this paper, and the participants for their tolerance of a time-consuming experiment. This research was supported by the University of Illinois Graduate College
Research Board.

5 0

comparisons of these persons with recognized delinquents are at worst causally meaningless and at best significantly biased. In fact, such comparisons might very well tell us more about law-enforcing rather than law-breaking activities or why some delinquents are caught while others are not.

In general, the self-report studies of delinquency support the biblical dictum that "many are called but few are chosen." Nearly all juveniles are delinquent to some degree, most of them engaging in delinquencies which remain hidden. While many such deviant acts are relatively non-serious, other repetitive and rather serious deviant acts also go undetected. The findings of self-report studies not only raise serious questions about the usefulness of etiological research based on official records, but they also lend support to a major contention of the interactionist-labeling perspective: Official records of deviant behavior are to be taken as problematic and may tell us more about the functioning of the agency or organization compiling them than about the behavior of the persons that they supposedly document.

In addition to the above research-oriented issues, two fundamental problems of the self-report method itself need to be considered. First, when respondents admit to having committed an offense, is their admission true? And second, to what extent do respondents either overestimate or underestimate their delinquent behavior? To overcome these problems, two different self-report techniques have been developed. One is the questionnaire technique which maintains complete anonymity and involves presenting a list of offense items to respondents and asking them to check those they have committed and how often they had committed them. This is the most frequently used method. The other technique is the interview method which consists of giving the respondent a pack of cards on each of which is written an offense category. The respondent then sorts the cards into those he has committed and those he has not. Following this, the interviewer asks detailed questions concerning the nature, frequency and circumstances of each act.

The following report by Clark and Tift addresses itself to two major issues raised by the use of self-report techniques. It examines whether some behaviors are under-reported and others over-reported during interviews or on questionnaires as well as the possibility of differential degrees of accuracy under varying circumstances and by offense. The report is also suggestive of ways to reduce the inaccuracies that exist. By manipulating or introducing the threat of exposure (via a polygraph examination), the authors introduce a constraint upon the respondent's freedom to lie. The general finding was that response accuracy was highly related to declared personal norms and reference group norms.

Under-reporting existed primarily for such offenses as truancy and stealing small amounts and over-reporting occurred primarily for offenses involving violence and sexual exploits in which the respondents were presumably living up to a masculine ideal and anticipated peer evaluations.

Because of well-known difficulties, sociologists have tended to avoid direct confrontation with the question of data validity. However, the few attempts that have been made in this respect have furnished every reason to suspect considerable inaccuracy in much of the data we frequently utilize. More specifically, the findings of the few validity studies of interview and questionnaire data

> "suggest that when people are being interviewed (or are filling out questionnaires) directly concerning behavior about which there is a strong expectation of social approval or disapproval, and in which there is considerable ego-involvement, they tend to err in the direction of idealizing their behavior,"[1]

Data obtained about deviant behavior via interviews and questionnaires are particularly vulnerable to challenge on the grounds of validity.

In recent years we have become highly sensitized to the great volume and variety of delinquent and criminal behavior which had been largely overlooked in prior analyses based upon official statistics.[2] Findings of studies of undetected crime and delinquency seem to have been so palatable to social scientists that little attention has been given to their accuracy—except to rephrase the question of how much more of such behavior might still lie unmeasured.[3]

The use of self-report techniques has raised the issue of whether some behaviors are *under-reported* and others *over-reported* during interviews or on questionnaires, as well as the possibility of *differential rates of accuracy* under varying circumstances and by offense, irrespective of the direction of possible inaccuracy.

To minimize gross inaccuracy, Nye and Short and others have built trap questions into their techniques to detect the random response-giver, the over-conformer, and the exaggerator.[4] Other attempts have been made to reduce respondents' concern about the identifiability of responses.[5] However, these procedures have not been designed to examine systematically the nature of the errors that are detected.

The Study

The study reported here was designed to test experimentally the accuracy of anonymous questionnaire responses by utilizing data obtained via a poly-graph examination as external validity criteria.[6] In the first of two preliminary studies, university students were asked to suggest behaviors which other students might tend to under- or over-report having done. In the second study, they were asked to estimate the amount of "normative pressure" on persons of their age and sex to respond in either direction on these items and items from other research of undetected delinquency. A final questionnaire was then constructed consisting of five seven-item groups reflecting consensus on their potential under- or over-reportability (Table 1).

All male students ($N=45$) in the discussion sections of an introductory sociology course at a major Midwestern university were given the final questionnaire.[7] Respondents were asked to admit the frequency of having committed each behavior *since they had entered high school*—a compromise between having age-specific data but little volume of reported deviance, and having data covering the student's entire life with the attendant greater ambiguity in recall.

After completion of the questionnaire (in pencil), respondents were told of a second phase of the study which would require approximately one hour and for which each participant would receive eight dollars. While maintaining questionnaire anonymity through a number identification system, students' names and telephone numbers were obtained. Personal "interviews" were scheduled by telephone during the ensuing two weeks, but respondents were not aware of the nature of phase two until they appeared for this "interview."[8]

During the "interview" the respondent was informed that our primary interest was in the accuracy of his questionnaire. In asking for his utmost cooperation in making his responses accurate, we strongly alluded to the likelihood of inaccurate responses being given on questionnaires administered in group situations. The respondent was then asked to select his questionnaire (using his identification number known only to him) from the entire collection of questionnaires and to make whatever modifications (in private) that were necessary to bring it to 100 per cent accuracy. Before he proceeded, he was advised that in order for us to have maximum confidence in his responses we would like him to take voluntarily a polygraph examination on his final responses, and the nature of such an examination was briefly discussed. (None of the respondents refused to continue participation, $N=40$.) He was assured that no probing of any type would occur beyond establishing the frequency of his involvement. The respondent then made the necessary modifications to his questionnaire and was afterwards introduced to the polygraph examiner who completed the examination.[9]

The respondents' initial responses had been surreptitiously recorded, and changes made during the polygraph examination were made in ink by the examiner. Therefore, we secured three different sets of responses: (1) initial

TABLE 1. Reporting Error and Per Cent Admitting Behavior For Self-Report Deviant Behavior Items

Deviant Behavior Items	REPORTING ERROR (PER CENT)[1]			Per cent admitting behavior[2]
	Accurate	Over-reported	Under-reported	
1. Run away from home	100.0	0.0	0.0	12.5
2. Attacked someone with the idea of taking his (her) life	100.0	0.0	0.0	0.0
3. Attempted to take my own life	100.0	0.0	0.0	2.5
4. Used force to get money or valuables from another person	95.0	2.5	2.5	2.5
5. Gotten a female other than my wife pregnant	95.0	2.5	2.5	7.5
6. Bribed or attempted to bribe a police officer or another type of official	95.0	5.0	0.0	7.5
7. Visited a house of prostitution	95.0	2.5	2.5	17.5
8. Carried a razor, switchblade, or gun as weapon	92.5	7.5	0.0	12.5
9. Taken part in gang fights	92.5	5.0	2.5	10.0
10. Used or sold narcotic drugs	92.5[3]	0.0[3]	5.0[3]	10.0
11. Taken things of large value (worth more than $50) that did not belong to me	92.5	5.0	2.5	5.0
12. Broken into and entered a home, store, or building	92.5	2.5	5.0	20.0
13. Struck my girlfriend or wife	92.5	2.5	5.0	15.0
14. Had a steady girlfriend	90.0	2.5	7.5	90.0
15. "Beaten up" on someone who hadn't done anything to me	90.0	5.0	5.0	10.0
16. Defied my parents' authority to their face	85.0	7.5	7.5	57.5
17. Taken a car for a ride without the owner's knowledge	85.0[3]	2.5[3]	7.5[3]	17.5
18. Attempted to force or forced a female to have sexual intercourse with me	85.0[3]	2.5[3]	7.5[3]	15.0
19. Driven a motor vehicle in an unauthorized drag race	80.0	5.0	15.0	45.0
20. Witnessed a crime and neither reported it nor made sure someone else had	80.0[3]	7.5[3]	7.5[3]	17.5
21. Had sex relations with a person of the same sex	80.0	5.0	15.0	22.5
22. Started a fist fight	80.0	17.5	2.5	22.5
23. Purposely damaged or destroyed public or private property that did not belong to me	77.5	10.0	12.5	55.0

24. Driven a car without a driver's license or permit (Do not include driver's training courses)	77.5[3]	2.5[3]	17.5[3]	62.5
25. Falsified information while filling out an application form or report	75.0	0.0	25.0	57.5
26. Taken things from someone else's desk or locker at school without permission	72.5	2.5	25.0	47.5
27. Gambled for money or something else with persons other than my family members	67.5	7.5	25.0	80.0
28. Had sex relations with a person of the opposite sex (other than my wife)	67.5	15.0	17.5	55.0
29. Masturbated	65.0	5.0	30.0	95.0
30. Bought or drunk beer, wine, or liquor illegally	65.0	2.5	32.5	95.0
31. Taken things of medium value (worth between $2 and $50) that didn't belong to me	65.0	2.5	32.5	45.0
32. Driven a motor vehicle at extreme speeds	52.5[3]	2.5[3]	40.0[3]	85.0
33. Had in my possession pictures, books, or other materials which were obviously obscene and prepared to arouse someone sexually	50.0[3]	7.5[3]	12.5[3]	50.0
34. Skipped school without a legitimate excuse	40.0[3]	2.5[3]	55.0[3]	85.0
35. Taken little things (worth less than $2) that didn't belong to me	32.5	5.0	62.5	87.5

Note: The items were presented to the respondents in five seven-item groups (one group per page) in the following order:

Group 1—35, 23, 25, 8, 22, 31, 1
Group 2—34, 24, 16, 26, 17, 33, 9
Group 3—21, 29, 3, 10, 11, 18, 2
Group 4—14, 12, 15, 20, 13, 4, 5
Group 5—30, 28, 6, 32, 7, 19, 27

1. Reporting error was determined by comparing responses on the initial questionnaire to final responses. A behavior is "over-reported" if the admitted frequency of commission is grea₊er in the initial questionnaire than in the final response. Conversely, a behavior is "under-reported" if the initial admitted frequency is less than in the final response. Accurate responses are those which remained unchanged between the first questionnaire and final polygraph interview. The three percentages add to 100.0.

2. In general, it appears that accuracy is directly related to seriousness of offense. It is possible that this relationship may be spurious because the lower reported incidence of the more serious offenses provides less opportunity for changes in responses to occur. However, because there is also the possibility to over-admit behavior on an item, items were ordered by the percentage of accurate responses. These percentages are based on the final responses.

3. Percentages do not add to 100.0 because of inaccuracies arising from respondents misunderstanding the meaning of an item.

responses to the classroom-administered questionnaire, (2) responses made after a private "interview" in which subjects were asked to re-consider their initial responses prior to a polygraph examination, and (3) responses made during the polygraph examination.

Findings

Overall validity. By the time the polygraph examination was completed, all respondents had made corrections to their questionnaire responses. About 58 per cent of the total number of changes between the initial questionnaire responses and the final responses were made at the time of the personal "interview" and 42 per cent during the polygraph examination.[10]

Three-fourths of all changes increased the frequency of admitted deviance, the remainder were in the opposite direction. In fact, all respondents under-reported the frequency of their misconduct on at least one item but only one-half over-reported on at least one item.

The validity of the initial responses on the questionnaire, based upon the number of items initially answered correctly (as determined by the polygraph) divided by the total number answered was 81.5 per cent. Respondents ranged from 47 to 97 per cent. There was a mean of 6.5 and a median of 6 changes on each questionnaire. (Calculated similarly, the validity of the "interview" responses was 92.3 per cent.) More narrowly, the validity of initial responses based only upon changes out of or into the zero category of frequency was about 92 per cent with the three-to-one ratio remaining between under-reporting and over-reporting.

We *tentatively* conclude that there is substantial empirical evidence that these questionnaire data are externally valid for the population covered and the conditions under which it was given. However, since this collection of items *in toto* has no particular theoretical relevance to the analysis of misconduct, we must examine the validity of the responses to individual items and groups of items which have been used previously as deliquency scales.

Item validity. Individual item accuracy (see Table 1) ranged from 33 to 100 per cent. Items 19, 21, 24, 25, 26, 27, 29, 30, 32, 34, and 35 were rather consistently under-reported; item 22 was frequently over-reported; and items 23 and 28 were both under- and over-reported. The reader will quickly recognize many of these items as parts of the Nye-Short seven-item general delinquency scale[11] and the Dentler-Monroe five-item adolescent theft scale.[12]

Scale validity. The question arises, then, as to what effect our validity findings have on the scale characteristics of these two Guttman-type scales. Should the items be differentially accurate, the predictive quality of the scale would be modified. This does not necessarily refute the utility of the scales as presently constructed, but it suggests the *possibility* that they can be made more useful if based upon more valid data. The Nye-Short scale consists of items 24, 35, 30, 23, 34, 28, and 16 (arranged in the scale order published in Nye and Short).[13] Item accuracy for our population ranged from 33 to 85 per cent with a mean of 64 per cent. The Dentler-Monroe adolescent theft scale, which consists of items 35, 26, 31, 17, and 11 (arranged similarly), had a mean accuracy of 71 per cent and ranged from 33 to 93 per cent).[14]

In regard to scalability (both after the initial and final responses), one item in each of the scales (Nye-Short item 30, Dentler-Monroe 11) did not meet the distribution-of-responses criterion required, a not too surprising finding when one considers the characteristics of our population.[15]

The Nye-Short items did not scale in the order indicated when either the initial or final responses were used. When the items were rearranged (items 35, 34, 29, 23, 16, and 24) the maximum reproducibility coefficient (0.85) was obtained with the initial responses. Using the final responses, the maximum coefficient of reproducibility (0.86) was obtained by using the same order, although any arrangement of the last four items produced the same coefficient. Further, with both the initial and final responses the number of respondents fitting pure scale types was inadequate. For these reasons, we conclude that the Nye-Short items did not "scale."

The Dentler-Monroe items fared much better. With the exception of item 11 which failed to meet the required response distribution, the items met all the requirements of Guttman-type scaling using both the initial and final responses. Using the published order of items the coefficient of reproducibility was .94. However, by using only four items there is a risk of overcapitalizing on chance in achieving such a coefficient.[16]

The data presented in Table 2, however, demonstrate that while there is a significant difference between original and final scale scores on both the Dentler-Monroe and Nye-Short scales, there is a high rank correlation between the ordering of subjects on the original questionnaire and the final ordering of subjects: Dentler-Monroe r=0.81 and Nye-Short r=0.80.

Factors Related to Systematic Error

Conformity to personal norms. Assuming that deviant behavior may be in conflict with norms to which individuals generally subscribe, we would expect persons in threatening situations to make errors in the direction of the norms. Such was the case in this study. Respondents were questioned on their feelings about the acceptability of the behavior described in each of the items. In 53 of 80 instances (66 per cent) in which respondents did not initially admit an act but later did, they stated the act was "never permissible" accord-

TABLE 2. Dentler-Monroe and Nye-Short Scale Scores Using Responses From Initial Interview and Final Interview

	Dentler-Monroe Scale Scores[a]			Nye-Short Scale Scores[b]	
Respondent	Initial interview	Final interview	Respondent	Initial interview	Final interview
1	5	4	1	14	14
2	4	4	2	12	12
3	3	3	12	12	13
4	3	3	18	11	12
5	3	3	3	11	12
6	3	4	24	11	11
7	3	4	6	11	10
8	3	2	4	9	9
9	2	3	9	9	9
10	2	2	10	9	10
11	2	3	17	9	10
12	2	2	30	9	12
13	2	3	31	9	10
14	2	3	5	9	10
15	2	4	19	8	9
16	2	2	22	8	8
17	2	3	35	8	9
18	1	1	40	8	10
19	1	1	21	7	7
20	1	1	25	7	10
21	1	1	13	7	13
22	1	2	15	7	10
23	1	1	20	6	6
24	1	2	8	6	9
25	1	2	7	6	9
26	1	3	26	6	12
27	1	3	16	6	8
28	1	1	28	6	8
29	1	1	27	5	12
30	1	2	14	5	7
31	1	1	29	5	6
32	1	2	23	4	8
33	1	1	34	3	5
34	0	0	33	3	4
35	0	1	11	2	5
36	0	0	37	2	5
37	0	1	32	2	6
38	0	1	39	1	3
39	0	0	38	1	3
40	0	1	36	0	2

a Dentler-Monroe scale scores were derived by dichotomizing responses into "no" and "admitted act at least once." See Robert A. Dentler and Lawrence J. Monroe, "Early Adolescent Theft," *American Sociological Review, 26* (October, 1961) pp. 733-744. Using a matched-pairs design, there is a significant difference between the original scale scores and the final corrected scale scores ($t=4.417$, $p<.001$). However, the association between the two sets of scores is high—the Spearman rank correlation coefficient, corrected for ties, is 0.81.

b Nye-Short scale scores were derived by trichotomizing responses into "not admitted," "once or twice," and "three or more" except the item concerning heterosexual activity which was trichotomized into "not admitted," "once through four times," "more than four." See F. Ivan Nye and James F. Short, Jr., "Scaling Delinquent Behavior," *American Sociological Review 22* (June, 1957) pp. 326-331. Using a matched-pairs design, there is a significant difference between the original scale scores and the final corrected scale scores ($t=6.59$, $p<.001$). However, the association between the two sets of scores is high—the Spearman rank correlation coefficient, corrected for ties, is 0.80.

ing to their own feelings.[17] Further, in 20 of the 26 instances (77 per cent) in which respondents initially admitted acts in spite of their not having committed them, respondents reported the behavior was personally "permissible in a few circumstances" or "in many circumstances."[18]

Conformity to group norms. Based upon the voluminous literature which suggests that commitment to group norms helps determine public behavior, we first assumed that responding to questionnaires did not represent total escape from the respondent's meaningful group attachments, and then hypothesized that errors would fall in the direction of perceived group norms. Our data tend to support this hypothesis.

In 29 of the 80 instances (36 per cent) in which respondents did not initially admit an act but later did, they stated that the act was "never permissible" according to the perceived standards of their reference group. (Reference group was operationally defined here as "the group of guys you have generally done things with.") The direct relevance of these data to the explanation of under-reporting errors is difficult to assess because every instance of group support coincided with a case of normative personal support. However, in 23 of the 26 instances (89 per cent) in which respondents initially admitted acts in spite of their not having committed them, respondents perceived group support for such acts. There is strong evidence that errors on questionnaires are directly associated with perceived discrepancies between individual acts and personal and group norms. The errors represent an attempt to make reported behavior compatible with perceived norms.

Involvement in misconduct. A positive relationship between the amount of misconduct ultimately admitted and reporting errors was expected and obtained. However, this relationship was thought to be spurious because the greater the number of items which applied to a person, the greater his opportunity to make errors in the under-reported direction. Because of this, the sample was divided into "high changers" and "low changers" on the basis of an error *rate*—the number of errors divided by number of items admitted. (The number of errors is the sum of the number of items changed between initial and final responses minus the over-reporting errors which were resolved to the zero category. The number of items admitted is based on final responses.) Average delinquency scores, shown in Table 3, indicate no significant relationship between error rate and amount of admitted misconduct. We must conclude from this comparison that there is no relationship between questionnaire validity (accuracy) and extent of involvement in deviant behavior.

Other indices. We also found that a general tendency to lie on other parts of our total questionnaire (as measured by a lie scale from the MMPI) was not related to inaccurate reporting on our deviant behavior items. In fact, we found no "liars" in our population if one used the traditional lie scale cutting-points.

TABLE 3. Mean Deliquency Scores for High and Low Response Changers

	Mean Delinquency Scores	
Items Included	High Changers	Low Changers
All items, except 14	54.4	55.4
Dentler-Monroe items	8.0	9.6
Nye-Short items	23.9	24.2

Note: Mean delinquency scores were computed by scoring frequency of commission as follows: "1-2" was given a value of 2; "3-4" a value of 4; and "over 4" a value of 6. These values were then averaged for the groups indicated. High and low response changers were determined on the basis of an error rate comparing first interview with final interview. See text for further detail.

The data also indicate that while all of our respondents held some positive evaluation of the efforts of social scientists, the more positive the evaluation, the lower the reporting error.

Further, our data suggest that the upwardly mobile, the religious and those with rural or small city residency are more likely than others to under-report their deviant behavior, although these relationships did not reach statistical significance. Another interesting finding suggests that items concerning homosexual behavior are more likely to elicit erroneous responses from single men than from married men, while the opposite is true on items concerning illicit heterosexual activity.

Conclusions

The main finding of this study is that self-reporting of delinquency is rather accurate when a wide range of behaviors is considered simultaneously, but that there is differential validity on specific questionnaire items. Those items most frequently used on delinquency scales were found to be rather inaccurate. These findings dictate the need for concern for the validity of indicators and the patterns of response bias to self-report data-gathering techniques. Hopefully, this type of study provides encouragement for further validity studies varying the area of investigation, the identifiability of the respondent, the degree of threat involved in the item content, the research situation, the social characteristics of respondents, and the type of self-report technique used.[19] It has been demonstrated by others that followup measures which differ from the initial measures probably enhance the validity of self-report data.[20] This study revealed that a particular type of personal interview, following group-administered anonymous self-report questionnaires, was beneficial in improving data validity.

Self-report techniques are well suited for etiological research, and it is time for some causal propositions to be operationalized and tested using these techniques. Validity studies such as ours can point out which qualitative items are accurate enough to use and what methodological procedures elicit the least amount of respondent bias. The latter finding is important in itself, yet has even greater importance for assessing the quality of inferential leaps made from samples to populations and from indicators to concepts in testing theoretical propositions.

This study might also provoke further investigations dealing with the relationships between normative structure and behavior, which has been suggested here as crucial in affecting the direction of reporting error. Inferences such as this may help in reinterpreting, for example, the research findings of a higher degree of delinquency involvement in an institutionalized population compared to a non-institutionalized population, or those in the lower class compared to those in the middle class. Assuming there are differences between the groups with respect to normative acceptance of the behavior items, employing the self-report technique to measure delinquency involvement may magnify behavioral differences, i.e., the institutionalized or lower-class persons may under-report considerably less (or over-report more) than the non-institutionalized or middle-class respondents.

Notes

1. Eleanor E. Maccoby and Nathan Maccoby, "The Interview: A Tool of Social Science," in Gardner Lindzey (ed.), *Handbook of Social Psychology*, vol. I, Reading, Massachusetts: Addison-Wesley, p. 482.

2. F. Ivan Nye and James F. Short, "Scaling Delinquent Behavior," *American Sociological Review*, 22 (June, 1957), pp. 326-331; Robert A. Dentler and Lawrence J. Monroe, "Early Adolescent Theft," *American Sociological Review*, 26 (October, 1961), pp. 733-743; Fred J. Murphy, Mary M. Shirley, and Helen L. Witner, "The Incidence of Hidden Delinquency," *American Journal of Orthopsychiatry*, 16 (October, 1946), pp. 686-696; John P. Clark and Eugene P. Wenninger, "Socio-Economic Class and Area as Correlates of Illegal Behavior Among Juveniles," *American Sociological Review*, 27 (December, 1962), pp. 826-834; James S. Wallerstein and Clement Wyle, "Our Law-Abiding Lawbreakers," *Probation*, (April, 1947), pp. 107-112; Maynard L. Erikson and Lamar T. Empey, "Court Records: Undetected Delinquency and Decision Making," *Journal of Criminal Law, Criminology and Police Science*, 54 (December, 1963), pp. 458-469; Edward E. Schwarz, "A Community Experiment in the Measurement of Juvenile Delinquency," *Yearbook of the National Probation Association*, 1945; Albert J. Reiss and Albert L. Rhodes, "The Distribution of Juvenile Delinquency in the Social Class Structure," *American Sociological Review*, 26 (October, 1961), pp. 720-732; William R. Arnold, "Continuities in Research: Scaling Delinquent Behavior," *Social Problems*, 13 (Summer, 1965), pp. 59-65.

3. For an exception to this appraisal see Robert H. Hardt and Sandra J. Peterson, "How Valid are Self-Report Measures of Delinquent Behavior?," Youth Development Center, Syracuse University, paper presented at the annual meeting of the Eastern Sociological Society, Philadelphia, April 16, 1966.

4. Nye and Short, *op. cit.*

5. For a discussion of this see Robert H. Hardt and George E. Bodine, *Development of Self-Report Instruments in Delinquency Research: A Conference Report,* Syracuse, New York: Syracuse University Press, 1965, pp. 22-23; Gene F. Summers and Andre D. Hammonds, "Toward a Paradign for Respondent Bias in Survey Research," paper presented at the annual meeting of the American Sociological Association, Chicago, 1965, pp. 3-4; and Claire Selltiz, Marie Jahoda, Morton Deutsch, and Stuart W. Cook, *Research Method in Social Relations,* New York: Holt, Rinehart and Winston, 1962, ch. 7.

6. The polygraph is a relatively simple instrument which measures certain physiological reactions of the person being tested. It is a diagnostic tool which indicates whether a person believes what he is saying. There are several conditions in which the polygraph examination can be rendered nearly or completely invalid: (1) *physiological abnormalities* such as excessively high or low blood pressure, heart diseases, respiratory disorders, or practically any painful ailment; (2) *extreme nervousness;* (3) *mental abnormalities* such as pronounced neuroses, psychoses, abnormally low intelligence, self-hypnosis, temporary amnesia, or pathological lying; (4) *unresponsiveness* resulting from extreme fatigue or mental exhaustion, being under the influence of alcohol or a number of drugs, or even modified yoga, muscle tension, or exciting imagery; and (5) *bodily movement* such as any physical or muscular activity that affects blood pressure. See *Use of Polygraph as "Lie Detectors" by the Federal Government,* Part 3; Panel Discussion with Scientists, Hearings before a Subcommittee of the Committee on Government Operations, House of Representatives, 86th Congress, Second Session, April 29-30, 1964, Washington: United States Government Printing Office, 1964, pp. 12-13. These conditions permit the individual to mislead the examiner. We had no reason to believe that any of these conditions significantly affected our results.

7. The respondents were all male undergraduates with a mean age of 20; all but two were white (two were Negroes). Thirty were single, five engaged or "pinned," and five were married. One-half were from large cities or their suburbs, sixteen were from small urban areas, two from rural non-farm areas, the remaining two from farms. As an index of social class the Duncan Socio-Economic Index Scores based on occupation of father was used, giving the following distribution: 0-23, 4; 24-47, 10; 48-71, 15; 72-96, 7; and unclassified, 4. See Albert J. Reiss, Jr., Otis Dudley Duncan, Paul K. Hatt, and Cecil C. North, *Occupation and Social Status,* New York: The Free Press of Glencoe, 1961, esp. pp. 109-161.

8. As is evident later, these were not interviews in the usual sense in that the respondent was not interviewed directly about his past deviant behavior. However, no other term seems more appropriate. The personal engagement was focused upon the establishment of rapport, the giving of information about the remainder of the experiment, and the appeal for continued participation. Forty of the original 45 were scheduled for this interview. Two were not reached by telephone and three stated their academic schedules were too demanding to allow participation. (The experiment was conducted during the final week of scheduled classes.)

9. The polygraph can indicate whether the person is responding emotionally but not why. When an indication of deception occurred with one of our respondents the examiner asked the respondent if he wanted to make a change in his response. Almost all respondents made changes. We, of course, have made the assumption that the difference in both quality and quantity of deviance between that admitted on our initial questionnaire and that detected on the polygraph can

be explained by the greater accuracy of the polygraph procedure. The accuracy of the polygraph can be challenged when it is employed under certain conditions. The question of polygraph validity is a judgmental question. It would be better to ask what is the degree of validity and under what circumstances was this validity obtained? For example, some studies show that the more motivated the subject is, the easier it is to detect deception. (See *Use of Polygraph as "Lie Detectors" by the Federal Govrnmnt, op. cit.*, p. 305.) It is also standard procedure, and one which we used, that a belief in the ability of the polygraph to detect deceptions must be established by the examiner. The examiner, like the instruments used, the social characteristics of the respondents, sample of questions, etc., is a crucial variable. The polygraph examiner in our study was a highly qualified licensed polygraph examiner with 18 years of experience who is employed by the State Bureau of Criminal Investigations. Some recent studies show that the polygraph can be used to detect deception (of the type which can be arranged to permit experimentation) by objective criteria in 90 percent or more of the cases. (See Joseph F. Kubis, "Studies in Lie Detection: Computer Feasibility Considerations," *RATC-TR 62-205*, June, 1962; David T. Lykken, "The GSR in the Detection of Guilt," *Journal of Applied Psychology*, 43 (1950), pp. 385-388; Henry V. Baesen, Chia-Mon Chung, and Chen-Ya Yang, "A Lie Detection Experiment," *Journal of Criminal Law and Criminology*, 39 (1948), pp. 532-537. Also see, *Use of Polygraphs as "Lie Detectors" by the Federal Government, op. cit.*, pp. 438-439 and 441-442, for a review of other studies on the polygraph. When used as a self-report technique we believe the data elicited are more accurate than the initial questionnaire data and in turn more accurate than the "interview" follow-up data. Although there may be some error in the quantity and quality of data gathered in this study, we feel we can safely say that our respondents believed the answers they gave to be accurate.

10. The changes reported do not reflect changes that were made due to clarification and explanation by the interviewer or polygraph examiner, nor do they include changes where blanks were left in the original questionnaire, nor where the respondent checked the category "over 4" but did not make an estimate of frequency. The reliability of the polygraph was also estimated by asking 10 of the 40 respondents to return again for a retest of the polygraph examination, answering the identical questions. Appointments were set up for these ten persons immediately after the first polygraph examination although they were tested a few days later and again paid eight dollars. Reliability was 99.7 per cent.

11. Nye and Short, *op. cit.*

12. Dentler and Monroe, *op. cit.*

13. Nye and Short, *op. cit.*

14. Dentler and Monroe, *op. cit.*

15. Matilda White Riley, John W. Riley, Jr., and Jackson Toby, *Sociological Studies in Scale Analysis,* New Brunswick, N. J.: Rutgers University Press, 1954, p. 279.

16. Samuel A. Stouffer, *Social Research to Test Ideas,* New York: Free Press of Glencoe, 1962, p. 276.

17. The 80 instances involved 34 different respondents.

18. The 26 instances involved 15 different respondents.

19. Summers and Hammonds, *op. cit.*

20. Winston Ehrmann, *Premarital Dating Behavior,* New York: Bantam Books, 1960; and James Walters, "Relation Between Reliability of Responses in Family Life: Research and Method of Data Collection," *Marriage and Family Living*, 22 (August, 1960), pp. 232-237.

DAVID LANDY
and
ELLIOT ARONSON

The Influence of the Character of the Criminal and His Victim on the Decisions of Simulated Jurors*

According to popular conceptions, the criminal trial is symbolic of justice in America. Presumably all parties in the judicial process—lawyers, defendants, victims, witnesses, jurors and judges—are collectively engaged in the pursuit of "truth" and "justice." The criminal trial, however, like any system of human action, involves variations in perceptions and behaviors similar to that found in any social situation. Although the proverb that "Justice is blind" may sometimes prevail it seems likely that factors other than the defendant's complicity or "real guilt" also influence the sanctioning process. For example, the rather harsh sentences accorded black defendants when white victims are involved suggests that sentencing practices are influenced by the interplay between defendant and victim characteristics. Along these same lines, other research has shown that the sentencing practices of judges often vary considerably and that these variations are related to background and attitudinal configurations.

As suggested above, factors that are likely to influence sentencing practices of *jurors* (although in most jurisdictions judges assign sentences, in some jurisdictions juries do so and in still others juries do so in specific kinds of cases) are the relative attractiveness or status of either the defendant or the victim. An attractive or high-status defendant, for ex-

Reprinted by permission of Academic Press, Inc. from David Landy and Elliot Aronson, "The Influence of the Character of the Criminal and His Victim on the Decisions of Simulated Jurors," *Journal of Experimental Social Psychology*, 1969, 5:141-152.

*This study was supported by a grant from the National Institute of Mental Health (MH 12357) to Elliot Aronson.

ample, is likely to elicit responses from jurors wherein an acceptable justification or set of mitigating circumstances is found for the behavior. These responses then necessitate only the mildest of sanctions or no sanctions at all. In similar fashion, an attractive or high status victim is likely to elicit reactions of liking and sympathy such that the defendant's actions are seen by the jurors as being inexcusable and deserving of punishment. The unattractive victim, on the other hand, is less likely to elicit such feelings of liking or sympathy and, in fact, may even be seen as deserving of the injury received. Lastly, the behavior of the unattractive or low-status defendant is likely to be seen as being consistent with the kind of person he "really" is. That is, "bad" behavior and "bad" people go together. If such a definition exists in the courtroom situation then the unattractive defendant is likely to be seen as being more responsible for his behavior and deserving of harsher sanctions.

The following study by Landy and Aronson deals with some of the issues just discussed and supports the major arguments advanced above. In two separate experiments subjects were presented with a standardized description of a crime of negligent homicide by way of an automobile. In Experiment I the victim of the crime was presented to one-half of the subjects as an attractive person and to the other half of the subjects as an unattractive person. In Experiment II the attractiveness of the defendant was also systematically varied. The actual circumstances of the crime were, of course, identical for all experimental conditions. The subjects were asked to sentence the defendant to a specific number of years of imprisonment.

As predicted, the results suggest that both the character of the defendant and the character of the victim are important variables influencing the severity of the sentence imposed. Experiment I showed that subjects in the Attractive Victim condition sentenced the defendant to a greater number of years of imprisonment than subjects in the Unattractive Victim condition. In Experiment II subjects in the Unattractive Defendant condition sentenced the defendant more severely than subjects in the Attractive Defendant condition.

This article neatly illustrates the use of experimental techniques through the use of paper-and-pencil procedures. The findings are consistent with other studies presented throughout the course of this book which demonstrate that the more powerful and privileged within our society have distinct advantages in being able to avoid the deviant label and in getting their way. On the other hand, less powerful and less privileged persons are more susceptible to deviant imputations and thereby accrue a disproportionate share of the negative sanctions imposed within the society.

Several writers have commented on the irrational tendency of people to exaggerate a person's causal responsibility for an event while underestimating the role of other causal factors which are logically involved in the occurrence of that event (Heider, 1944, 1958; Jones and Davis, 1965). This tendency to perceive persons as causal origins often influences the manner in which we evaluate or judge other individuals. That is, we often judge a person in terms of the consequences or effects of which we perceive him to be the causal origin. This occurs even in situations were there are many factors beyond the person's control which, from a logical point of view, are responsible for the specific effects.

For example, an experiment by Walster (1966) demonstrated that the more serious the consequences of an accident, the greater was the tendency for subjects to assign responsibility for the accident to someone who could *possibly* be held responsible for it. In Walster's experiment subjects heard a tape-recorded description of an accident in which a car owner parked his uninsured car at the top of a hill. The hand brake cable of the car broke and the car started to roll down the hill. For some of the subjects the damage caused by the car was described as having been minimal—the car was stopped by a tree stump and was slightly dented. For other subjects the damage was described as having been serious—the car rolled all the way down the hill, crashing through the window of a store and injuring two people. The subjects did not perceive the car owner as being more careless when the consequences of the accident were serious. They did, however, apply more strict moral standards in assessing his behavior, feeling that he was under greater moral obligation to have had auto insurance and to have had his brakes checked more frequently when the consequences of the accident were severe than when they were mild.

The fact that greater responsibility was attributed to the car owner when the effects of the accident were serious raises an interesting question concerning the judgment and punishment of criminal behavior. It is likely that people somehow view a crime as being more serious if the victim of the crime is a good, attractive person. If this is the case, one might ask whether individuals have a tendency to judge a criminal defendant more harshly when the *victim* of the crime is an attractive individual than when the victim is an unattractive individual. While "the law" makes no such distinction (i.e., a criminal is not held to be more responsible, guilty, or deserving of punishment the more sympathetic and attractive his victim), it is quite possible that the decision of a jury will be affected by the character of the victim in a criminal case.

This possibility apparently has not escaped the attention of criminals' counsel. Percy Foreman, a noted criminal defense lawyer, has claimed that "The best defense in a murder case is the fact that the deceased should have been killed regardless of how it happened" (Smith, 1966). In one case in which Foreman represented a woman who had confessed to shooting her husband, Foreman so effectively villified the victim that he felt "The jury was ready to dig up the deceased and shoot him all over again" (Smith, 1966). The jury did acquit his client.

The present research deals with the relationship between the personal characteristics of the victim of a crime and the desire or tendency of individuals to punish the person accused of committing that crime. In Experiment I the personal characteristics of the victim of a criminal offense are varied. We have predicted that when the victim of a criminal offense is presented as having positive characteristics, subjects will be more severe in their "sentencing" of the defendant than when the victim of the identical offense is presented as having negative characteristics.

While the present research is not directly concerned with the law or legal system *per se,* it does have obvious implications for both. The juridical analog seems to provide the most logical means of testing our hypothesis. For obvious reasons, however, we were unable to utilize real juries in actual criminal trials. The investigator of legal processes and judicial decision is confronted with numerous social, economic, and methodological difficulties (Kalven and Zeisal, 1966; Zeisal, 1962; Strodtbeck, 1962; James and Strodtbeck, 1957; Redmount, 1961). An attempt to manipulate variables within the context of an actual trial would be impossible. In addition, since there are a multiplicity of factors entering into a determination of guilt, we wanted to employ a situation in which there was little or no doubt in the minds of our subjects about the guilt of the defendant, i.e., a situation in which it would be clear that he had actually perpetrated the offense. We could then ask our subjects to sentence the defendant to what they felt was an appropriate number of years of imprisonment. This would provide us with a continuous variable, indicating severity of punishment, for our major dependent variable. Furthermore, we wanted to be able to control the circumstances of the crime so that it would not only be identical for all subjects but also be completely independent of the characteristics of the victim.

Experiment I

Method

Subjects were 261 male and female sophomores at the University of Texas who had agreed to participate in a study dealing with "Juridicial Judgment" in order to fulfill a requirement in their introductory psychology course. Twelve experimental sessions were scheduled on 4 consecutive days with from 20 to 30 subjects participating in each session.

The experimental sessions were all held in a university classroom. At the start of each session the experimenter greeted the subjects and then made the following comments:

"We are interested in studying the manner in which people judge various criminal offenses. I am going to give each of you a booklet which contains a brief account of a criminal offense. When you have finished reading the case account, you will be asked to give your personal opinion concerning the case. That is, we want you to sentence the defendant described in the case account to a specific number of years of imprisonment. Take as much time as you want in reading and contemplating the case before you finally sentence the defendant. Remember that we are interested in your personal opinion, so please give your own personal judgment and not how you feel others might react to the case or how you feel you should react to it. One other thing—in making your sentence, consider the question of parole as being beyond your jurisdiction. That is, sentence the defendant irrespective of whether or not you feel he should have the opportunity for parole after a certain number of years in prison."

The experimenter then passed out copies of a case account of a negligent automobile homocide. These were identical for all subjects except in one respect: In approximately one-half of the case accounts the victim of the negligent homocide was presented as an unattractive individual, while in the other half of the case accounts the victim was presented as an attractive individual. The assignment of subjects to either the Attractive or Unattractive Victim condition was, of course, random. There were 129 subjects in the Attractive Victim condition and 132 subjects in the Unattractive Victim condition.

The description of the crime as presented in the case account is presented below:

"John Sander was driving home from an annual Christmas office party on the evening of December 24 when his automobile struck and killed a pedestrian by the name of Martin Lowe. The circumstances leading to this event were as follows: The employees of the insurance office where Sander worked began to party at around 2:00 p.m. on the afternoon of the 24th. By 5:00 p.m. some people were already leaving for home, although many continued to drink and socialize. Sander, who by this time had had several drinks, was offered a lift home by a friend who did not drink and who suggested that Sander leave his car at the office and pick it up when he was in 'better shape.' Sander declined the offer, claiming he was 'stone sober' and would manage fine. By the time Sander had finished another drink, the party was beginning to break up. Sander left the office building and walked to the garage where he had parked his car, a four-door 1965 Chevrolet. It had just started to snow. He wished the garage attendant a Merry Christmas and pulled out into the street. Traffic was very heavy at the time. Sander was six blocks from the garage when he was stopped by a policeman for reckless driving. It was quite apparent to the officer that Sander had been drinking, but rather than give him a ticket on Christmas Eve, he said that he would let Sander off if he would promise to leave his car and take a taxi. Sander agreed. The officer hailed a taxi and Sander got into it. The minute the taxi had turned a corner, however, Sander told the driver to pull over to the curb and let him out. Sander paid the driver and started back to where he had parked his own car. Upon reaching his car he proceeded to start it up and drove off. He had driven four blocks from where the police officer had stopped him when he ran a red light and struck

Lowe, who was crossing the street. Sander immediately stopped the car. Lowe died a few minutes later on the way to the hospital. It was later ascertained that internal hemorrhaging was the cause of death. Sander was apprehended and charged with negligent homicide. The police medical examiner's report indicated that Sander's estimated blood alcohol concentration was between 2.5 and 3.0% at the time of the accident."

Manipulation of the Description of the Victim

The next paragraph in the case account contained a description of the victim, which differed for subjects in each of the two experimental conditions.

Attractive victim. "The victim, 48-year-old Martin Lowe, was a senior partner of a successful stock brokerage firm and an active member of the community welfare board. He was a widower and is survived by his son and daughter-in-law, Mr. and Mrs. Thomas Lowe. At the time of the accident the victim was on his way to the Lincoln Orphanage, of which he was a founding member, with Christmas gifts."

Unattractive victim. "The victim, 48-year-old Martin Lowe, was a notorious hoodlum and ex-convict who had been convicted of assault and extortion. He was a henchman for a crime syndicate which had been under police investigation for some time. A loaded 32-caliber pistol was found on his body."

The final paragraph of the case account contained a description of the defendant, which was the same for all subjects. The defendant was described as a 37-year-old insurance adjustor and divorcee. While he had no previous criminal record, he did have several serious violations on his traffic record.

The last page of the case account booklet contained instructions to the subjects to judge and sentence the defendant. In these, the subjects were requested to consider the crime as being punishable for from 1 to 60 years of imprisonment, and to sentence the defendant to a specific number of years of imprisonment according to their own personal judgment. They were told to take as much time as they wanted in making their decision.

When all of the subjects had completed sentencing the defendant, the experimenter collected the booklets. He then explained the nature of the experiment to the subjects.

Results

Each subject sentenced the defendant in the automobile homocide case to a specific number of years of imprisonment. We predicted that those subjects to whom the victim of the crime had been described as possessing positive characteristics would sentence the defendant to a greater number of years of imprisonment than those subjects to whom the victim had been presented as possessing negative characteristics. The results of the study lend support to this prediction. The mean sentence of subjects in the Attractive Victim condition was 15.77 years, while the mean sentence of subjects in the Unattractive

Victim condition was 12.90 years. However, this difference did not reach the conventional level of significance, ($F = 3.18$, 1 and 257 df, $p < .08$). This F ratio is the result of a two-way analysis of variance in which the nature of the victim was one factor and sex was the other factor. As expected, there were no systematic effects due to sex. The main effect for sex yielded $F = 1.05$ (1 and 257 df, $p < .31$). The interaction yielded $F < 1$.

Experiment II

Because of the marginal nature of the above results, we repeated the experiment with some slight modifications designed to make the manipulation more powerful. In addition, we manipulated the character of the defendant in order to assess the effect of this variable on the judgment of the subjects.

It is a common belief that jurors in a criminal trial are often influenced by the personal characteristics of the *defendant*. That is, they have a tendency to be more lenient in their decision when the defendant possesses certain positive characteristics and more severe when he possesses certain negative characteristics, even when these are apparently unrelated to the offense or circumstances in which it took place.

There is, in fact, some empirical evidence which indicates that sentiments about the defendant—his court appearance, family, occupation, etc.—may actually influence the decision of a jury. In a large-scale study of the decisions of judges and juries, Kalven and Zeisal (1966) asked judges to report by mail questionnaire on criminal cases which were tried before them with juries. The judges reported the actual verdict handed down by the jury, what their own verdict would have been had the case been tried before them without a jury, and the reasons which they thought accounted for disagreements when the two verdicts differed. In a sample of 962 cases in which the judge and jury disagreed about the verdict, the judges attributed 11% of the disagreements to factors related to the impression created by the defendant. In another sample of 293 disagreement cases in which judges were asked to indicate on the questionnaire whether they felt the impression made by the defendant was sympathetic, average, or unattractive, 14% of the disagreements were attributed to sentiments about the defendant.

These results seem to indicate that an attractive defendant can move the jury to be more lenient than the judge would have been, i.e., acquit rather than convict. Conversely, an unattractive defendant can presumably move the jury to be more severe than the judge would have been, i.e., convict rather than acquit. Still, the investigators note that the defendant factor rarely accounted for judge-jury disagreements in and of itself, but rather, acted in conjunction with other variables such as (a) disparity in the quality of the prosecution and defense counsel and (b) the ambiguity of the evidence presented during the trial. There is, of course, no information presented with regard to the extent which the judge himself is motivated in his decision by feelings about the defendant. However, the assumption is that the judge is less influenced than the jury by such sentiments. His primary concern is with the law and he is probably less swayed than the jury by extra-legal factors.[1]

In Experiment II the characteristics of both the defendant and the victim are varied. We have predicted that the more unattractive the presentation of the defendant, the more severe will be the sentence and the nature of the victim is, of course, the same as that in Experiment I—the more attractive the victim, the more severe the sentence.

Method

Subjects were 116 male and female students in two sections of an introductory government course at the University of Texas. The regular class instructor—the same individual for both sections—served as the experimenter.[2] The experimental sessions took place during regular class meetings and the subjects were not given any indication that they were participating in an experiment.

The basic case account of the automobile homocide offense presented to the subjects was nearly identical to that presented in Experiment I. In the present experiment, however, both the nature of the defendant and the nature of the victim were systematcially varied in a 2×3 design with two levels of victim character: Attractive and unattractive; and three levels of defendant character: Attractive, unattractive, and neutral. In addition, the descriptions of the defendant and victim were interpolated throughout the case account instead of appearing complete at the end of the account. This was done in order to make the personal characteristics of the defendant and victim salient throughout the description of the crime. It was also felt that this was a more subtle way of providing the subjects with the information about the principals involved in the case.

At the start of each of the two experimental class sessions, the instructor informed the students that he was going to give each of them a booklet containing a brief account of a criminal offense. He continued with instructions and remarks similar to those employed by the experimenter in the first study. When he completed these introductory comments, the instructor passed out the copies of the case account, randomly assigning each student to one of the six experimental conditions. There were 21 subjects in the Neutral Defendant-Attractive Victim conditions, 23 subjects in the Neutral Defendant-Unattractive Victim condition, and 18 subjects in each of the remaining four conditions (Attractive Defendant-Attractive Victim; Unattractive Defendant-Attractive Victim; Attractive Defendant-Unattractive Victim; Unattractive Defendant-Unattractive Victim).

Below are the aggregate descriptions of the defendant and the victim. Again, the subjects were not presented with them in this fashion, but with each sentence or descriptive phrase inserted at the appropriate place in the case account, depending on the condition to which the subject had been assigned. The descriptions were based, in part, on the comments made by the judges in Kalven and Zeisal's (1966) study concerning the characteristics of individual defendants which appeared to influence jury sentiments.

Attractive victim. "Lowe is a noted architect and prominent member of the community. He had designed many well-known buildings throughout the state . . . was an active member of the community welfare board. At the time of the incident, Lowe was on his way to the Lincoln Orphanage, of which he was a founding member, with Christmas gifts. He is survived by his wife and two children, ages 11 and 15."

Unattractive victim. "Lowe is a notorious gangster and syndicate boss who had been vying for power in the syndicate controlling the state's underworld activities. He was best known for his alleged responsibility in the Riverview massacre of five men. At the time of the incident, Lowe was carrying a loaded 32-caliber pistol which was found on his body. He had been out of jail on bond, awaiting trial on a double indictment of mail fraud and income tax evasion."

Attractive defendant. "Sander is a sixty-four-year-old insurance adjustor who has been employed by the same insurance firm for 42 years. Sander was friendly with everyone and was known as a good worker. Sander is a widower, his wife having died of cancer the previous year, and he is, consequently, spending Christmas Eve with his son and daughter-in-law. When the incident occurred, Sander's leg banged the steering column, reaggravating a gun wound which had been the source of a slight limp and much pain. Sander's traffic record shows he has received three tickets in the past five years, two of which were moving violations."

Unattractive defendant. "Sander is a thirty-three-year-old janitor. In the building where Sander has been working as a janitor for the past two months, he was not known by many of the firm employees, but was nevertheless invited to join the party. Sander is a two-time divorcee, with three children by his first wife, who has since remarried. He was going to spend Christmas Eve with his girlfriend in her apartment. The effect of the incident on Sander was negligible; he was slightly shaken up by the impact, but suffered no major injuries. Sander has two misdemeanors on his criminal record in the past five years—breaking and entering and a drug violation. His traffic record shows three tickets in the same space of time."

Neutral defendant. "Sander is employed in the area. He went to the office party in the insurance firm headquarters shortly after the party had begun. After the party Sander was heading in the direction of home. When the incident occurred, Sander was slightly shaken up by the impact, but suffered no major injuries. His traffice record shows he has received three traffic tickets in the past five years, two of which were moving violations."

The case accounts ended as follows: "Sander, who had stopped his car at the scene of the accident, was apprehended and charged with negligent automobile homicide, a crime which in the State is punishable by imprisonment of one to twenty-five years."

Following the description of the offense was a page of instructions requesting the subjects to judge and sentence the defendant. The subjects were requested to consider the crime of negligent automobile homocide as punishable for from 1 to 25 years imprisonment, and to sentence the defendant to a specific number of years of imprisonment, acording to their *own personal judgment.* They were told to take as much time as they wanted in making their decision.

The last page of the case account booklets contained several additional questions pertaining to the subject's feeling about the guilt of the defendant, and his impressions of the defendant and the victim. Each of these questions was answered on a 9-point scale appropriately labeled at the end points.

Results and Discussion

In order to assess the effectiveness of the character descriptions of the defendant and the victim, we asked the subjects to indicate their impressions of the defendant and the victim on a 9-point scale on which "9" meant "extremely negative (unfavorable)" and "1" meant "extremely positive (favorable)." The mean impression rating of the victim for the subjects in the Attractive Victim (AV) conditions was 2.52, while the mean impression rating of the victim for subjects in the Unattractive Victim (UV) conditions was 7.64. This difference was significant at beyond the .001 level of probability ($F = 354.21$, 1 and 111 df). The mean impression ratings of the defendant were as follows: For subjects in the Attractive Defendant (AD) conditions, 5.53; for subjects in the Neutral Defendant (ND) condtions, 6.04; and for subjects in the Unattractive Defendant (UD) conditions, 7.08. An analysis of variance performed on these data yielded $F = 8.11$ (2 and 111 df, $p < .001$). It is thus apparent that the character descriptions of the defendant and the victim had their intended effect.

The subjects were also requested to rate how guilty they felt the defendant was. We, of course, expected that there would be no differences in the subjects' guilt ratings of the defendant across experimental conditions and that the defendant would be perceived as having been definitely guilty of the crime. On a scale where "9" meant "definitely guilty of the crime," the subjects' guilt ratings of the defendant ranged from a mean of 8.00 (for subjects in the ND-UV condition) to a mean of 8.67 (for subjects in the AD-UV condition). The difference betwen these two extremes did not reach the conventional level of significance ($t = 1.47$, 39 df). The null hypothesis, of course, cannot be proved; nevertheless, the guilt rating data does afford some support regarding the subjects' uniform perception of the defendant's guilt.

With regard to the effect of the character description of the victim on the severity of sentence passed on the defendant, the results of Experiment II parallel those of Experiment I. Table 1 presents the means and standard deviations of the sentences made by the subjects in each of the experimental conditions.

An examination of this table indicates that, as predicted, the average sentence made by subjects in the AV conditions, 10.55 years imprisonment, was greater than the average sentence made by the subjects in the UV conditions, 8.48 years imprisonment. An analysis of variance yields an F ratio of 2.79

for the main effect due to the character of the victim. This only reaches the .09 level of significance (1 and 111 df). While the data in both Experiments I and II lend directional support to the hypothesis concerning the relationship between the character of the victim and the severity of sentencing, in neither experiment does the magnitude of the obtained differences between the AV and UV conditions reach the conventional level of significance. We, therefore, transformed the sentences in the two experiments to standard scores ($M = 50, S = 10$) and performed an analysis on the combined standardized data. It will be recalled that while the basic case account and procedure was similar in both experiments, the range of possible sentences differed. In Experiment I it was from 1 to 60 years and in Experiment II it was from 1 to 25 years. The transformation to standard scores made the data of the two experiments comparable.

TABLE 1. Means and Standard Deviations of the Sentences (expressed as years of imprisonment) Made by Subjects in Each of the Experimental Conditions of Experiment II

		VICTIM		
		Attractive	Unattractive	Total
Defendant				
Attractive	M	8.72	8.44	8.58
	σ	4.18	6.60	
	N	18.	18.	36.
Neutral	M	9.05	7.39	8.22
	σ	9.01	7.63	
	N	21.	23.	44.
Unattractive	M	13.89	9.61	11.75
	σ	5.76	5.98	
	N	18.	18.	36.
Total	M	10.55	8.48	
	N	57.	59.	

With the data of Experiments I and II combined, the mean standardized sentence of the 186 subjects in the AV condition was 51.42; the mean standardized sentence of the 191 subjects in the UV condition was 48.92. The analysis performed on the combined data showed this difference to be significant at beyond the .03 level of probability ($F = 5.09$, 1 and 374 df).

We now turn to the data concerning the influence of the defendant's character on the severity of sentences made by the subjects. The data indicate that subjects in the UD conditions were more severe in their sentences than subjects in either the ND or AD conditions, even though the crime committed was identical in all conditions. Again, looking at Table 1, we see that the mean sentence given to the defendant by subjects in the AD conditions was 8.58 years, the mean sentence given by the subjects in the ND conditions was 8.22 years, and the mean sentence given by subjects in the UD conditions was 11.75 years. The analysis of variance yielded a significant main effect due to the defendant's character factor ($F = 3.27$, 2 and 111 df, $p < .05$). While the mean sentence given by subjects in the ND conditions is slightly smaller than that given by subjects in the AD conditions, the difference does not approach statistical significance. The AD versus ND contrast produced a $t < 1$ (79 df). The contrast comparing the AD and ND versus the UD conditions is significant ($t = 2.51$, 115 df, $p < .05$, two-tailed test). There was no significant interaction between the defendant's and the victim's character factors ($F < 1$).

One reason that the subjects were more lenient on the neutral and attractive defendants is that subjects in the ND and AD conditions may have found it easier to identify with the defendant than could subjects in the UD condition. That is, the subjects may have found it easier to imagine themselves involved in a similar situation when the defendant was attractive or neutral simply because they had potentially more in common with the defendant in those conditions.

It may also be that subjects not only perceive the crime as being more serious when the victim is attractive as opposed to unattractive, but that they also view the defendant as being more unattractive when the victim is attractive. This latter possibility receives some support from the impression ratings of the defendant. When the victim was presented as being an attractive person, the subjects' impression of the defendant was significantly less favorable than when the victim was presented as an unattractive person. The mean impression rating of the defendant for subjects in the AV conditions was 6.53; for subjects in the UV conditions it was 5.9 ($F = 3.77$, 1 and 111 df, $p < .05$).

If this was simply the result of a contrast effect, i.e., a tendency to exaggerate the difference between the characters of the defendant and the victim, one would expect a similar difference in the impression ratings of the *victim* made by subjects in the AD and UD conditions. No such difference was manifest. For subjects in the AD conditions, the mean impression rating of the victim was 5.23, for subjects in the UD conditions it was 5.31.

Taken as a whole, our results suggest that both the character of the defendant and the character of the victim are important variables in the severity of the sentence imposed. While the results of these laboratory experiments may have important implications for actual jury trials, a direct and literal extrapolation would be imprudent. Regardless of how seriously our subjects took their task, the fact remains that college students sitting in a classroom are not identical to actual jurors sitting in judgment at a real trial. At the same time, we are encouraged by the fact that in the absence of extraneous stimuli, our results paralleled some of the findings of Kalven and Zeisal (1966) in their examination of actual cases.

References

Gaudet, F. J. Individual differences in the sentencing tendencies of judges. *Archives of Psychology,* 1938, 32, No. 230.

Heider, F. Social perception and phenomenal causality. *Psychological Review,* 1944, 51, 358-374.

Heider, F. *The psychology of interpersonal relations.* New York: Wiley, 1958.

James, R. M., and Strodtbeck, F. L. An attempted replication of a jury experiment by use of radio and newspaper. *Public Opinion Quarterly,* 1957, 21, 313-318.

Jones, E. E., and Davis, K. E. From acts to dispositions: the attribution process in person perception. In L. Berkowitz (Ed.), *Advances in experimental social psychology,* Vol. II. New York: Academic Press, 1965. Pp. 219-266.

Kalven, H., Jr., and Ziesal, H. *The American jury.* Boston: Little, Brown, 1966.

Redmount, R. S. Psychology and the law. In H. Toch (Ed.), *Legal and criminal psychology.* New York: Holt, 1961, Pp. 22-50.

Smith, M. Percy Foreman: top trial lawyer. *Life,* 1966, 60, 92-101.

Strodtbeck, F. Social process, the law, and jury functioning. In W. M. Evan (Ed.), *Law and sociology.* New York: Free Press of Glencoe, 1962. Pp. 144-164.

Walster, E. Assignment of responsibility for an accident. *Journal of Personality and Social Psychology,* 1966, 3, 73-79.

Zeisal, H. Social research and the law: the ideal and the practical. In W. M. Evan (Ed.), *Law and sociology.* New York: Free Press of Glencoe, 1962. Pp. 124-143.

Notes

1. Extra-legal factors often do affect judges' decisions. Evidence of this was found in the considerable individual differences between judges with regard to the severity of sentences (number of penal sentences passed) which they impose on convicted criminals for the same type of offense, in the same criminal court (time and locale constant). Experience does not appear to be an important factor in accounting for these inter-judge differences. Judges come onto the bench with the same individual tendencies which they maintain even over a ten-year period (see Guadet, 1938).

2. The authors would like to express their appreciation to Dr. Stuart Pullen for his cooperation and assistance.

DEREK L. PHILLIPS

Rejection: A Possible Consequence of Seeking Help for Mental Disorders*

In reacting to deviance, members of the social audience seem particularly influenced by knowledge of the deviant's previous contact with social control agencies. Knowledge that someone doing deviant things has sought outside help is likely to structure the evaluations of that person with the result that the person's deviance takes on different meanings than it would have if no outside help had been sought. Phillips directly confronts this problem by examining the effect that different kinds of help-sources have on the rejection of mentally ill persons.

Taking as given the fact that a person has been labeled as mentally ill, Phillips uses an experimental interview situation to examine the relationship between use of various mental health sources and rejecting behavior by others. The findings support the major hypothesis that individuals exhibiting *identical behavior* are increasingly rejected as they are perceived as persons who have not sought help, as persons seeing a clergyman, as persons seeing a physician, and so on. Using a psychiatrist or a mental hospital had the greatest impact on rejection patterns, a finding of particular interest to students of deviance.

Reprinted by permission of the American Sociological Association from Derek Phillips, "Rejection: A Possible Consequence of Seeking Help for Mental Disorders," *American Sociological Review*, Vol. 28, 1963, pp. 963-972.

*This investigation was carried out during the tenure of a Predoctoral Fellowship from the National Institute of Mental Health. The writer wishes to thank C. Richard Fletcher, Phillip S. Hammond, and Elton F. Jackson for their helpful suggestions.

Phillips interprets these findings as indicating that use of professional help sources provides the audience member with information which serves to identify the "mentally ill" individual as someone with a serious problem, as someone who cannot handle his own problems. These identifications increase the likelihood of rejection of that person.

Further analysis of the relationship between rejection and help-source showed that: (1) among respondents who had first-hand experiences with relatives who had sought help for an emotional problem, greater rejection occurred under the circumstances of seeking no help or going only to a clergyman; and (2) among respondents who did not adhere to the norm of self-reliance, greater rejection occurred when no help was sought. These findings underscore a basic dimemma confronting those defined as mentally ill: A person cannot avoid rejection by some members of the social audience once he has been identified as mentally ill. If he seeks psychiatric help he will be rejected by members of the community (and society at large) whereas if he seeked no help at all he increases the possibility of rejection by relatives. Either way, the deviant loses.

> The nonconformist, whether he be foreigner or 'odd ball,' intellectual or idiot, genius or jester, individualist or hobo, physically or mentally abnormal —pays a price for 'being different' unless his peculiarity is considered acceptable for his particular group, or unless he lives in a place or period of particularly high tolerance or enlightenment.[1]

The penalty that *mentally ill* persons pay for "being different" is often rejection by others in the community. Following the increased interest of social scientists in the public's attitudes toward the mentally ill,[2] this research investigates some of the factors involved in the rejection of mentally ill individuals.

This paper presents the results of a controlled experiment in influencing people's attitudes toward individuals exhibiting symptoms of mental illness. The research attempts to determine the extent to which people's attitudes toward an individual exhibiting disturbed behavior are related to their knowledge of the particular help-source that the individual is using or has used. The term "help-source" here refers to such community resources as clergymen, physicians, psychiatrists, marriage counselors, mental hygiene clinics, alcohol clinics, and mental hospitals, each of which is frequently concerned with persons having emotional problems.

Most studies concerned with attitudes toward the mentally ill have focused on the individual's behavior as the sole factor determining whether or not he is rejected by others. Other research has considered the importance of psychiatric treatment or hospitalization in *identifying* the individual as mentally ill and, subsequently, leading to his rejection.[3] But as far as could be determined, no study has been made of the importance of utilizing other help-sources in determining or influencing public attitudes toward individuals exhibiting disturbed behavior.

In a number of studies respondents have been asked whether they considered various *descriptions* to be those of mentally ill persons, and some respondents were found unable to recognize certain serious symptoms of disturbed behavior. Star, for example, asking 3500 respondents about six case abstracts of mentally ill persons, found that 17 per cent of the sample said that none of these imaginery persons was sufficiently deviant to represent what they meant by mental illness. Another 28 per cent limited their concept of mental illness to the paranoid, the only description where violence was a prominent feature of the behavior.[4] Elaine and John Cumming, asking questions about the same six descriptions of deviant behavior, found that the majority of people dismissed the descriptions, even when they were clinically grave, as normal, with such comments as "It's just a quirk, it's nothing serious."[5]

Sharply in disagreement with these findings, however, are the results of studies by Lemkau and Crocetti, and by Dohrenwend, Bernard and Kolb. Using three of the Star abstracts, Lemkau and Crocetti found that 91 per cent of their sample identified the paranoid as mentally ill, 78 per cent identified the simple schizophrenic, and 62 percent identified the alcoholic.[6] Dohrenwend and his associates, interviewing "leaders in an urban area," used the six Star abstracts. They report that "all saw mental illness in the description of paranoid schizophrenia; 72 per cent saw it in the example of simple schizophrenia; 63 per cent in the alcoholic; about 50 per cent in the anxiety neurosis and in the juvenile character disorder; and 40 per cent in the compulsive-phobic."[7] These findings, although somewhat inconsistent, do indicate some public ignorance concerning the signs and symptoms of mental illness. More important here, they tell us nothing about how the public *feels* toward the individuals in these case abstracts.

Hospitalization is another cue that has been found to influence recognition of a person as mentally ill. The Cumming's state, "Mental illness, it seems, is a condition which afflicts people who must go to a mental institution, but up until they go almost anything they do is fairly normal."[8]

Apparently some people can correctly identify symptoms of mental illness and others cannot, while for some the mentally ill are only those who have been in a mental hospital. But it seems equally important to ask whether people *reject* individuals displaying symptoms of mental illness or those who have been hospitalized. In part, the task of this research was to determine the extent to which people reject various descriptions of disturbed behavior. An additional cue—the *help-source* that the individual described is utilizing—was presented to the respondents in order to ascertain the importance of the help-source in determining rejection of mentally ill individuals. Four help-sources that people with mental disorders often consult[9]—the clergyman, the physician, the psychiatrist, and the mental hospital—were represented.

Several recent studies have been concerned with the help-sources that people suggest using for mental disorders, as well as the ones they actually have used.[10] Considerable evidence from these studies indicates that people have strong negative attitudes toward psychiatrists and mental hospitals and toward individuals using either of these help-sources.[11] But there seems to be no evidence of negative attitudes toward clergymen or physicians, or toward people consulting these two help-sources. Further, the fact that people with emotional problems are more likely to consult clergymen and physicians than psychiatrists and mental hospitals[12] suggests the absence of strong negative attitudes toward the latter and those uilizing them. Gurin points out that they ". . . are the areas most people turn to with their personal problems; they are the major 'gatekeepers' in the treatment process, either doing the treating themselves or referring to a more specialized professional resource."[13] Both the clergyman and the physician are professionally involved in what are usually defined as "the private affairs" of others. They have, what Naegele calls ". . . legitimate access to realms beyond public discussion."[14]

Although it is probably true that the public does not hold negative attitudes toward clergymen and physicians, I suggest that an individual consulting either of these help-sources may more often lose face, and more often be regarded as deviant, than an individual exhibiting the same behavior who does not consult one of these professional resources. How does this come to be so?

As Clausen and Yarrow point out, "There is an ethic of being able to handle one's own problems by oneself, which applies not only to psychiatric problems."[15] Similarly, Ewalt says, "One value in American culture compatible with most approaches to a definition of positive mental health appears to be this: An individual should be able to stand on his own two feet without making undue demands or impositions on others."[16] In another statement of this view, Kadushin reports that, in answer to the question "Would you tell people in general that you came here?" (the Peale-Blanton Religio-Psychiatric Clinic), a respondent replied ". . . I wouldn't tell people in general. I know that there's still a stigma attached to people who seek psychiatric aid, and I guess I'm ashamed that I couldn't manage my own problem."[17]

Thus, an outside observer's knowledge that a person is consulting any of the four help-sources discussed may have at least two important consequences for the individual with a behavior problem: (1) He is defined as someone who *has* a problem. Moreover, the further along the continuum from clergyman to mental hospital the individual moves, the more his problem is seen as a serious one, and individuals consulting a psychiatrist or a mental hospital are very often defined as "mentally ill" or "insane." (2) The individual is defined as unable to handle his problem by himself.

I am suggesting that the reported inability of some persons to recognize certain serious symptoms of disturbed behavior is due to difficulty in evaluating an individual's behavior, and that knowledge about what help-source the individual is utilizing helps others decide whether he is "deviant" or has a problem that he cannot cope with himself. And an important social consequence for the person who, because of his behavior or choice of help-source, is defined as deviant may be *rejection*.

These considerations led to formulation of the following hypothesis: Individuals exhibiting identical behavior will be increasingly rejected as they are described as not seeking any help, as utilizing a clergyman, a physician, a psychiatrist, or a mental hospital.

Method

To test this hypothesis, interviews were conducted with a systematic sample[18] of 300 married white females selected from the address section of the City Directory of Branford, a southern New England town of approximately 17,000 population.[19] The sample was so small that the need to control for a number of variables was obvious. Thus, males,[20] non-whites, and unmarried respondents were excluded from the sample.

The interviews took place in the respondents' homes and were of 20 to 40 minutes duration. Each respondent was given five cards, one at a time, describing different behaviors. The interviewer read each description aloud from the interview schedule as the respondent followed by reading the card.

Case abstract (A) was a description of a paranoid schizophrenic, (B) an individual suffering from simple schizophrenia, (C) an anxious-depressed person, (D) a phobic individual with compulsive features, and (E) a "normal" person. The first four abstracts were, in the main, the same as those developed by Shirley Star, formerly of the National Opinion Research Center in Chicago.[21] The fifth abstract, that of the "normal"[22] individual, was developed expressly for this research.[23]

The five case abstracts were presented in combination with information about what help-source an individual was utilizing, in the following manner:

(1) Nothing was added to the description of the behavior—this was, of course, the absence of any help.

(2) Affixed to the description was the statement: "He has been going to see his clergyman regularly about the way he is getting along."

(3) Affixed to the description was the statement: "He has been going to see his physician regularly about the way he is getting along."

(4) Affixed to the description was the statement: "He has been going to see his psychiatrist regularly about the way he is getting along."

(5) Affixed to the description was the statement: "He has been in a mental hospital because of the way he was getting along."

This research required an experimental design permitting classification of each of the two independent variables (behavior and help-source) in five categories.[24] Observations for all possible combinations of the values of the two variables would have been desirable, but this clearly was not feasible. Hence the observations were arranged in the form of a Graeco-Latin Square [25] so as to obtain a large amount of infomation from a relatively small number of observations. Specifically, this type of design enables us to discover: (a) the influence of different types of behavior in determining rejection, and (b) the influence of different help-sources in determining rejection.

The 300 respondents were divided at random into five groups of 60 individuals each. Every individual in each group saw five combinations of behavior and help-source, but no group or individual saw any given behavior or any given help-source more than once. In order to assure that the rejection rates were not affected by the *order* in which individuals saw the combinations, the experiment was designed so that each behavior and each help-source was seen first by one group, second by another, third by another, fourth by another, and last by the remaining group.[26]

Thus, in the Graeco-Latin Square design, three variables were considered (behavior, help-source, and order). The data were classified in five categories on each of these variables. See Figure 1, where letters in each cell indicate a description of behavior, and the numbers in each cell indicate the help-source utilized. In the top left-hand cell, for example, the letter A indicates that the paranoid schizophrenic was the description seen first by Group 1, and that he was described as seeing help-source 1 (that is, he was not described as seeking any help). Similarly, in the bottom right-hand cell, the letter D indicates that the phobic-compulsive person was the abstract seen fifth by Group 5, and that he was described as consulting help-source 3 (a physician).

FIGURE 1. The Graeco-Latin Square Design[a]

| | Order | | | | |
	1	2	3	4	5
Group 1	A1	B2	C3	D4	E5
Group 2	B3	C4	D5	E1	A2
Group 3	C5	D1	E2	A3	B4
Group 4	D2	E3	A4	B5	C1
Group 5	E4	A5	B1	C2	D3

a N for each cell in the table is 60.

After reading each combination of behavior and help-source, the respondents were asked a uniform series of questions. These questions made up a social distance scale, indicating how close a relation the respondent was willing to tolerate with the individuals in the case abstracts. This scale was used as the measure of *rejection,* the dependent variable in the research.

The social distance scale consisted of the following items: (1) "Would you discourage your children from marrying someone like this?" (2) "If you had a room to rent in your home, would you be willing to rent it to someone like this?" (3) "Would you be willing to work on a job with someone like this?" (4) "Would you be willing to have someone like this join a favorite club or organization of yours?" (5) "Would you object to having a person like this as a neighbor?"[27]

The range of possible scores for each combination of help-source and behavior was from zero (when no items indicated rejection) through five (when all items indicated rejection). A test of reproducibility was applied and the resulting coefficient was .97, indicating that the scale met acceptable standards; i.e., was a unidimensional scale.

It should be emphasized that each combination of behavior and help-source was seen by 60 respondents. It also bears repeating that each respondent was presented with five combinations of behavior and help-source. Thus, each respondent contributed a rejection score (on the social distance scale) to each of five cells out of the 25 cells in Figure 1. An analysis of variance of the form generally applied to planned experiments was carried out.[28]

TABLE 1. Rejection Scores[a] for Each Help-Source and Behavior Combination[b]

Help-Source Utilized

Behavior	No help	Clergyman	Physician	Psychiatrist	Mental Hospital	Total
Paranoid Schizophrenic	3.65	3.33	3.77	4.12	4.33	3.84
Simple Schizophrenic	1.10	1.57	1.83	2.85	3.68	2.21
Depressed-Neurotic	1.45	1.62	2.07	2.70	3.28	2.22
Phobic-Compulsive	.53	1.12	1.18	1.87	2.27	1.39
Normal Individual	.02	.22	.50	1.25	1.63	.72
Total	1.35	1.57	1.87	2.56	3.04	—

$$F = 23.53, p < .001$$

a Rejection scores are represented by the mean number of items rejected on the Social Distance Scale.
b N for each cell in the table is 60.

Results and Discussion

Table 1 presents the mean rejection rate for each combination of behavior and help-source. An individual exhibiting a given type of behavior is increasingly rejected as he is described as seeking no help, as seeing a clergyman, as seeing a physician, as seeing a psychiatrist, or as having been in a mental hospital. The relation between the dependent variable (help-source) and the dependent variable (rejection) is statistically significant at the .001 level. Furthermore, the reversal in the "paranoid schizophrenic" row is the only one among 25 combinations.[29]

The relation between the other independent variable (behavior) and rejection is also significant at the .001 level. In fact, the F obtained for the relation between behavior and rejection (F = 64.52 is much higher than the F obtained for the relation between help-source and rejection (F = 23.53). In other words, when a respondent was confronted with a case abstract containing both a description of their individual's behavior and information about what help-source he was utilizing, the description of behavior played a greater part (i.e., accounted for more variance) than the help-source in determining how strongly she rejected the individual described.

As was indicated earlier, the main purpose of this presentation is to show the extent to which attitudes toward an individual exhibiting symptoms of mental illness are related to knowledge of the particular help-source that he is utilizing. The importance of the type of behavior is of secondary interest here; I have investigated the relation between behavior and rejection mainly to ascertain the *relative* importance of each of the two elements presented in the case abstracts. The relation between behavior and rejection will be fully treated in a future paper.

The totals at the bottom of Table 1 show that the largest increase in the rejection rates occurs when an individual sees a psychiatrist. That is, the rejection rate of individuals described as consulting a physician (1.87) differs from the rejection rate for individuals described as consulting a psychiatrist (2.56) to a degree greater than for any other comparison between two adjacent help-sources. The second largest over-all increase in rejection occurs when the individual is described as having been in a mental hospital, and the smallest net increase (.20) occurs when the individual sees a clergyman, compared to seeking no help at all.

Probably the most significant aspect of the effect of help-source on rejection rates is that, for four of the five case abstracts, the biggest increase in rejection occurs when the individual is described as consulting a psychiatrist, and in three of the five abstracts the second largest increase occurs when the individual is depicted as having been in a mental hospital. Not only are individuals increasingly rejected as they are described as seeking no help, as seeing a clergyman, a physician, a psychiatrist, or a mental hospital, but they are *disproportionately* rejected when described as utilizing the latter two help-sources. This supports the suggestion made earlier that individuals utilizing psychiatrists and mental hospitals may be rejected not only because they have a health problem, and because they are unable to handle the problem themselves, but also because contact with a psychiatrist or a mental hospital defines them as "mentally ill" or "insane."

Despite the fact that the "normal" person is more an "ideal type" than a normal person, when he is described as having been in a mental hospital he is rejected more than a psychotic individual described as not seeking help or as seeing a clergyman, and more than a depressed-neurotic seeing a clergyman. Even when a normal person is described as seeing a psychiatrist, he is rejected more than a simple schizophrenic who seeks no help, more than a phobic-compulsive individual seeking no help or seeing a clergyman or physician.

As was noted previously, there is one reversal in Table 1. The paranoid schizophrenic, unlike the other descriptions, was rejected more strongly when he was described as not utilizing any help-source than when he was described as utilizing a clergyman. The paranoid was described in the case abstract as suspicious, as picking fights with people who did not even know him, and as cursing his wife. His behavior may be so threatening and so obviously deviates from normal behavior, that the respondents feel that he is socially less objectionable when he takes a step to help himself. In other words, the individual *obviously* in need of professional help is in a sense "rewarded" for seeking at least one kind of help, that of the clergyman. And though the paranoid schizophrenic is increasingly rejected when he is described as utilizing a physician, a psychiatrist, and a mental hospital, the relative amount of increase is much less than for the other four case abstracts.

Mentally ill persons whose behavior does not deviate markedly from normal role-expectations may be assigned responsibility for their own behavior. If so, seeking any professional help is an admission of inability to meet this responsibility. An individual whose behavior is markedly abnormal (in this instance, the paranoid schizophrenic) may not, however, be considered responsible for his behavior or for his recovery, and is, therefore rejected less than other individuals when he seeks professional help.

Controls

To determine whether the findings were spurious, the relation between help-source and rejection was observed under several different controls. The association was maintained within age groups, within religious affiliation groups, within educational attainment groups, and within groups occupying different positions in the status hierarchy.[30] The association was also maintained within groups differing in authoritarianism.[31]

But when (1) experience with someone who had sought help for emotional problems[32] and (2) attitude toward the norm of self-reliance,[33] were controlled, the relation between help-source and rejection was specified.

Table 2 presents the rejection rates for respondents reporting a relative who sought help, those reporting a friend who sought help, and those who

TABLE 2. Rejection Scores[a] for All Cases by Help-Source and Acquaintance with Help-Seekers

Help-Source Utilized	ACQUAINTANCE		
	Relative (N=37)	Friend (N=73)	No one (N=190)
No help-source	2.35	1.45	1.12
Clergyman	2.06	1.45	1.51
Physician	1.30	1.58	2.09
Psychiatrist	2.08	2.53	2.66
Mental Hospital	2.38	2.82	3.25

a Rejection scores are represented by the mean number of items rejected on the Social Distance Scale.

knew no one who sought help for emotional problems. For ease of presentation and interpretation, the rejection rates for the five case abstracts have been combined.[34]

There are two points of interest in Table 2. One is the difference in rejection rates *among* the three groups of respondents. But because these interesting differences are peripheral to the central concern here, I will focus, instead, on the second point of interest. This is the consistent increase—*within* two of the three groups of respondents—in rejection scores for persons not seeking any help, utilizing a clergyman, a physician, a psychiatrist, or a mental hospital.

Respondents *not* acquainted with a help-seeker as well as those acquainted with a help-seeking *friend* adhere to the pattern of rejection previously demonstrated in Table 1. But respondents with a help-seeking *relative* deviate markedly from this pattern. They reject persons not seeking help more than they do persons consulting a clergyman, physician, or psychiatrist, and almost as much as those utilizing a mental hospital. And they reject persons consulting a clergyman more than those consulting a physician.

Perhaps respondents with help-seeking relatives are more able to recognize the behavior in the abstracts as that of persons who *need* help and therefore they reject them strongly when they do not seek help. A similar explanation may apply to the rejection of persons using a clergyman. That is, these

TABLE 3. Rejection Scores[a] for All Mentally Ill Cases by Help-Source and Acquaintance with Help-Seekers

Help-Source Utilized	ACQUAINTANCE		
	Relative (N=37)	Friend (N=73)	No one (N=190)
No help-source	2.81	1.64	1.16
Clergyman	2.20	1.65	1.86
Physician	1.51	1.91	2.46
Psychiatrist	2.45	2.88	2.90
Mental Hospital	3.04	3.14	3.51

a Rejection scores are represented by the mean number of items rejected on the Social Distance Scale.

respondents may see the clergyman as not being what Parsons calls "technically competent help"[35] and equate seeing him with not seeking help. The comparatively low rejection of persons consulting a physician may reflect the respondents' belief that a physician is one of the professional resources that one *should* utilize for emotional problems, and that a physician brings the least stigma to the user; whereas the psychiatrist and the mental hospital, though both competent resources, tend to stigmatize the user much more.[36]

The reader will recall that one of the case abstracts presented to the respondents was that of a "normal" individual. Since respondents with a help-seeking relative may reject the non-help-seeking cases because they are recognized as needing help, including the description of the normal person may "distort" the findings. The rejection rates for the four mentally ill abstracts have, therefore, been separated from those for the normal person and presented in Table 3. Inspection of this table reveals the same pattern found in Table 2, except that the rejection rate for persons utilizing each help-source is somewhat higher than in Table 2.[37]

Turning now to the relation between adherence to the norm of self-reliance and rejection of persons described as using the various help-sources, the data in Table 4 indicate that the association between help-source and rejection is maintained even among those who do not strongly adhere to the norm of self-reliance.[38] Among respondents agreeing either strongly or somewhat to the norm of self-reliance there is a consistent increase in rejection of persons as they moved from no help to the mental hospital. Respondents *not* adhering to the norm of self-reliance, however, reject persons not seeking help more than they do persons seeking a clergyman or a physician.[39]

TABLE 4. Rejection Scores[a] for All Cases by Help-Source and Adherence to the Norm of Self-Reliance

Help-Source Utilized	ADHERENCE TO NORM OF SELF-RELIANCE		
	Disagree (N=28)	Agree Somewhat (N=128)	Agree Strongly (N=144)
No help-source	1.79	1.39	1.22
Clergyman	1.68	1.56	1.52
Physician	1.67	1.87	2.00
Psychiatrist	2.43	2.52	2.65
Mental Hospital	2.64	3.09	3.23

a Rejection scores are represented by the mean number of items rejected on the Social Distance Scale.

This pattern is similar to the one followed by respondents who had help-seeking relatives (see Table 2),[40] and the same general interpretation may be appropriate. Respondents who do not agree that people should handle their own problems may view people seeing a clergyman as "handling their own problems." If this is true, then those not adhering to the norm of self-reliance would be expected to reject persons who see a clergyman, as well as those who seek no help.

Thus, for the great majority of respondents, who either (1) have not had experience with a relative who sought help for emotional problems, or (2) adhere to the norm of self-reliance, help-source and rejection are strongly associated.[41]

On the other hand, respondents who have had experience with a help-seeking relative deviate quite sharply from the rejection pattern of the majority, as do those who do not adhere to the norm of self-reliance. Nevertheless, this deviant pattern appears to make sense theoretically. Those acquainted with a help-seeking relative, having had more exposure to sick-role prescriptions, may be highly rejecting of persons not seeking help because they feel that people should seek "technically competent help." Respondents not adhering to the norm of self-reliance may reject non-help-seekers for a similar reason. They too may feel that handling one's own problems is inappropriate, and that people should seek competent help. And, as suggested previously, both groups may equate help from a clergyman with no help at all.[42]

Conclusions and Implications

On the basis of these findings from a southern New England town, the source of help sought by mentally disturbed individuals appears to be strongly related to the degree to which others in the community reject them. Individuals are increasingly rejected as they are described as utilizing no help, as utilizing a clergyman, a physician, a psychiatrist, or a mental hospital.

Controls for age, religion, education, social class, and authoritarianism failed to diminish the relationship, but controls for experience with an emotionally disturbed help-seeker and for adherence to the norm of self-reliance tended to specify it. Respondents who had had experience with a help-seeking relative deviated markedly from the pattern followed by the rest of the sample, as did respondents not adhering to the norm of self-reliance. Both of these groups rejected people seeking no help more than they did those consulting a clergyman or a physician, and respondents with help-seeking relatives also reject non-help-seekers more than those consulting a psychiatrist. Both groups rejected persons seeing a clergyman more than those seeing a physician.

The evidence presented here suggests that a mentally ill person who seeks help may be rejected by others in the community. The findings also have implications for what Mechanic and Volkart call "the inclination to adopt the sick role."[43] We can easily imagine an individual who, because he fears the stigma attached to the help-seeker, does not utilize a professional resource for his problems. Avoiding the possibility of rejection, he also denies himself technically competent help.[44]

Thus the utilization of certain help-sources involves not only a *reward* (positive mental health), but also a *cost* (rejection by others and, consequently, a negative self-image);[45] we need to assess the net balance of gains and losses resulting from seeking help for problems of disturbed behavior.

The present analysis has been concerned with the rejection of help-seekers in hypothetical situations. Future research should be designed so that it would be possible to examine the rejection of help-seekers in "real" situations. Hopefully, the present research will provide some understanding and raise significant questions about the consequences of seeking help for problems of disturbed behavior in our society.

Notes

1. Joint Commission on Mental Illness and Health, *Action for Mental Health,* New York: Science Editions, 1961, p. 69.

2. See, for example, John A. Clausen and Marian R. Yarrow, "Paths to the Mental Hospital," *The Journal of Social Issues,* 11 (November, 1955), pp. 25-32; Elaine and John Cumming, *Closed Ranks: An Experiment in Mental Health Education.* Cambridge: Harvard University Press, 1957; Bruce P. Dohrenwend, Viola W. Bernard, and Lawrence C. Kolb, "The Orientations of Leaders in an Urban Area Toward Problems of Mental Illness," *The American Journal of Psychiatry,* 118 (February, 1962), pp. 683-691; Howard E. Freeman and Ozzie G. Simmons, "Mental Patients in the Community," *American Sociological Review,* 23 (April, 1958), pp. 147-154; Gerald Gurin, Joseph Veroff, and Sheila Feld, *Americans View Their Mental Health,* New York: Basic Books, 1960; E. Gartly Jaco, *The Social Epidemiology of Mental Disorders,* New York: Russell Sage Foundation, 1960; Paul V. Lemkau and Guido M. Crocetti, "An Urban Population's Opinion and Knowledge about Mental Illness," *The American Journal of Psychiatry,* 118 (February, 1962), pp. 692-700; Jum C. Nunnally, Jr., *Popular Conceptions of Mental Health,* New York: Holt, Rinehart and Winston, 1961; Glen V. Ramsey and Melita Seipp, "Public Opinions and Information Concerning Mental Health," *Journal of Clinical Psychology,* 4 (October, 1948), pp. 397-406; Charlotte Green Schwartz, "Perspectives on Deviance—Wives' Definitions of Their Husbands' Mental Illness," *Psychiatry,* 20 (August, 1957), pp. 275-291; Shirley Star, "The Place of Psychiatry in Popular Thinking," paper presented at the meeting of the American Association for Public Opinion Research, Washington, D.C., May 1957; Julian L. Woodward, "Changing Ideas on Mental Illness and Its Treatment," *American Sociological Review,* 16 (August, 1951), pp. 443-454.

3. See Clausen and Yarrow, *op. cit.,* and Cumming and Cumming, *op. cit.*

4. Star, *op. cit.*

5. Elaine and John Cumming, "Affective Symbolism, Social Norms, and Mental Illness," *Psychiatry,* 19 (February, 1956), pp. 77-85.

6. Lemkau and Crocetti, *op. cit.,* p. 694.

7. Dohrenwend, Bernard and Kolb, *op. cit.,* p. 635.

8. Cumming and Cumming, *Closed Ranks, op. cit.,* p. 102.

9. See, for example, Gurin, *et al., op. cit.*

10. Dohrenwend, *et al., op. cit.;* Gurin, *et al., op. cit.;* Ramsey and Seipp, *op. cit.;* Woodward, *op. cit.*

11. Clausen and Yarrow, *op. cit.;* Cumming and Cumming, *op. cit.;* Frederick C. Redlich, "What the Citizen Knows About Psychiatry," *Mental Hygiene,* 34 (January, 1950), pp. 64-70; Star, *op. cit.*

12. Gurin, *et al., op. cit.* p. 307.

13. *Ibid.,* p. 400.

14. Kasper D. Naegele, "Clergymen, Teachers, and Psychiatrists: A Study in Roles and Socialization," *The Canadian Journal of Economic and Political Science,* 22 (February, 1956), p. 48.

15. Clausen and Yarrow, *op. cit.,* p. 63.

16. Jack K. Ewalt, intro., Marie Jahoda, *Current Concepts of Positive Mental Health,* New York: Basic Books, 1958, p. xi.

17. Charles Kadushin, "Individual Decisions to Undertake Psychotherapy," *Administrative Science Quarterly,* 3 (December, 1958), p. 389.

Gurin, *et al.,* report that 25 per cent of their respondents who had problems but did not utilize help tried to solve the problems by themselves, *op. cit.,* pp. 350-351.

18. The sample was drawn from the address section of the Directory, with every 15th address marked for interview. The first address was drawn randomly from the first 15 entries; thereafter every 15th address was included until the total sample of 300 was obtained.

19. Twenty-eight of the households drawn in the original sample refused to be interviewed. In each of these cases, a substitution was made by selecting an address at random from the same street. Four of these substitutes refused to be interviewed, necessitating further substitution. Also requiring substitution were three addresses that could not be located and six wives of household heads who were divorced, separated, or widowed, rather than married. Selecting substitutes from the same neighborhood was done on the assumption that persons living in the same neighborhood would resemble one another in certain important ways; they were more likely, than people living in different neighborhoods, to be of similar socio-economic status. Although the possibility of bias still exists, so few substitutions were necessary that, hopefully, the effect is minimal.

20. In a pre-test with a sample of 32 women and 28 men, no significant differences were found between the rejection rates of men and women.

21. Star, *op. cit.*

22. The normal person was described as follows: "Here is a description of a man. Imagine that he is a respectable person living in your neighborhood. He is happy and cheerful, has a good enough job and is fairly well satisfied with it. He is always busy and has quite a few friends who think he is easy to get along with most of the time. Within the next few months he plans to marry a nice young woman he is engaged to."

23. My purpose was to determine (a) whether the rejection of the mentally ill descriptions might in part be accounted for by individuals who rejected everyone regardless of behavior; and (b) whether the utilization of a help-source alone could influence rejection, or whether it was the "combination" of deviant behavior and the use of a help-source that led to rejection.

24. The advantages of including tests of different combinations of two or more variables within one experiment have been cited by several writers concerned with

experimental design. For example, D. J. Finney, *The Theory of Experimental Design*, Chicago: The University of Chicago Press, 1960, p. 68, notes the following advantages: "(1) To broaden the basis of inferences relating to one factor by testing that factor under various conditions of others; (2) To assess the extent to which the effects of one factor are modified by the level of others; (3) To economize in experimental material by obtaining information on several factors without increasing the size of the experiment beyond what would be required for one or two factors alone."

25. For two excellent explanations of the Graeco-Latin Square design see, Finney, *op. cit.*, and E. F. Lindquist, *Design of Experiments in Psychology and Education*, Boston: Houghton Mifflin, 1953.

26. In addition, to 50 per cent of the respondents, the paranoid, the depressed individual, and the "normal" person were presented as males, with the simple schizophrenic and the phobic-compulsive individual presented as females. The other half of the sample saw a reversed order—the simple schizophrenic and the compulsive individuals as males, and the paranoid, depressed, and "normal" persons as females. Since both the male case abstracts and the female case abstracts were rejected in accordance with the pattern shown in Table 1, they will not be discussed further in this paper. The findings for the *differences* in the *absolute* rejection of males and females exhibiting a given behavior and utilizing the same help-source will be the subject of a forthcoming paper.

27. The above order duplicates the order of "closeness" represented by the scale. The items, however, were administered to each respondent in a random fashion.

28. See, for example, Lindquist, *op. cit.*, chs. 12 and 13.

29. Following Lindquist, neither orders nor interaction was found to be statistically significant at the .20 level. See Lindquist, *op. cit.*, pp. 273-281.

30. For details of the classification procedures, see pp. 82-88 of the author's doctoral dissertation, of which this research is a part: "Help-Sources and Rejection of the Mentally Ill," unpublished Ph.D. Disertation, Yale University, 1962.

31. For details of the authoritarian scale, see *ibid.*, p. 77.

32. The question was: "We've been talking about people with worries and problems. Have any of your close friends or relatives had any psychiatric treatment or gone to a hospital or professional person, or community agency, regarding emotional problems?" If the respondent answered in the affirmative, she was asked who this person was.

33. Attitude toward self-reliance was measured by the respondent's reaction to the following statement: "People should be expected to handle their own problems," with a choice of four responses—strongly agree, agree somewhat, disagree somewhat, and strongly disagree.

34. Because our primary interest is in the effect of help-source rather than behavior, rejection rates will hereafter be presented in combined form only.

35. Talcott Parsons, *The Social System*, Glencoe, Ill.: The Free Press, 1950, p. 437. Parsons states that ". . . the fourth closely related element [in the sick role] is the obligation—in proportion to the severity of the condition, of course—to seek *technically competent* help, namely in the most usual case, that of a physician and to *cooperate* with him in the process of trying to get well." He makes this point again in "Definitions of Health and Illness in the Light of American Values and Social Structure," in E. Gartly Jaco (ed.), *Patients, Physicians and Illness*, Glencoe, Ill.: The Free Press, 1953, pp. 165-187.

36. We might expect those with help-seeking friends to reject in the same pat-

tern as those with help-seeking relatives. Although both groups of respondents have had experience with someone who sought help, those whose experience was with friends probably were not so involved in the other's welfare and therefore had less intimate a knowledge of the help-sources people consult for emotional problems.

37. This is not surprising in light of the generally low rejection of the "normal" person.

38. Only 9 per cent disagreed (either somewhat or strongly) with the statement about people handling their own problems. This finding lends support to the proposition that people in our society are expected to handle their own problems.

39. Again we ignore differences *among* the various groups of respondents. Our primary interest is in determining whether the relation between help-source and rejection is maintained *within* each group.

40. It should be recalled that the latter respondents also rejected persons not seeking help more than persons seeing a psychiatrist; the findings with respect to experience with a help-seeking relative and non-adherence to the norm of self-reliance are not entirely similar.

41. It would have been desirable to control for experience and attitude toward self-reliance simultaneously, but there were too few (13) respondents who reported experience with a help-seeking relative *and* did not adhere to the norm of self-reliance.

42. The small number of respondents with a help-seeking relative (37), and the small number not adhering to the norm of self-reliance (28), make these findings, as well as their interpretation, highly tentative.

43. David Mechanic and Edmund A. Volkart, "Stress, Illness, and the Sick Role," *American Sociological Review,* 26 (February, 1961), pp. 51-58.

44. Jaco, *op. cit.,* points out that "If mental disease carries a stigma in a particular community, it is likely that many families will use extreme measures to conceal the fact that a member is mentally ill; even to the extent of preventing him from obtaining psychiatric treatment in that area." (p. 18)

45. For an interesting presentation of cost and reward, see George C. Homans, *Social Behavior: Its Elementary Forms,* New York: Harcourt, Brace & World, 1961, ch. 5.

B. Quasi-Experiments

H. LAURENCE ROSS
DONALD T. CAMPBELL
GENE V. GLASS

Determining the Social Effects of a Legal Reform: The British "Breathalyser" Crackdown of 1967

Quasi-experimental designs involve attempts to approximate experimental designs in situations where researchers take advantage of "naturally" occurring phenomena or phenomena that are implemented by persons other than the researchers and in situations where the random assignment of subjects cannot be achieved. While quasi-experiments may lack some of the rigor possible in full-fledged experimental designs they have some distinct advantages over non-experimental designs in that they enable the researcher to take advantage of some of the aspects of experiments. In addition, the researcher can bolster confidence in his findings by taking into consideration and evaluating the operation of various reasons for his findings *other than the ones that he has hypothesized.* Quasi-experiments, then, involve before-after measurements combined with efforts to rule out alternative explanations for the findings that are obtained.

Within the deviance framework, quasi-experiments are highly appropriate to the assessment of what have come to be called "legal impact" studies

"Determining the Social Effects of a Legal Reform: The British 'Breathalyser' Crackdown of 1967," by H. L. Ross, D. T. Campbell, and G. V. Glass is reprinted from *American Behavioral Scientist* Vol. 13, No. 4 (March/April 1970) pp. 493-509 by permission of the Publisher, Sage Publications, Inc.

Author's Note: *This study was supported in part by National Science Foundation Grant G51309X.*

in the sociology of law. The precise time of passage and implementation of statutes and policies frequently can be identified and data providing indications of the conduct falling within the purview of the statutes or policies are also often available. As is the case with all behavioral science research, however, the adequacy of the knowledge produced through quasi-experiments is heavily dependent upon the resourcefulness and ingenuity of the researcher.

A key issue within legal impact studies is that of deterrence. Do alterations in laws, sanctions, enforcement policies, surveillance tactics and the like produce concomitant changes in the deviant participation of the population? Deterrence is firmly entrenched in the American legal system. It has been said that if Americans don't like something their standard procedure is to pass a law outlawing it. A typical procedure used to reduce criminal behavior is to increase the penalties for those acts that are regarded as occurring too frequently. When downtown crime rates are regarded as too high more police are assigned to the downtown areas and sometimes more lights are installed. Quasi-experimental designs enable one to evaluate the effectiveness of these kinds of changes.

Although the research is not extensive at this time, there is some indication that changes in statutes and surveillance are most likely to be effective when they are specifically concerned with *instrumental* activities. Instrumental activities consist especially of rationally motivated acts which are designed to accomplish some material gain or other goal. That is, the activity is simply a means to another end. Speeding, shoplifting, running a stop light, illegal parking, income tax evasion and most white-collar crimes are examples of instrumental crimes.

On the other hand, changes are generally thought to be largely ineffective in deterring *expressive* activities. These consist of activities that are rewarding in and of themselves and are thought to involve less rational calculation and planning. Examples include most homicide, sex offenses, assault, drug use, drunkenness and mentally disordered behavior. These behaviors appear to be relatively unaffected by changes in laws, increases or decreases in sanctions, alterations in surveillance, or other legal actions.

The study reported below provides an excellent illustration of quasi-experimental research. Ross, Campbell and Glass attempt to assess the effectiveness of the British Road Safety Act of 1967 in accomplishing its intent to lower traffic fatalities by getting drunken drivers off the roads. It should be noticed that the authors use fatalities and serious casualities as their measure of the dependent variable and that before and after measures of the independent and dependent variables are provided. Their findings show that the casualty rate decreased significantly and

that this drop persisted when the influence of other factors was considered. The decrease remained significant even when time of day, weekends, commuting hours and the like were controlled.

Still this is not sufficient to conclude that the crackdown produced the decrease. The authors then discuss other alternatives that might have been
responsible for the decrease in casualties under the rubric of "threats
to validity." Several alternatives are analyzed and are ruled out as
plausible explanations for the findings. The result is that, at least in this
instance, an alteration in statutes did deter the phenomenon it was
designed to deal with.

This study is significant in several ways. First, it serves as an outstanding
illustration of how good quasi-experimental research should be conducted and provides sets of rules for doing so. Second, the findings are
of interest in that they demonstrate the possible effects that alterations
in the legal structure can have upon deviant conduct. Finally, the findings
support the notion that instrumental activities (drunken driving) may
indeed be influenced by changes in statutes or policies.

The social effects of a legal reform are examined in this paper utilizing the
Interrupted Times-Series research design, a method of analysis that has broad
potential use in studies of legal change more generally. A previous demonstration of the applicability of this design to the sociology of law concerned
the Connecticut crackdown on speeders see (Campbell and Ross, 1968; Glass,
1968). In that study, the substantive findings were that the crackdown had
little effect on the highway death rate, and that it introduced certain unexpected and undesirable changes into the legal process in Connecticut. The
present study concerns a similar attempt to lower the highway death rate
through changes in the law, specifically the British Road Safety Act of 1967.
Critical scrutiny of the data indicates that in this instance the legal change
quite impressively achieved its goal.

The British crackdown attempted to get drunken drivers off the road, and
thus took aim at a scientifically demonstrated correlate of automobile accidents. The Connecticut crackdown, in contrast, was based on commonsense
considerations unsupported even by correlational studies. Its sponsors
claimed success prematurely, before such possibilities as random variation
and statistical regression could be ruled out as explanations of an apparently
striking decline in accident rate. In the present study, similar claims turned
out to be justified.

In presenting this report, we hope for two consequences. Substantively,
we hope that officials concerned with traffic safety will consider adopting a
legal reform which has proved in one notable instance to be effective in re-

ducing traffic deaths; methodologically, we hope to increase awareness of the need of hard-headed evaluation of legal and administrative reforms, and of the value of experimental and quasi-experimental designs for this purpose.

Interrupted Time-Series Analysis

The Interrupted Time-Series is a quasi-experimental design (Campbell and Stanley, 1966; Campbell, 1969) for studying the effect of a given "treatment" on a variable that is repeatedly measured over a period of time before and after the application of the treatment. Like all quasi-experimental techniques, the time-series design is a substitute for an unfeasible true experiment. The true experiment requires randomized assignments of subjects to experimental and control groups, but the time-series design can be used, albeit with greater equivocality, in situations lacking randomization.

The essence of an Interrupted Time-Series design is the extension of a typical before-and-after study to a series of observations at various times removed from the experimental treatment, both before and after. To illustrate, the typical before-and-after study concerns only points immediately prior and subsequent to the treatment, as in Figure 1, which compares accidental deaths in Connecticut before and after the crackdown on speeding. It is very difficult to interpret any change from before to after the treatment for various reasons, discussed in more detail in our full presentations. Briefly, these reasons are:

(1) History. The change observed may be due to simultaneous events other than the experimental treatment.

(2) Maturation. The change may be part of some long-term trend.

(3) Instrumentation. The measured change may be based on a change in the means of measuring, rather than in the thing being measured.

(4) Testing. The change may be caused by the initial measurement rather than by the treatment.

(5) Instability. The apparent change may be no more than chance or random variation.

(6) Regression. If the group was selected because it was extreme on some measure, statistical reasoning indicates that it will appear less extreme on subsequent tests, even though the intervening treatment may be completely ineffectual.

A study of Figures 1 and 2 of Campbell and Ross (1968: 38, 42) will illustrate the relevance of time-series data to four of these six threats to validity. In this Connecticut case, maturation and testing are pretty well ruled out by the extended data series inasmuch as *both* posit processes that would have existed in prior years and inasmuch as the 1955-1956 drop is not interpretable as a continuation of trends manifest in 1951-1955. History and instrumentation are not controlled by this design, but an examination of plausible alternative causes such as winter weather and possible changes in record-keeping make this implausible as rival explanations of the 1955-1956 drop. It is on the threats of instability and regression that the time-series presentation exposes weaknesses invalidating the public pronouncements of the Connecticut experiment.

Instability was a possibility totally neglected. *All* of the 1955-1956 change was attributed to the crackdown; the Governor of Connecticut stating, "With a saving of forty lives in 1956, a reduction of 12.3% from the 1955 motor vehicle death toll, we can say the program is definitely worthwhile." When the prior years are examined it becomes obvious that the 1955-1956 shift is typical of the usual annual shifts, rather than being exceptionally large. The problem of regression was likewise overlooked. When a treatment is applied because of extremity on some score (e.g., remedial reading courses applied to persons because of their low reading comprehension scores) it is likely that subsequent scores will on the average be less extreme due to statistical regression alone, even if the treatment has had no effect. The problem of regression is not easy to communicate briefly. It will be helpful to think of a time-series that fluctuates completely at random. If one moves along the series, selecting points that are extraordinarily high, on the average subsequent points will be lower, less extreme and closer to the general trend. In the Connecticut case it appears certain that the great 1954-1955 increase instigated the crackdown. Thus the point where the treatment was instigated was selected for its height. Therefore, a good part of the 1955-1956 decrease must be attributed to statistical regression.

Legal change is a subject for which the Interrupted Time-Series design seems eminently suited. True experiments can seldom be performed in the law because all persons receive the treatment at the same time or because, even if only some receive it, legal or practical considerations prevent the necessary randomization. If a policy strikes a legislature or an administrative body as being a good idea, it is adopted wholesale; if it seems unpromising at first glance, it may not be tried at all. Moreover, even when a change is adopted "experimentally," it is seldom applied at random to one group of people and not to another similarly situated group. The experimental change is typically put into full-scale effect for either an arbitrarily limited time or for a single jurisdiction chosen nonrandomly from among many others. The time-series design is appropriate in these circumstances.

The opportunity to work with time-series design in studies of legal change is enhanced by the fact that there are numerous series of data that are routinely gathered by governmental bureaus and agencies. Examples are general and specific crime rates, institutional commitments, case loads, economic indexes, and accident rates. Because these data are routinely gathered, their measurement is not taken by participants as a cue that a study is being done (Webb et al., 1966). Generalization to other groups involves fewer theoretical problems than for laboratory experiments because of the much greater similarity between field of experimentation and field of application.

The special relevance of time-series data for questions of legal impact has no doubt frequently been recognized, even though simple before-and-after figures, or percentage change from the previous year remain the commonest means of reporting. Time-series data have been employed by Stieber (1949) and Rose (1952) in studies of the effects of compulsory arbitration; by Wolf, Luke and Hax, (1959), Rheinstein (1959) and Glass (forthcoming) in studies of divorce law; and by Walker (1965) and Schuessler (1969) in studies of the effects of capital punishment. But the formal development of the method, the analysis of its strengths and pitfalls, the development of appropriate tests of significance, are all too recent for method to have received the widespread application it deserves. We have previously reported a negative application, primarly rejecting the Connecticut claims. In the present paper we report an optimistic one, in which effects claimed in press releases stand up under scientific scrutiny.

Alcohol and Traffic Accidents

The Legislation and Background

The sponsors of the British Road Safety Act of 1967 based their action on a voluminous scientific literature which showed association between accidents, particularly serious ones, and blood alcohol, particularly in high concentrations. In a recent review of the literature, three studies of fatal accidents were cited in which the proportion of drivers with alcohol in their bloodstreams ranged from 55 to 64%. In single-vehicle accidents, three other studies revealed alcohol in from 71 to 83% of the victims (Automobile Manufacturers Association, 1966). One of the latter studies matched the deceased drivers with a sample obtained later of drivers in the same location at the same hour. Only 23% of the controls had a concentration of .02% or more of alcohol in their blood, compared with 71% of the deceased drivers.

There were similar findings in reports of several correlational studies of nonfatal accidents. The U.S. Department of Transportation recently issued a report containing the following summary:

> Scientific investigation of actual crashes and the circumstances in which they occur and laboratory and field experiments show very clearly that the higher a driver's blood alcohol concentration:
>
> —the disproportionately greater is the likelihood that he will crash;

—the greater is the likelihood that he himself will have initiated any crash in which he is involved; and
—the greater is the likelihood that the crash will have been severe.
[House Committee on Public Works, 1968: 15]

The British government, then, had a good theoretical basis on which to form their program of control. The attempt was further justified by claims of success in similar programs in the Scandinavian countries (Andanaes, 1966). The state of knowledge about alcohol and accidents is quite different from the existing knowledge about the effect of speed, which indicates no simple relationship with accidents.

Since 1925, it had been an offense in Britain to drive while under the influence of alcohol. However, as one British lawer explained:

> I knew only too well how easy it was to secure acquittal from a charge of drunken driving in the United Kingdom. The form one adopted for the defense was always to insist on a jury trial; the evidence as to drunkenness was always given by the Police Surgeon who had the drunken man carry out some rather extraordinary tests, many of which perfectly sober people could not carry out. You would inevitably find that your jury consisted of people like myself, honest, law-abiding citizens who both drove motor cars and also drank alcohol. The inevitable reaction of juries faced with a case of this nature was "there but [for] the Grace of God go I . . . Not Guilty" [Insurance Institute for Highway Safety, 1968: 40].

Legislation in 1962 permitted blood and urine tests, with certain presumptions to be raised in the event of the driver's refusal to cooperate. The stimulus for additional legislation was a continued rise in automobile-related deaths and serious injuries. Deaths had peaked in 1966 at 7,985, a culmination of a steady rise throughout the 1950s and 1960s. Injuries peaked a year earlier, but remained quite high (384,000) in 1966.

The new legislation, put into effect on October 9, 1967, was not particularly radical as compared, for instance, with Scandinavian procedures, or even with the laws in several American states. However, the Act was well publicized in Britain and included the following features:

(1) The criterion of impairment was set at a blood alcohol level of .08%. This is a more stringent standard than that prevailing in most American states, but less so than that prevailing in Norway and Sweden (.05%) or in Czechoslovakia, Bulgaria, and East Germany (.03%). A blood alcohol level of .08% might be barely reached if a 160-pound man drank three drinks in quick succession on an empty stomach (Campbell, 1964).

(2) Police were authorized to give an on-the-scene breath test. This test, called the Breathalyser, gave its name to the crackdown in the British press. The test may be administered to a driver if "the constable has reasonable cause— (a) to suspect him of having alcohol in his body;

or (b) to suspect him of having committed a traffic offense while the vehicle was in motion." The test may also be given to any driver involved in an accident. A driver who fails the breath test is brought to the police station for a (more accurate) blood or urine test, on the basis of which a charge is made.

(3) A mandatory punishment was instituted, consisting of "disqualification" (license suspension) for one year and a fine of £100 or imprisonment for up to four months, or both. Severe penalties were also instituted for failure to submit to the breath test or to either the blood or urine tests.

(4) The specific starting date for the new regulations was given advance publicity. This provides an essential aspect making the study interpretable. A very gradual change of enforcement would have produced results indistinguishable from a gradual change in long-term trends.

Although official publicity campaigns greatly increased public awareness of the new procedures and penalties, particularly of the on-the-scene breathalyzer test, enforcement was probably not much increased. During the first six months after the act was initiated, only 20,000 drivers had to take the test, and fewer than half of them failed it. A report commissioned by the Insurance Institute for Highway Safety states "that in reality [the British driver's] chances of being apprehended for driving after drinking are no greater than they were before" (Bennett and Westwick, 1968: 10).

Claimed Results

As in the case of the Connecticut crackdown, the fact of fewer casualties in the period immediately following the institution of the reform was interpreted as evidence of an effect. The Ministry of Transport in its official press releases was considerably more restrained than the governor of Connecticut had been, but its claims were based on much the same kind of reasoning. For instance, a press release of March 21, 1968, was headlined: "Road Casualties in 1967 Lowest Figure for Nine Years." This release documented the fact that in the last three months of 1967 casualties had declined by sixteen percent and deaths had declined by twenty-three percent; readers were reminded that the Road Safety Act came into force on the 9th of October. On December 11, 1968, the Ministry of Transport issued a press release headline: "First Twelve Months of 'Breath Test.' 1,152 Fewer Dead on Roads." Although the term "cause" was never used, the report contains statements about "casualty savings" and "gaining safety from the new legislation." The magnitude of the shift, particularly in the night hours when the casualty rate declined by a third, makes the British interpretation less offensive than the official line in Connecticut. Our statistical analyses, in fact, support the press releases. But the claims failed to indicate that thought had been given to such obvious alternative causes of the decline as instability of the casualty rate, regression from peak statistics, and other safety-related events taking place at the same time.

Interrupted Time-Series Analysis
of the Breathalyser Crackdown

The Statistics

A graphic presentation of some of our time-series analysis of the Breathalyser crackdown is shown in Figure 1. Our analyses are based upon statistics

Editor's Note: Figure 1 has been corrected according to instructions from the senior author.

made available to us by the British Ministry of Transport, including break-downs going beyond the data reported in their press releases, some of which were made especially at our request.[1] We report here only a portion of our analyses, selected so as to display the major results and to illustrate the method. For the full presentation, including alternative analyses, see Glass et al, (forthcoming).

All hours and days. Data on total monthly casualty rates by seriousness of casualty are available back to 1961. For the present analysis, we have focused upon the combination "fatalities plus serious casualties," since spe-cific hour and day analyses, to be discussed later, were only available in that form. These data have been smoothed in two stages: first, the rates for months of 28, 29, and 30 days in length have been extrapolated to 31-day equivalents (by multiplying the obtained rates by 31/28, and so forth). Second, a yearly cycle of seasonal variations has been removed. (In this cycle, January is low-est, August through December high.) The average monthly rate prior to the crackdown has been used to compute a monthly correction such that the mean annual correction is zero. These corrections have been added to, or sub-tracted from, the 31-day rates. The crackdown began on October 9, 1967. In order to plot October as a purely posttreatment value, an additional prorating has been employed.[2] Without the prorating, October 1967 would have had a plotted value of 7681, instead of 7226 shown.

Visual inspection of the all-hours-and-days graph supports the hypothesis that the crackdown had an effect. A simple nonparametric consideration offers further confirmation: the September-October drop of 1967 is the largest one-month shift not only for the three years plotted in Figure 1, but also for the total series going back to January 1961. The odds against this are 93 to 1. This holds true even if the uncorrected value for October 1967 is used. The most sophisticated test of significance in this situation is that devel-oped by Box and Tiao (1965).[3]

Taking out the annual seasonal cycle is a problematic matter (and even more so in the shorter series that follows). Our procedure is only one of many, all of which are unsatisfactory in one way or another. Can the effect be noted in these all-hours-and-days data without the annual cycle being removed? Only if one compensates for it by eye, or by seasonally controlled compari-sons. The largest shifts in the uncorrected data tend to be the annual Decem-ber-January drops, four out of seven larger than our focal September-October 1967. On the other hand, the 1967 September-October drop of 1,654 (or of 1,199 if October be left with the eight precrackdown days uncorrected for) greatly exceeds the seven other September-October shifts, being three times as large as the largest of them.

Week-end nights. Going back continuously until January 1966, the Ministry of Transport has monthly statistics by hours of the week. From their analyses and press releases, it was apparent that Friday and Saturday nights, from 10:00 P.M. to 4:00 A.M. the following morning, were the hours in which the effect of the Breathalyser was strongest. The bottom time-series in Figure 1 depicts these data. Here, the figures have been prorated to four Fridays and four Saturdays each month. Rather than attempt to estimate seasonal cycles on the basis of these few data, it seemed appropriate to use the monthly corrections based on all hours and days, proportionately reduced in magnitude.

These data provide striking evidence of efficacy. The casualty rate seems to initially drop some forty to forty-five percent, and to level off with a net reduction of perhaps thirty percent.

The September-October 1967 drop is four times as large as any other month-to-month change. The Box and Tiao statistics produces t in excess of 6.50 for likely magnitudes of effect, for which the chance probability is less than .0000001.

For these weekend nights, the data are convincing visually even when seasonal corrections are not made. Even then, the 1967 September-October drop far exceeds any other month-to-month change, including the December-January ones.

We have chided the typical administrator for being too quick to announce success without taking into account instability, and without adequate sampling time periods before and after the legal change. But when does the administrator have enough evidence? This is in part a function of the prior instability of the series, and in part a function of the magnitude of the change. In the present instance, using the Box and Tiao test and the common acceptance level of a chance probability of less than .01, the administrator could have announced a significant drop after only one posttreatment month. As a matter of fact, after only one month the t value was 8.63 where $p < .01 = 2.86$, $p < .001 = 3.88$. Even for the all-hours-and-days data, he would have had to wait only one month, at which time the t value was 3.27.

Commuting hours as a control. While both series of data considered so far indicate that the crackdown had an immediate effect, it becomes important to know to what extent that effect has been sustained. Such considerations involve inferences as to what the long-term trends would have been without the crackdown. On the basis of increased traffic volume, one would expect a steady rise. On the basis of increased availability of divided and limited access highways, one would expect a decline. The trend was actually downward 1961-1963, markedly upward 1963-1965, and slightly downward from January, 1966 until the crackdown. Thus there are no grounds here for extrapolation.

What one needs in such cases is a "control group" or some other control comparison. In the Connecticut case, we were able to use data from adjacent and similar states for this purpose, assuming similar weather, vehicles, and safety changes in the absence of a crackdown. Such comparisons never achieve the effectivenes of the randomly assigned control groups of true experiments, but are nonetheless useful. Because of differences in drinking and closed hours, as well as rate of automobilization and highway construction, Irish or Belgian data would be of less use as a control than were other states for Connecticut, but they would still be of value.

But control data series need not come solely from different persons, groups or populations. In the present situation, a valuable comparison would come from those high accident hours least likely to be affected by drinking. Commuting hours during which British pubs and bars are closed seemed ideal. Casualties on the five working days between the hours of 7:00 to 10:00 A.M. and 4:00 to 5:00 P.M. were chosen (pubs close after lunch at 2:30 P.M.). These monthly rates were prorated to 23 working days per month. These data showed a distinctly different annual cycle than did the all-hours-and-days data; rather than January being the lowest month, August was, whereas August was the highest in the all-hours-and-days cycle. November and December were high in both cycles. These differences made it inappropriate to use the 1961-1967 annual cycle used for the other two curves. Since the commuting-hour data showed much the same cycle each of the three years (except that the high was November rather than December in 1968) and since there was only trivial indication of effect, the three years of these data were averaged to get the annual cycle, which was then removed from the series.

In Figure 1, the middle line represents the resulting commuting-hours series. There is visibly no effect of the crackdown, nor does the Box and Tiao test show one, when applied to the series as graphed, or to an alternate way of removing the annual cycle. (The graphed approach would have some bias in the direction of minimizing the September-October 1967 shift.)

Ideally, this commuting-hour series would provide a control comparison against which we could decide whether or not the Breathalyser enforcement was being maintained or had abated. Insofar as it is relevant for this purpose, the crackdown had a maximum impact for the first three or four months and has leveled off since. But at the end of 1968 there was still a definite saving of some thirty percent in the weekend-night rates.

The appropriateness of the comparison is weakened by the dissimilarity shown in its annual cycle. Yet it is the nearest thing we have. If it is to be of value we need to do better than has been done here with the annual trend. Data subsequent to the crackdown continue to be collected, and four or five years from now we will have available a better estimate of the commuting-hour annual cycle.

The Threats to Validity

In the presentation of the Interrupted Time-Series design at the beginning of this paper, we listed six threats to validity. In the presentation so far of the British crackdown, we have paid attention primarily to the threat of instability—the only one, it should be remembered, to which tests of significance are relevant.

Reviewing the other threats, *maturation* seems out: the October 1967 drop is not plausibly interpretable as part of a general trend manifested prior to the crackdown. *Testing* and *instrumentation* seem unlikely: the procedures for recording and publicizing traffic casualties were well established prior to the crackdown and did not change on account of the crackdown. But this is not a trivial matter. The official categories of "seriously injured" and "slightly injured" obviously call for a judgment the threshold for which could change if the record-keepers were strongly motivated to make a good show. Crime rates, for example, have shown such fluctuations (Etzioni, 1968; Campbell, 1969: 415). In this regard it is comforting to note that for the all-days-and-hours figures, for which fatalities are separately available, they show as marked effects as do serious injuries. (In the crime studies cited, homicides and murders were markedly less susceptible to recording bias than were lesser crimes. See Campbell, 1969.) *Regression* seems implausible here, for, in marked contrast to the Connecticut case, the crackdown was not a reaction to a peak crisis, but rather to a chronic condition, as inspection of the series indicates.

There remains the catchall category labeled *history*—discrete events other than the experimental treatment that occurs simultaneously with them. In quasi-experimental thinking, when a set of hypotheses cannot be ruled out mechanically through design, the researcher bears the burden of seeking out the reasonable hypotheses included therein and ruling them out or allowing for them individually. The following explanations have been suggested as possible alternative or additional explanations of the change in the British casualty rate in October of 1967 (Bennett and Westwick, 1968).

(1) *The publicizing of crackdown.* The government conducted a two-phase publicity campaign concerning the crackdown, from September 25 through December 21, 1967. This large-scale effort involved several hundred thousand pounds spent for paid advertising, in addition to donations of large amounts of free time by public radio and television. The campaign publicized and explained the crackdown.

Although the publicity campaign may have helped the crackdown produce its effect—indeed, it may be considered as a part of the crackdown—the continued lower casualty rate is inconsistent with the idea that the publicity campaign acted independently. It seems reasonabls to posit that the publicity campaign made the crackdown more effective, and to expect that the effect of the crackdown might be increased with additional campaigns. An additional reason for doubting the independent effect of the publicity campaign is the known ineffectiveness of most safety publicity; a similar safety campaign conducted in Britain in 1964, on the same scale and with the same media as the 1967 campaign, had no notable effect on the casualty rate.

(2) *Improvements in traffic controls.* Within the past two or three years, there have been some important improvements in traffic control in Britain. For instance, the priority of vehicles at traffic circles has been resolved, and signs posted accordingly; "halt" and "yield" signs had been posted to control entry to major arteries; and intersections known to be dangerous had been reworked.

Perhaps part of the observed change in the casualty rate is due to these efforts, but the introduction of reforms in traffice control can best be conceived as a gradual program rather than as a sudden one, whereas the change in the data is abrupt. In addition, traffic signs would not be expected to have a greater effect at night than during the day.

(3) *Tire inspection.* New tires must now meet the standards of the British Standards Association. However, since the proportion of vehicles with new tires increases very gradually, the comments concerning the traffic control program apply here and rule out explaining much of the observed change in these terms.

(4) *Reduction in two-wheeled vehicles.* Motorcycles and motor scooters have a high accident rate; the number of these vehicles in use is alleged to have decreased very sharply in 1967, one estimate being as much as thirty percent (Bennett and Westwick, 1968). The reduction is said to be due to a temporary increase in the purchase tax on these vehicles, which was rescinded in 1968.

The factual basis of this explanation is challenged by statistics maintained by the Ministry of Transport showing that the use of motorcycles and motor scooters declined only about fourteen percent in 1967. This decline was part of a general, long-term decline in the use of these vehicles, and was about average in amount. A decline of this form is unlikely to produce an abrupt effect in a casually related variable. Just to be sure, we have examined all-hours-and-days figures separately for cars and for two-wheeled motor vehicles. The sharp October 1967 drop exists in both series, but is much more marked for four-wheeled cars.

(5) *Improvement in traffic law enforcement in London* has been suggested as a cause of the decline. Since there is no demonstrated sharp and direct relationship between law enforcement and accident rates, this explanation can be discounted.

(6) *Highway traffic* has grown less rapidly in Britain since 1965 than before that date. However, since growth has continued, albeit at a

slower pace, an absolute decrease in the number of accidents does not seem reasonably explained by this fact. The actual volume of traffic in Britain increased by six percent in 1967.

(7) *British insurance companies* offer an enormous discount for claim-free driving. However, this is no innovation, and any effect that it might have on casualties would not be expected to follow the form of our data.

Conclusion

The Interrupted Time-Series design used in this study of the British crackdown on drinking and driving has ruled out a wide variety of potential alternative explanations of the observed decline in casualties. The only serious contenders to the hypothesis that the crackdown saved lives and injuries are a group of hypotheses each of which refers to a simultaneous event that might be expected to have a similar effect. However, close attention to each of these rules them out as plausible explanations of much of the change observed at the time of the crackdown. Our conclusion is that the crackdown, with its attendant publicity, did save lives and prevent injuries, and that it continues to have an important beneficial effect on British highways.

Substantively, we have shown that a relatively simple and inexpensive legal reform has produced the results for which it was intended. We believe that the British Act, with appropriate modifications, would meet the requirements of constitutionality in the United States; and although direct generalization is not possible, we can see no reasons why such action would not have a similarly beneficial effect in this country. Officials charged with responsibility for highway safety might well be urged to consider this adoption.

Methodologically, we have demonstrated a technique for evaluating the effect of social changes generally and legal changes in particular. This technique ought to be used more frequently than it is at present by both pure and applied social research. The student of society does not need experimental control to assess the effect of a change, providing he knows the limits of the techniques he uses and proceeds sensibly rather than mechanically. If the resulting knowledge is imperfect, the same problem applies in a slightly lesser degree to the best controlled laboratory experiments when one tries to generalize beyond the laboratory. In contrast, the ability to generalize to a large population outside the laboratory is inherent in this and other quasi-experiment techniques where the basic experiment itself is conducted in a similar field situation. Uniqueness in such settings make it of course desirable to have replications and cross-validations.

The administrator who wants to adopt an innovation such as this should introduce it in such a way that its effectiveness can be reconfirmed in his own setting. For this purpose, where the Interrupted Time-Series is all that is feasible, rules should be kept in mind. First, an abrupt, strong, dateable point of impact should be sought, since gradual innovation cannot be distinguished from secular trends. Second, the available time-series records should be continued so as to preserve comparability. Third, the innovation should be introduced when the problem is at a chronic level, rather than in response to crisis. Fourth, the administrator should seek out control series, from adjacent political units or from subset data within his own polity.

Notes

1. For these data, we are indebted to N. F. Digance and J. M. Munden, Directorate of Statistics, Ministry of Transport, London. Their help is gratefully acknowledged.

2. This prorating procedure assumed that the rate for the first nine days of October 1967 was characteristic of October 1961-1966 and of the year 1967. The average October value was 9042. January-September of 1967 ran 1.058 times the average January-Septmber 1.058 × 9042 = anticipated October 1967 of 9566, 8/31 of which is 2468. The actual total for October 1967 was 8269, of which we assume that 8269 − 2468 = 5801 occurred during October 9 to 31. Expanding 5801 for 23 days to a 31-day month produces 7814. (This is then corrected for seasonal trend by subtracting 588 to achieve the plotted point of 7226.) It is obvious here, in the monthly prorating to 31 days, and in the prorating of weekends below, that for a scientific or legislatively authoritative analysis, we should have been given access to records by days rather than by months. However, this was not feasible.

3. Their model assumes that the time-series is subjected to an influence at each time which tends to move the series up or down, and that in the long run these influences—if they could be examined individually—would follow a normal distribution. Though a new influence enters maximally at each point, the effect of the influence is felt on the series at points beyond its initial appearance. Thus the statistical model specifically takes into account the nonindependence of adjacent observations in a time-series. It is with respect to this typical nonindependence of real data that attempts to solve the problems of time-series analysis with simple regression models fail. Data which conform to the statistical model will not show regular periodic cycles. Since most systems which are partially affected by weather and other annual phenomena shows yearly cycles, it is necessary to remove such cycles in the data before analysis. Subsidiary autocorrelation analyses verify the absence of cycles. Glass, Tiao, and Maguire (1970) have modified the model to allow for the data to show constant rates of "drift," increase or decrease, over time. It is this modified model which has been used here, applied to the total series, beginning January 1961. For all the likely values of the effect, the t values are 4.0 or larger, which indicates that the shift is of a magnitude that would occur by chance less than once in 10,000 similar series.

References

Andanaes, J. (1966) "The general preventive effects of punishment." Univ. of Pennsylvania Law Rev. 114 (March): 949-983.

Automobile Manufacturers Association, Inc. (1966) The State of the Art of Traffic Safety: A Critical Review and Analysis of the Technical Information on Factors Affecting Traffic Safety. Cambridge: Arthur D. Little.

Bennett, R. O. and E. H. Westwick (1968) "A report on Britain's road safety act of 1967." Prepared for the Insurance Institute of Highway Safety.

Box, G. E. P. and G. C. Tiao (1965) "A change in level of non-stationary time series." Biometrika 52: 181-192.

Campbell, D. T. (1969) "Reforms as experiments." Amer. Psychologist 24 (April): 404-429.

—and L. Poss (1968) "The Connecticut crackdown on speeding: time-series data in quasi-experimental analysis." Law & Society Rev. 3 (August): 33-53.

Campbell, D. T. and J. C. Stanley (1966) Experimental and Quasi-Experimental Designs for Research. Chicago: Rand-McNally.

Campbell, H. E. (1964) "The role of alcohol in fatal traffic 'accidents' and measures needed to solve the problem." Michigan Medicine 63 (October): 699-703.

Etzioni, A. (1968) "Shortcuts to social change?" The Public Interest 12: 40-51.

Glass, G. V. (1968) "Analysis of the Connecticut speeding crackdown as a time-series quasi-experiment." Law & Society Rev. 3 (August): 55-76.

—H. L. Ross, and D. T. Campbell (forthcoming) "Statistical analyses of the impact of the British road safety act of 1967."

Glass, G. V., G. C. Tiao, and T. O. Maguire (forthcoming) "Analysis of data on the 1900 revision of the German divorce laws as a quasi-experiment." Law & Society Rev.

Insurance Institute for Highway Safety (1968) Highway Safety, Driver Behavior: Cause and Effect. Washington.

Rheinstein, M. (1959) "Divorce and the law in Germany: a review." Amer. J. of Sociology 65: 489-498.

Rose, A. M. (1952) "Needed research on the mediation of labor disputes." Personnel Psychology 5: 187-200.

Schuessler, K. F. (1969) "The deterrent influence of the death penalty," pp. 378-388 in W. J. Chambliss (ed.) Crime and the Legal Process, New York: McGraw-Hill.

Stieber, J. W. (1949) Ten Years of the Minnesota Labor Relations Act. Minneapolis: Industrial Relations Center, University of Minnesota.

U.S. House Committee on Public Works (1968) 1968 Alcohol and Highway Safety Report. Washington: U.S. Government Printing Office.

Walker, N. (1965) Crime and Punishment in Britain. Edinburgh: Edinburgh Univ. Press.

Webb, E. J. et al. (1966) Unobtrusive Measures: Nonreactive Research in the Social Sciences. Chicago: Rand-McNally.

Wolfe, E., G. Luke, and H. Hax (1959) Scheidung und Scheidungsrecht: Grudfrägen der-Ehescheidung in Deutschland. Tubingen: J.C.B. Mohr.

BARRY SCHWARTZ

The Effect in Philadelphia of Pennsylvania's Increased Penalties for Rape and Attempted Rape*

In the preceding article by Ross, Campbell and Glass we saw that our common-sense ideas about being able to control another's conduct by threatening him with punishment were confirmed in the case of the British Road Safety Act of 1967. It will be recalled that the behavior in question in that study was classified as instrumental. The study by Barry Schwartz that is reproduced below is similar in that it is also a legal impact study. However, the behavior in question is classifiable as *expressive* behavior and, as we have indicated earlier, changes in statutes, sanctions, policies and so on have not been particularly effective in deterring expressive acts.

A typical way the politicians deal with criminal behavior, particularly when heinous acts occur, is to increase the penalties that can be administered to offenders committing the acts. Reactions of this sort are especially likely to take place as a consequence of spectacular acts of violence or sexual misconduct, such as a presidential assassination, multiple murders and the rape of a small child. This is illustrated in the following report by Schwartz who takes a forcible rape-homicide incident

Reprinted from Barry Schwartz, "The Effect in Philadelphia of Pennsylvania's Increased Penalties for Rape and Attempted Rape," *Journal of Criminal Law, Criminology and Police Science*, 1968, 59:509-515.

*The author wishes to express his appreciation to former Commissioner of Police Edward J. Bell for placing needed police data at his disposal. He is also indebted to the staff of the Research and Planning Division of the Philadelphia Police Department for their assistance.

110

as the starting point for his analysis of the effects of increased severity of sanctions upon the frequency and seriousness of forcible rape in Philadephia.

Again in this study we see an example of a quasi-experimental design, although many of the threats to validity suggested by Ross, Campbell and Glass are unmentioned. Also there is a less vigorous pursuit of alternative explanations. The results of the study show that neither the excitement leading up to the imposition of more severe penalties nor the actual imposition of such penalties affected the frequency or seriousness of rape in Philadelphia.

These findings are consistent with the contention that legal regulation is not particularly effective as a means of deterring expressive kinds of behavior. However given the nature of quasi-experimental research a variety of other factors possibly affecting the study's findings are worth considering. Official statistics on rape are notoriously deficient, for example, and may not reflect changes in frequency or severity even though such changes might have taken place. The public outcry and media attention to the problem of rape may have led to increased reporting of incidents of forcible rape and the increased reporting may have offset an actual decrease in the amount of rape taking place. Perhaps potential rapists were unaware of the severity of sanctions for forcible rape and the threat of severe sanctions did not enter their perceptual field prior to the commission of the act. Numerous other alternative explanations may be developed to account for the findings in terms other than the increased sanctions had no significant effect. Only as we can increasingly rule out these kinds of alternative explanations can we become more confident about the assertion that increasing severity of sanctions has little impact on the amount of severity of forcible rape.

Much work that can be included in the framework of quasi-experimental research is similarly problematic. The deterrent effects of capital punishment have been studied and debated for many years. Scientifically, we have no definitive answers to the question of whether capital punishment deters or not. At the most, we can indicate that it does not appear to deter, but even here we cannot be sure.

The paucity of solid evidence is particularly striking given that our criminal justice system is premised largely on the grounds that punishment deters and absolute punishment deters absolutely. Based on the pleasure-pain principle and assuming rational calculation by potential criminals, the threat of sanction should deter in that it results in pains that outweigh the pleasures to be gained from criminal activities. Thus it is assumed that negative sanctions will persuade rational men from committing criminal acts. As the Schwartz study indicates, however, this may be grossly incorrect.

Background

The Palm Sunday rape. On April 3rd, 1966, at approximately 3:00 a.m., three Negro men broke into a West Philadelphia home occupied by an eighty-year-old widow, her forty-four-year old daughter and fourteen-year-old granddaughter. During a period of forty minutes, the intruders viciously beat up and raped both women and the child, ransacked and looted the home. The grandmother was found unconscious by the police and lying in a pool of blood. The mother and daughter were hysterical. Each of three victims was ferociously dragged and thrown about (the fourteen-year-old had been pulled across the floor by her hair); the upstairs and downstairs were spattered with blood. The grandmother later died from her wounds.[1]

On April 14, after considerable public outrage (expressed most forcefully in *The Philadelphia Inquirer*), an end was put to all continuances on trials for those accused of crimes leading to bodily injury. This administrative shift was justified in terms of its deterrent value by one of Philadelphia's leading jurists:

"Let the word go out loud and clear to the lawless element in the city of Philadelphia that the arrest for any crime of violence will result in speedy arraignment and trial. Such action should serve not only to remove those convicted of such crimes in our community but—perhaps of equal importance—to deter others who might be so inclined."[2]

The District Attorney in Philadelphia applauded the new policy. "Once the pattern seeps down through the criminal element," he said, "they will think twice . . . and this will bring about the desired deterrent effect."[3] The District Attorney did admit that "the people we're dealing with in rape cases aren't quite as sensitive to what's being printed in the papers as the average public. . . . But it takes time to seep down . . . eventually these rapists are going to realize that such an attack is going to put them in prison for a good part of their lives."[4]

New penalties for rape. By the middle of April the Palm Sunday Rape in West Philadelphia had become a *cause célèbre* throughout the state. Legislators began to speak of doubling the existing penalties. On Monday, April 18th the Senate, in special legislative session, voted 48-0 for a bill which doubled the 15 year maximum sentence and provided for a $10,000 fine. This action was soon scuttled by the House, which set forth a more detailed and harsher measure providing for a maximum of life imprisonment and a $10,000 fine for those convicted of rape involving serious bodily injury. This latter proposal passed 202-0 after 64 minutes of debate.[5]

One legislator expressed the hope that a compromise between Senate and House could be "speedily agreed upon . . . so the women of our Commonwealth can walk our streets safely and live in their homes more securely."[6] Thus, public safety was seen to depend upon the passage of a new rape law, and tempers were running short. *The Philadelphia Inquirer* suggested that ". . . the maneuverings indicated a desire by both groups to seize political advantage in the battle over enactment of legislation in an effort to curb the growing number of rape cases."[7] Both the Governor and Senate Majority Leader accused the Democrats of exploiting the rape crisis for political gain. After further accusations and counter-accusations a compromise, modelled basically after the House proposal, was agreed upon.[8]

On May 12, 1966, Governor Scranton signed into law the compromise bill which amended the Pennsylvania Penal Code of 1939. The chief provisions of this new law call for differential maximum penalties for rape and attempted rape with and without bodily injury,[9] and for harsher penalties for those convicted of second and subsequent offenses in attempted rape. Perhaps the most important feature of this act is the setting of a *minimum* sentence of 15 years for rape involving injury. (In Pennsylvania the law in most cases only provides maximum penalties.)

The maximum sentence for rape with bodily injury was increased from 15 years to life imprisonment. For rape without injury the top penalty was raised from 15 to 20 years. The maximum punishment for attempted rape with bodily injury was increased from 5 to 15 years of imprisonment, and from 5 to 7 years for attempted rape without injury to the victim. However, for those at least twice convicted of attempted rape, the maximum sentence was increased from 5 years to life imprisonment. The new law also provides for increased maximum fines.[10]

Upon passage of the bill one of its three sponsors (a state senator from West Philadelphia) declared:

"The passage of this bill is a major breakthrough in the fight on crime throughout the State, and especially in Philadelphia, and will bring about a definite deterrent on future rapists.

"When the word is circulated among these vicious criminals that they will be swiftly and severely punished; when they get the message that our organized society will not tolerate the violation of our women, these men will think twice before committing these uncivilized acts."[11]

It is the purpose of the remainder of this paper to evaluate the effectiveness of the increased penalties for rape in Pennsylvania.

The Present Study

The rationale underlying this investigation is that the deterrent effect of the new penalties should affect the rate of rape and attempted rape most forcefully in the very community in which the celebrated Palm Sunday offense occurred. If the new law had a desirable effect, a perceptible drop in the monthly rape rates could be expected after May 12, 1966—or even in April, the period of greatest public outrage in which much well-publicized planning for the new penalties took place. Before analyzing the data we must point out that only negligible changes in the adult male population have occurred in Philadelphia during the period of time studied.[12] We may therefore work directly with frequencies.

Rapes and attempted rapes in 1965 and 1966. Police records of *combined* rape and attempted rape in the months of 1965 and 1966 immediately cast doubt upon the deterrent value of the new penal measures. This information is presented in Table I.

It can be seen that decreases of 16, 5 and 20 were found in April, May and June of 1966; however, the increases of 21, 5 and 3 in July, August and September disillusioned anyone who took the former decreases as indications of the deterrent effect of public attention and the rape legislation. Indeed, the number of rapes taking place after June 1st was 205 in *both* 1965 and 1966. On the basis of these figures, then, no long-run deterrent effect could be claimed.

Rapes and attempted rapes: 1958-1966. It may properly be argued that the monthly distribution of rape and attempted rape in 1965 was for some reason or other an unusual one, and therefore an unfair basis of comparison with the 1966 data. A more proper method would involve the enumeration of rape and attempted rape over a number of years and the expression of their monthly frequencies as a proportion of the trend (regression line) that best represents them.[13] This method would provide a distribtuion of values for each month of the year which are standardized with respect to seasonal variation. Such a procedure allows us to compare the monthly ratios of actual to

TABLE 1. Rapes and Attempted Rapes in Philadelphia: 1/65-12/66*

Month	1965	1966	Difference 1965-1966
January	47	42	—5
February	28	43	+15
March	29	40	+11
April	50	34	—16
May	51	46	—5
June	54	34	—20
July	42	63	+21
August	50	55	+5
September	45	48	+3
October	52	46	—6
November	41	43	+2
December	46	41	—5
Total	535	535	0

* Source: Philadelphia Police Department, *Major Crime* (Monthly Reports), January, 1966-December, 1966. (The 1965 data are included in the 1966 reports.)

trend for rape and attempted rape in 1966 with those of any other year. If the rape legislation produced a deterrent effect we would expect the ratios for the months following April or May of 1966 to be part of the lower tail of their respective distributions. In Figure 1 the 1966 values are circled.

The ratios of actual to trend in rape and attempted rape for 1966 are fairly consistent. Throughout the year values are found generally to be in the upper part of the distribution. The 1966 values are only found below the monthly means of the nine year period in April and June—and in neither of these months are the values extreme. In all other months, including May, 1966 (the month in which the legislation was passed) values are somewhat above average. If we compare the 1966 ratios of actual to trend before and after May or June we find nothing unusual in either set. There is certainly no indication of a decline in these values after the spring months.

Incidentally, the data at the bottom of Figure I enable us to evaluate the extent to which the year 1965 serves as an adequate base against which to judge the 1966 monthly breakdowns of rape and attempted rape. The 1965 ratios were below the mean of the nine year period in February, March, July, and August. It can also be seen that these ratios are highest not in July and

FIGURE 1. Ratios of Actual to Trend for Rapes and Attempted Rapes During a Period of 107 Months: 2/58-12/66

Month

Ratio	Jan.	Feb.	Mar.	Apr.	May	June	July	Aug.	Sept.	Oct.	Nov.	Dec.
1.50-1,59				/			⊘	/				
1.40-1.49						/			/	/		
1.30-1.39			/	/	//			/⊘		/	/	
1.20-1.29	/			//	//		/	//	/			
1.10-1.19	//				⊘		/	///	⊘	/⊘	/	/
1.00-1.09	/⊘	/⊘	//	/	/	//	//		///		/⊘	⊘
.90-.99			/⊘		//	///	//	/	//	//	//	//
.80-.89			/	⊘	//	⊘	/		/	/	//	///
.70-.79	//	///	/	//					/			/
.60-.69		///	/	/		/			/		/	/
.50-.59			/									
.40-.49			/									
.30-.39	/											
Mean	.94	.79	.81	1.05	1.06	1.03	1.13	1.23	1.02	1.08	.98	.88
1965	1.12	.67	.70	1.20	1.23	1.30	1.02	1.21	1.09	1.26	1.00	1.12
1966	1.03	1.05	.98	.84	1.13	.84	1.56	1.31	1.19	1.14	1.07	1.02

Source: Philadelphia Police Department, *Statistical Report*, 1961-1965; *Major Crime* (Monthly Reports), January 1966-December 1966. (Data for 1958-1960 are included in the 1961 *Statistical Report*.)

August as is the case in 1966 and for the mean of the nine year period, but in May, June and October. In this particular year, then, seasonal variations were atypical. Therefore, 1965 was not the best possible period to use as a base of comparison for the 1966 data.

Rape and attempted rape: 1966. Despite the fact that no reduction in the total number of rapes and attempted rapes appears to have been provoked by the imposition of harsher penalties, it is entirely possible that the *proportion* of forcible rapes has declined while the proportion of attempted rapes has increased. Since these modes of assault are confounded in the data published by the Philadelphia Police it was necessary to consult the Department's unpublished information in order to break down these totals.

All forcible and attempted rapes reported to the police between March 1, 1966 and July 31, 1966 were recorded. The justification for the use of this particular time interval is as follows: First, we have reason to suspect that sexual assaults may have decreased between April 3rd (the date of the Palm Sunday episode) and May 12th (date of the imposition of the more severe penalties). Public outrage had been very well articulated through the news media and may have served as a deterrent. Secondly, such administrative measures as the speeding-up of trials for those accused of crimes leading to bodily injury were explicitly imposed with a view to preventing violent offenses. Our choice of data enables us to compare the period of March 1st to April 3rd with that of April 3rd to May 12th with respect to the volumes of rape and attempted rape. But the major claim is for the new penalties themselves, which must be given sufficient time to prove themselves. As Philadelphia's District Attorney noted, it may take time for the news of the stiffer penalties to "seep down" to the criminal element. But if the May 12th legislation was effective one might expect that a reduction in the number of forcible rapes would be apparent by July 31st. In Table II we find the volumes of rape and attempted rape by age groups within the time intervals referred to.

Table II shows that the proportion of forcible rapes by adult offenders has not declined. In fact this proportion has risen slightly from .489 in Period 1 to .571 and .500 in Periods 2 and 3. But if we combine Periods 1 and 2 we find .529 of the total to consist of forcible rape by adults compared to .500 after May 12th (Period 3)—a hardly noticeable difference.

It may be yet argued that the new rape penalties could have brought about a deterrent effect by reducing the *seriousness* of forcible rapes. In other words, the imposition of harsher punishments may have no effect upon the volume of the offenses to which they are directed, but may succeed in reducing their intensity. This possibility was tested by drawing out the Police Investigation Reports on each of the 221[14] cases of rape and attempted rape reported to the Philadelphia Police between March 1st and July 31st of 1966. The description of the offense in all forcible rape cases was then examined and scored by the Sellin-Wolfgang Index.[15] The manner in which the events distributed themselves is shown in Table III.

TABLE II. Forcible and Attempted Rapes by Age Group of Offender: Philadelphia, 3/1/66-7/31/66

Offenses and Age Group of Offender	Period 1 March 1- April 3	Period 2 April 4- May 12	Period 3 May 13- July 31	Total
Forcible Rape				
Adult	22	24	67	113
Juvenile*	4	4	12	20
Unknown		2	7	9
Attempted Rape				
Adult	17	8	39	64
Juvenile	1	3	5	9
Unknown	1	1	4	6
Total	45	42	134	221
Forcible Rape by Adults; total	.489	.571	.500	.511

* Seventeen years of age and under; adult: Eighteen years of age and over.

TABLE III. Seriousness Scores of 113 Forcible Rapes Committed by Adult Offenders in Philadelphia: 3/1/66-7/31/66

Score	Period 1 March 1- April 3	Period 2 April 4- May 12	Period 3 May 13- July 31	Total
11	7	7	25	39⎱45
12	3	2	1	6⎰
13		2	7	9⎱35
14	6	4	16	26⎰
15		3	7	10⎱16
16	1	2	3	6⎰
17		1	7	8⎱11
18	2	1		3⎰
19				⎱4
20+	3	1		4⎰
Unknown		1	1	2
Total	22	24	67	113
Mean	15.18	13.70	13.32	13.77
Median	14.16	14.12	14.00	14.10

It can be seen that the scores in Table III are makedly skewed,[16] suggesting the median as the appropriate measure of central tendency. Clearly, the median seriousness scores are almost identical in each of the three time periods, which forces us to reject the idea that the new penalties could have brought about a deterrent effect by reducing the *seriousness* of forcible rapes.

On the other hand, the seriousness of a rape may be increased by theft or damages as well as by bodily injury. It is therefore possible for the *median* seriousness of this offense to remain constant over time while the bodily injury component decreases. A rapist, in other words, may not injure his victim by force of the more severe penalties for such an offense but compensate (as it

TABLE IV. Injury Scores of 113 Forcible Rapes Committed by Adult Offenders in Philadelphia: 3/1/66-7/31/66

Score	Period 1 March 1– April 3	Period 2 April 4– May 12	Period 3 May 13– July 31	Total
11 12	10	13	28	51⎫51 ⎭
13 14	4 3	6 1	13 18	23⎫45 22⎭
15 16	1 1	1 1	1 3	3⎫7 4⎭
17 18	1	1	3	5⎫5 ⎭
19 20+	1 1	1		2⎫3 1⎭
Unknown		1	1	2
Total	22	24	67	113
Mean	14.05	12.43	12.77	12.95
Median	13.25	11.88	13.38	13.24

TABLE V. Injury Classifications of 64 Attempted Rapes by Adult Offenders in Philadelphia: 3/1/65-7/31/66

Injury Group	Period 1 March 1– April 3	Period 2 April 4– May 12	Period 3 May 13– July 31	Total
No Injury	9	3	15	27
Minor Injury	6	2	11	19
Treated		3	10	13
Hospitalized	2		3	5
Total	17	8	39	64
Treated and Hospitalized as a Proportion of Total	.118	.375	.333	.281

were) for this renunciation by stealing from the victim, or by damaging her property in some way. Thus, it is necessary to isolate the injury component of the distribution of total scores set down in Table III. This is done in Table IV.

We find ourselves again compelled to reject the suggestion that more injury was inflicted upon the victim prior to the imposition of harsher penalties than after. As can be seen in Table IV the median injury score in Period 1 is

13.25 compared to 11.88 and 13.24 in the second and third periods.

The degrees of injury for attempted rape were obtained by classifying the data into the categories shown in Table V. Plainly enough, there is no indication that the proportion of treated and hospitalized victims decreased after April 3rd or May 12th.

Before concluding let us remind ourselves that the law now provides higher penalties for rapes and attempted rapes which create "a substantial risk of death or which causes serious permanent disfigurement or protracted loss or impairment of the function of any member or organ of the body." But it has not been possible to evaluate all of our cases according to this criterion—chiefly because we could not follow up the victims who had been treated or hospitalized.[17] For this reason, the distributions in Tables III and V are probably very slight underestimates of the true degree of seriousness. (This is of course true for each time period; the error does not, therefore, affect the propriety of our comparisons.)

Conclusion

We bring this investigation to a close by noting that Philadelphia found no relief from forcible and attempted rape either during the excitement leading up to the imposition of stronger penalties for these offenses or after the imposition itself. This holds true with respect to both the frequency and intensity of these crimes. We are therefore bound to conclude that Pennsylvania's new deterrent strategy against rape was a failure as far as Philadelphia is concerned.

The inefficacy of the new legislation should create much disappointment among those in Philadelphia who had taken for granted the deterrent impact of increased penalties. Of course, the question of deterrence was quite beside the point for those who supported the new legislation for the sake of a more perfect retribution, or with a view to the May primary elections. Whatever their motives, however, legislators and other officials are not to be held alone responsible for the misguidance to which the Philadelphia public was subjected. The criminological community could confront the legislator with few compelling arguments against his plans for greater and more costly penalties. Very little is actually know about the relationship between rape and penal sanction. Indeed, the deterrent effect of criminal law is a question which cuts across almost all modes of offense. Writes Adenaes:

"While general prevention has occupied and still occupies a central position in the philosophy of criminal law, in penal legislation and in the sentencing policies of the courts, it is almost totally neglected in criminology and sociology. It is a deplorable fact that practically no empirical research is being carried out on the subject. As long as no research results are available legis-lators and judges necessarily must base their decisions on common sense alone."[18]

This study is meant to contribute to the body of knowledge which Andenaes calls for.

Notes

1. *The Philadelphia Inquirer,* April 4, 1966, pp. 1; 31. The grandmother died on April 22, 1966.

2. *Ibid.,* April 14, 1966, p. 1.

3. *Ibid,* April 15, 1966, p. 10.

4. *The Evening Bulletin,* April 14, 1966, p. 1.

5. *The Philadelphia Inquirer,* April 19, 1966, pp. 1; 37. The other House pro-posals that were defeated involved a proposal to introduce the "cat-o-nine tails," and another to extend the death penalty to rapists. (*Ibid.,* May 11, 1966, p. 32.)

6. *Ibid.,* April 22, 1966, p. 7.

7. *Ibid.,* April 26, 1966, p. 11.

8. *Ibid.,* April 27, 1966, p. 6; May 10, 1966, p. 7. Interestingly, legislators had no special preference for either bill, despite the fact that the House and Senate versions differed broadly with respect to both the degree and structure of the rape penalties. Unanimity, then, was no measure of commitment in either House or Senate. The new rape penalties had definitely become a political issue which both parties were eager to exploit in the upcoming primaries.

9. Bodily injury refers to that which "creates a substantial risk of death or which causes serious permanent disfigurement or protracted loss or impairment of the function of any member or organ of the body." (*Purden's Pennsylvania Legis-lative Service,* 1966 Regular and Special Sessions, 1966, p. 27.)

10. For details of the 1939 Code and its amendment, see *Purdon's Pennsyl-vania Statutes Annotated,* Title 18 (Philadelphia: Bisel, 1963), pp. 210, 227; *Purdon's Pennsylvania Legislative Service,* 1966 Regular and Special Sessions, 1966, pp. 27-28.

11. *The Philadelphia Inquirer,* May 12, 1966, p. 42.

12. The number of males in Philadelphia between the ages of 15 and 54 has remained very stable. For the sake of completeness these estimates, which are available from 1960, are; 1960: 501,922; 1961: 528,100; 1962: 513,500; 1963: 514,700; 1964: 505,600; 1965: 524,900; 1966: 514,100. Sources: U.S. Bureau of the Census, *Characteristics of the Population,* Vol. I, Part 40, 1960, p. 243; Phila-delphia, Department of Public Health, Division of Statstics and Research, *Popula-tion Estimates,* 1962-1965, 1967; Philadelphia, Department of Public Health, Division of Statistics and Research, *Annual Statistical Report,* 1965, p. 1.

13. The values of a and b in this equation ($Y = a + bX$) are $Y = 44.065 + (-.075 X)$. Therefore, the trend in frequency of rape and attempted rape over the past nine years is decreasing slightly. The *annual* volumes of rape and at-tempted rape over the nine year period are:

1958:	556	1961:	500	1964:	461
1959:	642	1962:	523	1965:	535
1960:	529	1963:	460	1966:	535

In computing the line of best fit January, 1958 was omitted in order to make the number of months an odd number. This reduced computational labor.

This technique involves an examination of the regression line with a view to confirming or disconfirming a discontinuity at the cutting points implied in the hypothesis. As such, we are dealing with one mode of "Regression—Discontinuity Analysis." See *Campbell & Stanley, Experimental and Quasi-Experimental Designs for Research* 61-64 (1966).

14. As can be seen in Table 1, the Philadelphia Police reported only 217 cases of rape and attempted rape in their monthly *Major Crimes* reports. The small difference of 4 created by the 221 cases drawn by the investigator has chiefly to do with administrative lags. An investigation report, for example, may be returned to the arresting officer for more information and not be re-submitted in time for inclusion into the published monthly report in which it belongs.

15. *Sellin & Wolfgang, The Measurement of Delinquency* 401-412 (1964).

16. Professor Sellin has suggested that in evaluating the impact of crime control measures which have been established as a result of or in response to a particularly brutal or unusual offense, the offense itself be taken out of the data and not counted. The brunt of this rationale is seen in Table 3, whose first column contains the Palm Sunday offense. *The seriousness of this crime is so unusually high that it guarantees a reduction in seriousness in the periods following the one in which it itself occurred.* Notice, for example, that the *mean* seriousness score of 15.1S in Period 1 drops to 13.70 and 13.24 in Periods 2 and 3. If the Palm Sunday offense is removed, the mean of Period 1 drops to 13.95. (All means have been computed with ungrouped data.) However, we may retain this offense in our data as long as we employ the median as our measure of central tendency, for this is insensitive to the extreme or unusual values in a distribution.

17. The recorded seriousness score of the Palm Sunday event, for example, is 41. However, the eventual death of the grandmother (not recorded on the police Investigation Report) would increase this score. Other cases must surely exist whose more serious consequences are not felt until some time after their description and recording by the police.

18. Johannes Andenaes, *Punishment and the Problem of General Prevention,* a paper read before the International Society of Criminology, Montreal, 1965, p. 8. This same exhortation was made by Andenaes more than ten years earlier in his *General Prevention—Illusion or Reality?*, 43 J. Crim, L., C. & P.S. 176 (1952). See also Thorsten Sellin, *L'Effet Intimidant de la Peine, 4 Revue de Science Criminelle et de Droit Penal Comparé* 593 (1960). The lack of empirical data in respect to the deterrent effect of criminal law has also been discussed by John C. Ball, who presents a paradigm for future research in *The Deterrence Concept in Criminology and Law,* 46 J. Crim. L., C. & P.S. 347 (1955).

THE COMMISSION ON OBSCENITY
AND PORNOGRAPHY

Dirty Looks and Dirty Books

Responsibility for causing crime and delinquency has been laid periodically
at the doorstep of the mass media. At differing times extensive concern
has been exhibited over the assumed effects of comics, radio, movies
and television. Throughout, the harmful effects of viewing explicit sexual
materials have also been assumed and legal prohibitions have carefully
limited the production and availability of such materials.

Irrespective of definitions of obscenity or pornography, it is evident to all
that explicit sexual materials have become increasingly assimilated into
other "conventional" media content (movies and magazines) as well as
having been developed into a relatively large-scale industry separate
from conventional media channels (adult theaters and bookstores).

Rather than simply assuming that these materials have harmful consequences, the United States Congress in 1967 established a commission
to investigate the effects of obscene and pornographic materials upon
the American population. Under the auspices of this commission a siz-
able amount of research was conducted and in the end it constituted a
significant proportion of all sex-related research ever conducted in the
United States. In addition to surveys and experimental studies, some of
the research sponsored included quasi-experimental designs.

The portion of the report printed here takes advantage of the naturally
occurring increase in the availability of obscene and pornographic materials to attempt to discover whether increasing availability and use can

Reprinted from *The Report of the Commission on Obscenity and Pornography*, Washington, D.C.: U.S. Government Printing Office, 1970. p.p. 172, 182, 184-185, 241, 258-262,
269-274, 286-287.

account for such things as increases in crime, delinquency, sexual deviance and illegitimacy. Fortunately for research purposes Denmark at an identifiable point in time ceased to attempt to regulate obscenity and pornography by the use of legal prohibitions. Data from both the Danish and American experience are used to reach conclusions about effects.

The commission concluded that erotic materials do not constitute a major or significant cause of problematic behavior. These conclusions have been rejected by some members of the commission itself and by various governmental and religious leaders. Recent decisions of the Supreme Court (Miller vs. California, 1973) still demonstrate a reluctance to remove erotic materials from legal control.

Two interesting questions arise as a result of the commission's conclusions. First, why are behavioral science findings rejected in some instances (usually those in which they fail to confirm preconceptions extant in the population) and accepted in other instances (when they support existing preconceptions)? Granting that absolutely definitive knowledge may be an impossibility, what kinds of evidence about obscenity and pornography would be convincing and provide the basis for policy decisions?

Second, can you, on the basis of your readings about quasi-experimental designs, develop alternative explanations to reasonably account for the commission's findings? Are these alternative explanations more reasonable and adequate than those explanations offered by the Commission? If so, you have a good basis for accounting for the reluctance of many to accept the commission's conclusions.

Finally the public debate over pornography and obscenity points to the problematics of defining deviance as well as to the role of certain individuals and groups in the creation of "deviant" acts. To borrow a phrase from Howard Becker, anti-pornography campaigns are a moral enterprise involving *moral entrepreneurs* who are particularly active in the creation and enforcement of rules. While the reading below does not specifically address itself to moral entrepreneurship, the reader should keep in mind that the study of deviance must concern itself not only with the people who break the rules but also with those who make and enforce them. That is, the foci of deviance research and speculation are processes of, *and* responses to, differentially valuated phenomena. Reactions to, and interpretations of, the recent Supreme Court ruling on obscenity has already had the effect of underscoring this fundamental, yet often neglected notion.

Orientation to the Study of Effects

In July of 1968, the Commission established an Effects Panel, as one of four working Panels; and charged it with principal responsibility for three activities: (a) to review and evaluate existing research bearing on the effects of exposure to sexual stimuli; (b) to design a program of new research in the area; (c) to summarize, evaluate, and report the findings of these studies to the full Commission.

Conceptualizing Effects

The first task facing the Panel was to identify presumed effects of erotic materials and refine these for purposes of research. Two sources were consulted for guidance: (a) previous research in this area, and (b) the claims which had been made about the consequences of reading and viewing erotic material. Reviews of this literature generated several basic questions. If exposure to erotic materials does, in fact, have harmful effects, what kinds of effects are these and who experiences them? Distinctions can be made, for example, between "short-term" effects and "long-term" effects; between "direct" and "indirect" effects; and between effects upon conduct, and effects upon emotions, attitudes, opinions, and moral character. Are these effects experienced by adequately socialized "normal" individuals or only by persons who have already experienced some form of psychopathic or sociopathic condition? Are adults affected, or only children, or both? Various other questions can be asked, but these will perhaps suffice as examples.

Research Methods

A variety of research methods was judged to be potentially responsive to the Panel's goals, and the members of the Panel agreed not to recommend one or two to the exclusion of others. Rather, effects studies followed a "multiple method approach" so that alternative strategies might be used to complement and supplement one another. The following methods were employed: surveys employing various types of sampling procedures (as described immediately below) quasi- experimental studies of selected populations, studies of rates and incidence at the community level, and controlled experimental studies.

Quasi-experimental Methods

Although true experimental designs were not always possible, the Commission contracted for a number of studies which approximated experimental design through retrospective comparisons of matched groups. In these studies groups of individuals that manifested a supposed consequence of exposure to erotica (*e.g.,* juvenile delinquencies, sex offenders, etc.) were compared with groups, similar in most characteristics except the misbehavior, in terms of past experiences with erotic materials. Such studies attempted to determine the extent to which the past experiences of the groups were similar or different by comparing: sex offenders and sex deviants with matched nonsex offenders or nonoffender adult groups (Cook and Fosen, 1970; Goldstein, *et al.,* 1970;

Walker, 1970), and young male prisoners with matched nonoffender males (Davis and Braucht, 1970b).

The principal limitations of these studies are problems associated with adequate matching and reliance upon respondent reports, both of which complicate the inference of causality.

The logic of quasi-experimental analysis was extended to statistical comparisons of the incidence of delinquency and crime with estimates of the availability of erotic materials in both Denmark (Ben-Veniste, 1970; Kutschinsky, 1970c) and the United States (Kupperstein and Wilson, 1970). The limitations of these studies are those associated with analysis of social indicator statistics: the adequacy of available statistical records and the problematic success of including other relevant variables. These problems also impose severe limitations upon attempts to assert or refute causal relationships.

Exposure to Erotica and Character

Some psychologists have argued that hypotheses which predict that exposure to sex stimuli results in direct and substantial increases in rape, homosexuality, and other forms of sexual behavior are not plausible because they tend to discount the effects of ordinary socialization and other behavioral influences. It has been argued that if exposure to erotic material affects an individual at all, it would be a more subtle effect—the development of defective character. A recent study systematically investigated this problem (Davis and Braucht, 1970b).

Psychological inventories were developed to assess four aspects of moral and interpersonal character. Item scales were designed to assess moral "blindness," inclination to act upon a moral basis, level of moral reasoning, and quality of interpersonal character. The questionnaires also assessed respondents' experience with erotic materials and the extent to which family background and peer associations served as conforming or deviant influences. The inventories were administered to over 300 men between the ages of 18 and 30, including imprisoned offenders and university and theology students representing a range of ethnic groups.

Results of this study show that moral character was statistically unrelated to the amount of exposure to erotica ($r = -.14$), but associated with deviant home backgrounds[1] ($r = -.45$) and deviant peer influences[2] ($r = -.41$). Additional analysis revealed that character was unrelated to the age of first exposure to erotic materials, and that deviant homes and peers exerted a much stronger influence on both the amount of exposure and age of first exposure. The authors suggest that "these analyses provide no evidence for a detrimental effect of exposure to pornography on character" (Davis and Braucht, 1970b). The importance of peers in determining the age and amount of exposure to sex stimuli has been observed in several other studies (Report of the Traffic Panel, 1970).

Available research in this area suggests that exposure to erotica has no independent impact upon character.

Availability of Erotica, Juvenile Sex Crimes, and Illegitimacy

A recent study examined the relationship between increased availability of erotic material in the past decade and the national incidence of juvenile sex offenses during the same period (Kupperstein and Wilson, 1970). Police statistics were drawn from the Federal Bureau of Investigation's *Uniform Crime Reports*.[3] Analysis showed that the availability of sexual materials increased several fold from 1960 to 1969.[4] During that same period, and as shown in Table 26, the number of juvenile arrests for[5] *all* offenses, sexual and nonsexual, increased by 105 percent, and the number of such arrests for nonsexual crimes increased by 108 percent. During that same period, however, the number of juvenile arrests for sexual offenses *decreased* by four percent.

The decrease in juvenile arrests for sex offenses is in some part the product of a change in law enforcement policy resulting in the reduction of arrests for certain forms of homosexual behavior. Further, the overall decrease obscures an absolute increase of 86% in juvenile arrests for forcible rape and

TABLE 26. Number and Percent Change in Juvenile[1] Arrests: 1960 to 1969

Offense Category	1960	1969	Percent Change
All offenses, sexual and nonsexual	477,262	980,453	+105.4
All sex offenses	10,881	10,395	—4.5
Forcible rape	1,191	2,214	+85.9
Prostitution and commercialized vice	393	860	+118.9
Other sex offenses	9,297	7,321	—21.3
All nonsex offenses	466,381	970,058	+108.0

1. Under 18 years of age

Note: Compiled from Federal Bureau of Investigation, United States Department of Justice, *Uniform crime reports - 1969*. Washington, D.C.: U.S. Government Printing Office, 1970, 110.

a 119% increase in such arrests for prostitution and commercialized vice.[6] When population changes are taken into account, however, it becomes clear that the increases in juvenile arrests for these offenses are not so large as the absolute numbers suggest.[7] It is also worthy of note that juveniles accounted for a very small proportion of all arrests for prostitution and commercialized vice (1.5% in 1960 and 2.1% in 1969) and for about one-fifth of all arrests for forcible rape (17.3% in 1960 and 20.6% in 1969) and for other sex offenses (20.5% in 1960 and 19.5% in 1969). Thus, to the extent that arrest data are valid indicators of the changes in the nature and volume of crime, it appears that juveniles did not contribute substantially more to the sex crime rate in 1969 than they did in 1960.

In sum, then, while the availability of sexual materials increased several fold during the period from 1960 to 1969, and while juvenile arrests for all crimes more than doubled, juvenile arrests for sex crimes decreased. Despite the change in arrests for homosexual activity, and the increase in rape, these statistics do not provide support for the belief that increased availability of sexual materials leads to sex crime among juveniles. The data do not, however, *disprove* a connection between sexual material and forcible rape.

This review (Kupperstein and Wilson, 1970) also examined statistics on illegitimate births[8] between 1940 and 1969. When the first draft of this report was written, rates of illegitimate births had been made available by the Division of Vital Statistics of the United States Public Health Service for the period 1940 to 1965. Those data presented a clear and somewhat surprising picture. In relation to the 1960 to 1965 period, illegitimate birth rates for females 15-19 years rose from 15.7 to 16.7 (a 6.4% increase). Rate increases for *all* unmarried women 15 to 44, and indeed for almost every age group,[9] were higher, and in some cases vastly higher than the small increase among adolescent females. These 1940 to 1965 and 1960 to 1965 data accordingly cast extreme doubt on the thesis that increased availability of erotica was associated with increased illegitimate births among minors.

In late August, 1970, the Public Health Service released partial data on illegitimate births during the 1965 to 1968 period. These new data tremendously complicate the picture and render it impossible to come to any firm conclusion as to whether there is any relationship between increased availability of erotica and the rate of illegitimate births. In brief, the illegitimate birth rate among females 15-19 increased 18.6%, while illegitimacy rates for *every* older age group *dropped,* in some cases to a very marked degree (*e.g.,* by 24% among women aged 30-34). Put another way, the years 1965 to 1968 were marked by a virtual reversal of the 1960 to 1965 (or 1940 to 1965) trends for almost all age groups, and the reversals occurred in both directions, *i.e.,* minors went up, while the rate for everyone else went down (See Table 27). What is here manifested is not a simple change in rates but a wholly changed social picture.

The question which is virtually impossible to answer is whether the increased availability of erotica in the 1965 to 1968 period was related to this phenomenon. The picture is simply too complex and is necessarily a product of several causes. It is difficult to conceive, for example, that increased availability of erotica should have had one effect on minor girls and no similar effect—indeed, in a sense, the opposite effect—on all other women. Almost certainly, the increased availability of simple contraceptive methods and of abortion, and differences in such availability for different age groups, must be involved in the picture. The complexity of the phenomenon is further attested by the vast differences in illegitimate birth rates between such population

TABLE 27. Estimated Illegitimacy Rates and Percent Change, By Age of Mother: United States, 1940-1968

(Rates are illegitimate births per 1,000 females in specified age group)

Year	15-44 years	Age of Mother						
		10-14	15-19	20-24	25-29	30-34	35-39	40-44
1940	7.1	0.4	7.4	9.5	7.2	5.1	3.4	1.2
1950	14.1	0.6	12.6	21.3	19.9	13.3	7.2	2.0
1960	21.8	0.6	15.7	40.3	42.0	27.5	13.9	3.6
1961	22.6	0.6	16.0	41.2	44.8	28.9	15.1	3.8
1962	21.5	0.6	14.9	41.8	46.4	27.0	13.5	3.8
1963	22.5	0.6	15.3	39.9	49.4	33.7	16.1	4.3
1964	23.4	0.6	16.5	40.0	50.1	41.1	15.0	4.0
1965	23.4	0.7	16.7	38.8	50.4	37.1	17.0	4.4
1968	24.4	—*	19.8	37.3	38.6	28.2	14.9	3.8
Percent Change 1960-1965	+229.6	+75.0	+125.7	+224.2	+600.0	+627.4	+400.0	+266.7
Percent Change 1965-1968	+7.3	+16.7	+6.4	—3.7	+20.0	+34.9	+22.3	+22.2
Percent Change 1940-1969	+4.3	—*	+18.6	—3.9	—23.4	—24.0	—12.3	—13.6

*Figures not available

Note: Adapted from Public Health Service, United States Department of Health, Education and Welfare, Trends In Illegitimacy, United States 1940-1965. Washington, D.C.: U.S. Government Printing Office, 1968. Figures for 1968 received directly from the Public Health Service, Division of Vital Statistics.

groups as whites and blacks. In brief, the overall picture is simply too complex to lend itself to any simple, let alone single, explanation. In reference to the role of erotica, if any, all that can be said is that it seems unlikely that so complex a change could result from so specific an element. Whether it played any role at all is a question that simply cannot be answered on the basis of available data.

Erotica and Sexual Deviance

The belief that reading or viewing explicit sexual materials causes sex crimes is widespread among the American public. A recent survey of a representative sample of adults in the United States (Abelson, *et al.,* 1970) showed that 47% of the men and 51% of the women believed "sexual materials lead people to commit rape." Law enforcement officials, students of criminal behavior and other professionals working with criminals are also divided in their opinions about this relationship. Although some law enforcement officials attest to a causal relationship between exposure to pornography and the commission of sex offenses (Hoover, 1965), few psychiatrists and psychologists report having encountered such cases in their professional experience (Lipkin and Carns, 1970).

Availability of Erotica and Sex Offenses

Reports of increased availability of erotic materials coupled with reported statistical increases in sex crimes over the past decade may, in part, account for the public's apprehensions in this area. The Commission variously sponsored and performed several studies of the relationship between availability of erotic materials and the incidence of sex offenses in both the United States and Denmark.

The United States: 1960-1969

A recent analysis of national police statistics in the *Uniform Crime Reports* for the period 1960 to 1969 (Kupperstein and Wilson, 1970) showed that both the availability of erotic materials and the incidence of sex offenses

**TABLE 30. Number and Percent Change in Adult[1] Arrests for Sex Crimes:
1960 to 1969**

Offense Category	1960	1969	Percent Change
All offenses, sexual and nonsexual	2,846,479	3,145,763	+10.5
All sex offenses	66,860	79,069	+18.3
Forcible rape	5,671	8,533	+50.5
Prostitution and commercialized vice	25,240	40,405	+60.1
Other sex offenses	35,949	30,131	—16.2
All nonsex offenses	2,779,619	3,066,694	+10.3

1. 18 years of age and over

Note: Compiled from Federal Bureau of Investigation, United States Department of Justice, *Uniform crime reports - 1969,* Washington, D.C.: U.S. Government Printing Office, 1970, 110.

increased over the past decade. Increases in the availability of erotica,[10] however, generally outweighed the overall increase in adult arrests for sex offenses. With respect to sex offenses, there was an absolute increase of 50% in adult arrests for forcible rape and a 60% increase in adult arrests for prostitution and commercialized vice. At the same time, however, there was a *decrease* in arrests for all other sex offenses which may, at least in part, be attributable to a reduction in arrests of homosexuals (See Table 30).

FIGURE 9. Percentage Change in Number of Adult Arrests for, and Known Cases of Index Offenses, 1960-1969

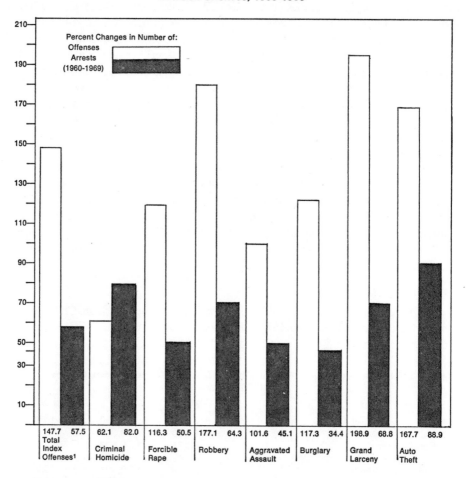

1. The seven offenses included in the FBI's crime index are: criminal homicide, forcible rape, aggravated assault, robbery, burglary, grand larceny, and auto theft.

Note: Adapted from Federal Bureau of Investigation, United States Department of Justice. *Uniform crime reports* - 1969. *Washington, D.C.: U.S. Government Printing Office, 1970, pp. 57, 110.*

Two other points regarding the offienses of forcible rape, prostitution and commercialized vice deserve mention here. First, these offenses, combined accounted for only 1.1% of all adult arrests in 1960 and 1.6% in 1969. Further, the number of known cases of and arrests for forcible rape increased less than did four out of the other six serious crimes which comprise at F.B.I. Crime Index[11] (See Figure 9) and less than such other serious offenses as narcotic drug law violations (adult arrests up 380.4% from 1960 to 1969) and weapons law violations (adult arrests up 129%).

TABLE 31. Percentage Change in Known Cases of and Arrests for
Forcible Rape 1960-1969

Unit of Court	1960	1969	Percent change
Number of forcible rapes known to police[1]	16,860	36,470	+116.3
Number per 100,000 inhabitants[1]	9.4	18.1	+92.6
Number per 100,000 male 10-49 years[2]	34.5	64.2	+86.1
Number of arrests for forcible rape[1]	6,862	10,747	+56.6
Number per 100,000 inhabitants[3]	3.8	5.3	+39.5
Number per 100,000 male 10-49 years[2]	14.5	19.0	+31.0

1. Federal Bureau of Investigation, United States Department of Justice. *Uniform crime reports 1969*. Washington, D.C.: U.S. Government Printing Office, 1970, 57, 110.
2. Based on figures supplied by the United States Department of Commerce, Bureau of the Census.
3. Adapted from *Uniform crime reports - 1969*.

Once again, however, the relatively crude comparisons of the absolute number of arrests or offenses over time may be misleading. The figures in Table 31 show that the differences in known cases and arrests for forcible rape between 1960 and 1969 become smaller as the index is refined. This would, of course, also be true for other crimes.

In sum, available evidence shows that although adult arrests for sex offenses have increased on the whole, the increase has not been as great for these offenses as for such other serious offenses as robbery and narcotic law violations. Further; arrests for sex offenses constituted no more than 2% of all adult arrests during the period studied. If the heightened availability of erotica were directly related to the incidence of sex offenses, one would have expected an increase of much greater magnitude than the available figures indicate. Thus, the data do not appear to support the thesis of a causal connection between increased availabiilty of erotica and the commission of sex offenses; that data do not, however, conclusively disprove such a connection.

Denmark: 1958-1969

In June, 1967, the Danish Parliament voted to remove erotic literature from its obscenity statute[12] and then, on June 1, 1969, repealed the statute, thus abolishing legal prohibitions against the dissemination of sexually explicit materials to persons sixteen years of age and older. Despite the general prohibition which existed prior to 1967, however, literary erotica has been available since 1965, and graphic material since 1967 (Ben-Veniste, 1970). Estimates furnished by producers of sexual materials indicated that dissemination of erotic literature, particularly paperback novels, began to increase during 1960, and reached a peak around 1967. By that time, an increase in production of explicit graphic materials apparently reduced consumer demand for literary erotica and the market for explicit graphic materials increased.[13]

**TABLE 32. Total Sex Crimes Reported to the Police in
Copenhagen, Denmark: 1958-1969**

Year	Total Crimes[1]	Percent increase or decrease over previous year
1958	982	-0-
1959	1,018	+3.66
1960	899	—11.69
1961	1,000	+11.23
1962	749	—25.10
1963	895	—19.49
1964	732	—18.21
1965	762	—4.10
1966	783	—2.75
1967	591	—24.52
1968	515	—12.86
1969	358	—30.48

1. Total reported sex crimes, 1958-1969 = 9284. These include: rape and attempted rape, coitus with minors, "indecent interference short of rape" with both minor girls and adult women, exhibitionism, peeping (voyeurism), homosexual offenses and verbal indecency. The original investigator omitted from his analysis, and without explanation, the "quasi-sex offenses" of bigamy, incest, livings off the earnings of a prostitute, inducing to prostitution, propositioning, and obscenity offenses (the latter eliminated by repeal of prohibitions against the dissemination of sexual materials).

Note: Adapted from Ben-Veniste, R. Pornography and sex crime—the Danish experience. *Technical reports of the Commission on Obscenity and Pornography.* Vol. 7.

Ben-Veniste (1970) compiled statistics on sex offenses reported to the police in Copenhagen, Denmark, over a twelve year period, 1958 to 1969. These figures show that the number of reported sex crimes declined during the period, even though pornography became increasingly available to the general public. As shown in Table 32, the sharpest continuous reduction in sex offenses began in 1967, and has continued through 1969. The onset of this decline occurred when prohibitions regarding dissemination of literary sexual materials were relaxed.

Further analysis found that all classes of sex crimes decreased, but that some decreased more than others. Rape and attempted rape decreased less than did exhibitionism or "unlawful interference short of rape" with children, and these latter offenses decreased less than voyeurism and homosexual offenses which showed the most dramatic decreases (see Table 33).

TABLE 33. Number and Percent Change in Sex Crimes Reported to Copenhagen Police, by Offense Category, 1958-1969

Offense Category	1958	1969	Percent Change
Heterosexual offenses	846	330	—61.0
Rape (including attempts)	52	27	—48.1
Intercourse on threat of violence or by fraud, etc.	11	8	—37.5
Unlawful interference short of rape with adult women	100	52	—48.0
Unlawful interference short of rape with minor girls	249	87	—65.1
Coitus with minors	30	19	—57.9
Exhibitionism	264	104	—60.6
Peeping	87	20	—77.0
Verbal indecency	53	13	—32.5
Homosexual offenses	128	28	—78.1

Note: Adapted from Ben-Veniste, R. Pornography and sex crime - the Danish experience. *Technical reports of the Commission on Obscenity and Pornography.* Vol. 7.

Additional studies (Ben-Veniste, 1970; Kutschinsky, 1970c) attempted to determine whether the reported decrease in sex offenses was attributable to changes in legislation, law enforcement procedures or practices, police reporting and data collection procedures or people's definition of sex crimes, their readiness to report offenses to the police, and their experience with such offenses. It was found that changes in the incidence of sex offenses could not be attributed to legislative change, alteration of law enforcement practices or modified police reporting and data collection procedures.[14] (Ben-Veniste, 1970). A survey (Kutchinsky, 1970c) of Copenhagen residents found that neither public attitudes about sex crimes nor willingness to report such crimes had changed sufficiently to account for the substantial decrease in sex offenses between 1958 and 1969.

Summary and Discussion

Analyses of the United State crime rates do not support the thesis of a causal connection between the availability of erotica and sex crimes among either juveniles or adults. Because of limitations in both the data and inferences which can validly be drawn from them, the data cannot, however, be said absolutely to disprove such a connection. Similar analyses for Denmark show that in that country the increased availability of erotica has been accompanied by a decrease in sex crimes.

Studies of juvenile delinquences indicate that their experience with erotica is generally similar to that of nondeliquents in reference to extent and amount of experience, age of first exposure, and arousal. Such small differences as exist appear to be products of age and subculture variables. Research does suggest that exposure to erotic materials may sometimes be part of a deviant life style and may reflect, rather than affect, the character, attitudes, and conduct of delinquent youth. There is no basis in the available data, however, for supposing that there is any independent relationship between exposure to erotica and delinquency.

Research to date thus provides no substantial basis for the belief that erotic materials constitute a primary or significant cause of the development of character deficits or that they operate as a significant determinative factor in causing crime and delinquency.

This conclusion is stated with due and perhaps excessive caution, since it is obviously not possible, and never would be possible, to state that never on any occasion, under any conditions, did any erotic material ever contribute in any way to the likelihood of any individual committing a sex crime. Indeed, no such statement could be made about any kind of nonerotic material. On the basis of the available data, however, it is not possible to conclude that erotic material is a significant cause of sex crime.

Notes

1. Six scales were developed as measures of deviance in the home. The components of the overall index included exposure to deviant models in the home, exposure to sexually deviant models in the family, absence of sanction networks within the family, perceived quality of mother-father relationships, and paternal-maternal warmth and fairness. See Davis and Braucht (1970b).

2. Four scales constituted an index of deviance in the neighborhood and peer group. The components included the extent of delinquency and crime in the neighborhood and peer group, and heterosexual and homosexual deviance in the peer group. See Davis and Braucht (1970b).

3. The Uniform Crime Reports present arrest statistics for three categories of sex offenses: (a) forcible rape (rape by force, assault to rape and attempted rape, excluding statutory offenses where no force is used and the victim is under age of consent); (b) prostitution and commercialized vice ("sex offenses of a commercialized nature and attempts, such as prostitution, keeping a bawdy house, procuring, or transporting women for immoral purposes"); and (c) other sex offenses ("statutory rape, offenses against chastity, common decency, morals and the like," including attempts).

4. See Report of the Traffic and Distribution Panel of the Commission on Obscenity and Pornography (1970).

5. Under 18 years of age.

6. It should be noted, however, that an accurate index of a given social phenomenon should be based on an appropriate age-, and where necessary, sex-specific rate, thus taking into account changes over time in the population of interest. In the case of illegitimacy (discussed below), the best index is based on the number of unmarried females in the population of childbearing age (15 to 44 years). In the case of forcible rape, the most appropriate base would consist of males in the population, 10 to 49 years of age. By definition, only males can be charged with this offense, and males in this age range accounted for 98% of all

arrests for forcible rape during the period under study (1960-1969). For all other sex offenses a reasonably accurate basis for estimating changes in volume and trends of juvenile arrests would be the number of juvenile males and females in the ten to seventeen year age category. The same kind of refinement calculated for all offenses would undoubtedly reduce the magnitude of the percentage increase of decrease over time. Sex offenses and illegitimacy were selected as a focus of refinement here because of the Commission's particular interest in their relationship to the availability of erotica.

7. The rate of juvenile arrests for forcible rape was 9.3 (per 100,000 males, 10 to 17 years) in 1960 and 13.9 in 1969. The rates (per 100,000 juveniles 10 to 17) of juvenile arrests for prostitution and commercialized vice are 1.5 in 1960 and 2.7 in 1969.

8. There are three different statistics variously used to estimate the volume and trends of illegitimate births. These statistics include: (a) the *number* of reported illegitimate births, (b) the *ratio* of illegitimate to total live births, and (c) the *rate* fo illegitimate births per 1,000 unmarried females of childbearing age (15-44 years). The illegitimacy rate, however, is the most reliable indicator and will be used as the basis for discussion here. Differences in calculations of percentage increases in terms of absolute number as opposed to rate may be illustrated as follows:

Age of Childbearing Females	Number of Illegitimate Births			Illegitimacy Rate		
	1960	1968	% Change	1960	1968	% Change
All ages (15-44)	224,300	339,200	+51.2	21.8	24.4	+11.9
Under 15 years	4,600	7,700	+67.4	0.6	0.7*	+16.7*
15-19 years	87,100	158,000	+81.4	15.7	19.8	+26.1

*Rates for age group under 15 years available only for the period 1960-1965.

Note—Adapted from Public Health Service, Division of Vital Statistics, United States Department of Health, Education and Welfare (1967, 1968). 1968 figures (unpublished) made available directly from the Division of Vital Statistics.

9. The rate decreased among women aged 20-24.

10. See Report of the Traffic and Distribution Panel of the Commission on Obscenity and Pornography (1970).

11. The F.B.I. Crime Index is comprised of the following offenses: criminal homicide, forcible rape, robbery, aggravated assault, burglary, larceny of $50 or over, and auto theft.

12. Sec. 234 of the Danish Penal Code.

13. As one researcher has noted, "spirited public discussion in the newspapers, radio and television alerted the populace to its accessibility. The existence of magazine vending machines outside some 'porno shops' and mail order solicitation in the daily newspapers has ensured that even the most inhibited consumer may purchase pornography with a minimum of anxiety" (Ben-Veniste, 1970).

14. With the exception of arrests for homosexual activity, which for several years reflected a change in the legal age of consent for homosexual relations and a short-lived police "crackdown" on homosexuals.

References

Abelson, H., Cohen, R., Heaton, E., & Slider, C. Public attitudes toward and experience with erotic materials. *Technical reports of the Commission on Obscenity and Pornography*. Vol. 6. Washington, D.C.: U.S. Government Printing Office, 1970.

Ben-Veniste, R. Pornography and sex crime—the Danish experience. *Technical reports of the Commission on Obscenity and Pornography*. Vol. 7. Washington, D.C.: U.S. Government Printing Office, 1970.

Cook, R. F., & Fosen, R. H. Pornography and the sex offender: Patterns of exposure and immediate arousal effects of pornographic stimuli. *Technical reports of the Commission on Obscenity and Pornography*. Vol. 7. Washington, D.C.: U.S. Government Printing Office, 1970.

Davis, K. E., & Braucht, G. N. Reactions to viewing films of erotically realistic heterosexual behavior. *Technical reports of the Commission on Obscenity and Pornography*. Vol. 8. Washington, D.C.: U.S. Government Printing Office, 1970(a).

Goldstein, M. J., Kant, H. S., Judd, L. L., Rice, C. J. & Green, R. Exposure to pornography and sexual behavior in deviant and normal groups. *Technical reports of the Commission on Obscenity and Pornography*. Vol. 7. Washington, D.C.: U.S. Government Printing Office, 1970.

Hoover, J. E. The fight against filth. Personally revised (1965) and distributed reprint of an article originally appearing in *The American Legion magazine*, 1961, 70(16), 48-49.

Kupperstein, L., & Wilson, W. C. Erotica and anti-social behavior: An analysis of selected social indicator statistics. *Technical reports of the Commission on Obscenity and Pornography*. Vol. 7. Washington, D.C.: U.S. Government Printing Office, 1970.

Kutschinsky, B. Sex crimes and Pornography in Copenhagen: A survey of attitudes. *Technical reports of the Commission on Obscenity and Pornography*. Vol. 7. Washington, D.C.: U.S. Government Printing Office, 1970(c).

Lipkin, M., & Carns, D. E. Poll of mental health professionals. Cited in the University of Chicago Division of the Biological Sciences and the Pritzker School of Medicine Reports, Chicago, Illinois, Winter 1970, 20,(1).

Traffic and distribution of sexually oriented materials in the United States: The report of the Traffic and Distribution Panel. *The report of the Commission on Obscenity and Pornography*. Washington, D.C.: U.S. Government Printing Office, 1970.

Walker, C. E. Erotic stimuli and the aggressive sexual offender. *Technical reports of the Commission on Obscenity and Pornography*. Vol. 7. Washington, D.C.: U.S. Government Printing Office, 1970.

C. Laboratory Experiments

STANLEY SCHACHTER

Obesity and Eating*

How an individual behaves in regard to food is, of course, the result of what
he has learned from his past experiences. Food choice and eating behavior are affected by both the variety and relative importance of learned
symbolic meanings. For example, for some people the "surroundings"
or "trappings" of a meal are of the utmost importance; for others, having
"what" they want matters most; to others, "quantity" is most important;
and for still others, "when" they eat is most important (e.g., food must
be immediately available at the first sign of hunger or meals must be
ready and be eaten at specific times).

A consideration of the meanings attached to food and eating has implications for the study of obesity, a socially defined condition of being excessively fat. While a fair amount has been written about the physiological, psychological and sociocultural factors thought to be associated
with obesity, relatively little research exists which deals with its social
psychological aspects. A major exception is the work of Stanley Schachter and his associates at Columbia University. As reported in the read-

Reprinted from Stanley Schacter, "Obesity and Eating," *Science*, Vol. 161, pp. 751-756,
23 August 1968. Copyright 1968 by the American Association for the Advancement of
Science.

*The author is professor of psychology at Columbia University, New York, N.Y.
This article is based on a speech delivered at a conference entitled "Biology and Behavior: Neurophysiology and Emotion," held at the Rockefeller University, New York,
on 10 December 1965, under the sponsorship of the Russell Sage Foundation and the
Rockefeller University.

ing below, they have conducted numerous experiments on obese and normal subjects to determine the effects of various social psychological factors on eating behavior.

The researchers manipulated such factors as gastric motility, food deprivation, circumstances of eating, time of eating and food taste, giving special attention to the cognitive and symbolic aspects of the eating situation for normal and obese individuals. The results showed that the stimuli that motivate the obese to eat are different from those motivating the individual of normal weight and that the set of bodily symptoms the person "labels" hunger also differs. Obese subjects were more influenced by "external cues" to eating, such as sight, smell, and taste of food, time of eating, and other people's actions than were normal subjects. At the same time, obese subjects were less influenced by their internal physiological state of hunger than were subjects of normal weight. Findings from a variety of non-experimental studies are also included in the Schachter report and confirm the general experimental findings.

In line with the interactionist perspective on deviance, the significance of Schachter's research is the conclusion that *different meanings* are attached to food and food-related activities by obese and normal individuals. That man's response to his environment is mediated by symbols and that humans act on the basis of their "definitions of the situation" rather than directly to physical stimuli is, of course, axiomatic to the interactionist position. Put simply, meaning intervenes between stimulus and response.

This view of obesity contrasts sharply with the more prevalent medical view (and with the personality problem approach) which sees the "problem" as residing in the physical makeup or internal physical and psychological states of the individual. The medical treatment of the obese usually concentrates on suppressing ravenous appetites and therapy usually consists of a strict dietary regimen, with or without the assistance of drugs. Results are generally unsatisfactory in that the percentage of failures is far higher than that of successes.

The high failure rate may be due to ignoring the importance of language and symbols in cognition and behavior by those who provide the treatment. In regard to obesity, as well as other deviant phenomena, the lesson is simple: instead of seeking answers and cures by "getting inside the individual" the major effort should be on "getting inside the symbol system" to find out the definitions of the situation operating. Specifically, in terms of obesity the effort would be to discover the learned definitions and meanings associated with the social objects of food and hunger, and of self in relation to them.

Finally, while obesity is a complex phenomenon having a variety of causes, the consequences of obesity as a basis of social differentiation are also worth considering. Being "fat" is socially defined as an undesirable attribute and fat individuals are often treated as social outcasts and second-class citizens. The consequences of these kinds of labeling and social reactions on self-attitudes and interpersonal relations have been noted in a variety of anecdotal and survey research. There is a remarkable similarity between these findings and those described by social psychologists who have studied prejudice and its effects on racial, ethnic and other deviant minorities. In both instances the expectation of rejection frequently results in withdrawal from normal activities, and once stigmatization occurs it serves to block acceptance in interpersonal relations. The similarity of self-attitudes and personality characteristics of the obese and other minorities underscores the commonality of their stigma and the consequent differentiation and rejection often experienced by minorities in general.

Current conceptions of hunger control mechanisms indicate that food deprivation leads to various peripheral physiological changes such as modification of blood constituents, increase in gastric motility, changes in body temperature, and the like. By means of some still debated mechanism, these changes are detected by a hypothalamic feeding center. Presumably some or all facets of this activated machinery lead the organism to search out and consume food. There appears to be no doubt that peripheral physiological changes and activation of the hypothalamic feding center are inevitable consequences of food deprivation. On the basis of current knowledge, however, one may ask, when this biological machinery is activated, do we necessarily describe ourselves as hungry, and eat? For most of us raised on the notion that hunger is the most primitive of motives, wired into the animal and unmistakable in its cues, the question may seem far-fetched, but there is increasing reason to suspect that there are major individual differences in the extent to which these physiological changes are associated with the desire to eat.

On the clinical level, the analyst Hilde Bruch (*1*) has observed that her obese patients literally do not know when they are physiologically hungry. To account for this observation she suggests that, during childhood, these patients were not taught to discriminate between hunger and such states as fear, anger, and anxiety. If this is so, these people may be labeling almost any state of arousal "hunger," or, alternatively, labeling no internal state "hunger."

If Bruch's speculations are correct, it should be anticipated that the set of physiological symptoms which are considered characteristic of food deprivation are not labeled "hunger" by the obese. In other words the obese literally may not know when they are physiologically hungry. For at least one of the presumed physiological correlates of food deprivation, this does appear to be the case. In an absorbing study, Stunkard (2, 3) has related gastric motility to self-reports of hunger in 37 obese subjects and 37 subjects of normal size. A subject, who had eaten no breakfast, came to the laboratory at 9 a.m.; he swallowed a gastric balloon, and for 4 hours Stunkard continuously recorded gastric motility. Every 15 minutes the subject was asked if he was hungry. He answered "yes" or "no," and that is all there was to the study. We have, then, a record of the extent to which a subject's self-report of hunger corresponds to his gastric motility. The results show (i) that obese and normal subjects do not differ significantly in degree of gastric motility, and (ii) that, when the stomach is not contracting, the reports of obese and normal subjects are quite similar, both groups reporting hunger roughly 38 percent of the time. When the stomach is contracting, however, the reports of the two groups differ markedly. For normal subjects, self-report of hunger coincides with gastric motility 71 percent of the time. For the obese, the percentage is only 47.6. Stunkard's work seems to indicate that obese and normal subjects do not refer to the same bodily state when they use the term *hunger*.

Effects of Food Deprivation and Fear

If this inference is correct, we should anticipate that, if we were to directly manipulate gastric motility and the other symptoms that we associate with hunger, we would, for normal subjects, be directly manipulating feelings of hunger and eating behavior. For the obese there would be no correspondence between manipulated internal state and eating behavior. To test these expectations, Goldman, Gordon, and I (4) performed an experiment in which bodily state was manipulated by two means—(i) by the obvious technique of manipulating food deprivation, so that some subjects had empty stomachs and others had full stomachs before eating; (ii) by manipulating fear, so that some subjects were badly frightened and others were quite calm immediately before eating. Carlson (5) has indicated that fear inhibits gastric motility; Cannon (6) also has demonstrated that fear inhibits motility, and has shown that it leads to the liberation, from the liver, of sugar into the blood. Hypoglycemia and gastric contractions are generally considered the chief peripheral physiological correlates of food deprivation.

Our experiment was conducted under the guise of a study of taste. A subject came to the laboratory in mid-afternoon or evening. He had been called the previous evening and asked not to eat the meal (lunch or dinner) preceding his appointment at the laboratory. The experiment was introduced as a study of "the interdependence of the basic human senses—of the way in which the stimulation of one sense affects another." Specifically, the subject was told that this study would be concerned with "the effects of tactile stimulation on the way things taste."

It was explained that all subjects had been asked not to eat a meal before coming to the laboratory because "in any scientific experiment it is necessary that the subjects be as similar as possible in all relevant ways. As you probably know from your own experience," the experimenter continued, "an important factor in determining how things taste is what you have recently eaten." The introduction over the experimenter then proceeded as follows.

For the "full stomach" condition he said to the subject, "In order to guarantee that your recent taste experiences are similar to those of other subjects who have taken part in this experiment, we should now like you to eat exactly the same thing they did. Just help yourself to the roast beef sandwiches on the table. Eat as much as you want—till you're full."

For the "empty stomach" condition, the subjects, of course, were not fed.

Next, the subject was seated in front of five bowls of crackers and told, "We want you to taste five different kinds of crackers and tell us how they taste to you." The experimenter then gave the subject a long set of rating scales and said, "We want you to judge each cracker on the dimensions (salty, cheesy, garlicky, and so on) listed on this sheet. Taste as many or as few of the crackers of each type as you want in making your judgments: the important thing is that your rating be as accurate as possible."

Before permitting the subject to eat, the experimenter continued with the next stage of the experiment—the manipulation of fear.

"As I mentioned," he said, "our primary interest in this experiment is the effect of tactile stimulation on taste. Electric stimulation is the means we use to excite your skin receptors. We use this method in order to carefully control the amount of stimulation you receive."

For the "low fear" condition the subject was told, "For the effects in which we are interested, we need to use only the lowest level of stimulation. At most you will feel a slight tingle. Probably you will feel nothing at all. We are only interested in the effect of very weak stimulation."

For the "high fear" condition the experimenter pointed to a large black console loaded with electrical junk and said, "That machine is the one we will be using. I am afraid that these shocks will be painful. For them to have any effect on your taste sensations, the voltage must be rather high. There will, of course, be no permanent damage. Do you have a heart condition?" A large electrode connected to the console was then attached to each of the subject's ankles, and the experimenter concluded, "The best way for us to test the effect of tactile stimulation is to have you rate the crackers now, before the electric shock, and then rate them again, after the shock, to see what changes in your rating the shock has made."

The subject then proceeded to taste and rate crackers for 15 minutes, under the impression that this was a taste test; meanwhile we were simply counting the number of crackers he ate (7). We then had measures of the amounts eaten by subjects who initially had either empty or full stomachs and who were initially either frightened or calm. There were of course, two types of subjects: obese subjects (from 14 percent to 75 percent overweight) and normal subjects (from 8 percent underweight to 9 percent overweight).

To review expectations: If we were correct in thinking that the obese do not label as hunger the bodily states associated with food deprivation, then our several experimental manipulations should have had no effects on the amount eaten by obese subjects; on the other hand, the eating behavior of normal subjects should have directly paralleled the effects of the manipulations on bodily state.

FIGURE 1. Effects of preliminary eating on the amounts eaten during the experiment by normal and obese subjects. Numbers in parentheses are numbers of subjects.

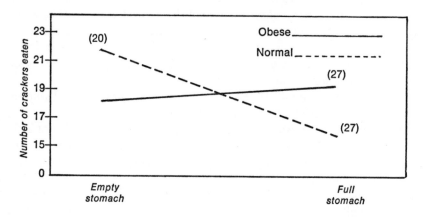

It will be a surprise to no one to learn, from Fig. 1, that the normal subjects ate considerably fewer crackers when their stomachs were full than when their stomachs were empty. The results for obese subjects stand in fascinating contrast. They ate as much—in fact, slightly more—when their stomachs were full as when they were empty (interaction $P < .05$). Obviously the actual state of the stomach has nothing to do with the eating behavior of the obese.

In Fig. 2, pertaining to the effect of fear, we note an analogous picture. Fear markedly decreased the number of crackers the normal subjects ate but had no effect on the number eaten by the obese (interaction $P < .01$). Again, there was a small, though nonsignificant, reversal: the fearful obese ate slightly more than the calm obese.

FIGURE 2. Effects of fear on the amounts eaten by normal and obese subjects. Numbers in parentheses are numbers of subjects.

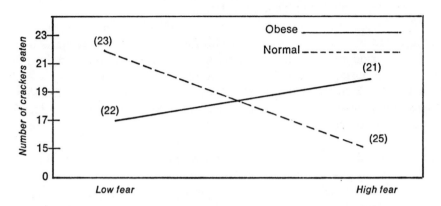

It seems clear that the set of bodily symptoms the subject labels "hunger" differs for obese and normal subjects. Whether one measures gastric motility, as Stunkard did, or manipulates it, as I assume my co-workers and I have done, one finds, for normal subjects, a high degree of correspondence between the state of the gut and eating behavior and, for obese subjects, virtually no correspondence. While all of our manipulations have had a major effect on the amounts eaten by normal subjects, nothing that we have done has had a substantial effect on the amounts eaten by obese subjects.

Effects of the Circumstances of Eating

With these facts in mind, let us turn to the work of Hashim and Van Itallie (8) of the Nutrition Clinic, St. Luke's Hospital, New York City. Their findings may be summarized as follows: virtually everything these workers do seems to have a major effect on the eating behavior of the obese and almost no effect on the eating behavior of the normal subject.

These researchers have prepared a bland liquid diet similar to commercial preparations such as vanilla-flavored Nutrament or Metrecal. The subjects are restricted to this monotonous diet for periods ranging from a week to several months. They can eat as much or as little of it as they want. Some of the subjects get a pitcher full and pour themselves a meal any time they wish. Other subjects are fed by a machine which delivers a mouthful every time the subject presses a button. With either feeding technique, the eating situation has the following characteristics. (i) The food itself is unappealing. (ii) Eating is entirely self-determined: whether or not the subject eats, how much he eats, and when he eats are matters decided by him and no one else. Absolutely no pressure is brought to bear to limit his consumption. (iii) The eating situation is devoid of any social or domestic trappings. It is basic eating: it will keep the subject alive, but it's not much fun.

To date, six grossly obese and five normal individuals have been subjects in these studies. In Fig. 3 the eating serves for a typical pair of subjects over a 21-day period are plotted. Both subjects were healthy people who lived in the hospital during the entire study. The obese subject was a 52-year-old woman, 5 feet 3 inches (1.6 meters) tall, who weighed 307 pounds (138 kilograms) on admission. The normal subject was a 30-year-old male, 5 feet 7 inches tall, who weighed 132 pounds.

The subject's estimated daily caloric intake before entering the hospital (as determined from a detailed interview) is plotted in Fig. 3. Each subject, while in the hospital but before entering upon the experimental regime, was fed a general hospital diet. The obese subject was placed on a 2400-calorie diet for 7 days and a 1200-calorie diet for the next 8 days. As may be seen in Fig. 3, she ate everything on her tray throughout this 15-day period. The normal subject was placed on a 2400-calorie diet for 2 days, and he too ate everything.

With the beginning of the experiment proper, the difference in the eating behavior of the two subjects was dramatic and startling. The food consumption of the obese subject dropped precipitately the moment she entered upon the experimental regime, and it remained at an incredibly low level for the duration of the experiment. This effect is so drastic that the weight of one obese subject who took part in the experiment for 8 months dropped from 410 to 190 pounds. On the other hand, the food consumption of the normal subject of Fig. 3 dropped slightly on the first 2 days, then returned to a fairly steady 2300 grams or so of food a day. The curves for these two subjects are typical. Each of the six obese subjects has manifested this marked and persistent decrease in food consumption during the experiment; each of the normal subjects has steadily consumed about his normal amount of food.

Before suggesting possible interpretations, I should note certain marked differences between these two groups of subjects. Most important, the obese subjects had come to the clinic for help in solving their weight problem and were, of course, motivated to lose weight. The normal subjects were simply volunteers. Doubtless this difference could account for the observed difference in eating behavior during the experiment, and if obese volunteers, unconcerned with their weight, are used as subjects of similar studies, we cannot be sure of the interpretation of this phenomenon. However, I think we should not, solely on grounds of methodological fastidiousness, dismiss these findings. It was concern with weight that brought these obese subjects to the clinic. Each of them, before entering the hospital and while in the hospital before being put on the experimental diet, was motivated to lose weight. Yet, despite this motivation, none of these subjects had been capable of restricting his diet at home, and each of them, when fed the general hospital diet, had eaten everything on his tray. Only when the food was dull and the act of eating was self-initiated and devoid of any ritual trappings did the obese subject, motivated or not, severely limit his consumption.

FIGURE 3. The effects of an emulsion diet on the amounts eaten by an obese and a normal subject.

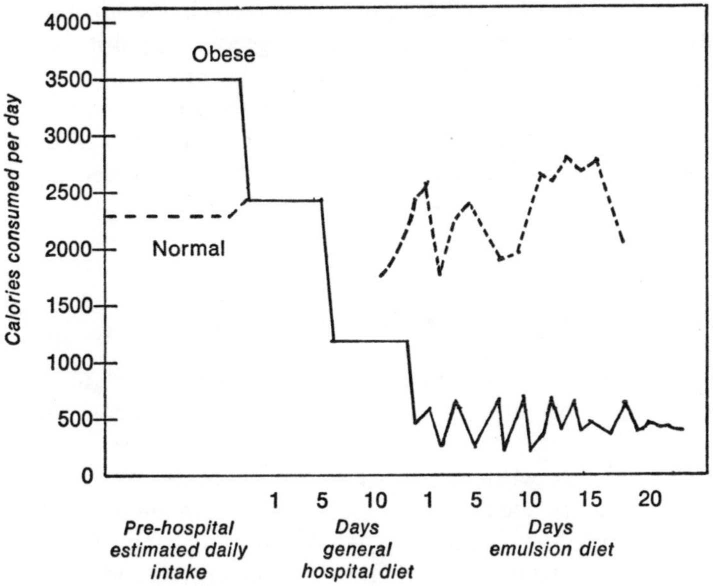

Internal and External Control

On the one hand, then, our experiments indicate virtually no relationship between internal physiological state and the eating behavior of the obese subject; on the other hand, these case studies seem to indicate a close tie between the eating behavior of the obese and what might be called the circumstances of eating. When the food is dull and the eating situation is uninteresting, the obese subject eats virtually nothing. For the normal subject, the situation is just the reverse: his eating beahavior seems directly linked to his physiological state but is relatively unaffected by the external circumstances or the ritual associated with eating.

Given this set of facts it seems clear that eating is triggered by different sets of stimuli in obese and normal subjects. Indeed, there is growing reason to suspect that the eating behavior of the obese is relatively unrelated to any internal state but is, in large part, under external control, being initiated and terminated by stimuli external to the organism. Let me give a few examples. A person whose eating behavior is under external control will stroll by a pastry shop, find the food in the window irresistible, and, even if he has recently eaten, go in and buy something. He will pass by a hamburger stand, smell the broiling meat, and, even though he has just eaten, buy a hamburger. Obviously such external factors—smell, sight, taste, other people's actions—to some extent affect anyone's eating. However, in normal individuals such external factors interact with internal state. They may affect what, where, and how much the normal individual eats, but they do so chiefly when he is in a state of physiological hunger. For the obese, I suggest, internal state is irrelevant and eating is determined largely by external factors.

This hypothesis obviously fits the data presented here, as well it should, since it is an *ad hoc* construction designed specifically to fit these data. Let us see, then, what independent support there is for the hypothesis, and where the hypothesis leads.

Effects of Manipulating Time

Among the multitude of external food-relevant cues, one of the most intriguing is the passage of time. Everyone "knows" that 4 to 6 hours after eating his last meal he should eat his next one. Everyone "knows" that, within narrow limits, there are set times for eating regular meals. We should, then, expect that if we manipulate time we should be able to manipulate the eating behavior of the obese subjects. In order to do this, Gross and I (9) simply gimmicked two clocks so that one ran at half normal speed and the other, at twice normal speed. A subject arrives at 5:00 p.m., ostensibly to take part in an experiment on the relationship of base levels of autonomic reactivity to personality factors. He is ushered into a windowless room containing nothing but electronic equipment and a clock. Electrodes are put on his wrists, his watch is removed "so that it will not get gummed up with electrode jelly," and he is connected to a polygraph. All this takes 5 minutes, and at 5:05 he is left alone, with nothing to do for a true 30 minutes, while ostensibly we are getting a record of galvanic skin response and cardiac rate in a subject at rest. There are two experimental conditions. In one, the experimenter returns after a true 30 minutes and the clock reads 5:20. In the other, the clock reads 6:05, which is normal dinner time for most subjects. In both cases the experimenter is carrying a box of crackers and nibbling a cracker as he comes into the room; he puts the box down, invites the subject to help himself, removes the electrodes from the subject's wrists, and proceeds with personality testing for exactly 5 minutes. This done, he gives the subject a personality inventory which he is to complete and leaves him alone with the box of crackers for another true 10 minutes. There are two groups of subjects—normal and obese—and the only datum we collect is the weight of the box of crackers before and after the subject has had a chance at it.

If these ideas on internal and external controls of eating behavior are correct, normal subjects, whose eating behavior is presumably linked to internal state, should be relatively unaffected by the manipulation and should eat roughly the same number of crackers regardless of whether the clock reads 5:20 or 6:05. The obese, on the other hand, whose eating behavior is presumably under external control, should eat very few crackers when the clock reads 5:20 and a great many crackers when it reads 6:05.

The data of Fig. 4 do indeed indicate that the obese subjects eat almost twice as many crackers when they think the time is 6:05 as they do when they believe it to be 5:20. For normal subjects, the trend is just the reverse (interaction $P = .002$)—an unanticipated finding but one which seems embarrassingly simple to explain, as witness the several normal subjects who thought the time was 6:05 and politely refused the crackers, saying, "No thanks, I don't want to spoil my dinner." Obviously cognitive factors affected the eating behavior of both the normal and the obese subjects, but there was a vast difference. While the manipulation of the clock served to trigger or stimulate eating among the obese, it had the opposite effect on normal subjects, most of whom at this hour were, we presume, physiologically hungry, aware that they would eat dinner very shortly, and unwilling to spoil their dinner by filling up on crackers.

Effects of Taste

In another study, Nisbett (10) examined the effects of taste on eating behavior. Nisbett reasoned that taste, like the sight or smell of food, is essentially an external stimulus to eating. Nisbett, in his experiment, also extended the range of weight deviation by including a group of underweight subjects as well as obese and normal subjects. His purpose in so doing was to examine the hypothesis that the relative potency of external versus internal controls is a dimension directly related to the degree of overweight. If the hypothesis was correct, he reasoned, the taste of food would have the greatest impact on the amounts eaten by obese subjects and the least impact on the amounts eaten by underweight subjects. To test this, Nisbett had his subject eat as much as they wanted of one of two kinds of vanilla ice cream; one was a delicious and expensive product, the other an acrid concoction of cheap vanilla and quinine which he called "vanilla bitters." The effects of taste are presented in Fig. 5, in which the subjects ratings of how good or bad the ice cream is are plotted against the amount eaten. As may be seen in Fig. 5, when the ice cream was rated "fairly good" or better, the obese subjects ate considerably more than the normal subjects did; these, in turn, ate more than the underweight subjects did. When the ice cream was rated "not very good" or worse, the ordering tended to reverse: the underweight subjects ate more than either the normal or the obese subjects. This experiment, then, indicates that the external, or at least nonvisceral, cue *taste* does have differential effects on the eating behavior of underweight, normal, and obese subjects.

The indications, from Nisbett's experiment, that the degree of dependence on external cues relative to internal cues varies with deviation from normal weight are intriguing, for, if further work supports this hypothesis, we may have the beginnings of a plausible explanation of why the thin are thin and the fat are fat. We know from Carlson's work (5) that gastric contractions cease after a small amount of food has been introduced into the stomach. To the extent that such contractions are directly related to the hunger "experience"—to the extent that a person's eating is under internal control—he should "eat like a bird," eating only enough to stop the contractions. Eating beyond this point should be a function of external cues— the taste, sight, and smell of food. Individuals whose eating is externally controlled, then, should find it hard to stop eating. This hypothesis may account for the notorious "binge" eating of the obese (11) or the monumental meals described in loving detail by students (12) of the great, fat gastronomic magnificoes.

This rough attempt to explain why the obese are obese in itself raises intriguing questions. For example, does the external control of eating behavior inevitably lead to obesity? It is evident, I believe, that not only is such a linkage logically not inevitable but that the condition of external control of eating may, in rare but specifiable circumstances, lead to emaciation. A person whose eating is externally controlled should eat and grow fat when food-related cues are abundant and when he is fully aware of them. However, when such cues are lacking or when for some reason, such as withdrawal or depression, the individual is unaware of the cues, the person under external control would, one would expect, not eat, and if the condition persisted, would grow "concentration-camp" thin. From studies of the clinical literature one does get the impression that there is an odd but distinct relationship between obesity and extreme emaciation. For example, 11 of 21 subjects of case studies discussed by Bliss and Branch in *Anorexia Nervosa* (13) were, at some time in their lives obese. In the case of eight of these 11 subjects, anorexia was preceded and accompanied by either marked withdrawal or intense depression. In contrast, intense attacks of anxiety or nervousness [states which our experiment (4) suggests would inhibit eating in normal individuals] seem to be associated with the development of anorexia among most of the ten subjects who were originally of normal size.

At this point, these speculations are simply idea-spinning—fun, but ephereal. Let us return to the results of the studies described so far. These can be quickly summarized as follows.

1) Physiological correlates of food deprivation, such as gastric motility, are directly related to eating behavior and to the reported experience of hunger in normal subjects but unrelated in obese subjects (*3, 4*).

2) External or nonvisceral cues, such as smell, taste, the sight of other people eating, and the passage of time, affect eating behavior to a greater extent in obese subjects than in normal subjects (*8-10*).

Obesity and Fasting

Given these basic facts, their implications have ramifications in almost any area pertaining to food and eating. And some of our studies have been concerned with the implications of these experimental results for eating behavior in a variety of nonlaboratory settings. Thus, Goldman, Jaffa, and I (*14*) have studied fasting on Yom Kippur, the Jewish Day of Atonement, on which the orthodox Jew is supposed to go without food for 24 hours. Reasoning that, on this occasion, food-relevant external cues are particularly scarce, one would expect obese Jews to be more likely to fast than normal Jews. In a study of 296 religious Jewish college students (defined as Jewish college students who had been to a synagogue at least once during the preceding year on occasions other than a wedding or a bar mitzvah), this proves to be the case, for 83.3 percent of obese Jews fasted, as compared with 69.8 percent of normal Jews. ($P < .05$).

Further, this external-internal control schema leads to the prediction that fat, fasting Jews who spend a great deal of time in the synagogue on Yom Kippur will suffer les from fasting than fat, fasting Jews who spend little time in the synagogue. There should be no such relationship for normal fasting Jews. Obviously, there will be far fewer food-related cues in the synagogue than on the street or at home. Therefore, for obese Jews, the likelihood that the impulse to eat will be triggered is greater outside of the synagogue than within it. For normal Jews, this distinction is of less importance. In or out of the synagogue, stomach pangs are stomach pangs. Again, the data support the expectation. When the number of hours in the synagogue is correlated with self-ratings of the unpleasantness of fasting, for obese subjects the correlation is -.50, whereas for normal subjects the correlation is only -.18. In a test of the difference between correlations, $P = .03$. Obviously, for the obese, the more time the individual spends in the synagogue, the less of an ordeal fasting is. For normals, the number of hours in the synagogue has little to do with the difficulty of the fast.

Obesity and Choice of Eating Place

In another study *(14)* we examined the relationship of obesity to choice of eating places. From Nisbett's findings on taste, it seemed a plausible guess

FIGURE 4. The effects of manipulation of time on the amounts eaten by obese and normal subjects.

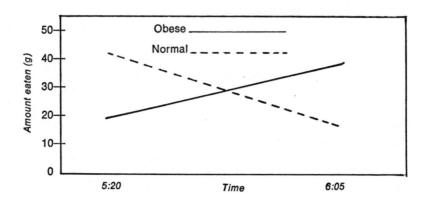

that the obese would be more drawn to good restaurants and more repelled by bad ones than normal subjects would be. At Columbia, students have the option of eating in the university dining halls or in any of the many restaurants that surround the campus. At Columbia, as probably at every similar institution in the United States, students have a low opinion of the institution's food. If a freshman elects to eat in a dormitory dining hall, he may, if he chooses, join a prepayment food plan at the beginning of the school year. Any time after 1 November he may, by paying a penalty of $15, cancel his food contract. If we accept prevailing campus opinion of the institution's food as being at all realistically based, we should anticipate that those for whom taste or food quality is most important will be the most likely to let their food contracts expire. Obese freshmen, then, should be more likely to drop out of the food plan than normal freshmen. Again, the data support the expectation: 86.5 percent of fat freshmen cancel their contracts as compared with 67.1 percent of normal freshmen ($P < .05$). Obesity does to some extent serve as a basis for predicting who will choose to eat institutional food.

Obesity and Adjustment to New Eating Schedules

In the final study in this series *(14)* we examined the relationship of obesity to the difficulty of adjusting to new eating schedules imposed by time-

FIGURE 5. The effects of food quality on the amounts eaten by obese, normal, and underweight subjects. Numbers in parentheses are numbers of subjects.

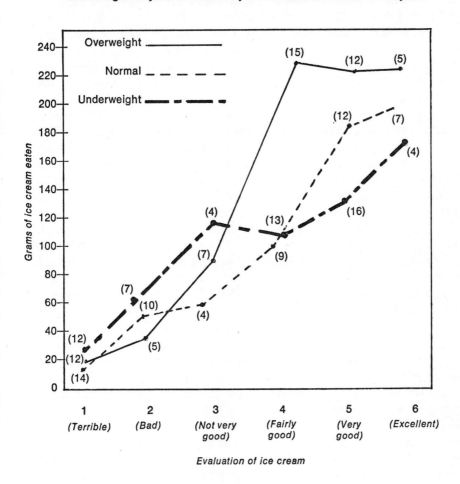

zone changes. This study involved an analysis of data collected by the medical department of Air France in a study of physiological effects of time-zone changes on 236 flight personnel assigned to the Paris-New York and Paris-Montreal flights. Most of these flights leave Paris around noon, French time; fly for approximately 8 hours; and land in North America sometime between 2:00 and 3:00 p.m. Eastern time. Flight-crew members eat lunch shortly after takeoff and, being occupied with landing preparations, are not served another meal during the flight. They land some 7 hours after their last meal, at a time that is later than the local lunch hour and earlier than the local dinner time.

Though this study was not directly concerned with eating behavior, the interviewers systematically noted all individuals who volunteered the information that they "suffered from the discordance between their physiological state and meal time in America" (*15*). One would anticipate that the fatter individuals, being sensitive to external cues (local meal hours) rather than internal ones, would adapt most readily to local eating schedules and be least likely to complain of the discrepancy between American meal times and physiological state.

Given the physical requirements involved in the selection of aircrews, there are, of course, relatively few really obese people in this sample. However, the results of Nisbett's experiment (*10*) indicate that the degree of reliance on external relative to internal cues may well be a dimension which varies with the degree of deviation from normal weight. It seems reasonable, then, to anticipate that, even within a restricted sample, there will be differences in response between the heavier and the lighter members of the sample. This is the case. In comparing the 101 flight personnel who are overweight (0.1 to 29 percent overweight) with the 135 who are not overweight (0 to 25 percent underweight), we find that 11.9 percent of the overweight complain as compared with 25.3 percent of the nonoverweight ($P < .01$). It does appear that the fatter were less troubled by the effects of time changes on eating than the thinner flyers (*16*).

These persistent findings that the obese are relatively insensitive to variations in the physiological correlates of food deprivation but highly sensitive to environmental, food-related cues is, perhaps, one key to understanding the notorious long-run ineffectiveness of virtually all attempts to treat obesity (*17*). The use of anorexigenic drugs such as amphetamine or of bulk-producing, nonnutritive substances such as methyl cellulose is based on the premise that such agents dampen the intensity of the physiological symptoms of food deprivation. Probably they do, but these symptoms appear to have little to do with whether or not a fat person eats. Restricted, low-calorie diets should be effective just so long as the obese dieter is able to blind himself to food-relevant cues or so long as he exists in a world barren of such cues. In the Hashim and Van Itallie study (*8*), the subjects did, in fact, live in such a world. Restricted to a Metrecal-like diet and to a small hospital ward, all the obese subjects lost impressive amounts of weight. However, on their return to normal living, to a man they returned to their original weights.

References and Notes

1. H. Bruch, *Psychiat. Quart.* 35, 458 (1961).
2. A. Stunkard, *Psychosomat. Med.* 21, 281 (1959).
3. — and C. Koch, *Arch. Genet. Psychiat.* 11, 74 (1964).

4. S. Schachter, R. Goldman, A. Gordon, *J. Personality Soc. Psychol.*, in press.

5. A. J. Carlson, *Control of Hunger in Health and Disease* (Univ. of Chicago Press, Chicago, 1916).

6. W. B. Cannon, *Bodily Changes In Pain, Hunger, Fear and Rage* (Appleton, New York, 1915).

7. It is a common belief among researchers in the field of obesity that the sensitivity of their fat subjects makes it impossible to study their eating behavior experimentally—hence this roundabout way of measuring eating: the subjects in this study are taking a "taste test," not "eating."

8. S. A. Hashim and T. B. Van Itallie, *Ann. N.Y. Acad. Sci.* 131, 654 (1965).

9. S. Schachter and L. Gross, *J. Personality Soc. Psychol.*, in press.

10. R. E. Nisbett, *Ibid.*, in press.

11. A. Stunkard, *Amer. J. Psychiat.* 118, 212 (1961).

12. L. Beebe, *The Big Spenders* (Doubleday, New York, 1966).

13. E. L. Bliss and C. H. Branch, *Anorexia Nervosa* (Hoeber, New York, 1960).

14. R. Goldman, M. Jaffa, S. Schachter, *J. Personality Soc. Psychol.*, in press.

15. J. Lavernhe and E. Lafontaine (Air France), personal communication.

16. Obviously, I do not mean to imply that the *only* explanation of the results of these three nonlaboratory studies lies in this formulation of the external-internal control of eating behavior. These studies were deliberately designed to test implications of this general schema in field settings. As with any field research, alternative explanations of the findings are legion, and, within the context of any specific study, impossible to rule out. Alternative formulations of this entire series of studies are considered in the original papers [see Schachter *et al.* (*4* and *9*), Nisbett (*10*), and Goldman *et al.* (*14*)].

17. A. Stunkard and M. McLaren-Hume, *Arch. Internal Med.* 103, 79 (1959); A. R. Feinstein, *J. Chronic Diseases* 11, 349 (1960).

18. Much of the research described in this article was supported by grants G23758 and GS732 from the National Science Foundation.

G. M. STEPHENSON
and
J. H. WHITE

An Experimental Study of Some Effects of Injustice on Children's Moral Behavior

In 1955, Albert Cohen set forth a theory of juvenile delinquency based upon social class. Limiting his concern to lower class delinquency, Cohen argued that lower-class boys suffered from a high degree of status frustration because of their class position. This led to an inversion of values —a reaction formation against middle-class values—with the result that the lower-class boy struck back through the adoption of opposite values. The status frustration and problems of adjustment associated with it led the boys to adopt a delinquent subculture of a collective solution. The subculture served to transmit delinquent values and delinquency was seen as the behavioral expression of the learned, inverted values.

The report by Stephenson and White suggests that the foregoing can be recast in terms of exchange theories of social interaction, these theories having as their basic premise the notion that participants in social interaction may perceive inequities or injustices in the distribution of rewards. The original thinking along hese lines grew out of research conducted by Samuel Stouffer and his colleagues. They formulated the concept of "relative deprivation" to refer to the phenomenon in question. In their research, for example, they found that army air corps men were less satisfied with opportunities for promotion than were those in the military police despite the fact that opportunities for promotion were vastly

Reprinted by permission of Academic Press, Inc. from G. M. Stephenson and J. H. White, "An Experimental Study of Some Effects of Injustice on Children's Moral Behavior," *Journal Experimental Social Psychology*, 1968, 4:460-469.

greater in the air corps. Relative deprivation suggests a resolution of this phenomenon by indicating that the men may have compared themselves with others like themselves. The greater prospect of promotion in the air corps, then, induced high expectations for promotion and subsequent dissatisfaction while in the military police the lower expectations for promotion resulted in less deprivation and, subsequently less dissatisfaction.

A similar idea has been advanced by George Homans in his discussion of "distributive justice." Using economic terminology, distributive justice refers to conditions where an individual's investments are balanced by his reward. A profit is a person's rewards minus costs incurred (where costs are anything given up in the process of interaction, including investments). Investments, in turn, include such things as one's social standing, experience, educational background and the like. Injustice, then, is the reaction to an imbalance between what an individual perceives to actually exist and what be believes should exist, particularly insofar as his own situation is concerned. The individual, then, acts to restore the balance by getting a fairer share of the rewards or in other ways doing away with the perceived injustices. Applying this thinking to lower class boys, it is suggested that perceived injustice exists when these boys compare their situation to middle class peers. The result is status frustration and delinquent activities constitute efforts to overcome the imbalance.

Stephenson and White attempt to test the deprivation or injustice hypothesis by manipulating injustice in the context of a model racing-car game. Four levels of justice were created: (1) a "privileged" group who raced cars all the time; (2) an "equity" group who raced half the time and retrieved cars half the time; (3) a "relatively deprived" group who retrieved all the time for adult racers; and (4) an "absolutel deprived" group who retrieved all the time for the privileged boys. All subjects were then given the opportunity to win prizes by cheating on a motor-racing quiz.

The findings generally confirm the injustice hypothesis in that cheating was greater in the absolutely than in the relatively deprived condition and more prevalent in the relatively deprived than in the equity condition. Contrary to expectations, boys in the privileged condition did not cheat less than those in the equity condition. Questionnaire data are used to explain this finding by showing that the boys in the equity condition did not perceive their situation as unjust. The authors conclude that the experiment gives support to the status-deprivation explanation of lower-class delinquency, nothing that if injustice perpetrated in the space of three one-minute car races was sufficient to produce cheating behavior then indeed the association between injustice and criminal behavior found in our society appears less remarkable.

This paper suggests that subcultural theories of delinquency that rely on the concept of "status deprivation" can be interpreted in terms of exchange theories of social interaction. Cohen (1956) has argued that working-class boys are deprived of prestige and material wealth in comparison with their middle-class contemporaries. Being denied access to a legitimate means of achievement through the education system, the working-class boy seeks an alternative source of status in the gang, which constitutes his delinquent subculture. Attacks on middle-class property and values are institutionalized, enabling the deprived boys to get back at the system that has frustrated them. Cohen claims that his theory explains the high incidence of delinquency among working-class boys, the apparent aimlessness of many delinquent acts, and their frequent occurrence within a group setting. Other theorists, such as Cloward and Ohlin (1960) and Downes (1965), have proposed modifications to Cohen's theory, but agree that deprivation is the basic motivation for delinquent actions.

It is both possible and fruitful to recast Cohen's theory in terms of exchange theories advanced by Thibaut and Kelley (1959), Homans (1961), and Blau (1964). Although these three theories differ in detail, all center on the notion that human behavior can be analyzed in economic terms. Any interaction between two or more people invokes an exchange of costs and rewards by the participants. Homans, whose theory will be used in this analysis, defines *rewards* as the activities of one person which bring about gratification of another's needs. *Costs* are either punishments (fatigue, anxiety) incurred during the course of an interaction, or rewards foregone by not engaging in an alternative activity. Homans introduces a third component—*investments*—to cover such attributes of the participants as their age, skills, and experience.

Homans regards *distributive justice* as an important principle governing social behavior. One individual in an exchange relationship with another will expect that their respective rewards, costs, and investments should be proportional: i.e., A's REWARDS — A's COSTS / A's INVESTMENTS = B's REWARDS — B's COSTS / B's INVESTMENTS. This principle also governs expectation when two individuals are rewarded by a third—their employer, for example. If the principle is violated, then the person to whose disadvantage it operates will feel angry, while the person in whose favor it operates will experience guilt. There is evidence from field studies (Stouffer *et al.,* 1949; Homans, 1954; Clark, 1958) and from experiments (Thibaut, 1950; Spector, 1956; Adams and Rosenbaum, 1962; Adams and Jacobson, 1964) that Homans' propositions are well founded. In order to avoid injustice, people will alter friendship choices, change their attitudes, increase their productivity, or behave in other ways that bring about distributive justice. In other words, injustice has the qualities of a motive.

The model of delinquency put forward by Cohen can be analyzed in terms of distributive justice (or, indeed, in terms of Stouffer's concept of relative deprivation or Thibaut and Kelley's theory of comparison levels). A working-class boy perceives that the rewards of middle-class boys whom he regards as having the same investments as himself are much greater. They live in better homes, have more possessions and greater status, and generally achieve where he does not. Society flouts the rule of distributive justice; the working-class boys experience anger and resentment. Delinquent acts are attempts to restore justice. For example, cheating and stealing may improve the rewards of working-class boys. In addition, "malicious" damage, in the form of destruction of middle-class property, increases the costs of the middle class and, thus, increases lower-class net outcomes. The experiments that follow put the rule of distributive justice to the test in relation to delinquent activities. With an equitable condition as the control, the effects of unjust conditions were contrasted, the dependent variable being cheating to gain prizes. The condition of absolute deprivation (boys working for other, privileged boys) was contrasted with a condition of relative deprivation in which boys worked for adults, whose investments (age, status) were greater than those of the privileged boys. According to Homans' theory, less injustice would be perceived in the latter condition. Thus, the first hypothesis was that absolutely deprived boys would cheat more than the relatively deprived, and the relatively deprived more than those treated equitably.

Whereas the deprived groups would feel angry, the privileged boys would feel guilty. Our second hypothesis asserted that privileged boys would restore equity by deliberately refraining from cheating, in consequence of which they would cheat less than would boys who were treated fairly.

Method

Experimental Conditions

Injustice was experimentally manipulated by involving subjects (10-year-old schoolboys) in a game in which some of them would have highly desirable roles, and other menial ones. A model electric racing-car game was used. This involved four parallel tracks in the form of a figure 8, on which ran four miniature racing cars, the speed of which could be varied by operators working alongside the track. Four experimental conditions were devised. In the *Absolute Deprivation* (AD) condition, groups of boys picked up cars when they came off the track for other boys who raced the cars. The latter were assigned to the *Privileged* (PR) condition. In the condition known as *Relative Deprivation* (RD) boys picked up cars for adults who raced the cars. In the *Equity* (E) condition, justice prevailed: one group raced while the other replaced the cars, and then the groups exchanged roles. The basic unit of racing was three races of 1 minute each.

Individual Testing Session

Immediately after the racing session, boys were taken to individual cubicles where they were given a questionnaire designed to assess the success of the experimental manipulation. Questions 1-3 concerned their enjoyment and evaluation of the game and their job in it. For these questions it was hoped simply to judge whether boys in the Deprived groups had enjoyed themselves less than the Privileged and Equity boys. Question 4 asked the boys how "fair" they thought the arrangements had been. AD and PR boys were expected to perceive the arrangements as "unfair," but for different reasons: the deprived boys feeling angry, the privileged, guilty. Similarly, it was expected that the AD and PR groups would be least anxious "to play with the same boys again" (question 5). After the questionnaire, a delinquent solution to the injustice was offered. The subjects were required to complete a "motor-racing quiz" consisting of eight multiple-choice (5 alternatives) questions; pre-testing had established the virtual impossibility of these questions for boys of this age group. They were told that a score of six out of eight would earn them a cardboard racing track and two model cars; a score of four, one model car only. They were required to mark their own answers from the back of the booklet. The probability of earning even the small prize by chance is less than 1 in 20.

Subjects

The experiment was conducted at five different Junior schools. Within each school all boys in their fourth year (10- to 11-year-olds) were tested. The boys were matched for ability and allocated randomly to the four experimental conditions. When boys had completed the experiment they were prevented from talking to those yet to be tested. A total of 132 boys was tested, of whom 12 were eliminated before the data were analyzed because they had not understood the instructions before completing the racing quiz. The numbers in the four conditions were: AD, 29; RD, 33; E, 29; and PR, 29.

Instructions

Boys were tested in groups of three or four to each experimental condition and were given the following instructions.

Common to all Conditions. We are from the University and we are interested in toys. We should like to find out what sort of toys boys of your age are interested in. Now when I was a boy, electric train sets were very popular, but nowadays racing cars seem to be more popular. We want to know just how popular they *really* are and how much boys like you enjoy them. We have brought some racing cars for you to see and afterwards we hope you will tell us how much you like them. We will ask you to fill in a form about it all.

Absolutely Deprived and Privileged. Four people can race together at any one time. We only have a short time so we have picked out _____, _____, _____, and _____ to do the racing. You will have RED, you BLUE, you GREEN, and you WHITE. You sit here with this throttle. This makes the cars go fast and slow. Be careful not to go too fast: the cars come off very easily at speed, especially round corners.

You four, your job is to pick the cars up when they come off the track. SIT HERE. You put the RED car back on the track marked with RED paper. Make sure you get the car on the right track. This peg goes in this slot. (DEMONSTRATE)

There will be three races of 1 minute each; the winner is the person who does the most laps. Have one or two practice laps.

Relatively Deprived. These four gentlemen are from the University and they are very good at this game. They are going to race these cars together and you are going to help them. _____ will have the RED car, _____ the BLUE, _____ the GREEN, and _____ WHITE. You sit here with this throttle. This makes the car go fast and slow. You have to be careful not to go too fast: the cars come off very easily at speed, especially round the corners.

You four, your job is to pick the cars up when they come off the track. SIT HERE. You put the RED car back on the track marked with RED paper. Make sure you get the car on the right track. This peg goes in this slot. (DEMONSTRATE)

Equity. Four people can race together at any one time. We have picked out _____, _____, _____, and _____ to race first; then they will change over with _____, _____, _____, and _____. You will have the RED, you BLUE, you WHITE, and you GREEN. You sit here with this throttle. This makes the car go fast and slow. Be careful not to go too fast: the cars come off very easily at speed, especially round the corners.

You four, your job is to pick the cars up when they come off the track. SIT HERE. You put the RED car on the track marked with RED paper. Make sure you get the car on the right track. This peg goes in this slot. (DEMONSTRATE)

There will be three races of 1 minute each. The winner is the person who does the most laps. Then we change round after 3 races and the boys picking up the cars will have 3 races. Have one or two practice laps.

Results and Discussion

Efficacy of the Experimental Manipulation

Answers to the questionnaire showed that boys in the Privileged and Equity conditions rated their experience more highly than boys in the two Deprivation conditions. The results are given in Table 1. Boys in all conditions thought the cars suitable, but boys in the PR and E conditions enjoyed themselves more ($\chi^2 = 4.82$, 1 *df, p* $< .05$),[1] and they liked the job better ($\chi^2 = 21.08$, 1 *df, p* $< .001$).

Replies to the question on "fairness" did not entirely fulfill expectations. While the differences between the AD, RD, and E conditions are in the predicted direction (the greater the deprivation, the greater the unfairness perceived), the Privileged boys did not think the game unfair. Indeed, of all groups, they thought it most fair, as is shown in Table 2. Yet the Privileged were not free of all embarrassment. As expected, they together with the AD boys, were less anxious to play again with each other (Table 2), although the difference between the AD and PR groups combined and the RD and E groups combined falls short of significance ($\chi^2 = 2.01$, 1 *df, p* $< .20$).

We may assume from these results that boys in the two Deprivation conditions were less content with their lot than were boys in the PR and E conditions, and that boys in the PR condition were on the whole happy to accept their privileges. We may, therefore, confirm the prediction that with respect to the two Deprivation and the Equity conditions the rank order of cheating will be AD $>$ RD $>$ E; for the Privileged boys, on the other hand, the attitude results suggest that this level of cheating is not likely to be lower than Equity level, and may even be higher, if they attempt to prolong their privileges by winning big prizes.

Patterns of Cheating

In the following analysis of results, boys who earned big prizes ("super-cheats") are differentiated from boys who earned small pizes ("cheats") and boys who earned no prize at all ("non-cheats"). Table 3 shows the percentage of super-cheats, cheats and non-cheats in the four experimental conditions. It is apparent that there is a steady increase in the total amount of cheating as we move from the E through the RD to the AD condition. The PR boys have the highest proportion of super-cheats, and a high proportion of non-cheats. Inspection shows that a majority of the Privileged boys who saw the arrangement as unfair did not cheat, whereas the opposite was true in the other conditions where unfairness was positively associated with cheating. Although this trend is not significant in itself, if the responses to the "fairness" question are combined with the answers to question 5 (in which a "no" response to seeing the other boys again is another indication of "guilt" in the Privileged

TABLE 1. Replies to Questionnaire on "Suitability," "Enjoyment," and "Liking" Questions by Boys in the Four Experimental Conditions

		Suitability of cars		Enjoyment this afternoon					Liking for job				
Condition	N	Yes	No	VM	Q	NS	NVM	NAA	VM	Q	NS	NR	NAA
AD	29	28	1	21	7	1	0	0	9	14	1	3	2
RD	33	31	2	25	7	1	0	0	13	16	3	1	0
E	28	28	0	25	3	0	0	0	20	5	1	0	2
PR	29	28	1	27	2	0	0	0	25	4	0	0	0

a VM = "very much," Q = "quite," NS = "not sure," NVM = "not very much," NAA = "not at all," NR = "not really."

TABLE 2. Replies to Questionnaire on "Fairness" and "Same Boys" Questions, by Boys in the Four Experimental Conditions

									No
			Fairness of arrangements				Same boys again?		
Condition	N	VF	QF	NS	RU	VU	Yes	No	No answer
AD	29	16	5	1	5	2	22	7	0
RD	33	18	9	3	2	1	27	6	0
E	28	17	8	0	0	3	23	4	1
PR	29	21	3	2	1	2	19	10	0

a VF = "very fair," QF = "quite fair," NS = "not sure,"
RU = "rather unfair," VU = "very unfair."

TABLE 3. Percentage of "Super-Cheats" (CC), Cheats (C), and "Non-Cheats" (NC) in the Four Experimental Conditions

Cheating category	AD N = 29	RD N = 33	E N = 28	PR N = 29
	55.0	42.5	34.5	58.5
CC	27.5	33.5	34.5	14.0
C	17.5	24.0	31.0	27.5
NC	100.0	100.0	100.0	100.0

group), the different pattern of results for the Privileged boys is more clearly revealed. Table 4 gives the results of an analysis in which a "justice" score of 2 was obtained if a subject said "yes" to playing with the same boys in the future and replied "very fair" in question 4, and a score of 1 or 0 if only one or neither question was answered positively. In the Privileged group there is a positive association between cheating and justice. Combining the cheating categories, chi-square indicates that this association is not significant ($\chi^2 =$ 1.87, 1 df, $p < .20$). In the other groups there is a contrary trend. The relation between justice and cheating is negative, and is significant ($\chi^2 = 4.95$, 1 df, $p < .05$). But, as we have seen, very few boys in the Privileged condition saw the situation as unfair. The rest presumably thought their privileged position just, and so cheated to maintain that position. As Homans said, the threshold for guilt is higher than that for anger. The manipulation was sufficient to make this group feel privileged, but was not effective in making them feel guilty.

TABLE 4. "Justice" Scores in Relation to Cheating: for PR Group, and for AD, RD, and E Groups Combined

	Group condition			
	AD, RD, and E		PR	
Cheating category	Number of subjects scoring:			
	1 and 0	2	1 and 0	2
CC	26	14	7	10
C	15	11	1	3
NC	7	15	6	2

Table 5 gives the rank order of cheating in the E, RD, and AD conditions for the five experiments in the different schools (obtained by scoring non-cheats 0, cheats 1, and super-cheats 2). A Friedman two-way analysis of variance by ranks gives a χ^2 value of 5.70, which is significant at the .05 level.

TABLE 5. Rank Order of Cheating in AD, RD, and E Conditions, for Five Schools

	Condition		
School	AD	RD	E
A	1	2	3
B	1	2	3
C	1.5	3	1.5
D	1	2	3
E	1.5	1.5	3
Mean rank	1.2	2.1	2.7

The rule of distributive justice receives strong support from these findings. The injustice experienced by those boys working for adults (RD condition) was less than that of boys working for the other boys (AD), but their total outcomes were made more nearly equal by their tendency to cheat less. Both these groups had lower profits than boys in the Equity condition, and they cheated more, in line with the theory that a just outcome would be sought after. Had we been wise before the event, we would have realized that the rule of distributive justice can make no firm prediction about cheating by boys in the Privileged condition, unless it is known in advance whether the guilt from being privileged is a higher cost than the shame of being a privileged person without a prize. It seems that the prospect for a Privileged person of being shamed was a cost not to be incurred except by the most susceptible conscience. Status congruence is a powerful motive.

By the same token, the results of these experiments give support to the status-deprivation accounts of delinquent behavior, and suggest one way in which survey data may be combined with experimental data in the elucidation of functional relationships suggested by survey results. It seems remarkable that injustice perpetrated in the space of three 1-minute toy-car races was sufficient to produce predictable differences in cheating for small gains. It does, however, make less remarkable the association between extended injustice and criminal behavior found in our society.

Note

1. In this and subsequent comparisons, a 2×2 contingency table was established by dichotomizing responses as close as possible to the median, correction for continuity being used in all cases.

References

Adam, J. S., and Jacobsen, Patricia R. Effects of wage inequities on work quality. *Journal of Abnormal and Social Psychology,* 1964, 69, 19-25.

Adams, J. S., and Rosenbaum, W. B. The relationship of worker productivity to cognitive dissonance about wage inequities. *Journal of Applied Psychology,* 1962, 46, 161-164.

Blau, P. M. *Exchange and power in social life.* New York: Wiley, 1964.

Clark, J. V. A preliminary investigation of some unconscious assumptions affecting labor efficiency in eight supermarkets. Unpublished D.B.A. thesis, Harvard Graduate School of Business Administration, 1958. Cited in G. C. Homans, *Social behaviour.* New York: Harcourt, 1961.

Cloward, R. A., and Ohlin, L. E. *Delinquency and opportunity.* New York: Macmillan, 1960.

Cohen, A. K. *Delinquent boys.* New York: Macmillan, 1956.

Downes, D. *The delinquent solution.* London: Routledge and Kegan Paul, 1965.

Homans, G. C. The cash posters: A study of a group of working girls. *American Sociological Review,* 1954, 19, 724-733.

Homans, G. C. *Social behaviour.* New York: Harcourt, 1961.

Spector, A. J. Expectations, fulfillment, and morale. *Journal of Abnormal and Social Psychology,* 1956, 52, 51-56.

Stouffer, S. A., Suchman, E. A., De Vinney, L. C., Starr, Shirley A., and Williams, R. M., Jr. *The American soldier: Adjustment during Army life.* Vol. 1. Princeton, New Jersey: Princeton Univ. Press, 1949.

Thibaut, J. An experimental study of the cohesivenes of underprivileged groups. *Human Relations,* 1950, 3, 251-278.

Thibaut, J., and Kelley, H. H. *The social psychology of groups.* New York: Wiley, 1959.

IRVING M. PILIAVIN
JANE ALLYN HARDYCK
and
ARLENE C. VADUM

Constraining Effects of Personal Costs on the Transgressions of Juveniles[1]

We have earlier argued that attempts to explain deviance on the basis of fixed physiological or psychological states or conditions have generally failed. One of the major criticisms of dispositional explanations is that these theories direct attention away from situational factors operating to influence deviant activities. Irrespective of the existence or operation of dispositions toward deviance, situational elements and immediate environmental contingencies are also operating—sometimes in the direction of deviant modes of expression and sometimes toward nondeviant modes.

The report by Piliavin, Vadum and Hardyck is one example of the nature and utility of a situational approach to deviance. They set forth a reward-cost model of delinquency which posits that everyone is capable of committing deviant acts (some more often and more seriously than others), and that what deters those who conform are subjectively experienced high costs attendant upon deviant activity. The motives giving rise to deviant acts are seen as growing out of relatively immediate situations.

In testing the reward-cost model the authors used high school males in setting up an experiment to examine the relationship between personal costs for deviance and cheating for monetary gain. An initial survey questionnaire was administered to determine personal cost factors and

From Irving M. Piliavin, Jane Allyn Hardyck, and Arlene C. Vadum, "Constraining Effects of Personal Costs on the Transgressions of Juveniles," *Journal of Personality and Social Psychology*, 1968, 10:227-231. Copyright 1968 by the American Psychological Association. Reprinted by permission.

subjects were then assigned to either a high or low cost group.

The findings support a situational approach to deviance in general and the reward-cost model in particular. As expected, low-cost boys cheated significantly more often than high-cost boys. The authors draw upon these findings for proposing an interesting approach to the prevention and control of juvenile delinquency. They propose increasing the costs of delinquency and the reward for conformity by means of a wage system wherein boys are given money on the condition that they keep out of trouble.

Most social scientists pay homage to Lewin as the founder of modern social research and pay lip service to his famous formulation: $B = f(P,E)$. Yet is is a curious fact that the great majority of theories for the explanation of deviant behavior still rely on various aspects of "P," ignoring the immediate situation, "E," as an important causal factor. Current theories of delinquency are an excellent case in point. Whether one refers to psychoanalytic theory, frustration-aggression theory, or the currently fashionable delinquent-subculture theory (Berkowitz, 1962; Cloward & Ohlin, 1960; Friedlander, 1947), one finds that he is dealing with a postulated fixed disposition toward crime residing in the individual as *the* major causal factor in the commission of deviant acts.

As has recently been pointed out (Becker, 1963; Matza, 1964), these theories all fail to account adequately for the known facts of male juvenile crime. First, few of the dispositions proposed have been found to be consistently related to delinquent behavior (Schuessler & Cressey, 1950). Second, even those dispositions which are found reliably to characterize juvenile offenders fail to account for one of the important dynamics of so-called delinquent careers—that most delinquents apparently become conforming in early adulthood (Berkowitz, 1962; Matza, 1964). Third, currently posited criminal dispositions fail to deal adequately with the repeated finding that the vast majority of adolescent boys engage in delinquency to some degree. A number of theories totally ignore this fact; others acknowledge it but then pass it off suggesting that the unlawful behavior of most boys is not of the same genus as that of "true" delinquents (Cloward & Ohlin, 1960). Finally, on heuristic grounds, criticism has been leveled at dispositional premises because they direct attention away from situational factors which may influence boys to commit crime. As Matza (1964) has pointed out, even the so-called serious delinquent engages in crime only rarely, and his illegal actions are typically purposive and situationally relevant. Thus, if dispositions toward crime are in fact operating, it seems likely that their behavioral expression must in some sense be strongly influenced by situational elements.

Briar and Piliavin (1965) have recently argued that a reward-cost formulation of the delinquent act avoids these shortcomings of contemporary dispositional delinquency theories. In its general form (Becker, 1960, 1964; Homans, 1961; Thibaut & Kelley, 1959) a reward-cost model of social elements involved in behavior. The Briar-Piliavin specification of the model assumes that any individual is capable of committing criminal acts and that the motives giving rise to these acts are engendered by the individual's contemporary situation. These motives, the satisfaction of which is conceptualized as anticipated reward, include the reasons offered by delinquents themselves for their illegal acts, for example, the desire for valued goods, the wish to harm a hated other, the hope for acceptance by peers, the wish for excitement, and so forth (Shaw, 1933; Yablonsky, 1962). Whether these motives are acted upon, however, is assumed to be dependent upon not only the strength of these motives but also on the individual's perception of potential costs. Given a particular reward value for an individual of a given act, the greater its potential costs the less likely it will be undertaken. While potential costs are probably numerous and varied, some of the more common ones include the punishments that may be inflicted by officialdom, the wrath of God, parental rejection, withdrawal of esteem by conventional friends, and the loss of educational and vocational opportunities.[2]

Although the Briar and Piliavin reward-cost formulation of delinquency appears to be more congruent than other theories with the general trends and patterns of juvenile crime, no direct test of the model has yet been reported. The research reported here is intended to test one proposition of the model, namely, that the greater an individual's potential costs in relation to the commission of a crime, the less is the likelihood that he will engage in crime. Although the realms in which these costs might be experienced are wide-ranging, for the purposes of the present research the measurements of potential costs was limited to two areas, family and school. Since these provide common and long-term bases for conventional expectations they suggest themselves as stable sources of potential costs for nonconformity among boys.

Method

An initial questionnaire survey of eleventh- and twelfth-grade males in a working-class community examined the relationship between boys' potential costs for engaging in illegal acts and their actual participation in these acts. The survey results (Piliavin, Vadum, & Hardyck, 1968) supported the prediction that high-cost boys engaged in crime less frequently than low-cost boys. Two of the scales used to assess potential costs, the Father Costs scale and the School-Teachers Costs scale, were strongly and positively associated with each of three criteria for delinquent behavior: self-reported criminal activity during the year preceding the survey, self-reported instances of police apprehension for delinquent acts, and official arrest records. The third scale, the Mother Costs scale, was positively related to the first and third of these criteria.

Despite these positive findings, the survey data by their nature contain ambiguities: the direction of causation cannot be determined and possible biases inhere in the criterion measures of delinquency. Thus, the findings that low-cost boys more often report being picked up by police and, according to official records, are more frequently arrested[3] may reflect only that these boys are dealt with more harshly for their crimes because they are less likely than high-cost boys to evince attitudes and emotions which evoke police leniency (Piliavin & Briar, 1964). Furthermore, the data obtained concerning self-reported crimes may indicate only that low-cost boys are less likely to hide their transgressions than are high-cost boys.

The experiment reported here was undertaken in order to avoid these problems of interpretation as well as to provide an opportunity for studying the effects of potential costs on boys' transgressions under controlled reward conditions. The transgression whose commission was to be observed was essentially fraud, that of cheating on a test for financial gain. It was hypothesized that low-cost boys cheat more frequently than high-cost boys over the entire experimental group and within delinquent as well as nondelinquent subgroups.

Subjects

Eighty-six boys who were members of the initial high school survey sample were selected for a 2 x 2 design: high versus low cost and delinquents versus nondelinquents. Subjects were assigned to the high (low) cost group on the basis of their being in the upper (lower) third of the initial high school sample on two cost scales and no lower (higher) than the middle third on the remaining scale. Self-reports on the survey questionnaire concerning apprehension by police for criminal activity provided the criterion for classifying subjects as delinquent or nondelinquent. Boys reporting one or more apprehensions were categorized as delinquent.

Potential Cost Scales

The three cost scales were intended to assess subjects' concern about maintaining parental and teacher respect and affection as well as the degree to which they depended upon direction from these adults.

Father Cost Scale

The score for each boy was his total score on six items pertaining to his relationship with his father. Two examples of items included in this scale are:

1. Being well thought of by my father
   a. Doesn't matter at all to me
   - •
   - •
   - •
   g. Means everything to me

2. When your father doesn't want you to do something you want to do, how often do you go ahead and do it anyway?
   a. Never
   - •
   - •
   - •
   g. Always

Mother Cost Scale

The score for each boy was obtained from an identical scale phrased in terms of mother's respect and approval.

School-Teacher Cost Scale

The score for each boy was his total score for eight items dealing with his concern over teachers' approval and school performance. Two of the items used in this scale were:

1. In general do you like or dislike school ?
   a. Like it
   - •
   - •
   - •
   c. Dislike it

2. Do you care what your teachers think of you?
   a. I care a lot
   - •
   - •
   - •
   c. I don't care much

In using these scales as measures of potential costs for transgressions three assumptions were required. First, it was premised that boys who evidence concern about parental and teacher evaluations regard loss of respect and/or affection from these adults as costly. Second, it was assumed that boys believe this loss of respect would be incurred if they transgressed and the transgression became known. Third, it was assumed that boys recognize some chance exists that any transgression they commit would become known by parents and/or teachers.

TABLE 1. Reliabilities and Intercorrelations of the Three Costs Scales

Scale	Father costs scale	Mother costs scale	School costs scale
Father costs	.79	.57	.36
Mother costs		.77	.22
School costs			.70[1]

Note.—N = 693.
1. Diagonal = Alpha reliabilities for each scale (Tryon, 1957).

While all three of these assumptions, particularly the first, seem quite plausible, no independent assessment of their validity was undertaken. To do so would have increased greatly the possibility of contaminating boys' self-reported deinquency on the survey questionnaire. The positive findings from the survey, however, lend some indirect support for the validity of these assumptions.

The alpha reliabilities (Tryon, 1957) and intercorrelations of the three scales are presented in Table 1. As may be seen from the table, the reliabilities are just barely adequate. As might be expected, the parental cost scales are more highly intercorrelated with one another than with the School-Teachers Cost scale.

Procedure

Subjects were telephoned and invited to participate in a study of "Gestalt Perception," for which they would be paid. When a subject arrived at the prearranged time, he was taken to a waiting room where he was joined by three other boys who were actually confederates of the experimenter.[4] When all four boys were present, the experimenter asked them to introduce themselves and then escorted them to the experimental testing room.

Task and Pretest Instructions

Gestalt Perception booklets were distributed to the boys, and it was explained that their task was to count and write down the number of times that a particular sequence of three letters appeared on each typed page of their booklet. Subjects were told that the test was not an intelligence test and had no relationship to academic performance and social or technical skills. The test simply measured the perception of letter sequences when these letters were embedded among other letters. Using the rationale that the counting became rather routine and might be somewhat boring for the subjects, they were offered $.50 for each page that they completed correctly.

It was then explained that each boy had been given a different form of the booklet and different sequence of letters but that all the boys would be given the same amount of time, 15 minutes, to work on the task. Finally, the experimenter announced that he would be leaving the room for the 15 minutes and that although he wasn't really certain, he thought that the boys should be able to finish counting about seven or eight pages in the allotted time. After answering any questions, the experimenter left the "subjects" alone to work on the task.

Although subjects were informed that they should be able to finish a substantial number of pages in the time allowed, a pretest had established that at best 1½-2 pages could be completed in that time and that the task was irritating and frustrating. Thus, if a subject worked honestly he could make perhaps $.50 or $1 for his efforts, but since the experimenter "wasn't sure" how many pages could be completed in the 15 minutes the subjects could make up to $5 by cheating. An opportunity to cheat was provided during the subsequent interactions between the subject and the three confederates.

Subject-Confederate Interaction

For approximately 2 minutes the group worked undisturbed at the counting. Then one confederate grumbled, "I'll never get eight pages of this done. I'd be lucky if I got two done at this rate."

"You can sure say that again," said a second confederate. No further interaction followed for about 1 minute.

Then the third confederate, who had refrained from speaking up until this time, "accidentally" broke his pencil, announced this to the group, and after looking around the room as if in search of either a pencil-sharpener or a pencil, walked up to a desk located at the front of the testing room, remarking that there might be one there. He searched the top middle drawer of the desk and, finding no pencil there, he opened a side drawer. In this drawer he "found" not only the pencil but also the answer key to all four forms of the perception test and announced this to the group.

Oh, I found one [a pencil]. [Pause] Hey, what do you know. Here's an answer sheet to these letters we're counting. It says Gestalt Perception Test Answer Sheet. I'll never get any eight pages done. I'm going to take down the right answers.

He then extended an invitation to each of the confederates in turn and finally to the subject to do the same. One confederate willingly acceded, saying, "Yah. Let me see it when you're done."

By contrast, the second confederate when asked whether he wanted it replied, "No, but you go ahead. I'm not going to do it, but I won't tell if anyone else does."

Finally, the subject was asked about whether he wanted the test key: "How about you? Do you want to copy them down?"

This constituted the only inducement which was offered the subject to cheat. He was not pressed in any way to accept, and he clearly had the opportunity of declining, as one confederate had done, or accepting, as the other had. This manipulation, it was hoped, would provide a situation which could not be classified as the Asch-like situation of a "minority of one against a unanimous majority [Asch, 1956]."

When the 15 minutes were up the experimenter returned, taking the subject and confederates to rooms for individual interviews. Any awareness of the experimental deception was then determined, and subjects were thoroughly debriefed. Finally, subjects were paid a standard amount for their participation and cautioned not to discuss the experiment for several weeks until it was completed. Nine subjects were eliminated because they acknowledged awareness of the nature of the deception employed.

Results and Discussions

As Table 2 indicates, the predictions concerning the influence of costs were confirmed: high-cost boys engaged in less cheating than did low-cost boys ($p < .01$). Furthermore, when delinquency is defined by self-reported apprehension by police (the criterion by which subjects were selected), the effect of costs within delinquent and nondelinquent subgroups approached conventional levels of significance. When the other two criteria of delinquency are used, the direction of differences between high- and low-cost boys within subgroups in all comparisons remains, although in only one instance is the difference significant.

A further finding is that the effect of delinquency as defined either by self-reported police apprehension or by self-reported commission of crimes is also significant ($p < .02$ and $p < .005$, respectively). Since the primary concern was not with assessing the influence of delinquency in the experimental situation, only one of the several alternative interpretations of this finding is mentioned. This interpretation is in terms of a secondary deviance phenomenon (Becker, 1963; Lemert, 1951). That is, police contact may lead to the realization that the costs actually incurred for delinquency are much lower than those previously anticipated. Consequently, on subsequent occasions where the opportunity is available, the likelihood of engaging in crime is increased.

The results of this experiment support those of the earlier survey which found that high-cost boys were less likely to report delinquent behavior and to have official police records. Although the cost scales employed in the study need further refinement and the use of additional domains of costs would no doubt result in a more valid cost index, the results of the study suggest considerable promise for a "utilitarian" model of delinquency.

Aside from its theoretical relevance, a reward-cost formulation of delinquency has some interesting practical implications for the control of juvenile crime. It suggests that this control might be achieved through increasing the

TABLE 2. Percentage of Subjects Cheating in an Experiment among High- and Low-Cost, Delinquent and Nondelinquent Boys, as Defined by Three Measures of Delinquency[a]

	Delinquency defined by:											
Subject	Self-reported police apprehension				Self-reported criminal acts[b]				Official arrest record			
	High cost	Low cost	χ^2, cost		High cost	Low cost	χ^2, cost		High cost	Low cost	χ^2, cost	
Nondelinquent	14.3 (21)	38.1 (21)	1.98[b] .08		17.2 (29)	35.3 (17)	ns		24.2 (33)	46.7 (30)	3.48[b] .05	
Delinquent	36.8 (19)	60.0 (25)	2.32[b] .07		50.0 (10)	60.0 (25)	ns		28.6 (7)	56.3 (16)	ns	
Overall χ^3, cost		5.56***				5.08**				5.56***		
Overall χ^2, delinquency		5.12**				9.29*****				1.19*		

a Five boys failed to respond to the question concerning commission of crimes.
b $\chi^2$1 Corrected for continuity.
* $p < .15$, one-tailed.
** $p < .02$, one-tailed.
*** $p < .01$, one-tailed.
**** $p < .005$, one-tailed.

costs of delinquency and the rewards of conformity. The most direct way of doing this requires the use of money wages to boys merely on condition that they keep out of trouble. A delinquency-control program based on this simple approach would provide an important test of the reward-cost framework.

Notes

1. This research was partially supported by a research grant from the Ford Foundation and from funds provided by an Institute of Social Sciences Grant from the University of California, Berkeley.

2. Although delinquency theories have not systematically incorporated the concept of costs, some have discussed the role of superego and internalized conventional values in constraining criminal acts. These concepts have not been very useful in delinquency research, however, and are, in any event, very narrow specification of the cost concept. At the least they fail to encompass the more calculative concerns that are involved in an actor's assessment of the consequences of his actions.

3. Police apprehension is distinguished from arrest in that the former often does not lead to the latter. Many boys who are picked up by police are released after the filing of an official incident report or simply after an informal warning. While arrest is the most drastic official action available to police in handling juveniles, it is but one of several dispositions available.

4. All three confederates were Caucasian. Eighteen Negro subjects appeared for the experiment and their data are included. Four of these boys were in the high-cost, delinquent group, five in the high-cost, nondelinquent group, six in the low-cost, delinquent group and three in the low-cost, nondelinquent group. The differences in cheating rates between delinquents and nondelinquents as well as between high-cost and low-cost boys are somewhat reduced by including these boys in the analysis.

References

Asch, S. E. Studies of independence and conformity: A minority of one against a unanimous majority. *Psychological Monographs,* 1956, 70 (9, Whole No. 416).

Becker, H. S. Notes on the concept of commitment. *American Journal of Sociology,* 1960, 66, 35-36.

Becker, H. S. *Outsiders: Studies in the sociology of deviance.* London: Free Press of Glencoe, 1963.

Becker, H. S. Personal change in adult life. *Sociometry,* 1964, 27, 40-53.

Berkowitz, L. *Aggression: A social psychological analysis.* New York: McGraw-Hill, 1962.

Briar, S., & Piliavin, I. M. Delinquency, situational inducements, and commitment to conformity. *Social Problems,* 1965, 12, 35-45.

Cloward, R. A., & Ohlin, L. E. *Delinquency and opportunity.* Glencoe, Ill.: Free Press, 1960.

Friedlander, K. *The psycholanalytic approach to juvenile delinquency.* New York: International Universities Press, 1947.

Homans, G. C. *Social Behavior: Its elementary forms.* New York: Harcourt, Brace & World, 1961.

Lemert, E. M. *Social pathology: A systematic approach to the theory of socio-pathic behavior.* New York: McGraw-Hill, 1951.

Matza, D. *Delinquency and drift.* New York: Wiley, 1964.

Piliavin, I. M., & Briar, S. Police encounters with juveniles. *American Journal of Sociology,* 1964, 70, 206-214.

Piliavin, I. M., Vadum, A. C., & Hardyck, J. A. Delinquency, personal costs, and parental treatment: A test of a cost-reward model. *Journal of Criminal Law, Criminology, and Police Science,* in press.

Schuessler, K. F., & Cressey, D. R. Personality characteristics of criminals. *American Journal of Sociology,* 1950, 55, 476-484.

Shaw, C. R. Juvenile delinquency—A group tradition. *Bulletin of the State University of Iowa,* 1933 (23 N.S. No. 700).

Thibaut, J. W., & Kelley, H. H. *The social psychology of groups.* New York: Wiley, 1959.

Tryon, R. C. Reliability and behavior domain validity: Reformulation and historical critique. *Psychological Bulletin,* 1957, 54, 229-249.

Yablonsky, L. *The violent gang.* New York: Macmillan, 1962.

STANLEY MILGRAM

Some Conditions of Obedience and Disobedience to Authority *

Picture the following situation. Two people come to a psychology laboratory
to take part in a study of memory and learning. They are met by an experimenter who assigns one of them the role of teacher and the other
the role of learner. The teacher's job is to teach the learner a simple
lesson and the teacher is told by the experimenter to give an electric
shock to the learner whenever the learner makes a mistake. To give him
the shock, the teacher is seated before an impressive shock generator.
It has thirty switches on it, ranging from 15 to 450 volts and accompanied
by markings that range from "slight shock" to "danger: severe shock."
Unknown to the teacher, the learner actually is an accomplice of the
experimenter and does not really receive the shocks. He has been
trained to groan, yell and beg to be let out of the experiment just as if he
were receiving them and by doing so convincingly creates the impression that the teacher is causing him great personal harm.

As will be seen in the following article by Stanley Milgram, the experiment
just described was indeed carried out. Its purpose was to see how far a
person would proceed in obeying the orders of a malevolent authority
to inflict "pain" upon an innocent victim. The experiment was set up
such that each time the victim gave an incorrect answer or failed to respond the teacher was to increase the voltage on the shock generator
and press the shock button. From this basic experimental design Mil-

Reprinted from Stanley Milgram, "Some Conditions of Obedience and Disobedience to
Authority," *Human Relations*, 1965, 18:57-75.

gram also created several different conditions involving variation in the degree of victim feedback and proximity between teacher and learner.

The results of the study were quite unexpected (alarmingly so) in that a substantial number of subjects administered shocks even to the maximum shock on the generator despite the painful cries for help from their victims. While this behavior depended somewhat on the degrees of victim feedback and proximity of the victim to the subject, a large number of subjects engaged in what might be interpreted as close-quarter assault on a seemingly innocent bystander.

While some observers may wish to interpret the shocking behavior engaged in by the subjects as requiring persons with twisted and sadistic personalities, this was far from the case. Rather ordinary citizens served as subjects in the study. Subsequent analyses revealed that there were few differences between backgrounds and personality characteristics of obedient and defiant subjects.

What the findings do clearly indicate is the crucial role of power and authority in affecting a person's definition of the situation and his present conduct. Moreover, the results are suggestive of the impact of immediate social influence on the emergent behavior in ongoing situations. Of special significance, perhaps, is the notion that once a person begins to engage in a certain line of conduct it may become extremely difficult to disengage himself from that activity. If Milgram had built only a single 450 volt switch into the shocking generator instead of the long row of switches, it is likely that few subjects would have been willing to administer even one shock to the victims. The progressive severity of the voltage, however, enabled the subject to initially inflict relatively little pain on the victim. Of course, once he had begun hurting the victim, it then became difficult to disengage himself from his course of action on the grounds of not wishing to harm the victim.

This emergent quality of behavior is also present in many other kinds of deviant activities, especially those that are group-based where the individual initially flirts or experiments with minor, non-serious deviant activities. Once begun, however, things may start to happen such that the situation may mushroom into a full-blown incident or series of incidents. Descriptions of the activities centered in the Watergate scandal and the My Lai massacre are illustrative of this point. Seymour Hersh (*My Lai 4,* New York: Random House, 1970, p. 43) quotes one My Lai participant as saying afterwards:

> It was like going from one step to another. . . . First, you'd stop the people, question them, and let them go. Second, you'd stop the people, beat up an old man, and let them go. Third, you'd stop the people, beat up an old man, and then shoot him. Fourth, you go in and wipe out a village.

The significance of the Milgram study for deviance research is that it underscores the need to study the emergent quality of human interaction in general and the immediate situational contexts of deviant conduct in particular. In addition, the study highlights the importance of power and authority relations in affecting definitions of the situation and thus influences the behavior itself. The kinds of research questions raised by the Milgram study are, of course, highly consistent with the interactionist-labeling perspective on deviance. As such, the Milgram study can be taken as illustrative of the kinds of variables emphasized by the perspective.

Finally, one might ask, "Who are the deviants in the study?" Are the deviants the obedient or the defiant subjects? Or, better still, is the experimenter the deviant for putting individuals through such an ordeal? We have chosen to call the obedient subjects the deviants—their deviance consisting of "hurting" or "assaulting" innocent victims. However, the issue clearly points to the problematics of defining deviance—for deviance, like beauty, is in the eyes of the beholder.

The situation in which one agent commands another to hurt a third turns up time and again as a significant theme in human relations. It is powerfully expressed in the story of Abraham, who is commanded by God to kill his son. It is no accident that Kierkegaard, seeking to orient his thought to the central themes of human experience, chose Abraham's conflict as the springboard to his philosophy.

War too moves forward on the triad of an authority which commands a person to destroy the enemy, and perhaps all organized hostility may be viewed as a theme and variation on the three elements of authority, executant, and victim.[2] We describe an experimental program, recently concluded at Yale University, in which a particular expression of this conflict is studied by experimental means.

In its most general form the problem may be defined thus: if X tells Y to hurt Z, under what conditions will Y carry out the command of X and under what conditions will he refuse. In the more limited form possible in laboratory research, the question becomes: if an experimenter tells a subject to hurt another person, under what conditions will the subject go along with this instruction, and under what conditions will he refuse to obey. The laboratory problem is not much a dilution of the general statement as one concrete expression of the many particular forms this question may assume.

One aim of the research was to study behavior in a strong situation of deep consequence to the participants, for the psychological forces operative in powerful and lifelike forms of the conflict may not be brought into play under diluted conditions.

This approach meant, first, that we had a special obligation to protect the welfare and dignity of the persons who took part in the study; subjects were, of necessity, placed in a difficult predicament, and steps had to be taken to ensure their wellbeing before they were discharged from the laboratory. Toward this end, a careful, post-experimental treatment was devised and has been carried through for subjects in all conditions.[3]

Terminology

If Y follows the command of X we shall say that he has obeyed X; if he fails to carry out the command of X, we shall say that he has disobeyed X. The terms *to obey* and to *disobey,* as used here, refer to the subject's overt action only, and carry no implication for the motive or experiential states accompanying the action.[4]

To be sure, the everyday use of the word *obedience* is not entirely free from complexities. It refers to action within widely varying situations, and connotes diverse motives within those situations: a child's obedience differs from a soldier's obedience, or the love, honor, and *obey* of the marriage vow. However, a consistent behavioral relationship is indicated in most uses of the term: in the act of obeying, a person does what another person tells him to do. Y obeys X if he carries out the prescription for action which X has addressed to him; the term suggests, moreover, that some form of dominance-subordination, or hierarchial element, is part of the situation in which the transaction between X and Y occurs.

A subject who complies with the entire series of experimental commands will be termed an *obedient* subject; one who at any point in the command series defies the experimenter will be called a *disobedient* or *defiant* subject. As used in this report, the terms refer only to the subject's performance in the experiment, and do not necessarily imply a general personality disposition to submit to or reject authority.

Subject Population

The subjects used in all experimental conditions were male adults, residing in the greater New Haven and Bridgeport areas, aged 20 to 50 years, and engaged in a wide variety of occupations. Each experimental condition described in this report employed 40 fresh subjects and was carefully balanced for age and occupational types. The occupational composition for each experiment was: workers, skilled and unskilled: 40 per cent; white collar, sales, business: 40 per cent; professionals: 20 per cent. The occupations were intersected with three age categories (subjects in 20s, 30s, and 40s, assigned to each condition in the proportions of 20, 40, and 40 per cent respectively).

The General Laboratory Procedure[5]

The focus of the study concerns the amount of electric shock a subject is willing to administer to another person when ordered by an experimenter to give the 'victim' increasingly more severe punishment. The fact of administering shock is set in the context of a learning experiment, ostensibly designed to study the effect of punishment on memory. Aside from the experimenter, one naive subject and one accomplice perform in each session. On arrival each subject is paid $4.50. After a general talk by the experimenter, telling how little scientists know about the effect of punishment on memory, subjects are informed that one member of the pair will serve as teacher and one as learner. A rigged drawing is held so that the naive subject is always the teacher, and the accomplice becomes the learner. The learner is taken to an adjacent room and strapped into an 'electric chair'.

The naive subject is told that it is his task to teach the learner a list of paired associates, to test him on the list, and to administer punishment whenever the learner errs in the test. Punishment takes the form of electric shock, delivered to the learner by means of a shock generator controlled by the naive subject. The teacher is instructed to increase the intensity of electric shock one step on the generator on each error. The learner, according to plan, provides many wrong answers, so that before long the naive subject must give him the strongest shock on the generator. Increases in shock level are met by increasingly insistent demands from the learner that the experiment be stopped because of the growing discomfort to him. However, in clear terms the experimenter orders the teacher to continue with the procedure in disregard of the learner's protest. *Thus, the naive subject must resolve a conflict between two mutually incompatible demands from the social field. He may continue to follow the orders of the experimenter and shock the learner with increasing severity, or he may refuse to follow the orders of the experimenter and heed the learner's pleas. The experimenter's authority operates not in a free field, but against ever-mounting countervailing pressures from the person being punished.*

A few technical points need to be considered before the findings of the study are described. For the purpose of delivering shock, a simulated shock generator is used, with 30 clearly marked voltage levels that range from 15 to 450 volts (and each activated by one of 30 individual lever switches set in a horizontal line). The naive subject is given a sample shock of 45 volts to convince him of the authenticity of the instrument. The generator bears verbal designations that range from 'Slight Shock' to 'Danger: Severe Shock'.

The responses of the victim are standardized on tape, and each protest is coordinated to a particular voltage level on the shock generator. Starting with 75 volts the learner begins to grunt and moan. At 150 volts he demands to be let out of the experiment. At 180 volts he cries out that he can no longer stand the pain. At 300 volts he refuses to provide any more answers to the memory test, insisting that he is no longer a participant in the experiment and must be freed. In response to this last tactic, the experimenter instructs the naive subject to treat the absence of an answer as equivalent to a wrong answer, and to follow the usual shock procedure. The experimenter reinforces his demand with the statement: 'You have no other choice, you must go on!' (This imperative is used whenever the naive subject tries to break off the experiment.) If the subject refuses to give the next higher level of shock, the experiment is considered at an end. A quantitative value is assigned to the subject's performance based on the maximum intensity shock he administered before breaking off. Thus any subject's score may range from zero (for a subject unwilling to administer the first shock level) to 30 (for a subject who proceeds to the highest voltage level on the board). For any particular subject and for any particular experimental condition the degree to which participants have followed the experimenter's orders may be specified with a numerical value, corresponding to the metric on the shock generator.

This laboratory situation gives us a framework in which to study the subject's reactions to the principal conflict of the experiment. Again, this conflict is between the experimenter's demands that he continue to administer the electric shock, and the learner's demands, which become increasingly more insistent, that the experiment be stopped. The crux of the study is to vary systematically the factors believed to alter the degree of obedience to the experimental commands, to learn under what conditions submission to authority is most probable, and under what conditions defiance is brought to the fore.

Pilot Studies

Pilot studies for the present research were completed in the winter of 1960; they differed from the regular experiments in a few details: for one, the victim was placed behind a silvered glass, with the light balance on the glass such that the victim could be dimly perceived by the subject (Milgram, 1961).

Though essentially qualitative in treatment, these studies pointed to several significant features of the experimental situation. At first no vocal feedback was used from the victim. It was thought that the verbal and voltage designations on the control panel would create sufficient pressure to curtail the subject's obedience. However, this was not the case. In the absence of protests from the learner, virtually all subjects, once commanded, went blithely to the end of the board, seemingly indifferent to the verbal designations ('Extreme Shock' and 'Danger: Severe Shock'). This deprived us of an adequate basis for scaling obedient tendencies. A force had to be introduced that would strengthen the subject's resistance to the experimenter's commands, and reveal individual differences in terms of a distribution of break-off points.

This force took the form of protests from the victim. Initially, mild protests were used, but proved inadequate. Subsequently, more vehement protests were inserted into the experimental procedure. To our consternation, even the strongest protests from the victim did not prevent all subjects from administering the harshest punishment ordered by the experimenter; but the protests did lower the mean maximum shock somewhat and created some spread in the subject's performance; therefore, the victim's cries were standardized on tape and incorporated into the regular experimental procedure.

The situation did more than highlight the technical difficulties of finding a workable experimental procedure: it indicated that subjects would obey authority to a greater extent than we had supposed. It also pointed to the importance of a feedback from the victim in controlling the subject's behavior.

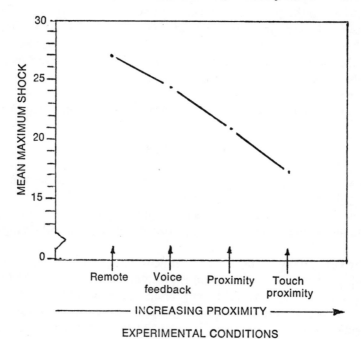

FIGURE 1. Mean Maxima in Proximity Series

One further aspect of the pilot study was that subjects frequently averted their eyes from the person they were shocking, often turning their heads in an awkward and conspicuous manner. One subject explained: 'I didn't want to see the consequences of what I had done.' Observers wrote:

> ... subjects showed a reluctance to look at the victim, whom they could see through the glass in front of them. When this fact was brought to their attention they indicated that it caused them discomfort to see the victim in agony. We note, however, that although the subject refuses to look at the victim, he continues to administer shocks.

This suggested that the salience of the victim may have, in some degree, regulated the subject's performance. If, in obeying the experimenter, the subject found it necessary to avoid scrutiny of the victim, would the converse be true? If the victim were rendered increasingly more salient to the subject, would obedience diminish? The first set of regular experiments was designed to answer this question.

Immediacy of the Victim

This series consisted of four experimental conditions. In each condition the victim was brought 'psychologically' closer to the subject giving him shocks.

In the first condition (Remote Feedback) the victim was placed in another room and could not be heard or seen by the subject, except that, at 300 volts, he pounded on the wall in protest. After 315 volts he no longer answered or was heard from.

The second condition (Voice Feedback) was identical to the first except that voice protests were introduced. As in the first condition the victim was placed in an adjacent room, but his complaints could be heard clearly through a door left slightly ajar, and through the walls of the laboratory.[6]

The third experimental condition (Proximity) was similar to the second, except that the victim was now placed in the same room as the subject, and 1½ feet from him. Thus he was visible as well as audible, and voice cues were provided.

The fourth, and final, condition of this series (Touch-Proximity) was identical to the third, with this exception: the victim received a shock only when his hand rested on a shockplate. At the 150-volt level the victim again demanded to be let free and, in this condition, refused to place his hand on the shockplate. The experimenter ordered the naive subject to force the victim's hand onto the plate. Thus obedience in this condition required that the subject have physical contact with the victim in order to give him punishment beyond the 150-volt level.

Forty adult subjects were studied in each condition. The data revealed that obedience was significantly reduced as the victim was rendered more immediate to the subject. The mean maximum shock for the conditions is shown in *Figure 1*.

Expressed in terms of the proportion of obedient to defiant subjects, the findings are that 34 per cent of the subjects defied the experimenter in the Remote condition, 37.5 per cent in Voice Feedback, 60 per cent in Proximity, and 70 per cent in Touch-Proximity.

How are we to account for this effect? A first conjecture might be that as the victim was brought closer the subject became more aware of the intensity of his suffering and regulated his behavior accordingly. This makes sense, but our evidence does not support the interpretation. There are no consistent differences in the attributed level of pain across the four conditions (i.e. the amount of pain experienced by the victim as estimated by the subject and expressed on a 14-point scale). But it is easy to speculate about alternative mechanisms:

Empathic cues. In the Remote and to a lesser extent the Voice Feedback condition, the victim's suffering possesses an abstract, remote quality for the subject. He is aware, but only in a conceptual sense, that his actions cause pain to another person; the fact is apprehended, but not felt. The phenomenon is common enough. The bombardier can reasonably suppose that his weapons will inflict suffering and death, yet this knowledge is divested of affect, and does not move him to a felt, emotional response to the suffering resulting from his actions. Similar observations have been made in wartime. It is possible that the visual cues associated with the victim's suffering trigger empathic responses in the subject and provide him with a more complete grasp of the victim's experience. Or it is possible that the empathic responses are themselves unpleasant, possessing drive properties which cause the subject to terminate the arousal situation. Diminishing obedience, then, would be explained by the enrichment of empathic cues in the successive experimental conditions.

Denial and narrowing of the cognitive field. The Remote condition allows a narrowing of the cognitive field so that the victim is put out of mind. The subject no longer considers the act of depressing a lever relevant to moral judgement, for it is no longer associated with the victim's suffering. When the victim is close it is more difficult to exclude him phenomenologically. He necessarily intrudes on the subject's awareness since he is continuously visible. In the Remote conditions his existence and reactions are made known only after the shock has been administered. The auditory feedback is sporadic and discontinuous. In the Proximity conditions his inclusion in the immediate visual field renders him a continuously salient element for the subject. The mechanism of denial can no longer be brought into play. One subject in the Remote condition said: 'It's funny how you really begin to forget that there's a guy out there, even though you can hear him. For a long time I just concentrated on pressing the switches and reading the words.'

Reciprocal fields. If in the Proximity condition the subject is in an improved position to observe the victim, the reverse is also true. The actions of the subject now come under proximal scrutiny by the victim. Possibly, it is easier to harm a person when he is unable to observe our actions than when he can see what we are doing. His surveillance of the action directed against him may give rise to shame, or guilt, which may then serve to curtail the action. Many expressions of language refer to the discomfort or inhibitions that arise in face-to-face confrontation. It is often said that it is easier to criticize a man 'behind his back' than to 'attack him to his face'. If we are in the process of lying to a person it is reputedly difficult to 'stare him in the eye'. We 'turn away from others in shame' or in 'embarrassment' and this action serves to reduce our discomfort. The manifest function of allowing the victim of a firing squad to be blindfolded is to make the occasion less stressful for him, but it may also serve a latent function of reducing the stress of the executioner. In sort, in the Proximity conditions, the subject may sense that he has become more salient in the victim's field of awareness. Possibly he becomes more self-conscious, embarrassed, and inhibited in his punishment of the victim.

Phenomenal unity of act. In the Remote conditions it is more difficult for the subject to gain a sense of *relatedness* between his own actions and the consequences of these actions for the victim. There is a physical and spatial separation of the act and its consequences. The subject depresses a lever in one room, and protests and cries are heard from another. The two events are in correlation, yet they lack a compelling phenomenological unity. The structure of a meaningful act—*I am hurting a man*—breaks down because of the spatial arrangement, in a manner somewhat analogous to the disappearance of phi phenomena when the blinking lights are spaced too far apart. The unity is more fully achieved in the Proximity conditions as the victim is brought closer to the action that causes him pain. It is rendered complete in Touch-Proximity.

Incipient group formation. Placing the victim in another room not only takes him further from the subject, but the subject and the experimenter are drawn relatively closer. There is incipient group formation between the experimenter and the subject, from which the victim is excluded. The wall between the victim and the others deprives him of an intimacy which the experimenter and the subject feel. In the Remote condition, the victim is truly an outsider, who stands alone, physically and psychologically.

When the victim is placed close to the subject, it becomes easier to form an alliance with him against the experimenter. Subjects no longer have to face the experimenter alone. They have an ally who is close at hand and eager to collaborate in a revolt against the experimenter. Thus, the changing set of spatial relations leads to a potentially shifting set of alliances over the several experimental conditions.

Acquired behavior dispositions. It is commonly observed that laboratory mice will rarely fight with their litter mates. Scott (1958) explains this in terms of passive inhibition. He writes: 'By doing nothing under . . . circumstances [the animal] learns to do nothing, and this may be spoken of as passive inhibition . . . this principle has great importance in teaching an individual to be peaceful, for it means that he can learn not to fight simply by not fighting.' Similarly, we may learn not to harm others simply by not harming them in everyday life. Yet this learning occurs in a context of proximal relations with others, and may not be generalized to that situation in which the person is physically removed from us. Or possibly, in the past, aggressive actions against others who were physically close resulted in retaliatory punishment which extinguished the original form of response. In contrast, aggression against others at a distance may have only sporadically led to retaliation. Thus the organism learns that it is safer to be aggressive toward others at a distance, and precarious to be so when the parties are within arm's reach. Through a pattern of rewards and punishments, he acquires a disposition to avoid aggression at close quarters, a disposition which does not extend to harming others at a distance. And this may account for experimental findings in the remote and proximal experiments.

Proximity as a variable in psychological research has received far less attention than it deserves. If men were sessile it would be easy to understand this neglect. But we move about; our spatial relations shift from one situation to the next, and the fact that we are near or remote may have a powerful effect on the psychological processes that mediate our behavior toward others. In the present situation, as the victim is brought closer to the man ordered to give him shocks, increasing numbers of subjects break off the experiment, refusing to obey. The concrete, visible, and proximal presence of the victim acts in an important way to counteract the experimenter's power and to generate disobedience.[7]

Closeness of Authority

If the spatial relationship of the subject and victim is relevant to the degree of obedience, would not the relationship of subject to experimenter also play a part?

There are reasons to feel that, on arrival, the subject is oriented primarily to the experimenter rather than to the victim. He has come to the laboratory to fit into the structure that the experimenter—not the victim—would provide. He has come less to understand his behavior than to *reveal* that behavior to a competent scientist, and he is willing to display himself as the scientist's purposes require. Most subjects seem quite concerned about the appearance they are making before the experimenter, and one could argue that this preoccupation in a relatively new and strange setting makes the subject somewhat insensitive to the triadic nature of the social situation. In other words, the subject is so concerned about the show he is putting on for the experimenter that influences from other parts of the social field do not receive as much weight as they ordinarily would. This overdetermined orientation to the experimenter would account for the relative insensitivity of the subject to the victim, and would also lead us to believe that alterations in the relationship between subject and experimenter would have important consequences for obedience.

In a series of experiments we varied the physical closeness and degree of surveillance of the experimenter. In one condition the experimenter sat just a few feet away from the subject. In a second condition, after giving initial instructions, the experimenter left the laboratory and gave his orders by telephone; in still a third condition the experimenter was never seen, providing instructions by means of a tape recording activated when the subject entered the laboratory.

Obedience dropped sharply as the experimenter was physically removed from the laboratory. The number of obedient subjects in the first condition (Experimenter Present) was almost three times as great as in the second, where the experimenter gave his orders by telephone. Twenty-six subjects were fully obedient in the first condition, and only 9 in the second (Chi square obedient *vs.* defiant in the two conditions, 1 d.f. $= 14.7; p < .001$). Subjects seemed able to take a far stronger stand against the experimenter when they did not have to encounter him face to face, and the experimenter's power over the subject was severely curtailed.[8]

Moreover, when the experimenter was absent, subjects displayed an interesting form of behavior that had not occurred under his surveillance. Though continuing with the experiment, several subjects administered lower shocks than were required and never informed the experimenter of their deviation from the correct procedure. (Unknown to the subjects, shock levels were automatically recorded by an Esterline-Angus event recorder wired directly into the shock generator; the instrument provided us with an objective record of the subjects' performance.) Indeed, in telephone conversations some subjects specifically assured the experimenter that they were raising the shock level according to instruction, whereas in fact they were repeatedly using the lowest shock on the board. This form of behavior is particularly interesting: although these subjects acted in a way that clearly undermined the avowed purposes of the experiment, they found it easier to handle the conflict in this manner than to precipitate an open break with authority.

Other conditions were completed in which the experimenter was absent during the first segment of the experiment, but reappeared at the point that the subject definitely refused to give higher shocks when commanded by telephone. Although he had exhausted his power via telephone, the experimenter could frequently force further obedience when he reappeared in the laboratory.

Experiments in this series show that the physical *presence* of an authority is an important force contributing to the subject's obedience or defiance. Taken together with the first experimental series on the proximity of the victim, it would appear that something akin to fields of force, diminishing in effectiveness with increasing psychological distance from their source, have a controlling effect on the subject's performance. As the victim is brought closer, the subject finds it harder to administer shocks to him. When the victim's position is held constant relative to the subject, and the authority is made more remote, the subject finds it easier to break off the experiment. This effect is substantial in both cases, but manipulation of the experimenter's position yielded the more powerful results. Obedience to destructive commands is highly dependent on the proximal relations between authority and subject.

Tensions

The description of final scores does not fully convey the character of the subjects' performance, and it would be useful to interrupt our reporting of quantitative relationships to remark on the subjects' general reaction to the situation.

One might suppose that a subject would simply break off or continue as his conscience and temperament dictated. Yet this is very far from what happened. There were powerful reactions of tension and emotional strain in a substantial proportion of the participants. Persons were observed to sweat, tremble, stutter, bite their lips, and groan as they found themselves increasingly implicated in the experimental conflict. Some sense of the subjects' mood can be gotten from a transcript of their remarks at break-off point. Here are the remarks of two defiant subjects:

Is he banging? . . . Is he hurt out there? Well, I don't want to be responsible for anything that happens to him. No, I can't go on with it. I don't know whether he's all right or not. I mean he may have a heart condition or something; I wouldn't feel right doing it. He's banging for help. He's evidently in trouble or he wouldn't bang . . . I don't see any sense to this —knocking him out or something. I just can't see it.

(Subject refuses to administer shocks)   [*Subject 0108*]

The man is banging. He wants to get out . . . I'm sorry. If the man wants to get out I'd just as soon stop . . . I don't want to administer any more [extremely excited] . . . I will gladly refund the check, but I will not harm this man . . . I'm sorry, I will not give him any more if he obviously wants to get out. There is no money in the world that will make me hurt another individual.   [*Subject 010X*]

And here is a transcript from an obedient subject. He began the experiment calmly, but became increasingly tense as the experiment proceeded.

After administering the 150-volt shock, he began to address the experimenter in agitated tones:

> *150 volts delivered.* You want me to keep going?
> *165 volts delivered.* That guy is hollering in there. There's a lot of them here. He's liable to have heart condition. You want me to go?
> *180 volts delivered.* He can't stand it! I'm not going to kill that man in there! You hear him hollering? He's hollering. He can't stand it. What if something happens to him? . . . I'm not going to get that man sick in there. He's hollering in there. You know what I mean? I mean I refuse to take responsibility. He's getting hurt in there. He's in there hollering. Too many left here. Geez, if he gets them wrong. There's too many of them left. I mean who is going to take responsibility if anything happens to that gentleman?
> [*The experimenter accepts responsibility.*] All right.
> *195 volts delivered.* You see he's hollering. Hear that. Gee, I don't know. [*The experimenter says: 'The experiment requires that you go on.'*]—I know it does, sir, but I mean—hugh—he don't know what he's in for. He's up to 195 volts.
> *210 volts delivered*
> *225 volts delivered*
> *240 volts delivered.* Aw, no. You mean I've got to keep going up with the scale? No sir. I'm not going to kill that man! I'm not going to give him 450 volts!
> [*The experimenter says: 'The experiment requires that you go on.*]—I know it does, but that man is hollering in there, sir . . .

Despite his numerous, agitated objections, which were constant accompaniments to his actions, the subject unfailingly obeyed the experimenter, proceeding to the highest shock level on the generator. He displayed a curious dissociation between word and action. Although at the verbal level he had resolved not to go on, his actions were fully in accord with the experimenter's commands. This subject did not want to shock the victim, and he found it an extremely disagreeable task, but he was unable to invent a response that would free him from *E*'s authority. Many subjects cannot find the specific verbal formula that would enable them to reject the role assigned to them by the experimenter. Perhaps our culture does not provide adequate models for disobedience.

One puzzling sign of tension was the regular occurrence of nervous laughing fits. In the first four conditions 71 of the 160 subjects showed definite signs of nervous laughter and smiling. The laughter seemed entirely out of place, even bizarre. Full-blown, uncontrollable seizures were observed for 15 of these subjects. On one occasion we observed a seizure so violently convulsive that it was necessary to call a halt to the experiment. In the post-experimental interviews subjects took pains to point out that they were sadistic types and that the laughter did not mean they enjoyed shocking the victim.

In the interview following the experiment subjects were asked to indicate on a 14-point scale just how nervous or tense they felt at the point of maximum tension *(Figure 2)*. The scale ranged from 'Not at all tense or nervous' to 'Extremely tense and nervous'. Self-reports of this sort are of limited precision, and at best provide only a rough indication of the subject's emotional response. Still, taking the reports for what they are worth, it can be seen that the distribution of responses spans the entire range of the scale, with the majority of subjects concentrated at the center and upper extreme. A further breakdown showed that obedient subjects reported themselves as having been slightly more tense and nervous than the defiant subjects at the point of maximum tension.

FIGURE 2. Level of Tension and Nervousness

LEVEL OF TENSION AND NERVOUSNESS REPORTED BY SUBJECT

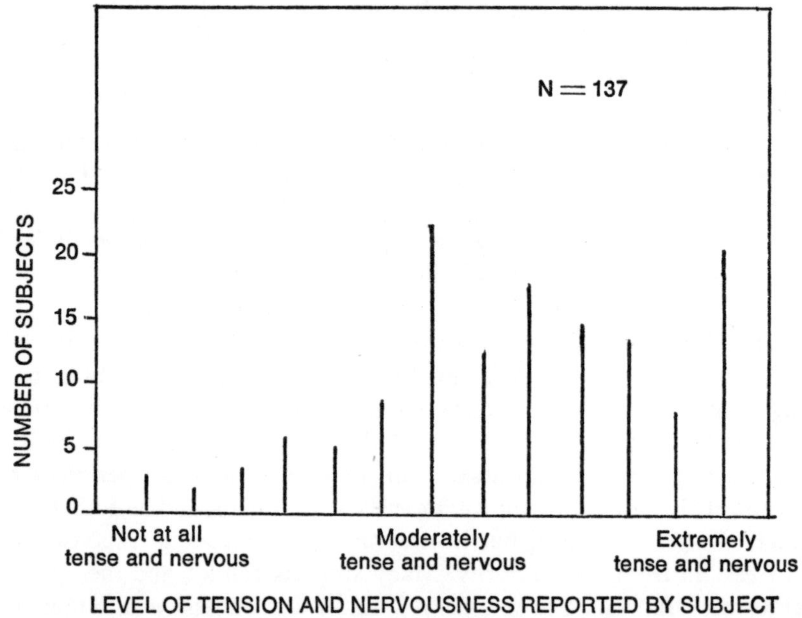

Figure 2 shows the self-reports on 'tension and nervousness' for 137 subjects in the Proximity experiments. Subjects where given a scale with 14 values ranging from 'Not at all tense and nervous' to Extremely tense and nervous'. They where instructed: 'Thinking back to that point in the experiment when you felt the most tense and nervous, indicate just how you felt by placing an X at the appropriate point on the scale.' The results are shown in terms of mid-point values.

How is the occurrence of tension to be interpreted? First, it points to the presence of conflict. If a tendency to comply with authority were the only psychological force operating in the situation, all subjects would have continued to the end and there would have been no tension. Tension, it is assumed, results from the simultaneous presence of two or more incompatible response tendencies (Miller, 1944). If sympathetic concern for the victim were the exclusive force, all subjects would have calmly defied the experimenter. Instead, there were both obedient and defiant outcomes, frequently accompanied by extreme tension. A conflict develops between the deeply ingrained disposition not to harm others and the equally compelling tendency to obey others who are in authority. The subject is quickly drawn into a dilemma of a deeply dynamic character, and the presence of high tension points to the considerable strength of each of the antagonistic vectors.

Moreover, tension defines the strength of the aversive state from which the subject is unable to escape through disobedience. When a person is uncomfortable, tense, or stressed, he tries to take some action that will allow him to terminate this unpleasant state. Thus tension may serve as a drive that leads to escape behavior. But in the present situation, even where tension is extreme, many subjects are unable to perform the response that will bring about relief. Therefore there must be a competing drive, tendency, or inhibition that precludes activation of the disobedient response. The strength of this inhibiting factor must be of greater magnitude than the stress experienced, else the terminating act would occur. Every evidence of extreme tension is at the same time an indication of the strength of the forces that keep the subject in the situation.

Finally, tension may be taken as evidence of the reality of the situations for the subjects. Normal subjects do not tremble and sweat unless they are implicated in a deep and genuinely felt predicament.

Background Authority

In psychophysics, animal learning, and other branches of psychology, the fact that measures are obtained at one institution rather than another is irrelevant to the interpretation of the findings, so long as the technical facilities for measurement are adequate and the operations are carried out with competence.

But it cannot be assumed that this holds true for the present study. The effectiveness of the experimenter's commands may depend in an important way on the larger institutional context in which they are issued. The experiments described thus far were conducted at Yale University, an organization which most subjects regarded with respect and sometimes awe. In post-experimental interviews several participants remarked that the locale and sponsorship of the study gave them confidence in the integrity, competence, and benign purposes of the personnel; many indicated that they would have shocked the learner if the experiments had been done elsewhere.

This issue of background authority seemed to us important for an interpretation of the results that had been obtained thus far; moreover it is highly relevant to any comprehensive theory of human obedience. Consider, for example, how closely our compliance with the imperatives of others is tied to particular institutions and locales in our day-to-day activities. On request, we expose our throats to a man with a razor blade in the barber shop, but would not do so in a shoe store; in the latter setting we willingly follow the clerk's request to stand in our stockinged feet, but resist the command in a bank. In the laboratory of a great university, subjects may comply with a set of commands that would be resisted if given elsewhere. *One must always question the relationship of obedience to a person's sense of the context in which he is operating.*

To explore the problem we moved our apparatus to an office building in industrial Bridgeport and replicated experimental conditions, without any visible tie to the university.

Bridgeport subjects were invited to the experiment through a mail circular similar to the one used in the Yale study, with appropriate changes in letterhead, etc. As in the earlier study, subjects were paid $4.50 for coming to the laboratory. The same age and occupational distributions used at Yale, and the identical personnel, were employed.

The purpose in relocating in Bridgeport was to assure a complete disassociation from Yale, and in this regard we were fully successful. On the surface, the study appeared to be conducted by RESEARCH ASSOCIATES OF BRIDGEPORT, an organization of unknown character (the title had been concocted exclusively for use in this study).

The experiments were conducted in a three-room office suite in a somewhat run-down commercial building located in the downtown shopping area. The laboratory was sparsely furnished, though clean, and marginally respectable in appearance. When subjects inquired about professional affiliations, they were informed only that we were a private firm conducting research for industry.

Some subjects displayed skepticism concerning the motives of the Bridgeport experimenter. One gentleman gave us a written account of the thoughts he experienced at the control board:

> . . . Should I quit this damn test? Maybe he passed out? What dopes we were not to check up on this deal. How do we know that these guys are legit? No furniture, bare walls, no telephone. We could of called the Police up or the Better Business Bureau. I learned a lesson tonight. How do I know that Mr. Williams [the experimenter] is telling the truth . . . I wish I knew how many volts a person could take before lapsing into unconsciousness . . .   [*Subject 2414*]

Another subject stated:

> I questioned on my arrival my own judgment [about coming]. I had doubts
> as to the legitimacy of the operation and the consequences of participa-
> tion. I felt it was a heartless way to conduct memory or learning pro-
> cesses on human beings and certainly dangerous without the presence of
> a medical doctor.   [*Subject 2440 V*]

There was no noticeable reduction in tension for the Bridgeport subjects.
And the subjects' estimation of the amount of pain felt by the victim was
slightly, though not significantly, higher than in the Yale study.

A failure to obtain complete obedience in Bridgeport would indicate that
the extreme compliance found in New Haven subjects was tied closely to the
background authority of Yale University; if a large proportion of the subjects
remained fully obedient, very different conclusions would be called for.

As it turned out, the level of obedience in Bridgeport, although somewhat
reduced, was not significantly lower than that obtained at Yale. A large proportion of the Bridgeport subjects were fully obedient to the experimenter's
commands (48 per cent of the Bridgeport subjects delivered the maximum
shock *vs.* 65 per cent in the corresponding condition at Yale).

How are these findings to be interpreted? It is possible that if commands
of a potentially harmful or destructive sort are to be perceived as legitimate
they must occur within some sort of institutional structure. But it is clear from
the study that it need not be a particularly reputable or distinguished institution. The Bridgeport experiments were conducted by an unimpressive firm
lacking any credentials; the laboratory was set up in a respectable office
building with title listed in the building directory. Beyond that, there was no
evidence of benevolence or competence. It is possible that the *category* of
institution, judged according to its professed function, rather than its qualitative position within that capacity, wins our compliance. Persons deposit
money in elegant, but also in seedy-looking banks, without giving much
thought to the differences in security they offer. Similarly, our subjects may
consider one laboratory to be as competent as another, so long as it *is* a scientific laboratory.

It would be valuable to study the subjects' performance in other contexts
which go even further than the Bridgeport study in denying institutional support to the experimenter. It is possible that, beyond a certain point, obedience
disappears completely. But that point had not been reached in the Bridgeport
office: almost half the subjects obeyed the experimenter fully.

Further Experiments

We may mention briefly some additional experiments undertaken in the

Yale series. A considerable amount of obedience and defiance in everyday life occurs in connection with groups. And we had reason to feel in the light of many group studies already done in psychology that group forces would have a profound effect on reactions to authority. A series of experiments was run to examine these effects. In all cases only one naive subject was studied per hour, but he performed in the midst of actors who, unknown to him, were employed by the experimenter. In one experiment (Groups for Disobedience) two actors broke off in the middle of the experiment. When this happened 90 per cent of the subjects followed suit and defied the experimenter. In another condition the actors followed the orders obediently; this strengthened the experimenter's power only slightly. In still a third experiment the job of pushing the switch to shock the learner was given to one of the actors, while the naive subject performed a subsidiary act. We wanted to see how the teacher would respond if he were involved in the situation but did not actually give the shocks. In this situation only three subjects out of forty broke off. In a final group experiment the subjects themselves determined the shock level they were going to use. Two actors suggested higher and higher shock levels; some subjects insisted, despite group pressure, that the shock level be kept low; others followed along with the group.

Further experiments were completed using women as subjects, as well as a set dealing with the effects of dual, unsanctioned, and conflicting authority. A final experiment concerned the personal relationship between victim and subject. These will have to be described elsewhere, lest the present report be extended to monographic length.

It goes without saying that future research can proceed in many different directions. What kinds of response from the victim are most effective in causing disobedience in the subject? Perhaps passive resistance is more effective than vehement protest. What conditions of entry into an authority system lead to greater or lesser obedience? What is the effect of anonymity and masking on the subject's behavior? What conditions lead to the subject's perception of responsibility for his own actions? Each of these could be a major research topic in itself, and can readily be incorporated into the general experimental procedure described here.

Levels of Obedience and Defiance

One general finding that merits attention is the high level of obedience manifested in the experimental situation. Subjects often expressed deep disapproval of shocking a man in the face of his objections, and others denounced it as senseless and stupid. Yet many subjects complied even while they protested. The proportion of obedient subjects greatly exceeded the expectations of the experimenter and his colleagues. At the outset, we had conjectured that subjects would not, in general, go above the level of 'Strong Shock'. In practice, many subjects were willing to administer the most extreme shocks available when commanded by the experimenter. For some subjects the experiment provides an occasion for aggressive release. And for others it demonstrates the extent to which obedient dispositions are deeply ingrained, and are engaged irrespective of their consequences for others. Yet this is not the whole story. Somehow, the subject becomes implicated in a situation from which he cannot disengage himself.

The departure of the experimental results from intelligent expectation, to some extent, has been formalized. The procedure was to describe the experimental situation in concrete detail to a group of competent persons, and to ask them to predict the performance of 100 hypothetical subjects. For purposes of indicating the distribution of break-off points judges were provided with a diagram of the shock generator, and recorded their predictions before being informed of the actual results. Judges typically underestimated the amount of obedience demonstrated by subjects.

In *Figure 3,* we compare the predictions of forty psychiatrists at a leading medical school with the actual performance of subjects in the experiment. The psychiatrists predicted that most subjects would not go beyond the tenth shock level (150 volts; at this point the victim makes his first explicit demand to be freed). They further predicted that by the twentieth shock level (300 volts; the victim refuses to answer) 3.73 per cent of the subjects would still be obedient; and that only a little over one-tenth of one per cent of the subjects would administer the highest shock on the board. But, as the graph indicates, the obtained behavior was very different. Sixty-two per cent of the subjects obeyed the experimenter's commands fully. Between expectation and occurrence there is a whopping discrepancy.

Why did the psychiatrists underestimate the level of obedience? Possibly, because their predictions were based on an inadequate conception of the determinants of human action, a conception that focuses on motives *in vacuo.* This orientation may be entirely adequate for the repair of bruised impulses as revealed on the psychiatrist's couch, but as soon as our interest turns to action in larger settings, attention must be paid to the situations in which motives are expressed. A situation exerts an important press on the individual. It exercises constraints and may provide push. In certain circumstances it is not so much the kind of person a man is, as the kind of situation in which he is placed, that determines his actions.

Many people, not knowing much about the experiment, claim that subjects who go to the end of the board are sadistic. Nothing could be more foolish as an overall characterization of these persons. It is like saying that a person thrown into a swift-flowing stream is necessarily a fast swimmer, or that he has great stamina because he moves so rapidly relative to the bank. The context of action must always be considered. The individual, upon entering the laboratory, becomes integrated into a situation that carries its own momentum. The subject's problem then is how to become disengaged from a situation which is moving in an altogether ugly direction.

The fact that disengagement is so difficult testifies to the potency of the forces that keep the subject at the control board. Are these forces to be conceptualized as individual motives and expressed in the language of personality dynamics, or are they to be seen as the effects of social structure and pressures arising from the situational field?

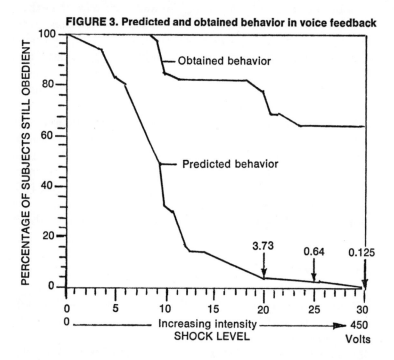

FIGURE 3. Predicted and obtained behavior in voice feedback

A full understanding of the subject's action will, I feel, require that both perspectives be adopted. The person brings to the laboratory enduring dispositions toward authority and aggression, and at the same time he becomes enmeshed in a social structure that is no less an objective fact of the case. From the standpoint of personality theory one may ask: What mechanisms of personality enable a person to transfer responsibility to authority? What are the motives underlying obedient and disobedient performance? Does orientation to authority lead to a shortcircuiting of the shame-guilt system? What cognitive and emotional defenses are brought into play in the case of obedient and defiant subjects?

The present experiments are not, however, directed toward an exploration of the motives engaged when the subject obeys the experimenter's commands. Instead, they examine the situational variables responsible for the elicitation of obedience. Elsewhere, we have attempted to spell out some of the structural properties of the experimental situation that account for high obedience, and this analysis need not be repeated here (Milgram, 1963). The experimental variations themselves represent our attempt to probe that structure, by systematically changing it and noting the consequences for behavior. It is clear that some situations produce greater compliance with the experimenter's commands than others. However, this does not necessarily imply an increase or decrease in the strength of any single definable motive. Situations producing the greatest obedience could do so by triggering the most powerful, yet perhaps the most idiosyncratic, of motives in each subject confronted by the setting. Or they may simply recruit a greater number and variety of motives involved—and it is far from certain that they can ever be known—action may be studied as a direct function of the situation in which it occurs. This has been the approach of the present study, where we sought to plot behavioral regularities against manipulated properties of the social field. Ultimately, social psychology would like to have a compelling *theory of situations* which will, first, present a language in terms of which situations can be defined; proceed to a typology of situations; and then point to the manner in which definable properties of situations are transformed into psychological forces in the individual.[9]

Postscript

Although a thousand adults were individually studied in the obedience research, and there were many specific conclusions regarding the variables that control obedience and disobedience to authority. Some of these have been discussed briefly in the preceding sections, and more detailed reports will be released subsequently.

There are now some other generalizations I should like to make, which do not derive in any strictly logical fashion from the experiments as carried out, but which, I feel, ought to be made. They are formulations of an intuitive sort that have been forced on me by observation of many subjects responding to the pressures of authority. The assertions represent a painful alteration in my own thinking; and since they were acquired only under the repeated impact of direct observation, I have no illusion that they will be generally accepted by persons who have not had the same experience.

With numbing regularity good people were seen to knuckle under the demands of authority and perform actions that were callous and severe. Men who are in everyday life responsible and decent were seduced by the trappings of authority, by the control of their perceptions, and by the uncritical acceptance of the experimenter's definition of the situation, into performing harsh acts.

What is the limit of such obedience? At many points we attempted to establish a boundary. Cries from the victim were inserted; not good enough. The victim claimed heart trouble; subjects still shocked him on command. The victim pleaded that he be let free, and his answers no longer registered on the signal box; subjects continued to shock him. At the outset we had not conceived that such drastic procedures would be needed to generate disobedience, and each step was added only as the ineffectiveness of the earlier techniques became clear. The final effort to establish a limit was the Touch-Proximity condition. But the very first subject in this condition subdued the victim on command, and proceeded to the highest shock level. A quarter of the subjects in this condition performed similarly.

The results, as seen and felt in the laboratory, are to this author disturbing. They raise the possibiilty that human nature, or—more specifically—the kind of character produced in American democratic society, cannot be counted on to insulate its citizens from brutality and inhumane treatment at the direction of malevolent authority. A substantial proportion of people do what they are told to do, irrespective of the content of the act and without limitations of conscience, so long as they perceive that the command comes from a legitimate authority. If in this study an anonymous experimenter could successfuly command adults to subdue a fifty-year-old man, and force on him painful electric shocks against his protests, one can only wonder what government, with its vastly greater authority and prestige, can command of its subjects. There is, of course, the extremely important question of whether malevolent political institutions could or would arise in American society. The present research contributes nothing to this issue.

In an article titled 'The Dangers of Obedience', Harold J. Laski wrote:

'. . . civilization means, above all, an unwillingness to inflict unnecessary pain. Within the ambit of that definition, those of us who heedlessly accept the commands of authority cannot yield claim to be civilized men.

'. . . Our business, if we desire to live a life, not utterly devoid of meaning and significance, is to accept nothing which contradicts our basic experience merely because it comes to us from tradition or convention or authority. It may well be that we shall be wrong; but our self-expression is thwarted at the root unless the certainties we are asked to accept coincide with the certainties we experience. That is why the condition of freedom in any state is always a widespread and consistent skepticism of the canons upon which power insists.'

Notes

1. This research was supported by two grants from the National Science Foundation: NSF G-17916 and NSF G-24152. Exploratory studies carried out in 1960 were financed by a grant from the Higgins Funds of Yale University. I am grateful to John T. Williams, James J. McDonough, and Emil Elges for the important part they played in the project. Thanks are due also to Alan Elms, James Miller, Taketo Murata, and Stephen Stier for their aid as graduate assistants. My wife, Sasha, performed many valuable services. Finally, I owe a profound debt to the many persons in New Haven and Bridgeport who served as subjects.

2. Consider, for example, J. P. Scott's analysis of war in his monograph on aggression:

'. . . while the actions of key individuals in a war may be explained in terms of direct stimulation to aggression, vast numbers of other people are involved simply by being part of an organized society.

'. . . For example, at the beginning of World War I an Austrian archduke was assassinated in Sarajevo. A few days later soldiers from all over Europe were marching toward each other, not because they were stimulated by the arch duke's misfortune, but because they had been trained to obey orders.' (Slightly rearranged from Scott (1958), *Aggression,* p. 103.)

3. It consisted of an extended discussion with the experimenter and, of equal importance, a friendly reconciliation with the victim. It is made clear that the victim did not receive painful electric shocks. After the completion of the experimental series, subjects were sent a detailed report of the results and full purpose of the experimental program. A formal assessment of this procedure points to its overall effectiveness. Of the subjects, 83.7 per cent indicated that they were glad to have taken part in the study; 15.1 per cent reported neutral feelings; and 1.3 per cent stated that they were sorry to have participated. A large number of subjects spontaneously requested that they be used in further experimentation. Four-fifths of the subjects felt that more experiments of this sort should be carried out, and 74 per cent indicated that they had learned something of personal importance as a result of being in the study. Furthermore, a university psychiatrist, experienced in outpatient treatment, interviewed a sample of experimental subjects with the aim of uncovering possible injurious effects resulting from participation. No such effects were in evidence. Indeed, subjects typically felt that their participation was instructive and enriching. A more detailed discussion of this question can be found in Milgram (1964).

4. *To obey* and *to disobey* are not the only terms one could use in describing the critical action of Y. One could say that Y is cooperating with X, or displays conformity with regard to X's commands. However, *cooperation* suggests that X agrees with Y's ends, and understands the relationship between his own behavior and the attainment of those ends. (But the experimental procedure, and, in particular, the experimenter's command that the subject shock the victim even in the absence of a response from the victim, preclude such understanding.) Moreover, cooperation implies status parity for the co-acting agents, and neglects the asymmetrical, dominance-subordination element prominent in the laboratory relationship between experimenter and subject. *Conformity* has been used in other important contexts in social psychology, and most frequently refers to imitating the judgements or actions of others when no explicit requirement for imitation has been made. Furthermore, in the present study there are two sources of social pres-

sure: pressure from the experimenter issuing the commands, and pressure from the victim to stop the punishment. It is the pitting of a common man (the victim) against an authority (the experimenter) that is the distinctive feature of the conflict. At a point in the experiment the victim demands that he be let free. The experimenter insists that the subject continue to administer shocks. Which act of the subject can be interpreted as conformity? The subject may conform to the wishes of his peer or to the wishes of the experimenter, and conformity in one direction means the absence of conformity in the other. Thus the world has not useful reference in this setting, for the dual and conflicting social pressures cancel out its meaning.

In the final analysis, the linguistic symbol representing the subject's action must take its meaning from the concrete context in which that action occurs; and there is probably no word in everyday language that covers the experimental situation exactly, without omissions or irrelevant connotations. It is partly for convenience, therefore, that the terms *obey* and *disobey* are used to describe the subject's actions. At the same time, our use of the words is highly congruent with dictionary meaning.

5. A more detailed account of the laboratory procedure can be found in Milgram (1963). A similar and independently evolved experimental procedure, employing a shock generator, victim, and learning task, was reported by Buss (1961). Buss used the technique for studying aggression, not obedience, and did not make use of the fundamental measure employed in the present study: break-off points. His investigation promises to be a useful complement to the present research.

6. It is difficult to convey on the printed page the full tenor of the victim's responses, for we have no adequate notation for vocal intensity, timing, and general qualities of delivery. Yet these features are crucial to producing the effect of an increasingly severe reaction to mounting voltage levels. (They can be communicated fully only by sending interested parties the recorded tapes.) In general terms, however, the victim indicates no discomfort until the 75-volt shock is administered, at which time there is a light grunt in response to the punishment. Similar reactions follow the 90- and 105-volt shocks, and at 120 volts the victim shouts to the experimenter that the shocks are becoming painful. Painful groans are heard on administration of the 135-volt shock, and at 150 volts the victim cries out, 'Experimenter, get me out of here! I won't be in the experiment any more! I refuse to go on!' Cries of this type continue with generally rising intensity, so that at 180 volts the victim cries out, 'I can't stand the pain', and by 270 volts his response to the shock is definitely an agonized scream. Throughout, he insists that he be let out of the experiment. At 300 volts the victim shouts in desperation that he will no longer provide answers to the memory test; and at 315 volts, after a violent scream, he reaffirms with vehemence that he is no longer a participant. From this point on, he provides no answers, but shrieks in agony whenever a shock is administered; this continues through 450 volts. Of course, many subjects will have broken off before this point.

A revised and stronger set of protests was used in all experiments outside the Proximity series. Naturally, new baseline measures were established for all comparisons using the new set of protests.

There is overwhelming evidence that the great majority of subjects, both obedient and defiant, accepted the victims' reactions as genuine. The evidence takes the form of: (a) tension created in the subjects (see discussion of tension); (b) scores on 'estimated pain' scales filled out by subjects immediately after the experiment; (c) subjects' accounts of their feelings in post-experimental interviews; and (d) quantifiable responses to questionnaires distributed to subjects several months after their participation in the experiments. This matter will be treated fully in a forthcoming monograph.

(The procedure in all experimental conditions was to have the naive subject announce the voltage level before administering each shock, so that—independently of the victim's responses—he was continually reminded of delivering punishment of ever-increasing severity.)

7. Admittedly, the terms *proximity, immediacy, closeness,* and *salience-of-the-victim* are used in a loose sense, and the experiments themselves represent a very coarse treatment of the variable. Further experiments are needed to refine the notion and tease out such diverse factors as spatial distance, visibility, audibility, barrier interposition, etc.

The Proximity and Touch-Proximity experiments were the only conditions where we were unable to use taped feedback from the victim. Instead, the victim was trained to respond in these conditions as he had in Experiment 2 (which employed taped feedback). Some improvement is possible here, for it should be technically feasible to do a proximity series using taped feedback.

8. The third condition also led to significantly lower obedience than this first situation, in which the experimenter was present, but it contains technical difficulties that require extensive discussion.

9. My thanks to Professor Howard Leventhal of Yale for strengthening the writing in this paragraph.

References

Buss, Arnold H. (1961). *The psychology of aggression.* New York and London: John Wiley.

Kierkegaard, S. (1843). *Fear and trembling.* English edition, Princeton: Princeton University Press, 1941.

Laski, Harold J. (1929). The dangers of obedience. *Harper's Monthly Magazine* 159, June, 1-10.

Milgram, S. (1961). Dynamics of obedience: experiments in social psychology. Mimeographed report, *National Science Foundation,* January 25.

Milgram, S. (1963). Behavioral study of obedience. *J. abnorm. soc. Psychol.* 67, 371-8.

Milgram, S. (1964). Issues in the study of obedience: a reply to Baumrind. *Amer. Psychol.* 19, 848-52.

Miller, N. E. (1944). Experimental studies in conflict. In J. McV. Hunt (Ed.), *Personality and the behavior disorders.* New York: Ronald Press.

Scott, J. P. (1958). *Aggression.* Chicago: University of Chicago Press.

CRAIG HANEY
CURTIS BANKS
and
PHILIP ZIMBARDO

Interpersonal Dynamics in a Simulated Prison

One of the major ways of handling deviants in our society is that of incarceration within an institution specially set aside to house problematic people. Perhaps the most intriguing of these institutions is the prison. Except for dramatic events such as riots and the taking of hostages, the public remains relatively unaware of the prison experience and pays little attention to the persistent efforts of prison reformers who argue that prisons are dehumanizing and overly punitive. An easy solution to prison problems would seem to lie in simply hiring sympathetic, understanding people to work in and run the prisons. What could be more simple?

Actually, however, things are not nearly as simple as they might appear to be at first glance. This is so because the prison is an excellent example of a complex social structure which inflences and limits the behavior of all who participate in it. The prisoner is injected forcefully and immediately into a new environment and suddenly becomes a member of an alien subculture. His community of peers consists of a group of people who may be totally different, but who now share a common identity, a common world view and a common language—prison slang. The inmate code, which the prisoner quickly learns, emphasizes loyalty to all other inmates and, conversely, resistance to the prison staff. Thus, the inmate structure makes for hostility and alienation irrespective of the good intention of any individual inmate.

From Craig Haney, Curtis Banks, and Philip Zimbardo, "Interpersonal Dynamics in a Simulated Prison," *International Journal of Criminology and Penology*, 1973, 1:69-97. Reprinted by permission of Academic Press (London) Limited.

The prison staff is faced with the difficult task of managing groups of people who have been involuntarily placed in their care. Usually one guard must manage and control the behavior of a relatively large number of inmates at any one time. Given that the inmates have been incarcerated against their will and that they are, by virtue of their criminal status, less than adequate persons (i.e., undesirably deviant), guards must work out relationships with each other and with the inmates in order that the work gets done and the custody of the institution is preserved.

The guard-inmate relationship is structured, then, irrespective of the individual proclivities of either guard or inmate. It is the structure that determines how prisoners will be treated and how dehumanizing the prison experience will be. The report that follows explores the guard-inmate relationship and provides a vivid description of the flavor and character of social life behind prison walls.

In order to assess the interpersonal dynamics in a prison environment, Haney, Banks and Zimbardo created a prison-like situation in which subjects role-played prisoners and guards for an extended period of time. They demonstrated in their experimental simulations that prisoners experienced a loss of personal identity and arbitrary control of their behavior. The guards, in contrast, experienced a marked gain in social power, status and group identification which made playing the role of guard rewarding. At least a third of the guards became more aggressive and dehumanizing toward prisoners than would ordinarily be expected in a simulation study.

The authors conclude that very few of the behaviors of prisoners and guards in the "mock" prison study could be attributed to personality trait differences which existed before subjects began to play their assigned roles. Rather, in accord with the interactionist-labeling perspective, the findings dramatically demonstrate the power of immediate social forces in determining human behavior. Moreover, the findings are suggestive of the impact that broader social structures have in influencing the social processes and patterns characteristic of correctional organizations in general and prisons in particular. Lastly, the report provides an excellent example of the usefulness of employing experimental techniques in the study of deviance, including even the study of deviance-processing agencies.

Introduction

After he had spent four years in a Siberian prison the great Russian novelist Dostoevsky commented, surprisingly, that his time in prison had created in him a deep optimism about the ultimate future of mankind because, as he put it, if man could survive the horrors of prison life he must surely be a "creature who could withstand anything". The cruel irony which Dostoevsky overlooked is that the reality of prison bears witness not only to the resilience and adaptiveness of the men who tolerate life within its walls, but as well to the "ingenuity" and tenacity of those who devised and still maintain our correctional and reformatory systems.

Nevertheless, in the century which has passed since Dostoevsky's imprisonment, little has changed to render the main thrust of his statement less relevant. Although we have passed through periods of enlightened humanitarian reform, in which physical conditions within prisons have improved somewhat and the rhetoric of rehabilitation has replaced the language of punitive incarceration, the social institution of prison has continued to fail. On purely pragmatic grounds, there is substantial evidence that prisons in fact neither "rehabilitate" nor act as a deterrent to future crime—in America, recidivism rates upwards of 75% speak quite decisively to these criteria. And, to perpetuate what is additionally an economic failure, American taxpayers alone must provide an expenditure for "corrections" of 1.5 billion dollars annually. On humanitarian grounds as well, prisons have failed: our mass media are increasingly filled with accounts of atrocities committed daily, man against man, in reaction to the penal system or in the name of it. The experience of prison undeniably creates, almost to the point of cliché, an intense hatred and disrespect in most inmates for the authority and the established order of society into which they will eventually return. And the toll which it takes on the deterioration of human spirit for those who must administer it, as well as for those upon whom it is inflicted, is incalculable.

Attempts to provide an explanation of the deplorable condition of our penal system and its dehumanising effects upon prisoners and guards, often focus upon what might be called the *dispositional hypothesis*. While this explanation is rarely expressed explicitly, it is central to a prevalent non-conscious ideology: that the state of the social institution of prison is due to the "nature" of the people who administer it, or the "nature" of the people who populate it, or both. That is, a major contributing cause to despicable conditions, violence, brutality, dehumanisation and degredation existing within any prison can be traced to some innate or acquired characteristic of the correctional and inmate population. Thus on the one hand, there is the contention that violence and brutality exist within prison because guards are sadistic, uneducated, and insensitive people. It is the "guard mentality", a unique syndrome of negative traits which they bring into the situation, that engenders the inhumane treatment of prisoners. Or, from other quarters comes the argument that violence and brutality in prison are the logical and predictable result of the involuntary confinement of a collective of individuals whose life histories are, by definition, characterised by disregard for law, order and social convention and a concurrent propensity for impulsiveness and aggression. Logically, it follows that these individuals, having proved themselves incapable of functioning satisfactorily within the "normal" structure of society, cannot do so either inside the structure provided by prisons. To control such men as these, the argument continues, whose basic orientation to any conflict situation is to react with physical power or deception, force must be met with force, and a certain number of violent encounters must be expected and tolerated by the public.

The dispositional hypothesis has been embraced by the proponents of the prison *status quo* (blaming conditions on the evil in the prisoners), as well as by its critics (attributing the evil to guards and staff with their evil motives and deficient personality structures). The appealing simplicity of this proposition localises the source of prison riots, recidivism and corruption in these "bad seeds" and not in the conditions of the "prison soil". Such an analysis directs attention away from the complex matrix of social, economic and political forces which combine to make prisons what they are—and which would require complex, expensive, revolutionary solutions to bring about any meaningful change. Instead, rioting prisoners are identified, punished, transferred to maximum security institutions or shot, outside agitators sought and corrupt officials suspended—while the system itself goes on essentially unchanged, its basic structure unexamined and unchallenged.

However, a critical evaluation of the dispositional hypothesis cannot be made directly through observation in existing prison settings, since such naturalistic observation necessarily confounds the acute effects of the environment with the chronic characteristics of the inmate and guard populations. To separate the effects of the prison environment *per se* from those attributable to à *priori* dispositions of its inhabitants requires a research strategy in which a "new" prison is constructed, comparable in its fundamental social-psychological milieu to existing prison systems, but entirely populated by individuals who are undifferentiated in all essential dimensions from the rest of society.

Such was the approach taken in the present empirical study, namely, to create a prison-like situation in which the guards and inmates were initially comparable and characterised as being "normal-average", and then to observe the patterns of behaviour which resulted, as well as the cognitive, emotional and attitudinal reactions which emerged. Thus, we began our experiment with a sample of individuals who did not deviate from the normal range of the general population on a variety of dimensions we were able to measure. Half were randomly assigned to the role of "prisoner", the others to that of "guard", neither group having any history of crime, emotional disability, physical handicap nor even intellectual or social disadvantage.

The environment created was that of a "mock" prison which physically constrained the prisoners in barred cells and psychologically conveyed the sense of imprisonment to all participants. Our intention was not to create a *literal* simulation of an American prison, but rather a functional representation of one. For ethical, moral and pragmatic reasons we could not detain our subjects for extended or indefinite periods of time, we could not exercise the threat and promise of severe physical punishment, we could not allow homosexual or racist practices to flourish, nor could we duplicate certain other specific aspects of prison life. Nevertheless, we believed that we could create a situation with sufficient mundane realism to allow the role-playing participants to go beyond the superficial demands of their assignment into the deep structure of the characters they represented. To do so, we established functional equivalents for the activities and experiences of actual prison life which were expected to produce qualitatively similar psychological reactions in our subjects—feelings of power and powerlessness, of control and oppression, of satisfaction and frustration, of arbitrary rule and resistance to authority, of status and anonymity, of machismo and emasculation. In the conventional terminology of experimental social psychology, we first identified a number of relevant conceptual variables through analysis of existing prison situations, then designed a setting in which these variables were made operational. No specific hypotheses were advanced other than the general one that assignment to the treatment of "guard" or "prisoner" would result in significantly different reactions on behavioural measures of interaction, emotional measures of mood state and pathology, attitudes toward self, as well as other indices of coping and adaptation to this novel situation. What follows is the mechanics of how we created and peopled our prison, what we observed, what our subjects reported, and finally, what we can conclude about the nature of the prison environment and the experience of imprisonment which can account for the failure of our prisons.

Method

Overview

The effects of playing the role of "guard" or "prisoner" were studied in the context of an experimental simulation of a prison environment. The research design was a relatively simple one, involving as it did only a single treatment variable, the random assignment to either a "guard" or "prisoner" condition. These roles were enacted over an extended period of time (nearly one week) within an environment which was physically constructed to resemble a prison. Central to the methodology of creating and maintaining a psychological state of imprisonment was the functional simulation of significant properties of "real prison life" (established through information from former inmates, correctional personnel and texts).

The "guards" were free with certain limits to implement the procedures of induction into the prison setting and maintenance of custodial retention of the "prisoners". These inmates, having voluntarily submitted to the conditions of this total institution in which they now lived, coped in various ways with its stresses and its challenges. The behaviour of both groups of subjects was observed, recorded and analysed. The dependent measures were of two general types: transactions between and within each group of subjects, recorded on video and audio tape as well as directly observed; individual reactions on questionnaires, mood inventories, personality tests, daily guard shift reports, and post experimental interviews.

Subjects

The 21 subjects who partcipated in the experiment were selected from an initial pool of 75 respondents, who answered a newspaper advertisement asking for male volunteers to participate in a psychological study of "prison life" in return for payment of $15 per day. Those who responded to the notice completed an extensive questionnaire concerning their family background, physical and mental health history, prior experience and attitudinal propensities with respect to sources of psychopathology (including their involvement in crime). Each respondent who completed the background questionnaire was interviewed by one of two experimenters. Finally, the 24 subjects who were judged to be most stable (physically and mentally), most mature, and least involved in anti-social behaviour were selected to participate in the study. On a random basis, half of the subjects were assigned the role of "guard", half to the role of "prisoner".

The subjects were normal, healthy males attending colleges throughout the United States who were in the Stanford area during the summer. They were largely of middle class socio-economic status, Caucasians (with the exception of one Oriental subject). Initially they were strangers to each other, a selection precaution taken to avoid the disruption of any pre-existing friendship patterns and to mitigate against any transfer ino the experimental situation of previously established relationships or patterns of behaviour.

This final sample of subjects was administered a battery of psychological tests on the day prior to the start of the simulation, but to avoid any selective bias on the part of the experimenter-observers, scores were not tabulated until the study was completed.

Two subjects who were assigned to be a "stand-by" in case an additional "prisoner" was needed were not called, and one subject assigned to be a "stand-by" guard decided against participating just before the simulation phase began—thus, our data analysis is based upon ten prisoners and eleven guards in our experimental conditions.

Procedure

Physical aspects of the prison

The prison was built in a 35-ft. section of a basement corridor in the psychology building at Stanford University. It was partitioned by two fabricated walls, one of which was fitted with the only entrance door to the cell block, the other contained a small observation screen. Three small cells (6 x 9 ft.) were made from converted laboratory rooms by replacing the usual doors with steel barred, black painted ones, and removing all furniture.

A cot (with mattress, sheet and pollow) for each prisoner was the only furniture in the cells. A small closet across from the cells served as a solitary confinement facility; its dimensions were extremely small (2 x 2 x 7 ft.) and it was unlit.

In addition, several rooms in an adjacent wing of the building were used as guards' quarters (to change in and out of uniform or for rest and relaxation), a bedroom for the "warden" and "superintendent", and an interview-testing room. Behind the observation screen at one end of the "yard" was video recording equipment and sufficient space for several observers.

Operational details

The "prisoner" subjects remained in the mock-prison 24 hours per day for the duration of the study. Three were arbitrarily assigned to each of the three cells; the others were on stand-by call at their homes. The "guard" subjects worked on three-man, eight-hour shifts; remaining in the prison environment only during their work shift, going about their usual lives at other times.

Role instruction

All subjects had been told that they would be assigned either the guard or the prisoner role on a completely random basis and all had voluntarily agreed to play either role for $15.00 per day for up to two weeks. They signed a contract guaranteeing a minimally adequate diet, clothing, housing and medical care as well as the financial remuneration in return for their stated "intention" of serving in the assigned role for the duration of the study.

It was made explicit in the contract that those assigned to be prisoners should expect to be under surveillance (have little or no privacy) and to have some of their basic civil rights suspended during their imprisonment, excluding physical abuse. They were given no other information about what to expect nor instructions about behaviour appropriate for a prisoner role. Those actually assigned to this treatment were informed by phone to be available at their place of residence on a given Sunday when we would start the experiment.

The subjects assigned to be guards attended an orientation meeting on the day prior to the induction of the prisoners. At this time they were introduced to the principal investigators, the "Superintendent" of the prison (P.G.Z.) and an undergraduate research assistant who assumed the administrative role of "Warden". They were told that we wanted to try to simulate a prison environment within the limits imposed by pragmatic and ethical considerations.

Their assigned task was to "maintain the reasonable degree of order within the prison necessary for its effective functioning", although the specifics of how this duty might be implemented were not explicitly detailed. They were made aware of the fact that while many of the contingencies with which they might be confronted were essentially unpredictable (e.g. prisoner escape attempts), part of their task was to be prepared for such eventualities and to be able to deal appropriately with the variety of situations that might arise. The "Warden" instructed the guards in the administrative details, including: the work-shifts, the mandatory daily completion of shift reports concerning the activity of guards and prisoners, the completion of "critical incident" reports which detailed unusual occurrences and the administration of meals, work and recreation programmes for the prisoners. In order to begin to involve these subjects in their roles even before the first prisoner was incarcerated, the guards assisted in the final phases of completing the prison complex —putting the cots in the cells, signs on the walls, setting up the guards' quarters, moving furniture, water coolers, refrigerators, etc.

The guards generally believed that we were primarily interested in studying the behaviour of the prisoners. Of course, we were equally interested in the effect which enacting the role of guard in this environment would have on their behaviour and subjective states.

To optimise the extent to which their behaviour would reflect their genuine reactions to the experimental prison situation and not simply their ability to follow instructions, they were intentionally given only minimal guidelines for what it meant to be a guard. An explicit and categorical prohibition against the use of physical punishment or physical aggression was, however, emphasised by the experiments. Thus, with this single notable exception, their roles were relatively unstructured initially, requiring each "guard" to carry out activities necessary for interacting with a group of "prisoners" as well as with other "guards" and the "correctional staff".

Uniform

In order to promote feelings of anonymity in the subjects each group was issued identical uniforms. For the guards, the uniform consisted of: plain khaki shirts and trousers, a whistle, a police night stick (wooden batons) and reflecting sunglasses which made eye contact impossible. The prisoners' uniforms consisted of loosely fitting muslin smocks with an identification number on front and back. No underclothes were worn beneath these "dresses". A chain and lock were placed around one ankle. On their feet they wore rubber sandals and their hair was covered with a nylon stocking made into a cap. Each prisoner was also issued a toothbrush, soap, towel and bed linen. No personal belongings were allowed in the cells.

The outfitting of both prisoners and guards in this manner served to enhance group identity and reduce individual uniqueness within the two groups.

The khaki uniforms were intended to convey a military attitude, while the whistle and night-stick were carried as symbols of control and power. The prisoners' uniforms were designed not only to deindividuate the prisoners but to be humiliating and serve as symbols of their dependence and subservience. The ankle chain was a constant reminder (even during their sleep when it hit the other ankle) of the oppressiveness of the environment. The stocking cap removed any distinctiveness associated with hair length, colour or style (as does shaving of heads in some "real" prisons and the military). The ill-fitting uniforms made the prisoners feel awkward in their movements, since these dresses were worn without undergarments, the uniforms forced them to assume unfamiliar postures, more like those of a woman than a man—another part of the emasculating process of becoming a prisoner.

Induction procedure

With the cooperation of Palo Alto City Police Department all of the subjects assigned to the prisoner treatment were unexpectedly "arrested" at their residences. A police officer charged them with suspicion of burglary or armed robbery, advised them of their legal rights, handcuffed them, thoroughly searched them (often as curious neighbors looked on) and carried them off to the police station in the rear of the police car. At the station they went through the standard routines of being fingerprinted, having an identification file prepared and then being placed in a detention cell. Each prisoner was blindfolded and subsequently driven by one of the experimenters and a subject-guard to our mock prison. Throughout the entire arrest procedure, the police officers involved maintained a formal, serious attitude, avoiding answering any questions of clarification as to the relation of this "arrest" to the mock prison study.

Upon arrival at our experimental prison, each prisoner was stripped, sprayed with a delousing preparation (a deodorant spray) and made to stand alone naked for a while in the cell yard. After being given the uniform described previously and having an I.D. picture taken ("mug shot"), the prisoner was put in his cell and ordered to remain silent.

Administrative routine

When all the cells were occupied, the warden greeted the prisoners and read them the rules of the institution (developed by the guards and the warden). They were to be memorised and to be followed. Prisoners were to be referred to only by the number on their uniforms, also in an effort to depersonalise them.

The prisoners were to be served three bland meals per day, were allowed three supervised toilet visits, and given two hours daily for the privilege of reading or letterwriting. Work assignments were issued for which the prisoners were to receive an hourly wage to constitute their $15 daily payment.

Two visiting periods per week were scheduled, as were movie rights and exercise periods. Three times a day all prisoners were lined up for a "count" (one on each guard work-shift). The initial purpose of the "count" was to ascertain that all prisoners were present, and to test them on their knowledge of the rules and their I.D. numbers. The first perfunctory counts lasted only about 10 minutes, but on each successive day (or night) they were spontaneously increased in duration until some lasted several hours. Many of the pre-established features of administrative routine were modified or abandoned by the guards, and some were forgotten by the staff over the course of the study.

Data Collection (Dependent Measures)

The exploratory nature of this investigation and the absence of specific hypotheses led us to adopt the strategy of surveying as many as possible behavioural and psychological manifestations of the prison experience on the guards and the prisoners. In fact, one major methodological problem in a study of this kind is defining the limits of the "data", since relevant data emerged from virtually every interaction between any of the participants, as well as from subjective and behavioural reactions of individual prisoners, guards, the warden, superintendent, research assistants and visitors to the prison. It will also be clear when the results are presented that causal direction cannot always be established in the patterns of interaction where any given behaviour might be the consequence of a current or prior instigation by another subject and, in turn, might serve as impetus for eliciting reactions from others.

Data collection was organised around the following sources:

(1) *Videotaping.* About 12 hours of recordings were made of daily, regularly occurring events, such as the counts and meals, as well as unusual interactions, such as prisoner rebellion, visits from a priest, a lawyer and parents, Parole Board meetings and others. Concealed video equipment recorded these events through a screen in the partition at one end of the cell-block yard or in a conference room (for parole meetings).

(2) *Audio recording.* Over 30 hours of recordings were made of verbal interactions between guards and prisoners on the prison yard. Concealed microphones picked up all conversation taking place in the yard as well as some within the cells. Other concealed recordings were made in the testing-interview room on selected occasions—interactions between the warden, superintendent and the prisoners' Grievance Committee, parents, other visitors and prisoners released early. In addition, each subject was interviewed by one of the experimenters (or by other research associates) during the study, and most just prior to its termination.

(3) *Rating scales.* Mood adjective checklists and sociometric measures were administered on several occasions to assess emotional changes in affec-

tive state and interpersonal dynamics among the guard and prisoner groups.

(4) *Individual difference scales.* One day prior to the start of the simulation all subjects completed a series of paper and pencil personality tests. These tests were selected to provide dispositional indicators or interpersonal behaviour styles—the *F* scale of Authoritarian Personality [1]), and the Machiavellianism Scale [2]—as well as areas of possible personality pathology through the newly developed Comrey Personality Scale [3]. The subscales of this latter test consist of :

(a) trustworthiness
(b) orderliness
(c) conformity
(d) activity
(e) stability
(f) extroversion
(g) masculinity
(h) empathy

(5) *Personal observations.* The guards made daily reports of their observations after each shift, the experimenters kept informal diaries and all subjects completed post-experimental questionnaires of their reactions to the experience about a month after the study was over.

Data analyses presented problems of several kinds. First, some of the data was subject to possible errors due to selective sampling. The video and audio recordings tended to be focussed upon the more interesting, dramatic events which occurred. Over time, the experimenters become more personally involved in the transaction and were not as distant and objective as they should have been. Second, there are not complete data on all subjects for each measure because of prisoners being released at different times and because of unexpected disruptions, conflicts and administrative problems. Finally, we have a relatively small sample on which to make cross-tabulations by possible independent and individual difference variables.

However, despite these shortcomings some of the overall effects in the data are powerful enough to reveal clear, reliable results. Also some of the more subtle analyses were able to yield statistically significant results even with the small sample size. Most crucial for the conclusions generated by this exploratory study is the consistency in the pattern of relationships which emerge across a wide range of measuring instruments and different observers. Special analyses were required only of the video and audio material, the other data sources were analysed following established scoring procedures.

Video Analysis

There were 25 relatively discrete incidents identifiable on the tapes of prisoner-guard interactions. Each incident or scene was scored for the presence of nine behavioural (and verbal) categories. Two judges who had not been involved with the simulation study scored these tapes. These categories were defined as follows:

Question. All questions asked, requests for information or assistance (excluding rhetorical questions).

Command. An order to commence or abstain from a specific behaviour, directed either to individuals or groups. Also generalised orders, e.g. "Settle down".

Information. A specific piece of information proffered by anyone whether requested or not, dealing with any contingency of the simulation.

Individuating reference. Positive: use of a person's real name, nickname or allusion to special positive physical characteristics. Negative: use of prison number, title, generalised "you" of reference to derogatory characteristic.

Threat. Verbal statement of contingent negative consequences of a wide variety, e.g. no meal, long count, pushups, lock-up in hole, no visitors, etc.

Deprecation insult. Use of obscenity, slander, malicious statement directed toward individual or group, e.g. "You lead a life of mendacity" or "You guys are really stupid."

Resistance. Any physical resistance, usually prisoners to guards, such as holding on to beds, blocking doors, shoving guard or prisoner, taking off stocking caps, refusing to carry out orders.

Help. Person physically assisting another (i.e. excludes verbal statements of support), e.g. guard helping another to open door, prisoner helping another prisoner in cleanup duties.

Use of instruments. Use of any physical instrument to either intimidate, threaten, or achieve specific end, e.g. fire extinguisher, batons, whistles.

Audio Analysis

For purposes of classifying the verbal behaviour recorded from interviews with guards and prisoners, eleven categories were devised. Each statement made by the interviewee was assigned to the appropriate category by judges. At the end of this process for any given interview analysis, a list had been compiled of the nature and frequencies of the interviewee's discourse. The eleven categories for assignment of verbal expressions were:

Questions. All questions asked, requests for information or assistance (excluding rhetorical questions).

Informative statements. A specific piece of information proffered by anyone whether requested or not, dealing with any contingency of the simulation.

Demands. Declarative statements of need or imperative requests.

Requests. Deferential statements for material or personal consideration.

Commands. Orders to commence or abstain from a specific behaviour, directed either to individuals or groups.

Outlook, positive/negative. Expressions of expectancies for future experiences or future events; either negative or positive in tone, e.g. "I don't think I can make it" *v.* "I believe I will feel better."

Criticism. Expressions of critical evaluation concerning other subjects, the experimenters or the experiment itself.

Statements of identifying reference, deindividuating/individuating. Statements wherein a subject makes some reference to another subject specifically by allusion to given name or distinctive characteristics (individuating reference), or by allusion to non-specific identity or institutional number (deindividuating reference).

Desire to continue. Any expression of a subject's wish to continue or to curtail participation in the experiment.

Self-evaluation, positive/negative. Statements of self-esteem or self-degradation, e.g. "I feel pretty good about the way I've adjusted" *v.* "I hate myself for being so oppressive."

Action intentions, positive/negative including "intent to aggress." Statements concerning interviewees' intentions to do something in the future, either of a positive, constructive nature or a negative, destructive nature, e.g. "I'm not going to be so mean from now on" *v* "I'll break the door down."

Results

Overview

Although it is difficult to anticipate exactly what the influence of incarceration will be upon the individuals who are subjected to it and those charged with its maintenance (especially in a simulated reproduction), the results of the present experiment support many commonly held conceptions of prison life and validate anecdotal evidence supplied by articulate ex-convicts. The evironment of arbitrary custody had great impact upon the affective states of both guards and prisoners as well as upon the interpersonal processes taking place between and within those role-groups.

In general, guards and prisoners showed a marked tendency toward increased negativity of affect and their overall outlook became increasingly negative. As the experiment progressed, prisoners expressed intentions to do harm to others more frequently. For both prisoners and guards, self-evaluations were more deprecating as the experience of the prison environment became internalised.

Overt behaviour was generally consistent with the subjective self-reports and affective expressions of the subjects. Despite the fact that guards and prisoners were essentially free to engage in any form of interaction (positive or negative, supportive or affrontive, etc.), the characteristic nature of their encounters tended to be negative, hostile, affrontive and dehumanising. Prisoners immediately adopted a generally passive response mode while guards assumed a very active initiating role in all interactions. Throughout the experiment, commands were the most frequent forms of verbal behaviour and, generally, verbal exchanges were strikingly impersonal, with few references to individual indentity. Although it was clear to all subjects that the experimenters would not permit physical violence to take place, varieties of less direct aggressive behaviour were observed frequently (especially on the part of guards). In lieu of physical violence, verbal affronts were used as one of the most frequent forms of interpersonal contact between guards and prisoners.

The most dramatic evidence of the impact of this situation upon the participants was seen in the gross reactions of five prisoners who had to be released because of extreme emotional depression, crying, rage and acute anxiety. The pattern of symptoms was quite similar in four of the subjects and began as early as the second day of imprisonment. The fifth subject was released after being treated for a psychosomatic rash which covered portions of his body. Of the remaining prisoners, only two said they were not willing to forfeit the money they had earned in return for being "paroled". When the experiment was terminated prematurely after only six days, all the remaining prisoners were delighted by their unexpected good fortune. In contrast, most of the guards seemed to be distressed by the decision to stop the experiment and it appeared to us that had become sufficiently involved in their roles so that they now enjoyed the extreme control and power which they exercised and were reluctant to give it up. One guard did report being personally upset at the suffering of the prisoners and claimed to have considered asking to change his role to become one of them—but never did so. None of the guards ever failed to come to work on time for their shift, and indeed, on several occasions guards remained on duty voluntarily and uncomplaining for extra hours—without additional pay.

The extremely pathological reactions which emerged in both groups of subjects testify to the power of the social forces operating, but still there were individual differences seen in styles of coping with this novel experience and in degrees of successful adaptation to it. Half the prisoners did endure the oppressive atmosphere, and not all the guards resorted to hostility Some guards were tough but fair ("played by the rules"), some went far beyond their roles to engage in creative cruelty and harassment, while a few were passive and rarely instigated any coercive control over the prisoners.

These differential reactions to the experience of imprisonment were not suggested by or predictable from the self-report measures of personality and attitude or the interviews taken before the experiment began. The standardised tests employed indicated that a perfectly normal emotionally stable sample of subjects had been selected. In those few instances where differential test scores do discriminate between subjects, there is an opportunity to, partially at least, discern some of the personality variables which may be critical in the adaptation to and tolerance of prison confinement.

Initial Personality and Attitude Measures

Overall, it is apparent that initial personality-attitude dispositions account for an extremely small part of the variation in reactions to this mock prison experience. However, in a few select instances, such dispositions do seem to be correlated with the prisoners' ability to adjust to the experimental prison environment.

Comrey Scale

The Comrey Personality Inventory [3] was the primary personality scale administered to both guards and prisoners. The mean scores for prisoners and guards on the eight sub-scales of the test are shown in Table 1. No differences between prisoner and guard mean scores on any scale even approach statistical significance. Furthermore, in no case does any group mean fall outside of the 40 to 60 centile range of the normative male population reported by Comrey.

TABLE 1. Mean scores for prisoners and guards on eight Comrey subscales

Scale	Prisoners	Guards
Trustworthiness—high score indicates belief in the basic honesty and good intentions of others	$x = 92.56$	$x = 89.64$
Orderliness—extent to which person is meticulous and concerned with neatness and orderliness	$x = 75.67$	$x = 73.82$
Conformity—indicates belief in law enforcement, acceptance of society as it is, resentment of nonconformity in others	$x = 65.67$	$x = 63.18$
Activity—liking for physical activity, hard work, and exercise	$x = 89.78$	$x = 91.73$
Stability—high score indicates calm, optimistic, stable, confident individual	$x = 98.33$	$x = 101.45$
Extroversion—suggests outgoing, easy to meet person	$x = 83.22$	$x = 81.91$
Masculinity—"people who are not bothered by crawling creatures, the sight of blood, vulgarity, who do not cry easily and are not interested in love stories"	$x = 88.44$	$x = 87.00$
Empathy—high score indicates individuals who are sympathetic, helpful, generous and interested in devoting their lives to the service of others	$x = 91.78$	$x = 95.36$

TABLE 2. Mean scores for "Remaining" v "Early released" prisoners on Comrey subscales

Scale	Remaining prisoners	Early released prisoners	Mean difference
Trustworthiness	93.4	90.8	+2.6
Orderliness	76.6	78.0	—1.4
Conformity	67.2	59.4	+7.8
Activity	91.4	86.8	+4.6
Stability	99.2	99.6	—0.4
Extroversion	98.4	76.2	+22.2
Masculinity	91.6	86.0	+5.6
Empathy	103.8	85.6	+17.2

Table 2 shows the mean scores on the Comrey sub-scales for prisoners who remained compared with prisoners who were released early due to severe emotional reactions to the environment. Although none of the comparisons achieved statistical significance, three seemed at least suggestive as possible discriminators of those who were able to tolerate this type of confinement and those who were not. Compared with those who had to be released, prisoners who remained in prison until the termination of the study: scored higher on conformity ("acceptance of society as it is"), showed substantially higher average scores on Comrey's measure of extroversion and also scored higher on a scale of empathy (helpfulness, sympathy and generosity).

F-Scale

The F-scale is designed to measure rigid adherence to conventional values and a submissive, uncritical attitude towards authority. There was no difference between the mean score for prisoners (4.78) and the mean score for guards (4.36) on this scale.

Again, comparing those prisoners who remained with those who were released early, we notice an interesting trend. This intra-group comparison shows remaining prisoners scoring more than twice as high on conventionality and authoritarianism ($\bar{x} = 7.78$) than those prisoners released early ($\bar{x} = 3.20$). While the difference between these means fails to reach acceptable levels of significance, it is striking to note that a rank-ordering of prisoners on the F-scale correlates highly with the duration of their stay in the experiment ($r_s = 0.898$, $P < 0.005$). To the extent that a prisoner was high in rigidity, in adherence to conventional values, and in the acceptance of authority, he was likely to remain longer and adjust more effectively to this authoritarian prison environment.

Machiavellianism

There were no significant mean differences found between guards ($\bar{x} = 7.73$) and prisoners ($\bar{x} = 8.77$) on this measure of effective interpersonal manipulation. In addition, the Mach Scale was of no help in predicting the likelihood that a prisoner would tolerate the prison situation and remain in the study until its termination.

This latter finding, the lack of any mean differences between prisoners who remained v. those who were released from the study, is somewhat surprising since one might expect the Hi Mach's skill at manipulating social interaction and mediating favourable outcomes for himself might be acutely relevant to the simulated prison environment. Indeed, the two prisoners who scored highest on the Machiavellianism scale were also among those adjudged by the experimenters to have made unusually effective adaptations to their confinement. Yet, paradoxically (and this may give the reader some feeling for the anomalies we encountered in attempting to predict in-prison behaviour from personality measures), the other two prisoners whom we categorised as having effectively adjusted to confinement actually obtained the lowest Mach scores of any prisoners.

Video Recordings

An analysis of the video recordings indicates a preponderance of genuinely negative interactions, i.e. physical aggression, threats, deprecations, etc. It is also clear that any assertive activity was largely the prerogative of the guards, while prisoners generally assumed a relatively passive demeanour. Guards more often aggressed, more often insulted, more often threatened. Prisoners, when they reacted at all, engaged primarily in resistance to these guard behaviours.

For guards, the most frequent verbal behaviour was the giving of commands and their most frequent form of physical behaviour was aggression. The most frequent form of prisoners' verbal behaviour was question-asking, their most frequent form of physical behaviour was resistance. On the other hand, the most infrequent behaviour engaged in overall throughout the experiment was "helping"—only one such incident was noted from all the video recording collected. That solitary sign of human concern for a fellow occurred between two prisoners.

Although question-asking was the most frequent form of verbal behaviour for the prisoners, guards actually asked questions more frequently overall than did prisoners (but not significantly so). This is reflective of the fact that the overall level of behaviour emitted was much higher for the guards than for the prisoners. All of those verbal acts categorised as commands were engaged in by guards. Obviously, prisoners had no opportunity to give commands at all, that behaviour becoming the exclusive "right" of guards.

Of a total of 61 incidents of direct interpersonal reference observed (incidents in which one subject spoke directly to another with the use of some identifying reference, i.e. "Hey, Peter"; "you there", etc.), 58 involved the use of some deindividuating rather than some individuating form of reference. (Recall that we characterised this distinction as follows: an individuating reference involved the use of a person's actual name, nickname or allusion to special physical characteristics, whereas a deindividuating reference involved the use of a prison number, or a generalised "you"—thus being a very depersonalising form of reference.) Since all subjects were at liberty to refer to one another in either mode, it is significant that such a large proportion of the references noted involved were in the deindividuating mode ($Z = 6.9$, $P < 0.01$). Deindividuating references were made more often by guards in speaking to prisoners than the reverse ($Z = 3.67, P < 0.01$). (This finding, as all prisoner-guard comparisons for specific categories, may oe somewhat confounded by the fact that guards apparently enjoyed a greater freedom to initiate verbal as well as other forms of behaviour. Note, however, that the existence of this greater "freedom" on the part of the guards is itself an empirical finding since it was not prescribed à priori.) It is of additional interest to point out that in the only three cases in which verbal exchange involved some individuating reference, it was prisoners who personalised guards.

A total of 32 incidents were observed which involved a verbal threat spoken by one subject to another. Of these, 27 such incidents involved a guard threatening a prisoner. Again, the indulgence of guards in this form of behaviour was significantly greater than the indulgence of prisoners, the observed frequencies deviating significantly from an equal distribution of threats across both groups ($Z = 3.88, P < 0.01$).

Guards more often deprecated and insulted prisoners than prisoners did of guards. Of a total of 67 observed incidents, the deprecation-insult was expressed disproportionately by guards to prisoners 61 times; ($Z = 6.72$, $P < 0.01$).

Physical resistance was observed 34 different times. Of these, 32 incidents involved resistance by a prisoner. Thus, as we might expect, at least in this reactive behaviour domain, prisoners responses far exceeded those of the guards ($Z = 5.14, P < 0.01$).

The use of some object or instrument in the achievement of an intended purpose or in some interpersonal interaction was observed 29 times. Twenty-three such incidents involved the use of an instrument by a guard rather than a prisoner. This disproportionate frequency is significantly variant from an equal random use by both prisoners and guards ($Z = 316, P < 0.01$).

Over time, from day to day, guards were observed to generally escalate their harassment of the prisoners. In particular, a comparison of two of the first prisoner-guard interactions (during the counts) with two of the last counts in the experiment yielded significant differences in: the use of deindividuating references per unit time ($\bar{x}_t = 0.0$ and $\bar{x}_{t_2} = 5.40$ respectively; $t = 3.65, P < 0.10$); the incidence of deprecation-insult per unit time $\bar{x}_{t_1} = 0.3$ and $\bar{x}_{t_2} = 5.70$, respectively; $t = 3.16, P < 0.10$). On the other hand, a temporal analysis of the prisoner video data indicated a general decrease across all categories over time: prisoners came to initiate acts far less frequently and responded (if at all) more passively to the acts of others—they simply *behaved less*.

Although the harassment by the guards escalated overall as the experiment wore on, there was some variation in the extent to which the three different guard shifts contributed to the harassment in general. With the exception of the 2:30 a.m. count, prisoners enjoyed some respite during the late night guard shift (10:00 p.m. to 6:00 a.m.). But they really were "under the gun" during the evening shift. This was obvious in our observations and in subsequent interviews with the prisoners and was also confirmed in analysis of the video taped interactions. Comparing the three different guard shifts, the evening shift was significantly different from the other two in resorting to commands; the means being 9.30 and 4.04, respectively, for standardised units of time ($t = 2.50, P < 0.05$). In addition, the guards on this "tough and cruel" shift showed more than twice as many deprecation-insults toward the prisoners (means of 5.17 and 2.29, respectively, $P < 0.20$). They also tended to use instruments more often than other shifts to keep the prisoners in line.

Audio Recordings

The audio recordings made throughout the prison simulation afforded one opportunity to systematically collect self-report data from prisoners and guards regarding (among other things) their emotional reactions, their outlook, and their interpersonal evaluations and activities within the experimental setting. Recorded interviews with both prisoners and guards offered evidence that: guards tended to express nearly as much negative outlook and negative self-regard as most prisoners (one concerned guard, in fact, expressed more negative self-regard than any prisoner and more general negative affect than all but one of the prisoners); prisoner interviews were marked by negativity in expressions of affect, self-regard and action intentions (including intent to aggress and negative outlook).

Analysis of the prisoner interviews also gave *post hoc* support to our informal impressions and subjective decisions concerning the differential emotional effects of the experiment upon those prisoners who remained and those who were released early from the study. A comparison of the mean number of expressions of negative outlook, negative affect, negative self-regard and intentions to aggress made by remaining *v.* released prisoners (per interview) yielded the following results: prisoners released early expressed more negative expectations during interviews than those who remained ($t = 2.32, P$ 0.10) and also more negative affect ($t = 2.17, P < 0.10$); prisoners released early expressed more negative self-regard, and four times as many "intentions to aggress" as prisoners who remained (although those comparisons fail to reach an acceptable level of significance).

Since we could video-record only public interactions on the "yard," it was of special interest to discover what was occurring among prisoners in private. What were they talking about in the cells—their college life, their vocation, girl friends, what they would do for the remainder of the summer once the experiment was over. We were surprised to discover that fully 90% of all conversations among prisoners were related to prison topics, while only 10% to non-prison topics such as the above. They were most concerned about food, guard harassment, setting up a grievance committee, escape plans, visitors, reactions of prisoners in the other cells and in solitary. Thus, in their private conversations when they might escape the roles they were playing in public, they did not. There was no discontinuity between their presentation of self when under surveillance and when alone.

Even more remarkable was the discovery that the prisoners had begun to adopt and accept the guards' negative attitude toward them. Half of all reported private interactions between prisoners could be classified as non-supportive and non-cooperative. Moreover, when prisoners made evaluative statements of or expressed regard for, their fellow prisoners, 85% of the time they were uncomplimentary and deprecating. This set of observed frequencies departs significantly from chance expectations based on a conservative binominal probability frequency ($P < 0.01$ for prison $v.$ non-prison topics; $P < 0.05$ for negative $v.$ positive or neutral regard).

Mood Adjective Self-reports

Twice during the progress of the experiment each subject was asked to complete a mood adjective checklist and indicate his current affective state. The data gleaned from these self-reports did not lend themselves readily to statistical analysis. However, the trends suggested by simple enumeration are important enough to be included without reference to statistical significance. In these written self-reports, prisoners expressed nearly three times as much negative as positive affect. Prisoners roughly expressed three times as much negative affect as guards. Guards expressed slightly more negative than positive affect. While prisoners expressed about twice as much emotionality as did guards, a comparison of mood self-reports over time reveals that the prisoners showed two to three times as much mood fluctuation as did the relatively stable guards. On the dimension of activity-passivity, prisoners tended to score twice as high, indicating twice as much internal "agitation" as guards (although, as stated above, prisoners were seen to be less active than guards in terms of overt behaviour).

It would seem from these results that while the experience had a categorically negative emotional impact upon both guards and prisoners, the effects upon prisoners were more profound and unstable.

When the mood scales were administered for a third time, just after the subjects were told the study had been terminated (and the early released subjects returned for the debriefing encounter session), marked changes in mood were evident. All of the new "ex-convicts" selected self-descriptive adjectives which characterised their mood as less negative and much more positive. In addition, they now felt less passive than before. There were no longer any differences on the sub-scales of this test between prisoners released early and those who remained throughout. Both groups of subjects had returned to their pre-experimental baselines of emotional responding. This seems to reflect the situational specificity of the depression and stress reactions experienced while in the role of prisoner.

Representative Personal Statements

Much of the flavour and impact of this prison experience is unavoidably lost in the relatively formal, objective analyses outlined in this paper. The following quotations taken from interviews, conversations and questionnaires provide a more personal view of what it was like to be a prisoner or guard in the "Stanford County Prison" experiment.

Guards

"They [the prisoners] seemed to lose touch with the reality of the experiment —they took me so seriously."

". . . I didn't interfere with any of the guards' actions. Usually if what they were doing bothered me, I would walk out and take another duty."

". . . looking back, I am impressed by how little I felt for them . . ."

". . . They [the prisoners] didn't see it as an experiment. It was real and they were fighting to keep their identity. But we were always there to show them just who was boss."

". . . I was tired of seeing the prisoners in their rags and smelling the strong odours of their bodies that filled the cells. I watched them tear at each other, on orders given by us."

". . . Acting authoritatively can be fun. Power can be a great pleasure."

". . . During the inspection, I went to cell 2 to mess up a bed which the prisoner had made and he grabbed me, screaming that he had just made it, and he wasn't going to let me mess it up. He grabbed my throat, and although he was laughing I was pretty scared. I lashed out with my stick and hit him in the chin (although not very hard) and when I freed myself I became angry."

Prisoners

". . . The way we were made to degrade ourselves really brought us down and that's why we all sat docile towards the end of the experiment."

". . . I realise now (after it's over) that no matter how together I thought I was inside my head, my prison behaviour was often less under my control than I realised. No matter how open, friendly and helpful I was with other prisoners I was still operating as an isolated, self-centered person, being rational rather than compassionate."

"... I began to feel I was losing my identity, that the person I call —— —— ——, the person who volunteered to get me into this prison (because it was a prison to me, it *still* is a prison to me, I don't regard it as an experiment or a simulation ...) was distant from me, was remote until finally I wasn't *that* person, I was 416. I was really my number and 416 was really going to have to decide what to do."

"I learned that people can easily forget that others are human."

Debriefing Encounter Sessions

Because of the unexpectedly intense reactions (such as the above) generated by this mock-prison experience, we decided to terminate the study at the end of six days rather than continue for the second week. Three separate encounter sessions were held, first, for the prisoners, then for the guards and finally for all participants together. Subjects and staff openly discussed their reactions and strong feelings were expressed and shared. We analysed the moral conflicts posed by this experience and used the debriefing sessions to make explicit alternative courses of action that would lead to more moral behaviour in future comparable situations.

Follow-ups on each subject over the year following termination of the study revealed the negative effects of participation had been temporary, while the personal gain to the subjects endured.

Conclusions and Discussion

It should be apparent that the elaborate procedures (and staging) employed by the experimenters to insure a high degree of mundane realism in this mock prison contributed to its effective functional simulation of the psychological dynamics operating in "real" prisons. We observed empirical relationships in the simulated prison environment which were strikingly isomorphic to the internal relations of real prisons, corroborating many of the documented reports of what occurs behind prison walls.

The conferring of differential power on the status of "guard" and "prisoner" constituted, in effect, the institutional validation of those roles. But further, many of the subjects ceased distinguishing between prison role and their prior self-identities. When this occurred, within what was a surprisingly short period of time, we witnessed a sample of normal, healthy American college students fractionate into a group of prison guards who seemed to derive pleasure from insulting, threatening, humiliating and dehumanising their peers—those who by chance selection had been assigned to the "prisoner" role. The typical prisoner syndrome was one of passivity, dependency, depression, helplessness and self-deprecation. Prisoner participation in the social reality which the guards had structured for them lent increasing validity to it and, as the prisoners became resigned to their treatment over time, many acted in ways to justify their fate at the hands of the guards, adopting attitudes and behaviour which helped to sanction their victimisation. Most dramatic and distressing to us was the observation of the ease with which sadistic behaviour could be elicited in individuals who were not "sadistic types" and the frequency with which acute emotional breakdowns could occur in men selected precisely for their emotional stability.

Situational v. Dispositional Attribution

To what can we attribute these deviant behaviour patterns? If these reactions had been observed within the confines of an existing penal institution, it is probable that a dispositional hypothesis would be invoked as an explanation. Some cruel guards might be singled out as sadistic or passive-aggressive personality types who chose to work in a correctional institution because of the outlets provided for sanctioned aggression. Aberrant reactions on the part of the inmate population would likewise be viewed as an extrapolation from the prior social histories of these men as violent, anti-social, psychopathic, unstable character types.

Existing penal institutions may be viewed as *natural experiments* in social control in which any attempts at providing a causal attribution for observed behaviour hopelessly confound dispositional and situational causes. In contrast, the design of our study minimised the utility of trait or prior social history explanations by means of judicious subject selection and random assignment to roles. Considerable effort and care went into determining the composition of the final subject population from which our guards and prisoners were drawn. Though case histories, personal interviews and a battery of personality tests, the subjects chosen to participate manifested no apparent abnormalities, anti-social tendencies or social backgrounds which were other than exemplary. On every one of the scores of the diagnostic tests each subject scored within the normal-average range. Our subjects then, were highly representative of middleclass, Caucasian American society (17 to 30 years in age), although above average in both intelligence and emotional stability.

Nevertheless, in less than one week their *behaviour* in this simulated prison could be characterised as pathological and anti-social. The negative, anti-social reactions observed were not the product of an environment created by combining a collection of deviant personalities, but rather, the result of an intrinsically pathological situation which could distort and rechannel the behaviour of essentially normal individuals. The abnormality here resided in the psychological nature of the situation and not in those who passed through it. Thus, we offer another instance in support of Mischel's [4] social-learning analysis of the power of situational variables to shape complex social behaviour. Our results are also congruent with those of Milgram [5] who most convincingly demonstrated the proposition that evil acts are not necessarily the deeds of evil men, but may be attributable to the operation of powerful social forces. Our findings go one step further, however, in removing the immediate presence of the dominant experimenter-authority figure, giving the subjects-as-guards a freer range of behavioural alternatives, and involving the participants for a much more extended period of time.

Despite the evidence favouring a situational causal analysis in this experiment, it should be clear that the research design actually *minimised* the effects of individual differences by use of a homogenous middle-range subject population. It did not allow the strongest possible test of the relative utility of the two types of explanation. We cannot say that personality differences do not have an important effect on behaviour in situations such as the one reported here. Rather, we may assert that the variance in behaviour observed could be reliably attributed to variation in situational rather than personality variables. The inherently pathological characteristics of the prison situation itself, at least as functionally simulated in our study, were a *sufficient* condition to produce aberrant, anti-social behaviour. (An alternative design which would maximise the potential operation of personality or dispositional variables would assign subjects who were extreme on pre-selected personality dimensions to each of the two experimental treatments. Such a design would, however, require a larger subject population and more resources than we had available.)

The failure of personality assessment variables to reliably discriminate the various patterns of prison behaviour, guard reactions as well as prisoner coping styles is reminiscent of the inability of personality tests to contribute to an understanding of the psychological differences between American P.O.W.s in Korea who succumbed to alleged Chinese Communist brain-washing by "collaborating with the enemy" and those who resisted [6]. It seems to us that there is little reason to expect paper-and-pencil behavioural reactions on personality tests taken under "normal" conditions to generalise into coping behaviours under novel, stressful or abnormal environmental conditions. It may be that the best predictor of behaviour in situations of stress and power, as occurs in prisons, is overt behaviour in functionally comparable simulated environments.

In the situation of imprisonment faced by our subjects, despite the potent situational control, individual differences were nevertheless manifested both in coping styles among the prisoners and in the extent and type of aggression and exercise of power among the guards. Personality variables, conceived as learned behaviour styles can act as moderator variables in allaying or intensifying the impact of social situational variables. Their predictive utility depends upon acknowledging the inter-active relationship of such learned dispositional tendencies with the eliciting force of the situational variables.

Reality of the Simulation

At this point it seems necessary to confront the critical question of "reality" in the simulated prison environment: were the behaviours observed more than the mere acting out assigned roles convincingly? To be sure, ethical, legal and practical considerations set limits upon the degree to which this situation could approach the conditions existing in actual prisons and penitentiaries. Necessarily absent were some of the most salient aspects of prison life reported by criminologists and documented in the writing of prisoners [7, 8]. There was no involuntary homosexuality, no racism, no physical beatings, no threat to life by prisoners against each other or the guards. Moreover, the maximum anticipated "sentence" was only two weeks and, unlike some prison systems, could not be extended indefinitely for infractions of the internal operating rules of the prison.

In one sense, the profound psychological effects we observed under the relatively minimal prison-like conditions which existed in our mock prison make the results even more significant and force us to wonder about the devastating impact of chronic incarceration in real prisons. Nevertheless, we must contend with the criticism that the conditions which prevailed in the mock prison were too minimal to provide a meaningful analogue to existing prisons. It is necessary to demonstrate that the participants in this experiment transcended the conscious limits of their preconceived stereotyped roles and their awareness of the artificiality and limited duration of imprisonment. We feel there is abundant evidence that virtually all of the subjects at one time or another experienced reactions which went well beyond the surface demands of role-playing and penetrated the deep structure of the psychology of imprisonment.

Although instructions about how to behave in the roles of guard or prisoner were not explicitly defined, demand characteristics in the experiment obviously exerted some directing influence. Therefore, it is enlightening to look to circumstances where role demands were minimal, where the subjects believed they were not being observed, or where they should not have been behaving under the constraints imposed by their roles (as in "private" situations), in order to assess whether the role behaviours reflected anything more than public conformity or good acting.

When the private conversations of the prisoners were monitored, we learned that almost all (a full 90%) of what they talked about was directly related to immediate prison conditions, that is, food, privileges, punishment, guard harassment, etc. Only one-tenth of the time did their conversations deal with their life outside the prison. Consequently, although they had lived together under such intense conditions, the prisoners knew surprisingly little about each other's past history or future plans. This excessive concentration on the vicissitudes of their current situation helped to make the prison experience more oppressive for the prisoners because, instead of escaping from it when they had a chance to do so in the privacy of their cells, the prisoners continued to allow it to dominate their thoughts and social relations. The guards too, rarely exchanged personal information during their relaxation breaks. They either talked about "problem prisoners", or other prison topics, or did not talk at all. There were few instances of any personal communication across the two role groups. Moreover, when prisoners referred to other prisoners during interviews, they typically deprecated each other, seemingly adopting the guards' negative attitude.

From post-experimental data, we discovered that when individual guards were alone with solitary prisoners and out of range of any recording equipment, as on the way to or in the toilet, harassment often was greater than it was on the "Yard". Similarly, video-taped analyses of total guard aggression showed a daily escalation even after most prisoners had ceased resisting and prisoner deterioration had become visibly obvious to them. Thus guard aggression was no longer elicited as it was initially in response to perceived threats, but was emitted simply as a "natural" consequence of being in the uniform of a "guard" and asserting the power inherent in that role. In specific instances we noted cases of a guard (who did not know he was being observed) in the early morning hours pacing the "Yard" as the prisoners slept— vigorously pounding his night stick into his hand while he "kept watch" over his captives. Or another guard who detained an "incorrigible" prisoner in solitary confinement beyond the duration set by the guards' own rules and then he conspired to keep him in the hole all night while attempting to conceal this information from the exerimenters who were thought to be too soft on the prisoners.

In passing, we may note an additional point about the nature of role-playing and the extent to which actual behaviour is "explained away" by reference to it. It will be recalled that many guards continued to intensify their harassment and aggressive behaviour even after the second day of the study, when prisoner deterioration became marked and visible and emotional breakdowns began to occur (in the presence of the guards). When questioned after the study about their persistent affrontive and harrassing behaviour in the face of prisoner emotional trauma, most guards replied that they were "just playing the role" of a tough guard, although none ever doubted the magnitude or validity of the prisoners' emotional response. The reader may wish to consider to what extremes an individual may go, how great must be the consequences of his behaviour for others, before he can no longer rightfully attribute his actions to "playing a role" and thereby abdicate responsibility.

When introduced to a Catholic priest, many of the role-playing prisoners referred to themselves by their prison number rather than their Christian names. Some even asked him to get a lawyer to help them get out. When a public defender was summoned to interview those prisoners who had not yet been released, almost all of them strenuously demanded that he "bail" them out immediately.

One of the most remarkable incidents of the study occurred during a parole board hearing when each of five prisoners eligible for parole was asked by the senior author whether he would be willing to forfeit all the money earned as a prisoner if he were to be paroled (released from the study). Three of the five prisoners said, "yes", they would be willing to do this. Notice that the original incentive for participating in the study had been the promise of money, and they were, after only four days, prepared to give this up completely. And, more surprisingly, when told that this possibility would have to be discussed with the members of the staff before a decision could be made, each prisoner got up quietly and was escorted by a guard back to his cell. If they regarded themselves simply as "subjects" participating in an experiment for money, there was no longer any incentive to remain in the study and they could have easily escaped this situation which had so clearly become aversive for them by quitting. Yet, so powerful was the control which the situation had come to have over them, so much a reality had this simulated environment become that they were unable to see that their original and singular motive for remaining no longer obtained, and they returned to their cells to await a "parole" decision by their captors.

The reality of the prison was also attested to by our prison consultant who had spent over 16 years in prison, as well as the priest who had been a prison chaplain and the public defender who were all brought into direct contact with our simulated prison environment. Further, the depressed affect of the prisoners, the guards' willingness to work overtime for no additional pay, the spontaneous use of prison titles and I.D. numbers in non role-related situations all point to a level of reality as real as any other in the lives of all those who shared this experience.

To understand how an illusion of imprisonment could have become so real, we need now to consider the uses of power by the guards as well as the effects of such power in shaping the prisoner mentality.

Pathology of Power

Being a guard carried with it social status within the prison, a group identity (when wearing the uniform), and above all, the freedom to exercise an unprecedented degree of control over the lives of other human beings. This control was invariably expressed in terms of sanctions, punishment, demands and with the threat of manifest physical power. There was no need for the guards to rationally justify a request as they do in their ordinary life and merely to make a demand was sufficient to have it carried out. Many of the guards showed in their behaviour and revealed in post-experimental statements that this sense of power was exhilarating.

The use of power was self-aggrandising and self-perpetuating. The guard power, derived initially from an arbitrary label, was intensified whenever there was any perceived threat by the prisoners and this new level subsequently became the baseline from which further hostility and harassment would begin. The most hostile guards on each shift moved spontaneously into the leadership roles of giving orders and deciding on punishments. They became role models whose behaviour was emulated by other members of the shift. Despite minimal contact between the three separate guard shifts and nearly 16 hours a day spent away from the prison, the absolute level of aggression as well as more subtle and "creative" forms of aggression manifested, increased in a spiralling function. Not to be tough and arrogant was to be seen as a sign of weakness by the guards and even those "good" guards who did not get as drawn into the power syndrome as the others respected the implicit norm of *never* contradicting or even interfering with an action of a more hostile guard on their shift.

After the first day of the study, practically all prisoner's rights (even such things as the time and conditions of sleeping and eating) came to be redefined by the guards as "privileges" which were to be earned for obedient behaviour. Constructive activities such as watching movies or reading (previously planned and suggested by the experimenters) were arbitrarily cancelled until further notice by the guards—and were subsequently never allowed. "Reward", then became granting approval for prisoners to eat, sleep, go to the toilet, talk, smoke a cigarette, wear glasses or the temporary diminution of harassment. One wonders about the conceptual nature of "positive" reinforcement when subjects are in such conditions of deprivation, and the extent to which even minimally acceptable conditions become rewarding when experienced in the context of such an impoverished environment.

We might also question whether there are meaningful non-violent alternatives as models for behaviour modification in real prisons. In a world where men are either powerful or powerless, everyone learns to despise the lack of power in others and in oneself. It seems to us, that prisoners learn to admire power for its own sake—power becoming the ultimate reward. Real prisoners soon learn the means to gain power whether through ingratiation, informing, sexual control of other prisoners or development of powerful cliques. When they are released from prison, it is unlikely they will ever want to feel so powerless again and will take action to establish and assert a sense of power.

The Pathological Prisoner Syndrome

Various coping strategies were employed by our prisoners as they began to react to their perceived loss of personal identity and the arbitrary control of their lives. At first they exhibited disbelief at the total invasion of their privacy, constant surveillance and atmosphere of oppression in which they were living. Their next response was rebellion, first by the use of direct force, and later with subtle divisive tactics designed to foster distrust among the prisoners. They then tried to work within the system by setting up an elected grievance committe. When that collective action failed to produce meaningful changes in their existence, individual self-interests emerged. The breakdown in prisoner cohesion was the start of social disintegration which gave rise not only to feelings of isolation but deprecation of other prisoners as well. As noted before, half the prisoners coped with the prison situation by becoming extremely disturbed emotionally—as a passive way of demanding attention and help. Others became excessively obedient in trying to be "good" prisoners. They sided with the guards against a solitary fellow prisoner who coped with his situation by refusing to eat. Instead of supporting this final and major act of rebellion, the prisoners treated him as a trouble-maker who deserved to be punished for his disobedience. It is likely that the negative self-regard among the prisoners noted by the end of the study was the product of their coming to believe that the continued hostility toward all of them was justified because they "deserved it" [9]. As the days wore on, the model prisoner reaction was one of passivity, dependence and flattened affect.

Let us briefly consider some of the relevant processes involved in bringing about these reactions.

Loss of personal identity. Identity is, for most people, conferred by social recognition of one's uniqueness, and established through one's name, dress, appearance, behaviour style and history. Living among strangers who do not know your name or history (who refer to you only by number), dressed in a uniform exactly like all other prisoners, not wanting to call attention to one's self because of the unpredictable consequences it might provoke—all led to a weakening of self identity among the prisoners. As they began to lose initiative and emotional responsivity, while acting ever more compliantly, indeed, the prisoners became deindividuated not only to the guards and the observers, but also to themselves.

Arbitrary control. On post-experimental questionnaires, the most frequently mentioned aversive aspect of the prison experience was that of being subjugated to the apparently arbitrary, capricious decisions and rules of the guards. A question by a prisoner as often elicited derogation and aggression as it did a rational answer. Smiling at a joke could be punished in the same way that failing to smile might be. An individual acting in defiance of the rules could bring punishment to innocent cell partners (who became, in effect, "mutually yoked controls") to himself, or to all.

As the environment became more unpredictable, and previously learned assumptions about a just and orderly world were no longer functional, prisoners ceased to initiate any action. They moved about on orders and when in their cells rarely engaged in any purposeful activity. Their zombie-like reaction was the functional equivalent of the learned helplessness phenomenon reported by Seligman and Groves [10]. Since their behaviour did not seem to have any contingent relationship to environmental consequences, the prisoners essentially gave up and stopped behaving. Thus the subjective magnitude of aversiveness was manipulated by the guards not in terms of physical punishment but rather by controlling the psychological dimension of environmental predictability. [11].

Dependency and emasculation. The network of dependency relations established by the guards not only promoted helplessness in the prisoners but served to emasculate them as well. The arbitrary control by the guards put the prisoners at their mercy for even the daily, commonplace functions like going to the toilet. To do so, required publicly obtained permission (not always granted) and then a personal escort to the toilet while blindfolded and handcuffed. The same was true for many other activities ordinarily practised spontaneously without thought, such as lighting up a cigarette, reading a novel, writing a letter, drinking a glass of water or brushing one's teeth. These were all privileged activities requiring permission and necessitating a prior show of good behaviour. These low level dependencies engendered a regressive orientation in the prisoners. Their dependency was defined in terms of the extent of the domain of control over all aspects of their lives which they allowed other individuals (the guards and prison staff) to exercise.

As in real prisons, the assertive, independent, aggressive nature of male prisoners posed a threat which was overcome by a variety of tactics. The prisoner uniforms resembled smocks or dresses, which made them look silly and enabled the guards to refer to them as "sissies" or "girls". Wearing these uniforms without any underclothes forced the prisoners to move and sit in unfamiliar, feminine postures. Any sign of individual rebellion was labelled as indicative of "incorrigibility" and resulted in loss of privileges, solitary confinement, humiliation or punishment of cell mates. Physically smaller guards were able to induce stronger prisoners to act foolishly and obediently. Prisoners were encouraged to belittle each other publicly during the counts. These and other tactics all served to engender in the prisoners a lessened sense of their masculinity (as defined by their external culture). It follows then, that although the prisoners usually outnumbered the guards during line-ups and counts (nine *v.* three) there never was an attempt to directly overpower them. (Interestingly, after the study was terminated, the prisoners expressed the belief that the basis for assignment to guard and prisoner groups was physical size. They perceived the guards were "bigger", when, in fact, there was no difference in average height or weight between these randomly determined groups.)

In conclusion, we believe this demonstration reveals new dimensions in the social psychology of imprisonment worth pursuing in future research. In addition, this research provides a paradigm and information base for studying alternatives to existing guard training, as well as for questioning the basic operating principles on which penal institutions rest. If our mock prison could generate the extent of pathology it did in such a short time, then the punishment of being imprisoned in a real prison does not "fit the crime" for most prisoners, indeed, it far exceeds it! Moreover, since prisoners and guards are locked into a dynamic, symbiotic relationship which is destructive to their human nature, guards are also society's prisoners.

Shortly after our study was terminated, the indiscriminate killings at San Quentin and Attica occurred, emphasising the urgency for prison reforms that recognise the dignity and humanity of both prisoners and guards who are constantly forced into one of the most intimate and potentially deadly encounters known to man.

Acknowledgments

This research was funded by an ONR grant: N00014-67-A-0112-0041 to Professor Philip G. Zimbardo.

The ideas expressed in this paper are those of the authors and do not imply endorsement of ONR or any sponsoring agency. We wish to extend our thanks and appreciation for the contributions to this research by David Jaffe who served as "warden" and pre-tested some of the variables in the mock prison situation. In addition, Greg White provided invaluable assistance during the data reduction phase of this study. Many others (most notably Carolyn Burkhart, Susie Phillips and Kathy Rosenfeld), helped at various stages of the experiment, with the construction of the prison, prisoner arrest, interviewing, testing, and data analysis—we extend our sincere thanks to each of these collaborators. Finally, we wish especially to thank Carlo Prescott, our prison consultant, whose personal experience gave us invaluable insights into the nature of imprisonment.

References

1. T. W. Adorno, E. Frenkel-Brunswick, D. J. Levinson & R.N. Sanford. *The Authoritarian Personality*. New York, Harper. 1950.

2. R. Christie & F. L. Geis (Eds). *Studies in Machiavellianism*. New York, Academic Press. 1970.

3. A. L Comrey. *Comrey Personality Scales*. San Diego, Educational and Industrial Testing Service. 1970.

4. W. Mischel. *Personality and Assessment*. New York, Wiley. 1968.

5. S. Milgram. Some conditions of obedience and disobedience to authority, *Human Relations* 1965, 18(1), 57-76.

6. G. Jackson. *Soledad Brother: the Prison Letters of George Jackson.* New York, Bantam Books. 1970.

7. E. Schein. *Coercive Persuasion.* New York, Norton. 1961.

8. H. Charriere. *Papillion.* Paris, Robert Laffont. 1969.

9. E. Walster. Assignment of responsibility for an accident, *Journal of Personality and Social Psychology* 1966, 3(1), 73-79.

10. M. E. Seligman & D. P. Groves. Nontransient learned helplessness, *Psychonomic Science* 1970, 19(3), 191-192.

11. D. C. Glass & J. E. Singer. Behavioural after effects of unpredictable and uncontrollable aversive events, *American Scientist* 1972, 6(4), 457-465.

D. Field Experiments

DARRELL J. STEFFENSMEIER
and
ROBERT M. TERRY

Deviance and Respectability: An Observational Study of Reactions to Shoplifting*

The interactionist-labeling perspective on deviance has focused attention away from the traditional etiological question of what makes social actors commit deviant acts and placed it more on the analysis of public reactions to deviance and on how social actors become defined and treated as deviant. One issue raised by this approach is: given that someone has engaged in deviant behavior, how does that become translated into a deviant? What factors lead to some acts being defined as deviant while others are simply ignored? Or, perhaps more importantly, why are some persons defined as deviant while others are not, even though the behavior engaged in is identical or essentially the same?

The following report by Steffensmeier and Terry deals specifically with these issues. As reported below, a field experiment was set up in which shoplifting incidents were staged in the presence of store customers who were in a position to observe and react to the shoplifting. Three variables were manipulated: (1) shoplifter's appearance—operationalized as hippie versus straight, (2) sex of shoplifter and (3) sex of subject.

The major finding of the field experiment was that hippie shoplifters were

Reprinted from Darrell J. Steffensmeier and Robert M. Terry, "Deviance and Respectability: An Observational Study of Reaction to Shoplifting," *Social Forces*, 1973, 51:417-426. Copyright © by The University of North Carolina Press.

*The authors are grateful for financial assistance provided by the Center for Research in Interpersonal Behavior and the Graduate College of the University of Iowa. We would also like to thank Renee Steffensmeier for critical readings of earlier drafts of this paper and Larry Rhoades for helpful suggestions regarding final editing.

much more likely to be reported for shoplifting than straight shoplifters, clearly demonstrating that imputation of a deviant label is often contingent upon much more than simply the fact of deviant behavior itself. The authors suggest that straight and hippie appearance constitute positive and negative identities which are important for structuring interaction between actors and audiences. By the mere fact of being a "hippie" the person has demonstrated his moral value, his lack of responsibility, from the dominant cultural perspective. A straight-appearing actor, on the other hand, is more likely to be viewed as basically stable, as ambitious and as a valuable contributor to the social system. When deviance is engaged in by the latter, his appearance is apt to serve as a buffer against deviant imputation—the deviance being judged as transient, situational or simply not serious enough to warrant intervention. In contrast, when deviance is engaged in by the hippie, his appearance increases his vulnerability to deviant imputation—the deviance being interpreted as more serious in nature and as indication of basic personality characteristics.

A major point made by Steffensmeier and Terry in the shoplifting report is that social identities have different meanings and differential values are placed on these meanings. These identities indicate "what kind of person" the individual is and a relative value is placed on that person concomitant with that identity. To predict whether a given behavior will be characterized as deviant, to determine what type of deviant label will be applied, and how it will be reacted to, knowledge of the actor's salient identities is crucial.

Lastly, in terms of the definition of deviance set forth in an earlier section, the differential reactions to hippie and straight shoplifters suggests that the hippie shoplifter can be viewed as sort of a "double-deviant." His deviance is double in that it consists of *both* engaging in deviant behavior, shoplifting, and in having a deviant attribute, namely, a hippie appearance.

The interactionist-labeling perspective in deviance asserts that audience responses to deviant acts are crucial to the understanding of deviant behavior. Furthermore, to understand audience response—reactions toward various types of deviance—investigators need to discover the meaning these behaviors have for potential reactors. These meanings may vary with the deviant's other social identities, with situational factors such as social support and social setting, and the characteristics of potential reactors. Although some research relates these variables to audience reactions, few studies have manipulated such variables within a field setting.

A growing body of observational field studies treats the reactions of official control agents such as the police (e.g., Black, 1970; Piliavin and Briar, 1964) and courts to deviant actors (Emerson, 1969). But such research has generally lacked the kind of control that allows for experimental manipulation of variables and the systematic examination of posited relationships. In addition, studies examining the reactions of the general public have been largely ignored. With few exceptions (e.g., Darley and Latane, 1968; Denner, 1968; Freed *et al.,* 1955; Lefkowitz *et al.,* 1955), there is a dearth of experimental field research that systematically examines posited relationships between reactions of the general public and deviant behavior.

Current thinking in Sociology indicates that the study of deviant behavior must overcome problems in the validity of official statistics (see, especially, Douglas, 1971a; Kitsuse and Cicourel, 1963; Wheeler, 1967), must recognize that while official control agents are important it is the general public that usually initiates responses to deviant behavior (e.g., Black, 1970), and must study deviance in its natural setting rather than as mediated through the official reports and actions of formal control agents (e.g., Douglas, 1971b; Humphreys, 1970).

This research attempts to shed some light on the nature and basis of reactions to a particular kind of deviance and, in doing so, tries to overcome the aforementioned problems by (1) using field research methods, (2) ascertaining responses of the general public to instances of deviant behavior in real life situations, and (3) making direct observations of behavior of members of the soical audience. Specifically, appearance and sex of the deviant are varied systematically in order to assess their effects upon the responses of the general public to observed instances of shoplifting.[1]

There is much theoretical support for the notion that the actor's social identity is a crucial determinant of reactions to deviant behavior (Douglas, 1970; Goffman, 1963; Lemert, 1951; Lofland, 1969). Two important aspects of social identity considered in this research are those of appearance and sex, both of which can be subsumed under the more abstract rubric of respectability.

Much of the literature in the interactionist-labeling perspective has argued that differential treatment is accorded persons with poor social backgrounds, less than perfect social indentities, or "bad" reputations. Many analyses of deviant categories are founded on the assumption that particular classes of people are more likely to perform deviant acts and to be particular types of deviant persons (Hughes, 1945; Kitsuse, 1962; Lofland, 1969; Scheff, 1966; Simmons, 1965; Sudnow, 1965). Such studies are highly consistent in arguing that respectability decreases the likelihood of deviant imputations, whereas "unrespectability" has the opposite effect.

In this research, appearance and sex are used as indicators of respectability. Reports by Ball (1970) and Cameron (1964) have noted that a respectable appearance serves as a buffer against a deviation imputation. Lefkowitz *et al.* (1955) found that a respectable appearance was influential in inducing others to engage in deviant behavior (jaywalking). In a field experiment, Bickman (1971) found that persons who appeared to be of low status were treated more dishonestly by experimental subjects than were those of apparently higher status. It has been noted that one's appearance (kinds of clothing, hair style, and the like) is part and parcel of being a particular kind of person and also indicates, in a general sense, an individual's attitude toward community norms (Carey, 1968; Stone, 1962). In the current scene, commonsense distinctions between hippie and straight appearances are especially noteworthy.

Another of actor's social identities thought to affect reactions to deviance is one's sex. Consistent research findings show that females are less severely dealt with by formal control agents than are males and some evidence exists to support the notion that public attitudes and reactions toward the sexes tend to favor females (Pollak, 1961; Reckles, 1961; Ward and Kassebaum, 1965). Schur (1969) has argued that the greater attitude of protectiveness taken toward women in our society and more generally the nature of their social roles and situations permit women to exploit their sex for criminal purposes and to engage in various kinds of criminal behavior with relatively little fear of detection or prosecution.

The effect of sex status on deviant imputation can be fitted into Goffman's discussion of social identities and more specifically into the rubric of respectability. Goffman (1963) argues that an individual's biography is composed of both past and present events and characteristics which function so as to establish an individual's social identity. The latter refers to those attributes others can observe, providing thereby a basis for classifying an actor as a particular kind of person. Such attributes as age and sex are of primary importance in making such categorizations. Although none of these variables is inherently bound to the notion of respectability, the deviant behavior literature rather clearly indicates that being a male tends to be viewed as an unfavorable attribute by social control agents and increases a person's vulnerability to the imputation of deviance.

Our third independent variable, sex of subject, is ambiguously grounded in research that generally indicates that females are less tolerant of deviance than are males (Phillips, 1964; Westie and Martin, 1959; Williams, 1964); although there is conflicting evidence (Whatley, 1959). Traditional sex role differences, theoretically at least, have emphasized more support of stability and the ongoing system among females than among males. Thus, females should be less accepting of nonconforming behavior than males (Parsons and Bales, 1955) and therefore should be more likely to report deviant acts.

Hypotheses

On the basis of the foregoing, the following hypotheses are the targets of inquiry:

1. *Store customers will be more likely to report a shoplifting incident when the shoplifter has a hippie rather than a straight appearance.*

2. *Store customers will be more likely to report a shoplifting incident when the shoplifter is male rather than female.*

3. *Female store customers will be more likely to report a shoplifting incident than male store customers.*

Methods

This research sought to discover factors related to reactions to shoplifting. "Reactions" was defined in terms of variations in the willingness of store customers to report behavior (shoplifting) which was blatantly illegal and deviant. In order to observe the reactions of a wide variety of subjects and simultaneously maintain some degree of control over the frequency of occurrence and consistency of the deviant behavior, a natural field experiment was designed. While this approach assured a rather high degree of external validity it presented some difficulties in settling on the variables determining societal reactions. For the experimental situation allowed us to investigate only those independent variables that were amenable to immediate observation in fleeting encounters: hence, sex and appearance.

The study was conducted in three preselected stores in a midwestern university city of *50,000*. The experiment can best be described as a rigged shoplifting incident—i.e., its occurrence was prearranged. The store's manager and personnel had complete knowledge of the experiment and the researchers had their full cooperation in staging the shoplifting incidents.

A. Shoplifting Sequence

The main concern of this research was the extent to which customers were willing to report shoplifting to store personnel. In order to control the frequency and consistency of the shoplifting situation three accomplices were employed. One accomplice played the part of a shoplifter and two more accomplices played the parts of store employees. The experimental procedure is best understood through a discussion of the roles played by the accomplices.

The first accomplice played the part of a shoplifter. This accomplice was to place himself under the direct observation of a customer (the subject), and then steal some item of merchandise in an obvious and deliberate manner.[2] Having done his shoplifting, the first accomplice moved to another location where he remained out of hearing distance but within eyesight of the subject. This procedure avoided the possible intimidation of the subject and simultaneously eased identification of the shoplifter if the subject showed a willingness to report the incident. The appearance and sex of the shoplifter were varied systematically.

The second and third research accomplices played the parts of store employees.[3] The principal task of the second accomplice or first store employee was to make himself readily available should the subject wish to report the shoplifting incident. As soon as the shoplifter moved away to another location (after he had shoplifted) the first store employee had instructions to move into the immediate vicinity of the subject and act as though he were arranging merchandise on the shelves or counters. The accomplice remained in the area for a brief period of time in order to allow the subject ample opportunity to report. If the subject reported, then the store employee was instructed to "apprehend" the shoplifter and both of them moved backstage.[4] If the subject did not report the shoplifting, the accomplice left the area and signaled to a third accomplice to intervene.

The third accomplice played the part of a second store employee. He was instructed to act more directly and vigorously in order to increase the likelihood of reporting. He asked the subject for assistance in identifying a possible shoplifter by prompting the subject in two different ways. The first prompting was as follows: "Good afternoon (evening), sir (madam), we have been watching so-and-so (identifying description) for shoplifting. Did you happen to see anything?" If, in response to his first prompting the subject reported the shoplifter, then the employee "apprehended" him and they moved backstage. If the subject did not respond to the first prompting, the same store employee was instructed to intervene more forcefully to elicit reporting from the subject. The second prompting was as follows: "Gee, I was quite sure I saw him (her) take something (specify item) and put it down his coat. You didn't happen to see anything suspicious, did you?" If the subject still did not report, the accomplice left the vicinity and there was no further prompting of the subject.

After the experiment was completed each subject was immediately debriefed by another research assistant. Every conceivable effort was made to clarify to the subject the nature and the purpose of the deception. In addition, an attempt was made to interview the subject briefly as to his perception of and reaction to the experiment.[5]

B. Operationalization of the Dependent Variable

The dependent variable in this research is willingness to report a shoplifting incident. On a higher theoretical level we are getting at the willingness of potential reactors to impute a deviant label to presumably deviant actors. The use of prompting as a device to obtain variation in the dependent variable was suggested by the previous research of Latane and Darley (1969) and Denner (1968). As operationalized in this research, willingness to report could achieve four possible values:

1. If the subject reported the shoplifting incident to the first store employee, this response was assigned a value of *high* willingness to report. As will be recalled, the first store employee took a passive stance toward the subject and made no direct attempt to encourage reporting. No prompting was used at this point.

2. If the subject reported the shoplifting incident to the second store employee in response to the first prompting, this behavior was held to indicate *medium high* willingness to report.

3. If the subject reported the shoplifting incident to the second store employee in response to the second prompting, this behavior was assigned a value of *medium low* willingness to report.

4. The catgegory of *low* willingness to report consisted of all subjects who did not report the shoplifting incident.

Table 1 gives the distributions obtained for the sample on the dependent variable, willingness to report. As can be seen, we got good variance in type of response. A good deal of reporting took place even without prompting.

C. Research Sites

Stores were selected on the basis of several criteria. We thought it important to use stores of differing size and degree of bureaucratization.[6] Also, the stores had to retail mechandise that would be easy and obvious to steal. We also sought stores that had customers who represented the nonstudent population of a university-dominated city.

TABLE 1. Frequency Distribution of Respondent Reporting Levels

Reporting	Total Sample (n = 212)	Adults (n = 191)	Students (n = 21)
High	62 (29.2)	61 (31.9)	1 (4.8)
Medium high	73 (34.4)	71 (37.2)	2 (9.5)
Medium low	28 (13.2)	25 (13.1)	3 (14.3)
Low	49 (23.1)	34 (17.8)	15 (71.4)

After considering these matters, we approached several store managers to determine their willingness to participate in the project. Some were encouraging and enthusiastic. Out of necessity, then, the stores finally selected as research sites were those at which most cooperation was offered. Fortunately, these stores varied along the relevant dimensions of size and bureaucratization. In addition, each store had certain unique features.

Store A was a small, older chain grocery store, located close to the downtown area. Patrons consisted largely of persons living in the immediate neighborhood, older people, and university students. Store B was a relatively new, large chain grocery store located in a fringe area shopping center. The patrons consisted chiefly of housewives. Store C was a very large discount department store located on the edge of the city. For a number of reasons (location, prices, variety of merchandise, store hours, etc.) this store was more likely to attract out-of-town customers than the other stores.[7]

We tried to get approximately equal numbers of subjects in each store. Except for persons later identified as college students, this aim was achieved, with 67 subjects exposed to shoplifting in Store A, 69 in Store B, and 55 in Store C. Since the stores differed in size and therefore in the number of customers during any given time period, trial runs were conducted on four separate occasions in Store A, on two separate occasions in Store B, and on one occasion in Store C. In addition, Store A was used to conduct all pretests for the experiment.

D. Experimental Design

A primary justification for the study of contrived rather than real shoplifting is the greater ability to manipulate the independent variables. Two identities of the shoplifters were systemtically varied—appearance and sex. In addition, sex of the subject (shopper) was also varied across experimental events. Each variable is dichotomized, resulting in an overall research design of the 2 x 2 x2 variety. Figure 1 illustrates the eight comparison groups produced by this design. Approximately 25 subjects are represented in each cell, with a total sample size of 212. Each subject was exposed to only one combination of the independent variables, sex of shoplifter and appearance of shoplifter. We tried to include proportionate numbers of male and female subjects from various age categories and backgrounds and to exclude persons who appeared to be college students. Of the total 212 subjects, 191 were classifiable as nonstudent adults. All future tabulations of experimental data are based on these 191 subjects.[8]

FIGURE 1. Representation of the Research Design

Sex of Shoplifter

	Male *Appearance of* *Shoplifter*		*Female* *Appearance of* *Shoplifter*	
Sex of Subject	*Hippie*	*Straight*	*Hippie*	*Straight*
Male				
Female				

E. Operationalizing the Independent Variables

The major independent variables in this research were appearance and

TABLE 2. Three-way Analysis of Variance of Reporting Levels and Tests for Interaction Effects for Appearance of Shoplifter, Sex of Shoplifter, and Sex of Subject*

Source	SS	DF†	MS	F	Prob.
Total	235.1296	$(npqr - 1) = 190$			
Main effects					
Appearance of shoplifter (A)	46.9782	$(q - 1) = 1$	46.9782	48.1186	$< .001$
Sex of shoplifter (B)	.0048	$(p - 1) = 1$	.0048	.0049	$> .05$ N.S.
Sex of subject (C)	2.7066	$(r - 1) = 1$	2.7066	2.7723	$> .05$ N.S.
Interactions					
AB interaction	.1688	$(q - 1)(p - 1) = 1$	.1688	.1728	$> .05$ N.S.
AC interaction	.5145	$(q - 1)(r - 1) = 1$	.5145	.5269	$> .05$ N.S.
BC interaction	4.6232	$(p - 1)(r - 1) = 1$	4.6232	4.7354	$.01 < p < .05$
ABC interaction	1.4594	$(q - 1)(p - 1)(r - 1) = 1$	1.4594	1.4948	$> .05$ N.S.
Error					
Error SS (W. cell)	178.6741	$pqr(n - 1) = 183$	.9763		

* The analysis of variance procedures used in Table 2 were based on the "method of expected equal frequencies." According to this procedure, if cell Ns do not differ markedly, a fairly simple weighting procedure can be used to estimate what the cell sums and sums of squared scores would be if all Ns had been the same. (See Kohout, forthcoming; Schuessler, 1971, for cogent discussions of the procedure involved.)

† In computing the degrees of freedom, q = levels of A, p = levels of B, r = levels of C, and n = the average cell frequency.

sex. Appearance was varied: hippie vs. straight. Sex was varied by using male and female shoplifters. Attributes of the shoplifter presentation types are as follows:

(1) *Hippie shoplifter:*

(a) *Male:* He wore soiled patched blue jeans, blue workman's shirt, and blue denim jacket; well-worn scuffed shoes with no socks. He had long and unruly hair with a ribbon tied around his forehead. He was unshaven and had a small beard.

(b) *Female:* She wore soiled patched blue jeans, blue workman's shirt, and dirty blue denim jacket; well-worn ragged tennis shoes with no socks. She had long unruly and ratted hair. She wore no makeup.

(2) *Straight shoplifter:*

(a) *Male:* He wore neatly pressed dress slacks, sport shirt and tie, sport jacket, shined shoes. He had short, trimly cut hair and was clean shaven.

(b) *Female:* She wore a dress, shined shoes or boots, a fur coat. Her hair was well-styled. She wore makeup and was well groomed.

Other than the induced differences of grooming and dress, the shoplifters were about the same age, same height and build, and attractiveness.

Results

Tables 2 and 3 analyze the effects on reporting levels of our three independent variables. Table 2 also shows the interaction effects among our three independent variables. The tests of hypotheses, which are treated separately below, are derived from the information presented in Tables 2 and 3.

TABLE 3. Summary Correlation Table*

Zero-order	First-order	Second-order
$r_{wy} = .465$ (appearance of shoplifter)	$r_{wy \cdot x} = .465$ $r_{wy \cdot z} = .471$	$r_{wy \cdot xz} = .471$
$r_{xy} = .012$ (sex of shoplifter)	$r_{xy \cdot w} = .016$ $r_{xy \cdot z} = .014$	$r_{xy \cdot wz} = .018$
$r_{zy} = .096$ (sex of subject)	$r_{zy \cdot w} = .127$ $r_{zy \cdot x} = .096$	$r_{zy \cdot wx} = .127$

* The measure of association reported is Pearson's coefficient of correlation.
z = sex of subject
x = sex of shoplifter
w = appearance of shoplifter
y = reporting level

Appearance and Reporting

Our hypothesis predicts that the level of reporting of a shoplifting incident will be higher for the hippie than for the straight shoplifter. The hypothesis is clearly supported in that the relationship ($r = 465$) is large and in the expected direction and the F-test results are highly significant. In line with previous arguments, the shoplifter's appearance provides the potential reactor with information that enables him to locate the actor on a high-low evaluative continuum. Apparently a hippie appearance constitutes a negative identity that results in a greater willingness on the part of subjects to report the hippie over the straight shoplifter and by extension, a greater willingness to impute a deviant label to a hippie rather than a straight actor. The effects of shoplifter's appearance on reporting levels is discussed in greater detail following presentation of other results.

Sex of Shoplifter and Reporting

Our hypothesis as to the effect of shoplifter's sex on reporting levels is not supported in the data. The relationship ($r = .012$) is in the expected direction but is so small as to be nonexistent. In addition, F-test results are not significant.

Explanations for this finding are easy to come by, although such explanations are speculative. First, the findings may be limited to shoplifting and may not be generalizable to other deviance. Also, the trend toward sexual equality may be narrowing sex differentials in attitudes and actions toward offenders and the protectiveness argument may be no longer feasible. Finally, findings of differential reactions to offenders on the basis of sex have focused upon the reactions of formal control agents rather than the general public. It may be that control agents discriminate whereas the public does not.

Sex of Subject and Reporting Levels

Our hypothesis asserts that females will be more likely to report than will males. The data offer little support for the hypothesis. As indicated in Tables

TABLE 4. Mean Reporting Levels for Combinations of Independent Variables

Rank Order	Sex of Subject	Sex of Shoplifter	Sex of Subject and Sex of Shoplifter	Appearance of Shoplifter	Mean Reporting Level
1	Female	Male	Opposite	Hippie	1.4347
2	Female	Female	Same	Hippie	1.5217
3	Male	Female	Opposite	Hippie	1.7173
4	Male	Male	Same	Hippie	1.9130
5	Female	Male	Opposite	Straight	2.2962
6	Male	Female	Opposite	Straight	2.5000
7	Female	Female	Same	Straight	2.8518
8	Male	Male	Same	Straight	2.9166

2 and 3, the relationship ($r = .096$) is in the expected direction, but it is so small that we reject the hypothesis. In addition, F-test results are not significant. Again, it is possible that changing cultural definitions of female social

roles and the increasing equalitarianism of women in general has had the effect of narrowing sexual differentials in reactions to deviance. Williams (1964) has argued that this is occurring with racial prejudice and discrimination, and a similar process might have produced these results with respect to deviance.

Interaction Effects

Table 2 shows the interaction effects on reporting levels of various combinations of our independent variables. Only the interaction effect between sex of shoplifter and sex of subject proved to be significant (*BC* Interaction: $.01 < p < .05$). This interaction effect can be explained ex post facto by means of further analyses. The cell means for combinations of the independent variables were used to rank-order reporting levels for various categories of shoplifters and subjects. In addition, a new variable was derived by combining the sex of subject and sex of shoplifter. The derived variable yields a dichotomy—opposite sex vs. same sex reporting. The results are presented in Table 4, a table which neatly summarizes the results of this research.

First, the appearance of the shoplifter has the strongest and most clear-cut effect on reporting levels. Hippie shoplifters are always more likely to be reported than straight shoplifters. Second, for hippie shoplifters, female subjects report more than male subjects, irrespective of sex of shoplifter. For straight shoplifters, subject's willingness to report is greater when the shoplifter is of the opposite, rather than the same sex. According to these rank orders, straight shoplifters who are the same sex as the subject-witness are the least likely of all shoplifters to be reported.

Within categories of shoplifter's appearance we have a case of specification. For the hippie shoplifter, sex of subject has an independent effect on reporting: females report more often than males. In the case of the straight shoplifter, the interaction of sex of subject and sex of shoplifter clearly affects the level of reporting. The simple finding of interaction between these two independent variables becomes more complicated than it at first appeared to be in Table 2.

This specification of different levels of reporting requires us to try to explain the results for each category, separately. For straight shoplifters, same sex reporting may be less than opposite sex reporting because subjects are more able to empathize with persons cf the same sex. Another possibility is that subjects are more likely to report a member of the opposite sex because they feel less threatened. That is, subjects may feel that they are less likely to be attacked (physically or verbally) in a highly visible public situation by a member of the opposite sex than by a member of the same sex.

On the other hand, female subjects are more likely than male subjects to report the shoplifter who is a hippie because they are probably more offended by the overt violation of community norms and are more threatened by such attacks on the social order of the community. Females therefore are more likely than males to sanction persons with a nonrespectable appearance. The possibility that female subjects are more concerned with the appearance of respectability and with maintenance of social order explains the differential in reporting between male and female subjects when the shoplifter is a hippie.

Discussion

The major results of this research are that sex of shoplifter and sex of subject had little effect on reporting levels, whereas appearance of shoplifter exerted a major independent effect on reporting levels. The importance of appearance merits further discussion: How to account for its significance?

The evidence presented clearly indicates that a hippie appearance constituted a highly salient basis for social differentiation. From the perspective of "middle class" America, hippies and other beatnik types are viewed as basically unstable, as lacking in ambition and ability, and as marginal contributors to the social system. By the mere fact of being a hippie the person has demonstrated his lack of moral worth, his unrespectability, from the dominant cultural perspective. As such, a hippie label represents a stigma, an extreme negative identity. Such an identity has been variously dealt with as a "master status" by Becker (1963), a "pivotal category" by Lofland (1969), or a "central trait" by Asch (1946). All of these concepts refer to a similar phenomenon: an extreme negative identity can exercise a disproportionate influence in structuring perceptions and behaviors and, in terms of this research, the reactions to shoplifting. A hippie identity or label constitutes, for many subjects in this research, a master status, a pivotal category, or a central trait, which greatly increases the individual's vulnerability to stigmatization as a deviant.[9]

Some anecdotal observations illustrate these notions. These observations also depict the less conscious, less deliberate reactions of the subjects to the hippie identity than to the straight identity. In general, most subjects appeared to be inclined *not* to report the shoplifting incident and to avoid getting involved. When they witnessed the incident and the shoplifter gave off no other negative cues or stimuli they were apt to hesitate. Hesitation of this sort was likely to result in disengagement and failure to report.

Subjects were more likely to hesitate when a shoplifter was straight rather than hippie. A number of subjects, for instance, indicated that they considered reporting the straight shoplifter but thought twice or hesitated before proceeding with a course of action. This "thinking twice" or hesitating then often resulted in their deciding simply to ignore the incident.

But in the case of hippie shoplifters, this hesitation was less likely to occur. That is, when witnessing a hippie shoplifting, the subject was not only more likely to consider reporting but he was also less likely to think twice about it and thus in reality he was more likely to proceed to report. The hippie appearance seemed to tip the scales in the direction of increased reporting.

Further support for the importance of appearance comes from the level of enthusiasm in reporting. In reporting the hippie shoplifter some subjects were very excited—even enthusiastic. Although not true of all subjects, reporting of hippie shoplifters (without prompting) frequently included such comments as "That hippie thing took a package of lunchmeat," or "That son of bitch hippie over there just stuffed a banana down his coat." For these subjects, the high levels of reporting of hippie shoplifters must be viewed within a particular situational context wherein his undoing was not simply a result of his being a shoplifter, but because he was both shoplifter *and* hippie.

Conclusions

Via the use of field research techniques combined with an experimental design we have provided clear support for the basic interactionist-labeling contention that the imputation of deviance resides not only in the *fact* of deviance per se; it also depends heavily on the meanings that the audience attach to the behavior and the actor. Willingness to report deviant acts can be assumed to depend on the "deviant's" other social identities, a significant clue to identity being provided by his appearance.

At the same time, however, some other identities that may seem to be important at first glance may actually prove to be unimportant aspects of the interpersonal relationships between offender and audience. This seemed to be the case with sex of shoplifter and sex of subject, although it is apparent that the complexity of the relationships involved necessitates additional research. Further research should also focus upon other aspects of the social identities of the offender, the situational contexts in which deviant acts occur, and the backgrounds and relevant identities of members of the social audience. At the very least we have demonstrated that in order to get at such problems it is possible and fruitful to utilize experimental field research techniques.

Notes

1. Theoretically the choice of shoplifting is predicated on the assumption that it is a form of deviant behavior which elicits variable social reactions that are usually mild to moderate. Moreover, shoplifting is a sufficiently problematic form of deviance to allow for other deviant identities to influence reactions to it. Several

practical considerations also determined the selection of shoplifting as the object of investigation. It was a behavior around which a field experiment could readily be constructed and that in turn allowed for the observation of a large number of subjects within a limited time period and simultaneously permitted the control and manipulation of the independent variables.

2. In the course of pretesting, we found that for subjects to be aware of the shoplifting as well as for them to be reasonably certain that it was shoplifting, our shoplifters had to be quite blatant and aggressive in their shoplifting. At least one member of the research team had to be reasonably certain that the subject saw the shoplifting.

3. The research accomplices who were assigned the roles of store employees were all males who appeared to be about *25-30* years old. To give as much credibility as possible to the experiment, these accomplices wore the same apparel as the regular store employees. In Stores A and B, long white aprons made the accomplices easily identifiable. However, in Store C regular employees were less well differentiated and thus some minor modifications were introduced in our accomplices in order to ensure their proper identification by subjects. These modifications did not seem to create any noticeable differences in the experimental situation that would affect our interpretation of the data.

4. Backstage refers to an area of the store reserved for store personnel where the researcher and his associates were able to record each event as it happened and plan for the next event without being observed by subjects.

5. Studying behavior in the natural environment raises ethical questions about the deception of subjects and the invasion of their privacy. Should people be used in a social-psychological experiment without their permission or awareness? The question is difficult to answer. We feel that in the case of this study the permission of the subjects was not crucial. None of the subjects expressed hostility toward the experiment and most were highly cooperative. Note, for example, that *178* of the *191* adult subjects completed the postexperimental interview, and *171* of these *178* consented either to a mailed questionnaire or home interview. Careful and thorough pretesting enabled us to avoid numerous problems.

6. Subsequent reports will deal with the effects on reporting levels of size of store and degree of bureaucratization of the store. In general, these variables had little effect on reporting levels and did not affect the relationships between reporting levels and the three variables discussed in this article.

7. Since two of the stores were grocery stores, most things stolen were food items. The remainder consisted of articles of clothing, small appliances, cosmetics, etc. The items shoplifted were of relatively small value, most retailing for less than *$3.00.*

8. A subject was operationally defined as a student if he/she indicated that he/she attended the university full- or part-time and was less than 26 years old. Pretesting indicated that students were highly unlikely to report, irrespective of prompting.

9. Related notions have been dealt with in exchange theory wherein perceived statuses or identities are characterized in terms of positive and negative credits. In dealing with reactions to deviance the reasoning is as follows: the higher the perceived status of an individual the greater his "stock" of esteem, or accumulation of credits. Being involved in visibly deviant behaviors, such as shoplifting, reduces the absolute level of these accumulated credits. However, if a high- (straight-appearing actor) and low- (hippie-appearing actor) status individual commit the same deviant act, the high-status person can retain some level of positive credits

while the low-status person can go to zero or minus quality of credits (Alvarez, 1968; Hollander, 1958; Homans, 1961). Thus having a high status or respectable identity served to "protect" the actor from being reported for shoplifting whereas having a low-status or less-than-respectable identity increases the likelihood of being reported. That is, a hippie appearance reduces actor's level of positive credits to a considerable degree, with the effect that when such an actor engages in deviant behavior, more positive credits are lost and his chances for being reported are greatly increased.

References

Alvarez, R. 1968. "Informal Reactions to Deviance in Simulated Work Organizations: A Laboratory Experiment." *American Sociological Review* 33 (December): 895-911.

Asch, S. E. 1946. "Forming Impressions of Personality." *Journal of Abnormal and Social Psychology* 41:258-90.

Ball, D. W. 1970. "The Problematics of Respectability." In Jack Douglas (ed.), *Respectability and Deviance*. New York: Basic Books.

Becker, Howard S. 1963. *Outsiders: Studies in the Sociology of Deviance*. New York: Free Press.

Bickman, L. 1971. "The Effect of Social Class on the Honesty of Others." *Journal of Social Psychology* 85:87-92.

Black, D. J. 1970. "Production of Crime Rates." *American Sociological Review* 35 (August): 733-48.

Black, D. J., and A. J. Reiss, Jr. 1970. "Police Control of Juveniles." *American Sociological Review* 35 (February): 63-77.

Cameron, Mary O. 1964. *The Booster and the Snitch*. Glencoe: Free Press.

Carey, James T. 1968. *The College Drug Scene*. Englewood Cliffs: Prentice-Hall.

Darley, J. M., and B. Latane. 1968. "Bystander Intervention in Emergencies: Diffusion of Responsibility." *Journal of Personality and Social Psychology* 8:377-83.

Denner, B. 1968. "Did a Crime Occur? Should I Inform Anyone? A Study of Deception." *Journal of Personality* 36:454-68.

Douglas, Jack (ed.). 1970. *Respectability and Deviance*. New York: Basic Books.

———. 1971a. *American Social Order*. New York: Free Press.

———. 1971b. (ed.). *Research on Deviance*. New York: Random House.

Emerson, Robert M. 1969. *Judging Delinquents*. Chicago: Aldine.

Freed, A., P. J. Chandler, R. R. Blake, and J. S. Mouton. 1955. "Stimulus and Background Factors in Sign Violation." *Journal of Personality* 23:499.

Goffman, Erving. 1963. *Stigma: Notes on the Management of Spoiled Identity*. Englewood Cliffs: Spectrum Books.

Hollander, E. P. 1958. "Conformity, Status, and Idiosyncrasy Credit." *Psychological Review* 65: 117-27.

Homans, George C. 1961. *Social Behavior: Its Elementary Forms*. New York: Harcourt, Brace & World.

Hughes, E. C. 1945. "Dilemmas and Contradictions of Status." *American Journal of Sociology* 50 (March): 353-9.

Humphreys, Laud. 1970. *Tearoom Trade*. Chicago: Aldine.

Kitsuse, J. I. 1962. "Societal Reaction to Deviant Behavior: Problems of Theory and Method." *Social Problems* 9:247-56.

Kitsuse, J. I., and A. Cicourel. 1963. "A Note on the Uses of Official Statistics." *Social Problems* 11:131-9.

Kohout, Frank J. 1972. *Applied Statistics*. Forthcoming.

Latane, B., and J. Darley. 1969. "Bystander Apathy." *American Scientist* 57:244-68.

Lefkowitz, M., R. R. Blake, and J. S. Mouton. 1955. "Status Factors in Pedestrian Violation of Traffic Signals." *Journal of Abnormal and Social Psychology* 51:704-705.

Lemert, Edwin. 1951. *Social Pathology*. New York: McGraw-Hill.

Lofland, John. 1969. *Deviance and Identity*. Englewood Cliffs: Prentice-Hall.

Parsons, Talcott, and Robert F. Bales. 1955. *Family Socialization and Interaction Process*. Glencoe: Free Press.

Phillips, D. L. 1964. "Rejection of the Mentally Ill: The Influence of Behavior and Sex." *American Sociological Review* 29 (October): 679-87.

Piliavin, I., and S. Briar. 1964. "Police Encounters with Juveniles." *American Journal of Sociology* 70 (November): 206-14.

Pollak, Otto. 1961. *The Criminality of Women*. New York: Perpetua Books.

Reckless, Walter. 1961. *The Crime Problem*. New York: Appleton-Century-Crofts.

Scheff, Thomas J. 1966. *Being Mentally Ill: A Sociological Theory*. Chicago: Aldine.

Schuessler, Karl. 1971. *Analyzing Social Data*. Boston: Houghton Mifflin.

Schur, E. M. 1969. "Reactions to Deviance: A Critical Assessment." *American Sociological Review*.

Simmons, J. L. 1965. "Public Stereotypes of Deviants." *Social Problems* 13:223-32.

Stone, G. P. 1962. "Appearance and the Self." In Aronld Rose (ed.), *Human Behavior and Social Processes*. Boston: Houghton Mifflin.

Sudnow, D. 1965. "Normal Crimes: Sociological Features of the Penal Code in a Public Defender Office." *Social Problems* 12:255-76.

Ward, David A., and Gene Kassebaum. 1965. *Women's Prison: Sex and Social Structure*. Chicago: Aldine.

Westie, F. R., and J. C. Martin. 1959. "The Tolerant Personality." *American Sociological Review* 24 (August): 521-28.

Whatley, C. D. 1959. "Social Attitudes Toward Discharged Mental Patients." *Social Problems* 6:313-20.

Wheeler, S. 1967. "Criminal Statistics: A Reformulation of the Problem." *Journal of Criminal Law, Criminology, and Police Science* 58: 317-24.

Williams, Robin M., Jr. 1964. *Strangers Next Door*. Englewood Cliffs: Prentice-Hall.

F. K. HEUSSENSTAMM

Bumper Stickers and the Cops

The contingencies of social control and the impact of law and law enforcement on the nature of deviance are important issues in the study of deviance. The distribution of deviance within the population is in part a
function of the ways in which laws are developed and applied differentially within the population. Groups and individuals vary in terms of a
vast variety of characteristics, backgrounds, political viewpoints, social
position and the like. Some of these variations increase the risk that one
will be identified and defined as deviant by control agents.
The police play a particularly crucial role in the identification and definition
of deviance in that their major responsibility consists of enforcing laws
and apprehending miscreants. Studies of police behavior have shown
that despite much official rhetoric about the uniform, impartial and "full
enforcement" activities of the police, their actual practices involve a
highly selective and discretionary application of statutes to persons. At
times, these applications appear to be based more upon the risk contingencies than upon the deviant behavior of the person.
Discretionary or selective enforcement of criminal laws is the rule rather
than the exception for police. Some think that not only is this necessary
in that total enforcement is an impossibility, but also that full enforcement would bring the justice system to a halt and jails and prisons would
overflow. On the other hand, as illustrated in the following report, dis-

Reprinted from F. K. Heussenstamm, "Bumper Stickers and the Cops," *Transaction*,
1971, 8:32-33.

cretionary practices may serve as a shield for discriminatory harassing procedures used by the police selectively against certain individuals and groups.

The article by Heussenstamm tests Black Panther charges of police harassment by having 15 drivers with no record of traffic violations for the preceding 12 months attach "Black Panther" bumper stickers to their cars. The drivers received a total of 33 traffic citations over a period of 17 days with the stickers on their cars. The experiment supported the charges of police harassment.

This research is part of a growing body of evidence about social control agencies and their operation. This evidence sheds considerable light on the structure and functions of social control on the one hand, and on the processes involved in the "creation" or "construction" of deviants on the other. In particular, an examination of the practices of the police vis à vis the public enables one to understand something about how a pool of deviants is created, this pool subsequently serving as the "list" of persons eligible for police attention and as the population of persons who are eligible to become deviants. While many people can become deviants, only some are chosen. Understanding police decision-making will help us to explain why and how some are chosen.

A series of violent, bloody encounters between police and Black Panther Party members punctuated the early summer days of 1969. Soon after, a group of black students I teach at California State College, Los Angeles, who were members of the Panther Party, began to complain of continuous harassment by law enforcement officers. Among their many grievances, they complained about receiving so many traffic citations that some were in danger of losing their driving privileegs. During one lengthy discussion, we realized that all of them drove automobiles with Panther Party signs glued to their bumpers. This is a report of a study that I undertook to assess the seriousness of their charges and to determine whether we were hearing the voice of paranoia or reality.

Recruitment advertising for subjects to participate in the research elicited 45 possible subjects from the student body. Careful screening thinned the ranks to 15—five black, five white, and five of Mexican descent. Each group included three males and two females. Although the college enrolls more than 20,000 students (largest minority group numbers on the west coast), it provides no residential facilities; all participants, of necessity then, traveled to campus daily on freeways or surface streets. The average round trip was roughly ten miles, but some drove as far as 18 miles. Eleven of the 15 had part-time jobs which included driving to and from work after class as well.

All participants in the study had exemplary driving records, attested to by a sworn statement that each driver had received no "moving" traffic violations in the preceding twelve months. In addition, each promised to continue to drive in accordance with all in-force Department of Motor Vehicles regulations. Each student signed another statement, to the effect that he would do nothing to "attract the attention" of either police, sheriff's deputies or highway patrolmen—all of whom survey traffic in Los Angeles county. The participants declared that their cars, which ranged from a "flower child" hippie van to standard American makes of all types, had no defective equipment. Lights, horns, brakes and tires were duly inspected and pronounced satisfactory.

The appearance of the drivers was varied. There were three blacks with processed hair and two with exaggerated naturals, two white-shirt-and-necktie, straight caucasians and a shoulder-length-maned hippie, and two mustached-and sideburn-sporting Mexican-Americans. All wore typical campus dress, with the exception of the resident hippie and the militant blacks, who sometimes wore dashikis.

A fund of $500 was obtained from a private source to pay fines for any citations received by the driving pool and students were briefed on the purposes of the study. After a review of lawful operation of motor vehicles, all agreed on the seriousness of receiving excessive moving traffic violations. In California, four citations within a twelve-month period precipitates automatic examination of driving records, with a year of probation likely, or, depending on the seriousness of the offenses, suspension of the driver's license for varying lengths of time. Probation or suspension is usually accompanied by commensurate increases in insurance premiums. Thus, the students knew they were accepting considerable personal jeopardy as a condition of involvement in the study.

Bumper stickers in lurid day-glo orange and black, depicting a menacing panther with large BLACK PANTHER lettering were attached to the rear bumper of each subject car and the study began. The first student received a ticket for making an "incorrect lane change" on the freeway less than two hours after heading home in the rush hour traffic. Five more tickets were received by others on the second day for "following too closely." "failing to yield the right of way," "driving too slowly in the high-speed lane of the freeway," "failure to make a proper signal before turning right at an intersection," and "failure to observe proper safety of pedestrians using a crosswalk." On day three, students were cited for "excessive speed," "making unsafe lane changes" and "driving erratically." And so it went every day.

One student was forced to drop out of the study by day four, because he had already received three citations. Three others reached what we had agreed was the maximum limit—three citations—within the first week. Altogether, the participants received 33 citations in 17 days, and the violations fund was exhausted.

Drivers reported that their encounters with the intercepting officers ranged from affable and "standard polite" to surly, accompanied by search of the vehicle. Five cars were thoroughly gone over and their drivers were shaken down. One white girl, a striking blonde and a member of a leading campus sorority, was questioned at length about her reasons for supporting the "criminal activity" of the Black Panther Party. This was the only time that an actual reference to the bumper stickers was made during any of the ticketings. Students, by prior agreement, made no effort to dissuade officers from giving citations, once the vehicle had been halted.

Pledges to Drive Safely

Students received citations equally, regardless of race or sex or ethnicity or personal appearance. Being in jeopardy made them "nervous" and "edgy" and they reported being very uncomfortable whenever they were in their automobiles. After the first few days, black students stopped saying "I told you so," and showed a sober, demoralized air of futility. Continuous pledges to safe driving were made daily, and all expressed increasing incredulity as the totals mounted. They paid their fines in person immediately after receiving a citation. One student received his second ticket on the way to pay his fine for the first one.

No student requested a court appearance to protest a citation, regardless of the circumstances surrounding a ticketing incident. When the investigator announced the end of the study on the eighteenth day, the remaining drivers expressed relief, and went straight to their cars to remove the stickers.

Some citations were undoubtedly deserved. How many, we cannot be sure. A tightly designed replication of this study would involve control of make and year of cars through the use of standard rented vehicles of low-intensity color. A driving pool of individuals who represented an equal number of both extreme-left and straight-looking appearance with matched age-range could be developed. Drivers could be assigned at random to pre-selected, alternate routes of a set length. Both left-wing and right-wing bumper stickers could also be attached at random after drivers were seated in their assigned vehicles and the doors sealed. In this way, no subject would know in advance whether he was driving around with "Black Panther Party" or "America Love It Or Leave It" on his auto. This would permit us to check actual driving behavior in a more reliable way. We might also wish to include a tape recorder in each car to preserve the dialogue at citation incidents.

No More Stickers

It is possible, of course, that the subject's bias influenced his driving, making it less circumspect than usual. But it is statistically unlikely that this number of previously "safe" drivers could amass such a collection of tickets without assuming real bias by police against drivers with Black Panther bumper stickers.

The reactions of the traffic officers might have been influenced, and we hypothesize that they were, by the recent deaths of police in collision with Black Panther Party members. But whatever the provocation, unwarranted traffic citations are a clear violation of the civil rights of citizens, and cannot be tolerated. Unattended, the ligitimate grievances of the black community against individuals who represent agencies of the dominant society contribute to the climate of hostility between the races at all levels, and predispose victims to acts of violent retaliation.

As a footnote to this study, I should mention that Black Panther bumper stickers are not seen in Los Angeles these days, although the party has considerable local strength. Apparently members discovered for themselves the danger of blatantly announcing their politics on their bumpers, and have long since removed the "incriminating" evidence.

ROBERT ROSENTHAL
and
LENORE JACOBSON[1]

Self-Fulfilling Prophecies in the Classroom:

Teachers' Expectations as Unintended Determinants of Pupils' Intellectual Competence

One of the major questions raised by the interactionist-labeling perspective is "What are the consequences of being defined and labeled as
deviant for the person's self-attitudes and interpersonal relations?" This
question obviously implies that the deviant's behavior can be substantially influenced by the perceptions and reactions of others. In order to
describe a specific aspect of this more general process, the term "self-
fulfilling prophecy" has become widely used. According to Merton, who
coined the term:

> The self-fulfilling prophecy is, in the beginning, a false definition of
> the situation evoking a new behavior which makes the originally false
> conception come true. The specious validity of the self-fulfilling
> prophecy perpetuates a reign of error. For the prophet will cite the
> actual course of events as proof that he was right from the very be-
> ginning. . . . Such are the perversities of social logic. (Robert K. Mer-
> ton, *Social Theory and Social Structure,* New York: The Free Press,
> 1957, p. 423.)

In particular, treating a person as though he were generally rather than specifically deviant is likely to result in the phenonmenon of the self-fulfilling

prophecy by setting in motion a number of processes which tend to shape the person along the lines of the images others have of him.

Considerable anecdotal evidence exists to support the existence of self-fulfilling prophecies although there is surprisingly little empirical evidence that does so. The recent experiment by Rosenthal and Jacobson reported below is a major exception. They attempted to assess the effects of teacher expectations on the performance of children on IQ tests and class work. Their study supports the notion that social expectations and beliefs can set in motion self-fulfilling prophecies, at least within the educational process.

When teachers were told that certain randomly selected students would increase their IQ levels during the year, the performanc of the designated students did tend to increase. As one would expect, this effect was greatest among the younger children. These findings are interpreted as indicating that the teachers were encouraging and friendly to the children from whom they expected better performances and these altered expectations and actions on the part of the teachers motivated the children to perform better.

Several methodological problems in this research should be noted. The reliability of the IQ test given and the mode of repeated administration of the tests may have biased the findings in the direction of producing more significant differences than really existed between the potentially bright students and other students. Also, while the interpretation of the authors makes sense, especially in the light of the interactionist-labeling perspective, the authors never directly observed whether or not the teachers did in fact act differently toward the children in the experimental group.

Despite these criticisms the basic comparison of experimental and control groups demonstrate striking differences, especially in the three early grades. The findings are suggestive of the effects of deviant labeling processes for self-attitudes, interpersonal relations and subsequent deviant careers.

Finally, the Rosenthal and Jacobson study is especially noteworthy because it deals with positive deviance and the effects of positive labels in generating desirable behavior. As such, it illustrates the similarity in the processes and consequences of social differentiation for both positive and negative varieties of deviant behavior.

With increasing concern over what can be done to reduce the disparity of opportunity of education, of intellectual motivation, and of competence that exists between the social classes and the colors of our school children, attention has been focused more and more on the role of the classroom teacher, and the possible effects of her values, her attitudes, and, especially, her beliefs and expectations. Asbell (1963), Becker (1952), Clark (1963), Gibson (1965), Harlem Youth Opportunities Unlimited (1964), Katz (1964), Kvaraceus (1965), MacKinnon, (1962), Riessman (1962, 1965), Rose (1956) and Wilson (1963) have all expressed their belief that the teacher's expectation of pupils' performance may serve as an educational self-fulfilling prophecy. The teacher gets less because she expects less—that is the essence of the positions cited.

The concept of the self-fulfilling prophecy has been applied in many contexts other than education. As early as 1898, Albert Moll mentioned ". . . the phophecy (which) causes its own fulfillment" (p. 244) as the source of cures of hysterical paralyses, insomnia, nausea, impotence and stammering. His particular interest was in the phenomenon of hypnosis. Subjects, he believed, behaved as they were expected to behave by the hypnotist. Some six decades later Orne (1959) showed that for the hypnosis situation, Moll was quite right.

In the analysis of large-scale social and economic phenomena, both Merton (1948) and Allport (1950) applied the concept of self-fulfilling prophecies. Merton used the concept to explain racial and religious prejudice and the collapse of economic systems. Allport suggested that nations that expect to go to war, do go to war. The expectation to wage war is communicated to the opponent-to-be who reacts by preparing for war, an act which confirms the first nation's expectation, strengthens it, leads to greater preparations for war, and so on, in a mutually reinforcing system of positive feedback loops. Nations expecting to remain out of wars sometimes seem to manage to avoid entering into them.

The self-fulfilling prophecy has been investigated in everyday life situations. Whyte (1943) in a study of a street-corner gang found that the group "knew how well a man should bowl." On a given evening the group "knew" that a given member would bowl well, and so he did. On another evening, the group "knew" that some member would bowl poorly, and so he did, even if he had bowled well the week before. The group, through its behavior toward the target member, fulfilled its prophecy for that member's performance.

The self-fulfilling prophecy has been observed in the world of work as well as in the word of recreation. Jastrow (1900) tells some details. The Hollerith tabulating machine had just been installed at the United States Census Bureau. The machine, something like a typewriter, required the clerks to learn a new skill which the inventor, Hollerith, regarded as quite demanding. He expected that a trained worker could punch about 550 cards per day. After two weeks the workers were adequately trained and began to produce about 550 cards per day. After a while the clerks began to exceed the expected performance, but only at great emotional cost. Workers became so tense trying to beat the expected limit that the Secretary of the Interior forbade the establishment of any minimum-performance criterion. This was seen as a step necessary to preserve the mental health of the establishment.

Then a new group of some two hundred clerks was brought in to augment the Hollerith machine work force. These clerks knew nothing of the work, had no prior training, and had never even seen the machines. No one had told these workers what the emotional cost of the work might be, nor of the upper limit of production which could be achieved. Within three days this new group was performing at the level which was reached only after seven weeks by the earlier, properly indoctrinated group. Whereas clerks from the initial group were exhausted from producing 700 cards per day, members of the new group began turning out three times that number without ill effects.

In the behavioral sciences the expectation of the experimenter or data-collector has been shown to affect the responses he obtains from his subjects (Rosenthal, 1966). In a variety of experimental tasks the paradigm has been the same. Half the experimenters are led to expect one type of response from their subjects; half are led to expect the opposite type of response. In some way these expectations turn out to function as self-fulfilling prophecies. Subjects contacted by experimenters expecting data Type X, give Type X responses. Subjects contacted by experimenters expecting data Type Y, give Type Y responses. Some of the studies of the self-fulfilling prophecy in experimental situations are particularly relevant to the theme of this chapter and will be described below.

The literature on the self-fulfilling prophecy in survey research is a venerable one. As early as 1929, Rice found that interviewers' expectations could be related to their respondents' replies. In a study of applicants for welfare funds, Rice found that the "causes" of destitution could be predicted from a knowledge of the interviewers' expectations. Thus, a prohibitionist interviewer obtained three times as many responses implicating Demon Rum as did a socialist interviewer who, in turn, obtained 50 percent more responses implicating industrial factors than did the prohibitionist interviewer. In this study as in most of the others reviewed, we cannot be certain whether a self-fulfilling prophecy accounted for the findings. Congruence of prophecy and prophesied behavior has been demonstrated. But the prophecy may have been based on the prior behavior of the person or persons whose behavior was prophesied so that the prophecy was, in a sense, "contaminated" by reality. If a physician predicts a patient's improvement, we cannot say whether the doctor is giving a sophisticated prognosis or whether the patient's improvement is based in part on the optimism engendered by the physician's prediction. If school children who perform poorly are those expected by their teachers to perform poorly, is the teacher's expectation the "cause" of the pupils' poor performance, or is the teacher's expectation rather an accurate prognosis of performance based on knowledge of past performance? To help answer this question, experiments are required in which the expectation is clearly the independent variable, uncontaminated by the past behavior of the person whose performance is predicted.

A recent experiment was designed to test the hypothesis that, within a given classroom, those children from whom the teacher expected greater growth in intellectual competence would show such greater growth (Rosenthal and Jacobson, 1966). The Harvard Test of Inflected Acquisition was administered to all the children in an elementary school in the spring of 1964. This test was purported to predict academic "blooming" or intellectual growth. The reason for administering the test in the particular school was ostensibly to perform a final check on the validity of the test, a validity which was presented as already well established. Actually, the Harvard Test of Inflected Acquisition was a standardized relatively nonverbal test of intelligence, Flanagan's (1960) Tests of General Ability.

Within each of the six grades of the elementary school, there were three classrooms, one each for children performing at above-average, average, and below-average levels of scholastic achievement. In each of the eighteen classrooms of the school about 20 percent of the children were designated as academic "spurters." The names of these children were reported to their new teachers in the fall of 1964 as those who, during the academic year ahead, would show unusual intellectual gains. The "fact" of their intellectual potential was established from their scores on the test for "intellectual blooming."

Teachers were cautioned not to discuss the test findings with either their pupils or the children's parents. Actually, the names of the 20 percent of the children assigned to the "spurting" condition had been selected by means of a table of random numbers. The difference, then, between these children earmarked for intellectual growth and the undesignated control children was in the mind of the teacher.

THE SCHOOL AS A WHOLE. Four months after the teachers had been given the names of the "special" children, all the children once again took the same form of the nonverbal test of intelligence. Four months after this retest, the children took the same test once again. This final retest was at the end of the school year, some eight months after the teachers had been given the expectation for intellectual growth of the special children. These retests were not, of course, explained as "retests" to the teachers but rather as future efforts to predict intellectual growth.

The intelligence test employed, while relatively nonverbal in the sense of requiring no speaking, reading, or writing, was not entirely nonverbal. Actually there were two subtests, one requiring a greater comprehension of English—a kind of picture vocabulary. The other subtest required less ability to understand any spoken language, but more ability to reason abstractly. For shorthand purposes we refer to the former as a *verbal* subtest and to the latter as a *reasoning* subtest. The pretest correlation between these subtests was +0.42.

Table 6.3 shows the means and standard deviations of gains in IQ and MA by the children of the control group and the experimental group after eight months. For the school as a whole, the children of the experimental groups did not show a significantly greater gain in verbal IQ and mental age than did the control-group children. However, in total IQ and mental age, and especially in the reasoning IQ and mental age, the experimental children gained more than did the control children. Even after the fourth-month retest this trend was already in evidence though the effects were smaller.

TABLE 6.3. Means and Standard Deviations of Gains in Intellectual Performance

| | | Control | | | Experimental | | Difference between | |
	N	Mean	S.D.a	N	Mean	S.D.	Means	pb
Verbal IQ	269	7.8	17.7	68	9.9	21.9	2.1	
Reasoning IQ	255	15.7	28.6	65	22.9	31.3	7.2	0.03
Total IQ	255	8.4	13.5	65	12.2	15.0	3.8	0.02
Verbal MA	269	1.8	1.8	68	2.0	2.2	0.2	
Reasoning MA	255	2.3	2.4	65	3.0	2.8	0.7	0.02
Total MA	255	1.8	1.3	65	2.1	1.4	0.3	0.02

a S.D., standard deviation.
b Error term for all tests of significance is mean square within treatments in classrooms.

Toward the end of the school year of this study, all teachers were asked to rate each of their pupils on the following variables: the extent to which they would be successful in the future, and the degree to which they could be described as interesting, curious, happy, appealing, adjusted, affectionate, hostile, and motivated by a need for social approval. A comparison of the experimental and control children on each of these variables was thought to be valuable to obtain some idea of the effect of the experimental treatment on behavior other than intellectual-test performance. In addition, it was thought that differences in teachers' perceptions of the experimental and control children might be suggestive of the mechanism whereby a teacher communicates her expectation to her pupils. There is, of course, no way to be sure that the children's behavior was accurately described by the teachers. If it were, and if the experimental- and control-group children differed in their classroom behavior, we would know at least that changes in intellectual ability were accompanied by changes in other classroom behavior. If the teachers' descriptions of the children's behavior were not accurate, any differences in the descriptions of the experimental and control children could be ascribed to a kind of halo effect. Such a halo effect might suggest the possibility that altered perceptions of children's behavior might be associated with differences in teachers' treatment of the children, such treatment differences leading to differences in intellectual performance and remaining to be discovered. In Table

6.4 are found the mean ratings of the children of each experimental condition on each of the nine characteristics described earlier.

The children from whom intellectual growth was expected were described as having a significantly better chance of becoming successful in the future, as significantly more interesting, curious, and happy. There was a tendency, too, for these children to be seen as more appealing, adjusted, and affectionate and as lower in the need for social approval. In short, the children from whom intellectual growth was expected became more intellectually alive and autonomous, or at least were so perceived by their teachers.

We have already seen that the children of the experimental group gained more intellectually so that the possibility exists that it was the fact of such gaining that accounted for the more favorable ratings of these children's behavior and aptitude. But a great many of the control-group children also gained in IQ during the course of the year. Perhaps those who gained more intellectually among these undesignated children would also be rated more favorably by their teachers. Such was not the case, however. The more the control-group children gained in verbal IQ the more they were regarded as less well-adjusted ($r = -0.13, p < 0.05$). Among the experimental-group children the greater their gains in verbal IQ the more they were regarded as more likely to be successful in the future ($r = +0.22, p < 0.10$), as happier ($r = +0.21, p < 0.10$), and as less affectionate ($r = -0.22, p < 0.10$).

Those children of the control group who gained more in reasoning IQ came to be regarded as less interesting ($r = -0.14, p < 0.05$) and less affectionate ($r = -0.13, p < 0.05$). The children of the experimental group who gained more in reasoning IQ came to be regarded as more likely to succeed ($r = +0.22, p < 0.10$), better adjusted ($r = +0.36, p < 0.01$), more affectionate ($r = +0.25, p < 0.05$) and as lower in their need for social approval ($r = -0.24, p < 0.10$). Relative to the control-group children who gained more in reasoning IQ, the experimental-group children who gained more in reasoning IQ were seen as significantly more interesting, more happy, better adjusted, and more affectionate.

TABLE 6.4. Mean Ratings by Teachers of Children in Experimental and Control Groups

Characteristics	Control	Experimental	Difference	p
Future success	5.53	6.48	0.95	0.0006
Interesting	5.46	6.43	0.97	0.0008
Curious	5.50	6.25	0.75	0.01
Happy	5.77	6.33	0.56	0.05
Appealing	5.78	6.23	0.45	0.14
Adjusted	5.67	6.04	0.37	0.22
Affectionate	5.72	6.01	0.29	0.28
Hostile	3.84	3.97	0.13	
Needs approval	5.35	4.97	—0.38	0.20

TABLE 6.5. Means and Standard Deviations of Gains in Total IQ for Six Grades

Grade	N	Control Mean	S.D.	N	Experimental Mean	S.D.	Difference between means	pa
1	48	12.0	16.6	7	27.4	12.5	15.4	0.002
2	47	7.0	10.0	12	16.5	18.6	9.5	0.02
3	40	5.0	11.9	14	5.0	9.3	0.0	
4	49	2.2	13.4	12	5.6	11.0	3.4	
5	26	17.5	13.1	9	17.4	17.8	— 0.1	
6	45	10.7	10.0	11	10.0	6.5	— 0.7	

a Error term for all tests of significance is mean square within treatments in classrooms.

From these results and from the similar results based on total-IQ gains it would seem that when children who are expected to grow intellectually do so, they are considerably benefited in other ways as well. When children who are not especially expected to develop intellectually do so, they seem either to show accompanying undesirable behavior, or at least are perceived by their teachers as showing such undesirable behavior. If a child is to show intellectual gains it seems to be better for his real or perceived intellectual vitality and for his real or perceived mental health if his teacher has been expecting him to gain intellectually. It appears that there may be hazards to unpredicted intellectual growth.

THE SIX GRADES. So far we have examined the effects of teachers' expectations only for the school as a whole. Table 6.5 shows the mean gains in total-IQ points from the pretest to the final posttest among experimental- and control-group children for each of the six grades. As we go from the higher grades to the lower grades we find the effects of teacher expectations increasing almost monotonically (*rho* = 0.94, *p* = 0.02) and only in the first and second grades do we find the total IQ changes to be affected to a statistically significant degree. In one of the three classrooms comprising the first grade, the control-group children gained an average of 16.2 IQ points, whereas the experimentals gained an average of 41.0 points, a difference of nearly 25 points ($p < 0.006$). The largest effect of teachers' expectations to occur in the second grade was in a classroom which found the control-group children gaining 4.3 IQ points while the experimental-group children gained 22.5 points, a difference of over 18 points ($p < 0.002$).

Another useful way to show the effects of teachers' expectations on their pupils' total-IQ gains is to show the percentage of experimental and control-group children who achieve various amounts of gain. In Table 6.6 such percentages are shown for the first and second grades only. Less than half the control-group children gained 10 or more total IQ points, but about four out of five experimental-group children did. Every fifth control-group child gained 20 or more total-IQ points, but nearly every second experimental-group child did. While only one out of twenty control-group children gained thirty or more total-IQ points, one out of five experimental-group children did.

Earlier it was noted that for the school as a whole the effects of teachers' expectations on children's gains in reasoning IQ were greater than they were on children's gains in verbal IQ. The results for grades and for classrooms were consistent with the over-all finding. On the whole, verbal IQ was not much affected by teachers' expectations. In only twelve of the eighteen classrooms was there a greater gain in verbal IQ among children from whom intellectual gains were expected ($p = 0.12$) and the bulk of the verbal-IQ gain favoring the experimental-group children occurred in the first two grades.

It was in the gains in reasoning IQ that the effect of teachers' expectations showed itself more clearly. Of the seventeen classrooms in which the posttest reasoning-IQ tests had been administered (one class was inadvertently not retested for reasoning IQ) fifteen showed greater gains among the children from whom intellectual growth had been expected ($p < 0.001$). Although the advantage in terms of gain in reasoning IQ of having been predicted to "spurt" was significant statistically only in the second grade, the absolute magnitude of advantage was not trivial in any of the first five grades. In fourteen of the seventeen classrooms in which the comparison was possible, the excess of reasoning-IQ gain of the experimental- compared to the control-group children was greater than the excess of verbal-IQ gain ($p = 0.006$).

**TABLE 6.6. Percentages of First- and Second-Grade Children Gaining
10 or more, 20 or more, 30 or more, Total IQ Points**

IQ Gain at Least:	Control N = 95	Experimental N = 19	p of difference
10 points[a]	49	79	0.02
20 points[b]	19	47	0.01
30 points	5	21	0.04

a Includes children gaining 20 and 30 points or more.
b Includes children gaining 30 points or more.

**TABLE 6.7. Differences in Mean Ratings by Teachers of Children in
Experimental and Control Groups in Six Grade Levels**

Characteristics	Grade Level					
	1	2	3	4	5	6
Future success	+2.4[d]	+1.7[c]	—0.0	+0.4	+0.6	+1.2[a]
Interesting	+3.0[e]	+0.9	+0.2	+0.3	+0.1	+1.8[c]
Curious	+2.4[c]	+1.1[a]	—0.5	+0.7	—0.8	+1.9[c]
Happy	+1.6[a]	+1.0	—0.5	+0.1	+0.5	+1.1
Appealing	+1.6[a]	+0.7	—1.3[b]	—0.1	—0.2	+2.2[d]
Adjusted	+2.2[b]	+0.9	—0.7	—0.2	+0.3	+0.7
Affectionate	+1.1	—0.1	—0.7	+0.8	—0.4	+1.2[a]
Hostile	+0.4	—0.2	+1.3[a]	—0.1	—0.4	—0.4
Needs approval	—2.2[b]	—1.0	—0.1	+0.6	—0.4	+0.3

a $p < .10$.
b $p < .05$.
c $p < .01$.
d $p < .005$.
e $p < .0005$.

How did the teachers' expectations come to serve as determinants of gains in intellectual performance? The most plausible hypothesis seemed to be that the children for whom unusual intellectual growth had been predicted would be more attended to by their teachers. If teachers were more attentive to the children earmarked for growth, we might expect that teachers might be robbing Peter to see Paul grow. With a finite amount of time to spend with each child, if a teacher gave more time to the children of the experimental group, she would have less time to spend with the children of the control group. If the teacher's spending more time with a child led to greater gains, we could test the "robbing-Peter" hypothesis by comparing the gains made by children of the experimental group with gains made by children of the control group in each class. The "robbing-Peter" hypothesis predicts a negative correlation. The greater the gains made by the children of the experimental group (with the implication of more time spent on them) the less should be the gains made by the children of the control group (with the implication of less time spent on them). In fact, however, the correlation was positive, large, and statistically significant ($rho = +0.57$, $p = 0.02$, two tail). The greater the gain made by the children of whom gain was expected, the greater the gain made in the same classroom by the children from whom no special gain was expected. The evidence presented that teachers did not take time from control-group children to spend with the experimental-group children is indirect. More direct evidence was available.

Some ten months after the posttest had been administered, each of the teachers was asked to estimate how much time, relatively, she had devoted to each of four children. All four of these children had been in her classroom the preceding academic year; two had been in the control group and two had been in the experimental group. There was one boy and one girl in each of these

TABLE 6.11. Differences in Time Spent with Children of the Experimental and Control Groups

	Mean Difference	Median Difference	N of Pairs[a]
	%	%	
All children	—2.6	0.0	31
Boys	+0.3	+5.0	15
Girls	—5.3	0.0	16
Fast track	—2.4	0.0	12
Medium track	—5.0	0.0	8
Slow track	—1.1	0.0	11
Grade 1	+5.0	0.0	6
Grade 2	—8.8	0.0	5
Grade 3	+10.0	+10.0	4
Grade 4	—3.3	0.0	6
Grade 5	—2.5	—2.5	4
Grade 6	—12.8	0.0	6

[a] No data were available from the two teachers who had left the school.

two subgroups. The boys of each group were matched on their pretest IQ, as were the girls. The mean difference in IQ was les than one-half point in favor of the children of the experimental group ($t < 0.71$). The specific question asked of the teacher was: Given a unit of time available to spend on these four children (100 percent), how much of that unit was spent with each child? For each matched pair of boys and girls the percentage of time allocated to the control-group child was subtracted from the percentage of time allocated to the experimental-group child. A positive difference score, then, meant that the experimental-group child was given more time by the teacher according to her own assessment. Table 6.11 shows the mean and median difference scores for the entire school, for boys and girls, for each of the three tracks, and for each of the six grades. None of the obtained mean differences was significantly different from zero. In fact, there was a slight tendency for the children of the experimental group to be given less time than the children of the control group ($t < 0.66$).

That the children of the experimental group were not favored with a greater investment of time seems less surprising in view of the pattern of their greater intellectual gains. If, for example, teachers had talked to them more we might have expected greater gains in verbal IQ but, we recall, the greater gains were found not in verbal but in reasoning IQ. It may be, of course, that the teachers were inaccurate in their estimates of time spent with each of the four children. Possibly direct observation of the teacher-pupil interactions would have given different results, but that method was not possible in the present study. Even direct observation by judges who could agree with one another might not have revealed a difference in the amounts of teacher time invested in each of the two groups of children. It seems plausible to think that it was not a difference in amount of time spent with the children of the two groups which led to the difference in their rates of intellectual development. It may have been more a matter of the type of interaction which took place between the teachers and their pupils which served as the determinant of the expected intellectual development.

By what she said, by how she said it, by her facial expressions, postures, and perhaps, by her touch, the teacher may have communicated to the children of the experimental group that she expected improved intellectual performance. Such communications together with possible changes in teaching techniques may have helped the child learn by changing his self-concept, his expectations of his own behavior, his motivation, as well as his cognitive skills. It is self-evident that further research is needed to narrow the range of possible mechanisms whereby a teacher's expectations become translated into a pupil's intellectual growth. It would be valuable, for example, to have sound films of teachers interacting with their pupils. We might then look for differences in the way teachers interact with those children from whom they expect intellectual growth compared to those from whom they expect less. On the basis of films of psychological experiments interacting with subjects from whom different responses are expected, we know that even in such highly standardized situations unintential communications can be incredibly subtle and complex (Rosenthal, 1966). How much more subtle and complex may be the communications between children and their teachers who are not constrained by the demands of the experimental laboratory.

Some Implications

The results of the experiment just now described provide further evidence that one person's expectations of another's behavior may serve as a self-fulfilling prophecy. When teachers expected that certain children would show greater intellectual development, those children did show greater intellectual development. The effect was in evidence, however, primarily at the lower-grade levels, and it is difficult to be certain why that was the case. A number of interpretations suggest themselves, and these are not mutually exclusive.

First, younger children are generally regarded as more malleable, less fixed, more capable of change. It may be, then, that the experimental conditions of this experiment were more effective with younger children simply because younger children are easier to change than older ones. (It should be recalled that when we speak here of change we mean it as change relative to control-group change. Table 6.5 shows that even fifth-graders can change dramatically in IQ, but there the change of the experimental-group children is not greater than the change of the control-group children.)

A second interpretation is that younger children within a given school have less well-established reputations within the school. It then becomes more credible to a teacher to be told that a younger child will show intellectual growth. A teacher may "know" an older child much better by reputation and be less inclined to believe him capable of intellectual growth simply on someone else's say-so.

A third interpretation is a combination, in a sense, of the first two. It suggests that younger children show greater gains associated with teachers' expectancies not because they necessarily *are* more malleable but rather because they are believed by teachers to be more malleable.

A fourth interpretation suggests that younger children are more sensitive to, and more affected by, the particular processes whereby teachers communicate their expectations to children. Within this interpretation, it is possible that teachers react to children of all grade levels in the same way if they believe them to be capable of intellectual gain. But perhaps it is only the younger children whose performance is affected by the special things the teacher says to them, the special ways in which she says them, the way she looks, postures, and touches the children from whom she expects greater intellectual growth.

A fifth interpretation suggests that the effects of teachers' expectations were more effective in the lower-grade levels not because of any difference associated with the children's age but rather with some correlated sampling errors. Thus it is possible that the children of the lower grades are the children of families which differ systematically from the families of the children of the higher-grade levels.

A sixth interpretation also suggests that the greater IQ gain in younger children attributable to teacher expectation is a result of sampling error, not in the sampling of children this time but in the sampling of teachers. It may be that in a variety of demographic, intellectual, and personality variables the teachers of the younger children differed from the teachers of the older children such that they may have (1) believed the communications about their "special" children more, or (2) been more effective communicators to their children of their expectations for the children's performance.

Those children from whom greater intellectual gains were expected showed advantages over their classmates other than greater gain in intellectual performance. They were also judged by their teachers to be more likely to succeed, to be more intellectually alive and to be more superior in their socioemotional functioning and mental health. These effects on teachers' perceptions of the children might have been reflective of either actual behavior differences in the children or of the operation of a halo effect. Even if these ratings reflected only halo effects, however, they may not be trivial in implications. Halo effects may determine not only teachers' perceptions of children but, as the results of this experiment suggest, the subsequent behavior of children as well.

The more the children who were expected to gain intellectually did so, the more favorably they were evaluated by their teachers. Not so, however, for the children who were not expected to show any particular growth in intellectual functioning. The trend, in fact, was for these children to be regarded less favorably the more they gained intellectually. That finding suggests the hypothesis that there may be hazards to unexpected intellectual growth. Classroom teachers may not be prepared to assimilate the unexpected classroom behavior of the intellectually upwardly mobile child.

Perhaps the most suitable summary of the hypothesis discussed in this chapter and tested by the described experiment has already been written. The writer is G. B. Shaw, the play is *Pygmalion,* and the speaker is Eliza Doolittle:

> You see, really and truly, apart from the things anyone can pick up (the dressing and the proper way of speaking, and so on), the difference between a lady and a flower girl is not how she behaves, but how she's treated. I shall always be a flower girl to Professor Higgins, because he always treats me as

a flower girl, and always will; but I know I can be a lady to you, because you always treat me as a lady, and always will.

Notes

1. Robert Rosenthal is at Harvard University, and Lenore Jacobson is in the South San Francisco Unified School District. Preparation of this chapter and much of the research reported was supported by the Division of Social Sciences of the National Science Foundation. An earlier draft of this chapter was the basis for a paper read at the annual meeting of the American Psychological Association, New York City, September 1966.

References

Allport, G. W. "The role of expectancy." In H. Cantril (ed.), *Tensions that cause wars.* Urbana, Ill.: University of Illinois, 1950, 43-78.

Asbell, B. Not like other children. *Redbook,* October, 1963.

Becker, H. S. Social class variations in the teacher-pupil relationship. *Journal of Educational Sociology,* 1952, 25, 451-465.

Bruner, J. S. *The process of education.* Cambridge, Mass.: Harvard University Press, 1960.

——. The growth of mind. *American Psychologist,* 1965, 20, 1007-1017.

Clark, K. B. "Educational stimulation of racially disadvantaged children." In A. H. Passow (ed.), *Education in depressed areas.* New York: Teachers College, Columbia University, 1963, 142-162.

Flanagan, J. C. *Tests of general ability: Technical report.* Chicago: Science Research Associates, 1960.

Flowers, C. E. Effects of an arbitrary accelerated group placement on the tested academic achievement of educationally disadvantaged students. Unpublished doctoral dissertation, Teachers College, Columbia University, 1966.

Gibson, G. Aptitude tests. *Science,* 1965, 149, 583.

Gruenberg, B. C. *The story of evolution.* Princeton, N. J.: Van Nostrand, 1929.

Harlem Youth Opportunities Unlimited, Inc. *Youth in the ghetto.* New York: HARYOU, 1964.

Hurwitz, Susan, and Virginia Jenkins. Effects of experimenter expectancy on performance of simple learning tasks. Unpublished paper, Harvard University, 1966.

Jastrow, J. *Fact and fable in psychology.* Boston: Houghton Mifflin, 1900.

Katz, I. Review of evidence relating to effects of desegragation on the intellectual performance of Negroes. *American Psychologist,* 1964, 19, 381-399.

Kvaraceus, W. C. Disadvantaged children and youth: Programs of promise or pretense? *Proceedings of the 17th annual state conference on educational research.* California Advisory Council on Educational Research, Burlingame: California Teachers' Association, 1965.

MacKinnon, D. W. The nature and nurture of creative talent. *American Psychologist,* 1962, 17, 484-495.

Marwit, S., and J. Marcia. Tester-bias and response to projective instruments. Unpublished paper, State University of New York at Buffalo, 1966.

Masling, J. Differential indoctrination of examiners and Rorschach responses. *Journal of Consulting Psychology*, 1965, 29, 198-201.

Merton, R. K. The self-fulfilling prophecy. *Antioch-Review*, 1948, 8, 193-210.

Moll, A. *Hypnotism*. Ed. 4. New York: Scribner's, 1898.

Orne, M. T. The nature of hypnosis: Artifacts and essence. *Journal of Abnormal and Social Psychology*, 1959, 58, 277-299.

——. On the social psychology of the psychological experiment: With particular reference to demand characteristics and their implications. *American Psychologist*. 1962, 17, 776-783.

Pfungst, O. *Clever Hans (the horse of Mr. von Osten): A contribution to experimental, animal, and human psychology*. Translated by C. L. Rahn. New York: Holt, Rinehart and Winston, 1911.

Rice, S. A. Contagious bias in the interview: A methodological note. *American Journal of Sociology*, 1929, 35, 420-423.

Riessman, F. *The culturally deprived child*. New York: Harper & Row, 1962.

——. Teachers of the poor: A five point plan. *Proceedings of the 17th annual state conference on educational research*. California Advisory Council on Educational Research. Burlingame: California Teachers' Association, 1965.

Rose, A. *The Negro in America*. Boston: Beacon Press, 1956.

Rosenthal, R. "The effect of the experimenter on the results of psychological research." In B. A. Maher (ed.), *Progress in experimental personality research*. New York: Academic Press, 1964, Vol. I, 79-114.

——. "Clever Hans: A case study of scientific method." Introduction to O. Pfungst, *Clever Hans;* New York: Holt, Rinehart and Winston, 1965, ix-xlii.

——. *Experimenter effects in behavioral research*. New York: Appleton-Century Crofts, 1966.

——, and K. L. Fode. The effect of experimenter bias on the performance of the albino rat. *Behavioral Science*, 1963, 8, 183-189.

——, and Lenore Jacobson. Teachers' expectancies: Determinants of pupils' IQ gains. *Psychological Reports*, 1966, 19, 115-118.

——, and R. Lawson. A longitudinal study of the effects of experimenter bias on the operant learning of laboratory rats. *Journal of Psychiatric Research*, 1964, 2, 61-72.

Sommer, R. Rorschach M responses and intelligence. *Journal of Clinical Psychology*, 1958, 14, 58-61.

Wartenberg-Ekren, Ursula. The effect of experimenter knowledge of a subject's scholastic standing on the performance of a reasoning task. Unpublished master's thesis, Marquette University, 1962.

Whyte, W. F. *Street corner society*. Chicago: University of Chicago Press, 1943.

Wilson, A. B. "Social stratification and academic achievement." In A. H. Passow (ed.), *Education in depressed areas*. New York: Teachers College, Columbia University, 1963, 217-235.

Wysocki, B. A. Assessment of intelligence level by the Rorschach Test as compared with objective tests. *Journal of Educational Psychology*, 1957, 48, 113-117.

RICHARD D. SCHWARTZ
and
JEROME H. SKOLNICK

Two Studies of Legal Stigma*

In recent years much deviance research and theory has focused on the
ways in which the stigmatizing processes of law enforcement activities
not only help reshape the deviant's own self-image, but also, interre-
latedly, how they may transform the identity of the deviant in the eyes
of others, thus making difficult an easy exit from a deviant status.

In particular, in passing through the criminal justice processes of arrest,
trial, conviction and/or imprisonment the deviant is likely to experience
considerable status degradation and many must consequently recast
their personal and social identities. Similar effects are likely to result
from being processed through a network of health and welfare agencies.
Once it is known that a person has had contact with an official agency
of social control, regardless of the outcome of that contact, other people
are likely to redefine him as the "kind of person" who is, or at least is
likely to be, a deviant.

The degree and impact of criminal stigmatization will, of course, vary according to such factors as social class, family background and age. In

Reprinted by permission of *The Society for the Study of Social Problems*. From Richard
D. Schwartz and Jerome H. Skolnick, "Two Studies of Legal Stigma," *Social Problems*,
1962, 10:133-138.

*Revised version of paper read at the Annual Meeting of the American Sociological
Association, August, 1960. This paper draws upon materials prepared by students of
the Law and Behavioral Science Division of the Yale Law School. We wish to acknowledge the contributions of Michael Meltzner, who assisted in the experiment, and especially that of Dr. Robert Wyckoff, who surveyed medical practitioners. We are indebted
to Donald T. Campbell and Hanan Selvin for valuable comments and suggestions.

the paper that follows, Schwartz and Skolnick demonstrate the differential impact of a criminal record on occupational opportunities for low and high-status offenders. In interviews with a group of doctors sued for malpractice the authors found that none indicated that their medical practice had been affected adversely regardless of whether they had won, lost or settled out of court.

Quite opposite findings emerged from the field experimental part of their study in which a researcher posing as an employment agent presented information on an applicant for an unskilled job to prospective employers. Four folders were prepared setting forth identical characteristics of the job applicant except that in one he had been sentenced for assault, in one he had been tried but acquitted, in one not only had he been acquitted but the judge had written a complimentary letter in his behalf, and in the final folder no mention was made of criminal activity or involvement. The field experiment was so designed that employers were listed randomly and visited for reactions to such an applicant. It was found that, in contrast to doctors, unskilled working-class persons are affected by real or alleged criminal involvement. The *extent* of criminal involvement, in turn, influenced the job opportunities of the unskilled.

For our purposes, the major finding of the Schwartz and Skolnick research is that high-status offenders are less penalized by a criminal conviction or charge than are low-status offenders. While the status reputations and occupational opportunities of doctors are not easily affected by criminal-labeling processes, unskilled suspected offenders are easily stigmatized as "suspicious" persons and job opportunities are markedly reduced, even when they have not been guilty of any offense. In documenting that would-be employers accept stigma in denying employment even when there is no factual basis for the stigma, Schwartz and Skolnick show that a criminal status may transcend truth or falsity and further that members of the general public can become defining agents long after official agents of social control have ceased their work with deviants.

Legal thinking has moved increasingly toward a sociologically meaningful view of the legal system. Sanctions, in particular, have come to be regarded in functional terms.[1] In criminal law, for instance, sanctions are said to be designed to prevent recidivism by rehabilitating, restraining, or executing the offender. They are also said to be intended to deter others from the performance of similar acts and, sometimes, to provide a channel for the expression of retaliatory motives. In such civil actions as tort or contract, monetary awards may be intended as retributive and deterrent, as in the use of punitive damages, or may be regarded as a *quid pro quo* to compensate the plaintiff for his wrongful loss.

While these goals comprise an integral part of the rationale of law, little is know about the extent to which they are fulfilled in practice. Lawmen do not as a rule make such studies, because their traditions and techniques are not designed for a systematic examination of the operation of the legal system in action, especially outside the courtroom. Thus, when extra-legal consequences—e.g., the social stigma of a prison sentence—are taken into account at all, it is through the discretionary actions of police, prosecutor, judge, and jury. Systematic information on a variety of unanticipated outcomes, those which benefit the accused as well as those which hurt him, might help to inform these decision makers and perhaps lead to changes in substantive law as well. The present paper is an attempt to study the consequences of stigma associated with legal accusation.

From a sociological viewpoint, there are several types of indirect consequences of legal sanctions which can be distinguished. These include differential deterrence, effects on the sanctionee's associates, and variations in the degree of deprivation which sanction imposes on the recipient himself.

First, the imposition of sanction, while intended as a matter of overt policy to deter the public at large, probably will vary in its effectiveness as a deterrent, depending upon the extent to which potential offenders perceive themselves as similar to the sanctionee. Such "differential deterrence" would occur if white-collar anti-trust violators were restrained by the conviction of General Electric executives, but not by invocation of the Sherman Act against union leaders.

The imposition of a sanction may even provide an unintended incentive to violate the law. A study of factors affecting compliance with federal income tax laws provides some evidence of this effect.[2] Some respondents reported that they began to cheat on their tax returns only *after* convictions for tax evasion had been obtained against others in their jurisdiction. They explained this surprising behavior by noting that the prosecutions had always been conducted against blatant violators and not against the kind of moderate offenders which they then became. These respondents were, therefore, unintentionally educated to the possibility of supposedly "safe" violations.

Second, deprivations or benefits may accrue to non-sanctioned individuals by virtue of the web of affiliations that join them to the defendant. The wife and family of a convicted man may, for instance, suffer from his arrest as much as the man himself. On the other hand, they may be relieved by his absence if the family relationship has been an unhappy one. Similarly, whole groups of persons may be affected by sanctions to an individual, as when discriminatory practices increase because of a highly publicized crime attributed to a member of a given minority group.

Finally, the social position of the defendant himself will serve to aggravate or alleviate the effects of any given sanction. Although all three indirect consequences may be interrelated, it is the third with which this paper will be primarily concerned.

Findings

The subjects studied to examine the effects of legal accusation on occupational positions represented two extremes: lower-class unskilled workers charged with assault, and medical doctors accused of malpractice. The first project lent itself to a field experiment, while the second required a survey design. Because of differences in method and substance, the studies cannot be as formal controls for each other. Taken together, however, they do suggest that the indirect effects of sanctions can be powerful, that they can produce unintended harm or unexpected benefit, and that the results are related to officially unemphasized aspects of the social context in which the sanctions are administered. Accordingly, the two studies will be discussed together, as bearing on one another. Strictly speaking, however, each can, and properly should, stand alone as a separate examination of the unanticipated consequences of legal sanctions.

Study I. The Effects of a Criminal Court Record on the
Employment Opportunities of Unskilled Workers

In the field experiment, four employment folders were prepared, the same in all respects except for the criminal court record of the applicant. In all of the folders he was described as a thirty-two year old single male of unspecified race, with a high school training in mechanical trades, and a record of successive short term jobs as a kitchen helper, maintenance worker, and handyman. These characteristics are roughly typical of applicants for unskilled hotel jobs in the Catskill resort area of New York State where employment opportunities were tested.[3]

The four folders differed only in the applicant's reported record of criminal court involvement. The first folder indicated that the applicant had been convicted and sentenced for assault; the second, that he had been tried for assault and acquitted; the third, also tried for assault and acquitted, but with a letter from the judge certifying the finding of not guilty and reaffirming the legal presumption of innocence. The fourth folder made no mention of any criminal record.

A sample of one hundred employers was utilized. Each employer was assigned to one of four "treatment" groups.[4] To each employer only one folder was shown; this folder was one of the four kinds mentioned above, the selection of the folder being determined by the treatment group to which the potential employer was assigned. The employer was asked whether he could "use" the man described in the folder. To preserve the reality of the situation and make it a true field experiment, employers were never given any indication that they were participating in an experiment. So far as they knew, a legitimate offer to work was being made in each showing of the folder by the "employment agent."

The experiment was designed to determine what employers would do in fact if confronted with an employment applicant with a criminal record. The questionnaire aproach used in earlier studies[5] seemed ill-adapted to the problem, since respondents confronted with hypothetical situations might be particularly prone to answer in what they considered a socially acceptable manner. The second alternative—studying job opportunities of individuals who had been involved with the law—would have made it very difficult to find comparable groups of applicants and potential employers. For these reasons, the field experiment reported here was utilized.

Some deception was involved in the study. The "employment agent"—the same individual in all hundred cases—was in fact a law student who was working in the Catskills during the summer of 1959 as an insurance adjuster. In representing himself as being both an adjuster and an employment agent, he was assuming a combination of roles which is not uncommon there. The adjuster role gave him an opportunity to introduce a single application for employment casually and naturally. To the extent that the experiment worked, however, it was inevitable that some employers should be led to believe that they had immediate prospects of filling a job opening. In those instances where an offer to hire was made, the "agent" called a few hours later to say that the applicant had taken another job. The field experimenter attempted in such instances to locate a satisfactory replacement by contacting an employment agency in the area. Because this procedure was used and since the jobs involved were of relatively minor consequence, we believe that the deception caused little economic harm.

As mentioned, each treatment group of twenty-five employers was approached with one type of folder. Responses were dichotomized: those who expressed a willingness to consider the applicant in any way were termed positive; those who made no response or who explicitly refused to consider the candidate were termed negative. Our results consist of comparisons between positive and negative responses, thus defined, for the treatment groups.

Of the twenty-five employers shown the "no record" folder, nine gave positive responses. Subject to reservations arising from chance variations in sampling, we take this as indicative of the "ceiling" of jobs available for this kind of applicant under the given field conditions. Positive responses by these employers may be compared with those in the other treatment groups to obtain an indication of job opportunities lost because of the various legal records.

Of the twenty-five employers approached with the "convict" folder, only one expressed interest in the applicant. This is a rather graphic indication of the effect which a criminal record may have on job opportunities. Care must be exercised, of course, in generalizing the conclusions to other settings. In this context, however, the criminal record made a major difference.

From a theoretical point of view, the finding leads toward the conclusion that conviction constitutes a powerful form of "status degradation"[6] which continues to operate after the time when, according to the generalized theory of justice underlying punishment in our society, the individual's "debt" has been paid. A record of conviction produces a durable if not permanent loss of status. For purposes of effective social control, this state of affairs may heighten the deterrent effect of conviction—though that remains to be established. Any such contribution to social control, however, must be balanced against the barriers imposed upon rehabilitation of the convict. If the ex-prisoner finds difficulty in securing menial kinds of legitimate work, further crime may become an increasingly attractive alternative.[7]

Another important finding of this study concerns the small number of positive responses elicited by the "accused but acquitted" applicant. Of the twenty-five employers approached with this folder, three offered jobs. Thus, the individual accused but acquitted of assault has almost as much trouble finding even an unskilled job as the one who was not only accused of the same offense, but also convicted.

From a theoretical point of view, this result indicates that permanent lowering of status is not limited to those explicitly singled out by being convicted of a crime. As an ideal outcome of American justice, criminal procedure is supposed to distinguish between the "guilty" and those who have been acquitted. Legally controlled consequences which follow the judgment are consistent with this purpose. Thus, the "guilty" are subject to fine and imprisonment, while those who are acquitted are immune from these sanctions. But deprivations may be imposed on the acquitted, both before and after victory in court. Before trial, legal rules either permit or require arrest and detention. The suspect may be faced with the expense of an attorney and a bail bond if he is to mitigate these limitations on his privacy and freedom. In addition, some pre-trial deprivations are imposed without formal legal permission. These may include coercive questioning, use of violence, and

TABLE 1. Effect of Four Types of Legal Folder on Job Opportunities (in per cent)

	No record	Acquitted with letter	Acquitted without letter	Convicted	Total
	(N=25)	(N=25)	(N=25)	(N=25)	(N=100)
Positive response	36	24	12	4	19
Negative response	64	76	88	96	81
Total	100	100	100	100	100

stigmatization. And, as this study indicates, some deprivations not under the direct control of the legal process may develop or persist after an official decision of acquittal has been made.

Thus two legal principles conflict in practice. On the one hand, "a man is innocent until proven guilty." On the other, the accused is systematically treated as guilty under the administration of criminal law until a functionary or official body—police, magistrate, prosecuting attorney, or trial judge or jury—decides that he is entitled to be free. Even then, the results of treating him as guilty persist and may lead to serious consequences.

The conflict could be eased by measures aimed at reducing the deprivations imposed on the accused, before and after acquittal. Some legal attention has been focused on pre-trial deprivations. The provision of bail and counsel, the availability of habeas corpus, limitations on the admissabiilty of coerced confessions, and civil actions for false arrest are examples of measures aimed at protecting the rights of the accused before trial. Although these are often limited in effectiveness, especially for individuals of lower socio-economic status, they at least represent some concern with implementing the presumption of innocence at the pretrial stage.

By contrast, the courts have done little toward alleviating the post-acquittal consequences of legal accusation. One effort along these lines has been employed in the federal courts, however, Where an individual has been accused and exonerated of a crime, he may petition the federal courts for a "Certificate of Innocence" certifying this fact.[8] Possession of such a document might be expected to alleviate post-acquittal deprivations.

Some indication of the effectiveness of such a measure is found in the responses of the final treatment group. Their folder, it will be recalled, contained information on the accusation and acquittal of the applicant, but also included a letter from a judge addressed "To whom it may concern" certifying the applicant's acquittal and reminding the reader of the presumption of innocence. Such a letter might have had a boomerang effect, by reemphasizing the legal involvement of the applicant. It was important, therefore, to determine empirically whether such a communication would improve or harm the chances of employment. Our findings indicate that it increased employment opportunities, since the letter folder elicited six positive responses. Even though this fell short of the nine responses to the "no record" folder, it doubled the number of the "accused but acquitted" and created a signficantly greater number of job offers than those elicited by the convicted record. This suggests that the procedure merits consideration as a means of offsetting the occupational loss resulting from accusation. It should be noted, however, that repeated use of this device might reduce its effectiveness.

The results of the experiment are summarized in Table 1. The differences in outcome found there indicate that various types of legal records are systematically related to job opportunities. It seems fair to infer also that the trend of job losses corresponds with the apparent punitive intent of the authorities. Where the man is convicted, that intent is presumably greatest. It is less where he is accused but acquitted and still less where the court makes an effort to emphasize the absence of a finding of guilt. Nevertheless, where the difference in punitive intent is ideally greatest, between conviction and acquittal, the difference in occupational harm is very slight. A similar blurring of this distinction shows up on a different way in the next study.

Study II. The Effects on Defendants of Suits for Medical Malpractice

As indicated earlier, the second study differed from the first in a number of ways: method of research, social class of accused, relationship between the accused and his "employer," social support available to accused, type of offense and its possible relevance to occupational adequacy. Because the two studies differ in so many ways, the reader is again cautioned to avoid thinking of them as providing a rigorous comparative examination. They are presented together only to demonstrate that legal accusation can produce unanticipated deprivations, as in the case of Study I, or unanticipated benefits, as in the research now to be presented. In the discussion to follow, some of the possible reasons for the different outcomes will be suggested.

The extra-legal effects of a malpractice suit were studied by obtaining the records of Connecticut's leading carrier of malpractice insurance. According to these records, a total of 69 doctors in the State had been sued in 64 suits during the post World War II period covered by the study. September, 1945 to September, 1959.[9] Some suits were instituted against more than one doctor, and four physicians had been sued twice. Of the total of 69 physicians, 58 were questioned. Interviews were conducted with the approval of the Connecticut Medical Association by Robert Wyckoff, whose extraordinary qualifications for the work included possession of both the M.D. and LL.B. degrees. Dr. Wyckoff was able to secure detailed response to his inquiries from all doctors contacted.

Twenty of the respondents were questioned by personal interview, 28 by telephone, and the remainder by mail. Forty-three of those reached practiced principally in cities, eleven in suburbs, and four in rural areas. Seventeen were engaged in general practice and forty-one were specialists. The sample proved comparable to the doctors in the State as a whole in age, experience, and professional qualifications.[10] The range was from the lowest professional stratum to chiefs of staff and services in the State's most highly regarded hospitals.

Of the 57 malpractice cases reported, doctors clearly won 38; nineteen of these were dropped by the plaintiff and an equal number were won in court by the defendant doctor. Of the remaining nineteen suits, eleven were settled out of court, for a nominal amount, four for approximately the amount the plaintiff claimed and four resulted in judgment for the plaintiff in court.

The malpractice survey did not reveal widespread occupational harm to the physician involved. Of the 58 respondents, 52 reported no negative effects of the suit on their practice, and five of the remaining six, all specialists, reported that their practice *improved* after the suit. The heaviest loser in court (a radiologist), reported the largest gain. He commented, "I guess all the doctors in town felt sorry for me because new patients started coming in from doctors who had not sent me patients previously." Only one doctor reported adverse consequences to his practice. A winner in court, this man suffered physical and emotional stress symptoms which hampered his later effectiveness in surgical work. The temporary drop in his practice appears to have been produced by neurotic symptoms and is therefore only indirectly traceable to the malpractice suit. Seventeen other doctors reported varying degrees of personal dissatisfaction and anxiety during and after the suit, but none of them reported impairment of practice. No significant relationship was found between outcome of the suit and expressed dissatisfaction.

A protective institutional environment helps to explain these results. No cases were found in which a doctor's hospital privileges were reduced following the suit. Neither was any physician unable later to obtain malpractice insurance, although a handful found it necessary to pay higher rates. The State Licensing Commission which is headed by a doctor, did not intervene in any instance. Local medical societies generally investigated charges through their ethics and grievance committees, but where they took any action, it was almost always to recommend or assist in legal defense against the suit.

Discussion

Accusation has different outcomes for unskilled workers and doctors in the two studies. How may these be explained? First, they might be nothing more than artifacts of research method. In the field experiment, it was possible to see behavior directly, i.e., to determine how employers act when confronted with what appears to them to be a realistic opportunity to hire. Responses are therefore not distorted by the memory of the respondent. By contrast, the memory of the doctors might have been consciously or unconsciously shaped by the wish to create the impression that the public had not taken seriously the accusation leveled against them. The motive for such a distortion might be either to protect the respondent's self-esteem or to preserve an image of public acceptance in the eyes of the interviewer, the profession, and the public. Efforts of the interviewer to assure his subjects of anonymity—intended to offset these effects—may have succeeded or may, on the contrary, have accentuated an awareness of the danger. A related type of distortion might have stemmed from a desire by doctors to affect public attitudes toward malpractice. Two conflicting motives might have been expected to enter here. The doctor might have tended to exaggerate the harm caused by an accusation, especially if followed by acquittal, in order to turn public opinion toward legal policies which would limit malpractice liability. On the other hand, he might tend to underplay extra-legal harm caused by a legally insufficient accusation in order to discourage potential plaintiffs from instituting suits aimed at securing remunerative settlements and/or revenge for grievances. Whether these diverse motives operated to distort doctors' reports and, if so, which of them produced the greater degree of distortion is a matter of speculation. It is only suggested here that the interview method is more subject to certain types of distortion than the direct behavioral observations of the field experiment.

Even if such distortion did not occur, the results may be attributable to differences in research design. In the field experiment, a direct comparison is made between the occupational position of an accused and an identical individual not accused at a single point in time. In the medical study, effects were inferred through retrospective judgment, although checks on actual income would have no doubt confirmed these judgments. Granted that income had increased, many other explanations are available to account for it. An improvement in practice after a malpractice suit may have resulted from factors extraneous to the suit. The passage of time in the community and increased experience may have led to a larger practice and may even have masked negative effects of the suit. There may have been a general increase in practice for the kinds of doctors involved in these suits, even greater for doctors not sued than for doctors in the sample. Whether interviews with a control sample could have yielded sufficiently precise data to rule out these possibilities is problematic. Unfortunately, the resources available for the study did not enable such data to be obtained.

A third difference in the two designs may affect the results. In the field experiment, full information concerning the legal record is provided to all of the relevant decision makers, i.e., the employers. In the medical study, by contrast, the results depend on decisions of actual patients to consult a given doctor. It may be assumed that such decisions are often based on imperfect information, some patients knowing little or nothing about the malpractice suit. To ascertain how much information employers usually have concerning the legal record of the employee and then supply that amount would have been a desirable refinement, but a difficult one. The alternative approach would involve turning the medical study into an experiment in which full information concerning malpractice (e.g., liable, accused but acquitted, no record of accusation) was supplied to potential patients. This would have permitted a comparison of the effects of legal accusation in two instances where information concerning the accusation is constant. To carry out such an experiment in a field situation would require an unlikely degree of cooperation, for instance by a medical clinic which might ask patients to choose their doctor on the basis of information given them. It is difficult to conceive of an experiment along these lines which would be both realistic enough to be vaild and harmless enough to be ethical.

If we assume, however, that these methodological problems do not invalidate the basic finding, how may it be explained? Why would unskilled workers accused but acquitted of assault have great difficulty getting jobs, while doctors accused of malpractice—whether acquitted or not—are left unharmed or more sought after than before?

First, the charge of criminal assault carries with it the legal allegation and the popular connotation of intent to harm. Malpractice, on the other hand, implies negligence or failure to exercise reasonable care. Even though actual physical harm may be greater in malpractice, the elements of intent suggests that the man accused of assault would be more likely to repeat his attempt and to find the mark. However, it is dubious that this fine distinction could be drawn by the lay public.

Perhaps more important, all doctors and particularly specialists may be immune from the effects of a malpractice suit because their services are in short supply.[11] By contrast, the unskilled worker is one of many and therefore likely to be passed over in favor of someone with a "cleaner" record.

Moreover, high occupational status, such as is demonstrably enjoyed by doctors,[12] probably tends to insulate the doctor from imputations of incompetence. In general, professionals are assumed to possess uniformly high ability, to be oriented toward community service, and to enforce adequate standards within their own organization.[13] Doctors in particular receive deference, just because they are doctors, not only from the population as a whole but even from fellow professionals.[14]

Finally, individual doctors appear to be protected from the effects of accusation by the sympathetic and powerful support they receive from fellow members of the occupation, a factor absent in the case of unskilled, unorganized laborers.[15] The medical society provides advice on handling malpractice actions, for instance, and referrals by other doctors sometimes increase as a consequence of the sympathy felt for the malpractice suit victim. Such assistance is further evidence that the professional operates as "a community within a community,"[16] shielding its members from controls exercised by formal authorities in the larger society.

In order to isolate these factors, additional studies are needed. It would be interesting to know, for instance, whether high occupational status would protect a doctor acquitted of a charge of assault. Information on this question is sparse. Actual instances of assaults by doctors are probably very rare. When and if they do occur, it seems unlikely that they would lead to publicity and prosecution, since police and prosecutor discretion might usually be employed to quash charges before they are publicized. In the rare instances in which they come to public attention, such accusations appear to produce a marked effect because of the assumption that the pressing of charges, despite the status of the defendant, indicates probable guilt. Nevertheless, instances may be found in which even the accusation of first degree murder followed by acquittal appears to have left the doctor professionally unscathed.[17] Similarly, as a test of the group protection hypothesis, one might investigate the effect of an acquittal for assault on working men who are union members. The analogy would be particularly instructive where the union plays an important part in employment decisions, for instance in industries which make use of a union hiring hall.

In the absence of studies which isolate the effect of such factors, our findings cannot readily be generalized. It is tempting to suggest after an initial look at the results that social class differences provides the explanation. But subsequent analysis and research might well reveal significant intra-class variations, depending on the distribution of other operative factors. A lower class person with a scarce specialty and a protective occupational group who is acquitted of a lightly regarded offense might benefit from the accusation. Nevertheless, class in general seems to correlate with the relevant factors to such an extent that in reality the law regularly works to the disadvantage of the already more disadvantaged classes.

Conclusion

Legal accusation imposes a variety of consequences depending on the nature of the accusation and the characteristics of the accused. Deprivations occur, even though not officially intended, in the case of unskilled workers who have been acquitted of assault charges. On the other hand, malpractice actions—even when resulting in a judgment against the doctor—are not usually followed by negative consequences and sometimes have a favorable effect on the professional position of the defendant. These differences in outcome suggest two conclusions: one, the need for more explicit clarification of legal goals; two, the importance of examining the attitudes and social structure of the community outside the courtroom if the legal process is to hit intended targets, while avoiding innocent bystanders. Greater precision in communicating goals and in appraising consequences of present practices should help to make the legal process an increasingly equitable and effective instrument of social control.

Notes

1. Legal sanctions are defined as changes in life conditions imposed through court action.
2. Richard D. Schwartz, "The Effectiveness of Legal Controls: Factors in the

Reporting of Minor Items of Income on Federal Income Tax Returns." Paper presented at the annual meeting of the American Sociological Association, Chicago, 1959.

3. The generality of these results remains to be determined. The effects of criminal involvement in the Catskill area are problably diminished, however, by the temporary nature of employment, the generally poor qualifications of the work force, and the excess of demand over supply of unskilled labor there. Accordingly, the employment differences among the four treatment groups found in this study are likely, if anything to be *smaller* than would be expected in industries and areas where workers are more carefully selected.

4. Employers were not approached in preselected random order, due to a misunderstanding of instructions on the part of the law student who carried out the experiment during a three and one-half week period. Because of this flaw in the experimental procedure, the results should be treated with appropriate caution. Thus, chi-squared analysis may not properly be utilized. (For those used to this measure, $P < .05$ for table 1.)

5. Sol Rubin, *Crime and Juvenile Delinquency*, New York: Oceana, 1958, pp. 151-156.

6. Harold Garfinkel, "Conditions of Successful Degradation Ceremonies," *American Journal of Sociology*, 61 (March, 1956), pp. 420-24.

7. Severe negative effects of conviction on employment opportunities have been noted by Sol Rubin, *Crime and Juvenile Delinquency*, New York: Oceana, 1958. A further source of employment difficulty is inherent in licensing statutes and security regulations which sometimes preclude convicts from being employed in their pre-conviction occupation or even in the trades which they may have acquired during imprisonment. These effects may, however, be counteracted by bonding arrangements, prison associations, and publicity programs aimed at increasing confidence in, and sympathy for, exconvicts. See also, B. F. McSally, "Finding Jobs for Released Offenders," *Federal Probation*, 24 (June, 1960), pp. 12-17; Harold D. Lasswell and Richard C. Donnelly, "The Continuing Debate over Responsibility: An Introduction to Isolating the Condemnation Sanction," *Yale Law Journal*, 68 (April, 1959), pp. 869-99; Johs Andeneas, "General Prevention—Illusion or Reality?", *J. Criminal Law*, 43 (July-August, 1952), pp. 176-98.

8. 28 United States Code, Secs. 1495, 2513.

9. A spot check of one county revealed that the Company's records covered every malpractice suit tried in the courts of that county during this period.

10. No relationship was found between any of these characteristics and the legal or extra-legal consequences of the lawsuit.

11. See Eliot Freidson, "Client Control and Medical Practice," *American Journal of Sociology*, 65 (January, 1960), pp. 374-82. Freidson's point is that general practitioners are more subject to client-control than specialists are. Our findings emphasize the importance of professional as compared to client control, and professional protection against a particular form of client control, extending through both branches of the medical profession. However, what holds for malpractice situations may not be true of routine medical practice.

12. National Opinion Research Center, "Jobs and Occupations: A Popular Evaluation," *Opinion News*, 9 (Sept., 1947), pp. 3-13. More recent studies in several countries tend to confirm the high status of the physician. See Alex Inkeles, "Industrial Man: The Relation of Status to Experience, Perception and Value," *American Journal of Sociology*, 66 (July, 1960), pp. 1-31.

13. Talcott Parsons, *The Social System*, Glencoe: The Free Press, 1951, pp. 454-473; and Everett C. Hughes, *Men and their Work*. Glencoe: The Free Press, 1958.

14. Alvin Zander, Arthur R. Cohen, and Ezra Stotland, *Role Relations in the Mental Health Professions*. Ann Arbor: Institute for Social Research, 1957.

15. Unions sometimes act to protect the seniority rights of members who, discharged from their jobs upon arrest, seek re-employment following their acquittal.

16. See William J. Goode, "Community Within A Community: The Professions," *American Sociological Review*, 22 (April, 1957), pp. 194-200.

17. For instance, the acquittal of Dr. John Bodkin Adams after a sensational murder trial, in which he was accused of deliberately killing several elderly women patients to inherit their estates, was followed by his quiet return to medical practice. *New York Times*, Nov. 24, 1961, p. 28, col. 7. Whether the British regard acquittals as more exonerative than Americans is uncertain.

BENJAMIN M. BRAGINSKY
and
DOROTHEA D. BRAGINSKY[1]

Schizophrenic Patients in the Psychiatric Interview:

An Experimental Study of Their Effectiveness at Manipulation

As we noted earlier in this book, many traditional assumptions and theories concerning deviance as well as practices implemented to deal with deviants may have to be discarded in the light of careful and critical research evidence. Braginsky and Braginsky report on research that challenges the traditional psychiatric view of mental illness, a view that characterizes the schizophrenic as an extremely ineffectual and helpless individual who is thought to be a passive victim of his environment, unable to either perform satisfactorily in interpersonal situations or to effectively control his future.

Using the concept of impression management, Braginsky and Braginsky examine whether or not chronic schizophrenic patients can effectively use this manipulative strategy in an evaluative interview situation. The authors administered mental status examinations to long-term open-ward schizophrenics. Patients were randomly assigned to one of three experimental conditions in which their perceptions of the purposes of the examinations were varied. Tape-recordings of the examinations were then presented to psychiatrists who rated the patients for psychopathology and need for hospital control.

The data supported the expectation that schizophrenics can effectively present themselves as "sick" or "healthy" and can make selections of strategy dependent upon what happens to be most suited to their personal interests and goals. The authors argue that these findings support their assumptions of patient effectiveness in implementing goals and demonstrate that mental patients are not necessarily helpless, ineffectual persons.

This study's documentation of impression management tactics on the part of schizophrenics underscores a fundamental notion of the interactionist-labeling perspective: deviant behavior must be explained within the same general framework used to explain other human behavior. Thus, it should not be so surprising that mental patients employ the widely used manipulative strategy of impression management to achieve goals. What is surprising, perhaps, is how successfully they do so.

The present investigation is concerned with the manipulative behavior of hospitalized schizophrenics in evaluative interview situations. More specifically, the study attempts to answer the question: Can schizophrenic patients effectively control the impressions (impression management, Goffman, 1959) they make on the professional hospital staff?

Typically, the mental patient has been viewed as an extremely ineffectual and helpless individual (e.g., Arieti, 1959; Becker, 1964; Bellak, 1958; Joint Commission on Mental Illness and Health, 1961; Redlich & Freedman, 1966; Schooler & Parkel, 1966; Searles, 1965). For example, Redlich and Freedman (1966) described the mental patient and his pathological status in the following manner: "There is a concomitant loss of focus and coherence and a profound shift in the meaning and value of social relationships and goal directed behavior. This is evident in the inability realistically to implement future goals and present satisfactions; they are achieved magically or through fantasy and delusion . . . [p. 463]." Schooler and Parkel (1966) similarly underline the mental patients' ineffectual status in this description: "the chronic schizophrenic is not Seneca's 'reasoning animal,' or Spinoza's 'social animal,' or even a reasonably efficient version of Cassirer's 'symbol using animal'. . . . Since he violates so many functional definitions of man, there is heuristic value in studying him with an approach like that which would be used to study an alien creature [p. 67]."

Thus, the most commonly held assumptions concerning the nature of the schizophrenic patient stress their ineffectuality and impotency. In this context one would expect schizophrenics to perform less than adequately in interpersonal situations, to be unable to initiate manipulative tactics, and certainly, to be incapable of successful manipulation of other people.[2]

In contrast to the above view of the schizophrenic, a less popular orientation has been expressed by Artiss (1959), Braginsky, Grosse, and Ring (1966), Goffman (1961), Levinson and Gallagher (1964), Rakusin and

Fierman (1963), Szasz (1961, 1965), and Towbin (1966). Here schizophrenics are portrayed in terms usually reserved for neurotics and normal persons. Simply, the above authors subscribe to the beliefs that: (*a*) the typical schizophrenic patient, as compared to normals, is not deficient, defective, or dissimilar in intrapsychic functioning; (*b*) the typical schizophrenic patient is not a victim of his illness; that is, it is assumed that he is not helpless and unable to control his behavior or significantly determine life outcomes; (*c*) the differences that some schizophrenic patients manifest (as compared to normals) are assumed to be more accurately understood in terms of differences in belief systems, goals, hierarchy of needs, and interpersonal strategies, rather than in terms of illness, helplessness, and deficient intrapsychic functioning. This orientation leads to the expectation that schizophrenic patients do try to achieve particular goals and, in the process, effectively manipulate other people.

There is some evidence in support of this viewpoint (e.g., Artiss, 1959; Braginsky, Holzberg, Finison, & Ring, 1967; Levinson & Gallagher, 1964). Furthermore, a recent study (Braginsky et al., 1966) demonstrated that schizophrenic patients responded, on a paper-and-pencil "mental status" test, in a manner that would protect their self-interests. Those who wanted to remain in the hospital (chronic patients) presented themselves as "sick," whereas those who desired to be discharged (first admissions) presented themselves as "healthy." That is, they effectively controlled the impressions they wished to make on others. Their manipulative performance, however, was mediated by an impersonal test.

Therefore, the following question is asked: Can schizophrenics engage in similar manipulative behaviors in a "face-to-face" interview with a psychologist? That is, will chronic schizophrenics who desire to remain in the hospital and live on open wards present themselves in an interview situation when they perceive that their open ward status is being questioned as (*a*) "healthy" and, therefore, eligible for open ward living, and in another interview situation when their residential status is being questioned as (*b*) "sick" and, therefore, ineligible for discharge? If so, are their performances convincing to a professional audience (i.e., psychiatrists)?

Method

A sample of 30 long-term (more than 2 continuous years of hospitalization) male schizophrenics living on open wards was randomly selected from ward rosters. Two days prior to the experiment the patients were told that they were scheduled for an interview with a staff psychologist. Although each patient was to be interviewed individually, all 30 were brought simultaneously to a waiting room. Each patient interviewed was not allowed to return to this room, to insure that patients who had participated would not communicate with those who had not.

Each patient was escorted to the interview room by an assistant, who casually informed the patient in a tone of confidentiality about the purpose of the interview (preinterview induction). Patients were randomly assigned by the assistant to one of three induction conditions (10 to each condition). The interviewer was unaware of the induction to which the patients were assigned, thereby eliminating interviewer bias.

Induction Conditions

Discharge induction. Patients were told: "I think the person you are going to see is interested in examining patients to see whether they might be ready for discharge."

Open ward induction.[3] Patients were told: "I think that the person you are going to see is interested in examining patients to see whether they should be on open or closed wards."

Mental status induction.[4] Patients were told: "I think the person you are going to see is interested in how you are feeling and getting along in the hospital."

After greeting each patient the interviewer asked: "How are you feeling?" Patients who responded only with physical descriptions were also asked: "How do you feel mentally?" whereas those who only gave descriptions of their mental state were asked: "How are you feeling physically?" The patients' responses were tape-recorded. The interview was terminated after 2 minutes,[5] whereupon the purpose of the experiment was disclosed.

Three staff psychiatrists from the same hospital separately rated each of the 30 tape-recorded interviews during two 40-minute sessions. The psychiatrists had no knowledge of the experiment, and they were unfamiliar with the patients; they were told by the experimenter that these were mental patients residing in the hospital and that as a group they represented a wide range of diagnostic categories.

The psychiatrists rated the patients on the following dimensions: (a) the patient's degree of psychopathology, using a five-point scale ranging from "not at all ill" to "extremely ill"; (b) the amount of hospital control a patient needed, ranging on an eight-point scale from complete freedom ("discharge") to maximum control ("closed ward, continual observation"); and (c) the structural or qualitative aspects of the patient's speech, such as pressure of speech, affect, volume, etc. The score for each patient's speech characteristic was based on the sum of the psychiatrist's rating of 14 Lorr scale items (Lorr, 1953). Each item was rated on an eight-point scale ranging from not at all atypical to extremely atypical verbal behavior.

Predictions

If long-term patients are both motivated to live on open wards and to remain in the hospital and if, in addition, they effectively engage in impression management in order to realize these desires, then the following would be expected:

1. Psychiatrists will rate patients in the discharge and the mental status conditions as being similar with respect to psychopathology and need for hospital control. Mental status interviews are generally used by the hospital to evaluate patients for discharge; therefore, the mental status and discharge conditions offer the same potential consequences for patients. Thus, patients in both conditions will give the impression of being "sick" and in need of hospital control in order to decrease the probability of discharge. The purpose of including the discharge induction was to present the consequences of the interview as explicitly as in the open ward induction.

2. Psychiatrists will rate the patients in the open ward condition significantly less mentally ill and less in need of hospital control than patients in the discharge and mental status conditions. That is, patients in the open ward condition will give the impression of being "healthy" in order to maximize their chances of remaining on an open ward.

Subjects

The mean age of the patients was 47.4 years ($SD = 8.36$). The mean educational level of the group was 8.05 years of schooling ($SD = 3.44$). The median length of hospitalization was 10 years. In terms of diagnostic categories, 43% of the sample was diagnosed as chronic undifferentiated schizophrenic, 37% as paranoid schizophrenic, 10% as catatonic, and the remaining 10% as simple schizophrenic. There were no differences between the three experimental groups on any of the above variables.

Results and Discussion

The reliability coefficients of the three psychiatrists' combined ratings of the patient interviews were as follows: (*a*) ratings of psychopathology—$r = .89, p < .01$; (*b*) need of hospital control—$r = .74, p < .01$; (*c*) normality of speech characteristics—$r = .65, p < .01$. Thus, is was concluded that there was significant agreement between the three psychiatrists.

The means of the psychopathology ratings by experimental condition are presented in Table 1. The ratings ranged 1-5. The analysis of variance of the data yielded a significant condition effect ($F = 9.38, p < .01$). The difference between the open ward and discharge conditions was statistically significant ($p < .01$; Tukey multiple-range test). In addition, the difference between the open ward and the mental status condition was significant ($p <$ .01). As predicted, there was no significant difference between the discharge and mental status conditions.

The means of the ratings of need for hospital control are presented in Table 1. These ratings ranged 1-8. The analysis of these data indicated a significant difference between the means ($F = 3.85, p < .05$). Again, significant differences (beyond the .05 level) were obtained between the open ward and the discharge conditions, as well as between the open ward and mental status conditions. No difference was found between the discharge and mental status conditions.

TABLE 1. Mean Psychopathology and Need-for-Hospital-Control Ratings by Experimental Condition

Rating	Open ward		Mental status		Discharge	
	M	SD	M	SD	M	SD
Psychopathology	2.63	.58	3.66	.65	3.70	.67
Need for hospital control	2.83	1.15	4.10	1.31	4.20	1.42

On the basis of these analyses it is clear that patients in the open ward condition appear significantly less mentally ill and in less need of hospital control than patients in either the discharge or mental status conditions. Obviously the patients in these conditions convey different impressions in the interview situation. In order to ascertain the manner by which the patients conveyed these different impressions, the following three manipulative tactics were examined: (*a*) number of positive statements patients made about themselves, (*b*) number of negative statements made about themselves (these include both physical and mental referents), and (*c*) normality of speech characteristics (i.e., how "sick" they sounded, independent of the content of speech). The first two indexes were obtained by counting the number of positive or negative self-referent statements a patient made during the interview. These counts were done by three judges independently, and the reliability coefficient was .95. The third index was based on the psychiatrists' ratings on 14 Lorr scale items of the speech characteristics of patients. A score was obtained for each patient by summing the ratings for the 14 scales.

Ratings of psychopathology and need for hospital control were, in part, determined by the frequency of positive and negative self-referent statements. The greater the frequency of positive statements made by a patient, the less ill he was perceived ($r = -.58, p < .01$) and the less in need of hospital control ($r = -.41, p < .05$). Conversely, the greater the frequency of negative statements, the more ill a patient was perceived ($r = .53, p < .01$) and the more in need of hospital control ($r = .37, p < .05$). It is noteworthy that patients were consistent in their performances; that is, those who tended to say positive things about themselves tended not to say negative things ($r =$ —.55, $p < .01$).

When self-referent statements were compared by condition, it was found that patients in the open ward condition presented themselves in a significantly more positive fashion than patients in the discharge and mental status conditions. Only 2 patients in the open ward condition reported have physical or mental problems, whereas 13 patients in the mental status and discharge conditions presented such complaints ($\chi^2 = 5.40$, $p < .05$).

The frequency of positive and negative self-referent statements, however, cannot account for important qualitative components of the impressions the patients attempted to convey. For example, a patient may give only one complaint, but it may be serious (e.g., he reports hallucinations), whereas another patient may state five complaints, all of which are relatively benign. In order to examine the severity of symptoms or complaints reported by patients, the number of "psychotic" complaints, namely, reports of hallucinations or bizzare delusions, was tallied. None of the patients in the open ward condition made reference to having had hallucinations or delusions, while nine patients in the discharge and mental status conditions spontaneously made such reference ($\chi^2 = 4.46$, $p < .05$).

In comparing the structural or qualitative aspects of patient speech no significant differences were obtained between experimental conditions. Patients "sounded" about the same in all three conditions. The majority of patients (80%) were rated as having relatively normal speech characteristics. Although there were no differences by condition, there was a significant inverse relationship ($r =$ —.35, $p < .05$) between quality of speech and the number of positive statements made. That is, patients were consistent to the extent that those who sounded ill tended not to make positive self-referent statements.

In summary then, the hypotheses were confirmed. It is clear that patients responded to the inductions in a manner which maximized the chances of fulfilling their needs and goals. When their self-interests were at stake patients could present themselves in a face-to-face interaction as either "sick" or "healthy," whichever was more appropriate to the situation. In the context of this experiment "sick" impressions were conveyed when the patients were faced with the possibility of discharge. On the other hand, impressions of "health" were conveyed when the patients' open ward status was questioned. Moreover, the impressions they conveyed were convincing to an audience of experienced psychiatrists.

One may argue, however, that the differences between the groups were a function of differential anxiety generated by the inductions rather than a function of the patients' needs, goals, and manipulative strategies. More specifically, the discharge and the mental status conditions would generate more anxiety and, therefore, more pathological behavior than the open ward condition. As a result, the psychiatrists rated the patients in the discharge and mental status conditions as "sicker" than patients in the open ward condition. According to this argument, then, the patients who were rated sick were, in fac, more disturbed, and those rated healthy were, in fact, less disturbed.

No differences, however, were found between conditions in terms of the amount of disturbed behavior during the interview. As was previously mentioned, the psychiatrists did not perceive any differences by condition in atypicality of verbal behavior. On the contrary, the patients were judged as sounding relatively normal. Thus, the psychiatrists' judgments of psychopathology were based primarily on the symptoms patients reported rather than on symptoms manifested. Patients did not behave in a disturbed manner; rather, they told the interviewer how disturbed they were.

The traditional set of assumptions concerning schizophrenics, which stresses their irrationality and interpersonal ineffectuality, would not only preclude the predictions made in this study, but would fail to explain parsimoniously the present observations. It is quite plausible and simple to view these findings in terms of the assumptions held about people in general; that is, schizophrenics, like normal persons, are goal-oriented and are able to control the outcomes of their social encounters in a manner which satisfies their goals.

Notes

1. The authors would like to express their appreciation to Doris Seiler and Dennis Ridley for assistance with the data collection.
2. This statement is explicitly derived from formal theories of schizophrenia and not from clinical observations. It is obvious to some observers, however, that schizophrenics do attempt to manipulate others. The discrepancy between these observations and traditional theoretical assumptions about the nature of schizophrenics is rarely, if ever, reconciled.
3. It may be suggested that the open ward induction was meaningless, since no patient enjoying open ward status would believe that he could be put on a closed ward on the basis of an interview. At the time this experiment was being conducted, however, this hospital was in the process of reorganization, and open and closed ward status was a salient and relevant issue.
4. Mental status evaluation interviews are typically conducted yearly. Thus, patients who have been in the hospital for more than a year expect to be interfor the purposes of determining their residency status.
5. Although, admittedly, psychiatrists would never base decisions concerning mental status and discharge on a 2-minute interview, it was adequate for the purposes of this study (namely, to determine if mental patients effectively engage in impression management). The 2-minute response to the single question provided sufficient information for psychiatrists to form reliable impressions of the patients. Interestingly, the typical mental status interview conducted by these psychiatrists is rarely longer than 30 minutes.

References

Arieti, S. *Amerian handbook of psychiatry.* New York: Basic Books, 1959.

Artiss, K. L. *The symptom as communication in schizophrenia.* New York: Grune & Stratton, 1959.

Becker, E. *The revolution in psychiatry.* London: Collier-Macmillan, 1964.

Bellak, C. *Schizophrenia: A review of the syndrome.* New York: Logos Press, 1958.

Braginsky, B., Grosse, M., & Ring, K. Controlling outcomes through impression-management: An experimental study of the manipulative tactics of mental patients. *Journal of Consulting Psychology,* 1966, 30, 295-300.

Braginsky, B., Holzberg, J., Finison, L., & Ring, K. Correlates of the mental patient's acquisition of hospital information. *Journal of Personality,* 1967, 35, 323-342.

Goffman, E. *The presentation of self in everyday life.* New York: Doubleday, 1959.

Goffman, E. *Asylums.* New York: Doubleday, 1961.

Joint Commission on Mental Illness and Health. *Action for mental health.* New York: Basic Books, 1961.

Levinson, D. S., & Gallagher, E. B. *Patienthood in the mental hospital.* Boston: Houghton-Mifflin, 1964.

Lorr, M. Multidimensional scale for rating psychiatric patients. *Veterans Administration Technical Bulletin,* 1953, 51, 119-127.

Rakusin, J. M., & Fierman, L. B. Five assumptions for treating chronic psychotics. *Mental Hospitals,* 1963, 14, 140-148.

Redlich, F. C., & Freedman, D. T. *The theory and practice of psychiatry.* New York: Basic Books, 1966, 29, 67-77.

Schooler, C., & Parkel, D. The overt behavior of chronic schizophrenics and its relationship to their internal state and personal history. *Psychiatry,* 1966, 29, 67-77.

Searles, H. F. *Collected papers on schizophrenia and related subjects.* New York: International Universities Press, 1965.

Szasz, T. S. *The myth of mental illness.* New York: Hoeber-Harper, 1961.

Szasz, T. S. *Psychiatric justice.* New York: Macmillan, 1965.

Towbin, A. P. Understanding the mentally deranged. *Journal of Existentialism,* 1966, 7, 63-83.

HENRY J. MEYER
EDGAR F. BORGATTA
and
WYATT C. JONES

Girls at Vocational High:

An Experiment in Social Work Intervention

A wide range of social agencies exist and have responsibility for the prevention, detection and control of deviance. Police, psychiatrists, social
workers, judges, probation and parole officers, and numerous correctional and mental health workers reflect the extent to which social intervention has become a formally recognized function within our society.
Empirically, social intervention efforts aimed at deviants and potential
deviants may tend to inhibit further deviant activities (usually the stated
objective of personnel within the social agencies), may have essentially
no effect, or may even contribute to additional deviant activities. The
likelihood of the latter is suggested as a strong possibility by scholars
of the interactionist-labeling perspective. This position, of course, means
that many have taken critical stances toward those involved in social
intervention with interactionists usually pointing out that evidence of
being able to prevent and/or control deviance has been unconvincing.
A major task of evaluation research is to identify the effects of treatment and
correctional experiences on deviants and to determine the effects of
intervention efforts. The following report directs itself to this issue by
using a well-designed field experiment to evaluate the effects of providing social work services to high school females identified as potential
deviants. Girls so defined were randomly assigned to either an experi-

Reprinted from Henry J. Meyer, Edgar F. Borgatta and Wyatt C. Jones, *Girls at Vocational High: An Experiment in Social Work Intervention*, New York: Russell Sage Foundation, 1965, pp. 15-16, 23-24, 26-27, 33-34, 37-38, 40, 42-46, 48, 158-174, 176-179,
200-204.

mental or control group. Girls in the experimental groups received a battery of services whereas those in the control group were left alone.

The results essentially showed that intervention had no significant effect on the girl's deviant careers. Using a variety of behavioral, attitudinal and personality measures, the authors found only minimal differences between the experimental and control subjects. They conclude that, in this instance at least, social intervention of the casework-counseling services variety with potential problem girls was largely ineffective.

While some may be disappointed with the results of this study, the study demonstrates how good evaluation research is done. In particular, it shows some of the kinds of evidence that can be used in evaluating social intervention and highlights the need for further research of this nature. The student should be aware of these issues and examine claims of helping, cure, successful treatment, etc., in light of rigorous research evidence rather than on the basis of claims made by practitioners with vested interests.

This report describes a study of the consequences of providing social work services to high school girls whose record of earlier performance and behavior at school revealed them to be potentially deviant. Over the course of four years girls with potential problems who entered a vocational high school in New York City were identified from information available to the school. From this pool of students a random sample of cases were referred to an agency where they were offered casework or group counseling services by professional social workers. A control group was also selected at random from the same pool of potential problem cases in order that a comparison could be made between girls who received service and similar girls who did not. Since all these girls were identified as potential problem cases, they may be considered latent or early detected deviants. Services to them consisted in efforts to interrupt deviant careers.

Youth Consultation Service is a nonsectarian, voluntary social agency in New York City that for more than fifty years has specialized in offering services to adolescent girls. The characteristic problems that bring troubled girls and young women between the ages of twelve and twenty-five to YCS are: out-of-wedlock pregnancy, school behavior problems, chronic truancy, unmanageability at home, "immoral conduct," incorrigibility, and "runaway." At the time this research was undertaken, the agency served approximately two hundred clients each year, of whom about two-fifths were unmarried mothers.

The major service offered to clients of the agency is casework, but since 1952 it has conducted a supplementary group-therapy program and has pioneered in group methods of treatment for unmarried mothers and adolescent girls with other behavior problems. In addition to the regular complement of psychiatric consultants, group-therapy consultants have been provided.

The Research Design

The basic plan of the research was a simple experimental design requiring random assignment of adolescent girls with potential problems (1) as clients of Youth Consultation Service to constitute an *experimental* sample, that is, to receive treatment, and (2) as members of a group of *control* cases, with no treatment provided by YCS. The comparison of these two groups of cases after the former was exposed to the services of the agency will constitute a test of the effects of that service, since in other respects the two groups may be assumed to begin equally and to differ in experiences only to the extent that the control cases have not had the services of YCS. It is to be noted that these are assumptions and therefore require some empirical examination if they are to be accepted with confidence.

In order to check these assumptions, as well as to provide information additional to the experimental test, it was arranged that the total school population from which experimental and control cases were chosen would be tested *prior* to random assignment and periodically throughout the study so that equivalence could be examined and change differentials noted. Similarly, it was arranged that the total school population as well as the experimental and control cases would be observed at a determinate follow-up point according to criteria that reflected a range of objectives contemplated by YCS in its services to the experimental sample.

Through additional procedures, including clearance with the Social Service Exchange and direct inquiry from both experimental and control subjects, an effort would be made to estimate whether YCS service did, in fact, constitute the primary variation in experience of the two groups of cases, or whether, for example, similar or comparable services might have been provided elsewhere for the control cases. In the strictest sense, therefore, the experimental test was not one of provision of service vs. withholding of service, but rather the known provision of service vs. unknown experiences excluding these specific services. This is a severe test of the impact of such services. But it is also a powerful one and the sort of question that is, in effect, asked of social agencies: "Have your services benefited clients more than no services or services provided on a casual and haphazard basis?"

Implementation of the Research Design

Selection of Experimental and Control Cases

The cooperating school—here called Vocational High—agreed with the agency that the girls selected by the research staff for referral would be encouraged to accept the help of Youth Consultation Service and that the necessary home permission for the girls to go to the agency would be sought by the school in cooperation with YCS. Vocational High also agreed that the girls selected could fit into their schoolday schedules the required appointments with caseworkers at the agency and (as group procedures developed) the scheduled group meetings. The school also accepted the condition that the project would continue through four years in order that the requisite numbers could be referred and observed throughout their high school years, normally the time between entrance and graduation from the school (tenth, eleventh, and twelfth grades).

The records of four entering cohorts of girls at Vocational High were screened and potential problem cases identified for each. Only those entering in the fall term were included in order to provide as long a time for treatment as possible. Approximately one-fourth of the cohort was included in the potential problem cases and from this pool a random procedure was used to select those to be referred to YCS, the number depending on the capacity of the agency to accept additions to its caseload. At the same time, and by the same random procedure, the control group was selected from the potential problem cases. A total of 200 referred girls and 200 in the control sample was set as the goal and, over the course of four years, 189 referrals and 192 control cases were actually included in the experimental and control samples.

Referral from the School

When YCS indicated that it could accept a number of clients for the project, the names of those selected were drawn from the pool and given both to the school guidance department and to the agency. Neither the school nor the agency was given the names of other girls who had been selected as control cases, and they were not informed of the students who constituted the rest of the potential problem cases.

The girls selected for referral had to be approached with an explanation of the program and invited to accept help from YCS. They had to obtain parental permission to leave the school premises during school hours and arrange appointments with the agency within their school schedules. In addition, they had to be given some rationale for this unusual attention directed toward them. Furthermore, in keeping with the design of the research, the entire entering class of girls, including the potential problem cases, were given a series of tests and asked to fill out questionnaires so that uniform information would be available to describe the experimental and control samples.

Acceptance at the Agency

Just as the school had no choice under the design of the project, with respect to which student it could refer to YCS, so, too, the agency relinquished its freedom to decide by its own criteria which girls it wished to accept for treatment. Both accepted this restriction to protect the validity of the experimental results from unknown selective processes that would affect the equivalence of the experimental and control cases. In the interest of the preventive goal of the project, it is also to be noted that the agency agreed to accept clients without the overt presenting problems customary for its intake, which is a novel situation for a voluntary social agency.

From the standpoint of evaluative research, the requirement of arbitrary referral and acceptance created an experimental population that could be expected to differ in some ways from the usual clientele of the agency, but in what ways it was not possible to say. One might speculate that Vocational High students were less motivated to accept help than clients who came on their own initiative. However, adolescent girls were often seen by YCS under conditions not likely to encourage positive motivation. They frequently came with problems and difficulties that were serious and with attitudes resistant or even hostile to adult help. The arbitrary referrals from Vocational High might not have been as visibly in need of help as some of the usual clients of YCS. But, as previously indicated, the preventive objective of the project accepted this as the major question to examine. That is, could help given *before* problems were clearly visible prevent them from developing? It was not the effectiveness of the agency with its usual clientele that was in question but rather the effectiveness of its special effort with a determinate clientele that was to be examined through the experimental project.

Research Data Obtained for the Study

With the focus of the research on evaluation of effectiveness by comparing referred and control samples, data on criteria of success and change were required.

For experimental and control cases alike, information was obtained about *school performance and behavior*. Did the student finish school or drop out? Was she ever suspended or expelled from school? Was she "truant" from school? Did she pursue the vocational training progam provided for her? Was her attendance at school good or poor? Was her school conduct satisfactory or unsatisfactory? Did she receive honors, awards, and good ratings for school service? Did teachers regard her as outstanding or as presenting a serious problem to them?

Some *out-of-school behavior* also is indicative of getting into trouble but this was more difficult to obtain without resources for an extended field follow-up. Out-of-wedlock pregnancy, however, was one event that became known to the school and represented unsatisfactory behavior and its was included among the criteria. Also, getting into trouble with police or becoming known through delinquent acts was a relevant negative behavioral criterion, and an effort was made to obtain information about this for experimental and control cases through use of the Social Service Exchange, in which contact with juvenile authorities as well as social agencies is recorded. In general, it might be expected that out-of-school serious trouble for a girl would result in her removal from school or impairment of her school record so that school continuity was considered a reflection at least in part of out-of-school situation.

It may be asked whether such behavioral and objective criteria as these can be expected to reflect the type of treatment offered by an agency such as YCS. From one point of view, the agency is not directing its primary effort to achieving school continuity and good behavior. It is more likely to see itself as seeking to achieve optimal functioning, healthy personalities, satisfactory interpersonal relations, and the like. It can certainly be argued, however, that the latter are not ends in themselves but are basic to "normal and appropriate" living and hence the more objective criteria are minimum secondary objectives of treatment.

Two direct measures of *personality change* were used, the Junior Personality Quiz and the Make A Sentence Test. The JPQ is a questionnaire containing items that have been selected through factor analysis to reflect twelve personality dimensions. This personality test was expressly developed for use with young adolescents between twelve and sixteen years of age. Its dimensions have meaningful relationship in content to the more fully developed 16 Personality Factor Test that has been widely used in studies of adult personality.

It may be argued that the type of treatment to which the adolescent girls referred to YCS were exposed cannot be expected to affect fundamental personality characteristics such as those presumably measured by these tests. Persons may not change basically from limited contact with social workers. This may very well be true but it is an open question and one on which light may be shed by examining these measures. Plausible differences to be expected from "healthier," "more normal," "less disturbed," "better functioning" persons may readily be hypothesized in terms of the categories of these tests and therefore they may suggest differences between treated and control cases that are in directions accepted as indicative of successful treatment.

A more superficial level of change for successfully treated adolescent girls might be expected to be reflected in *general attitudes* toward themselves and their situations. Particularly relevant attitudes might be those concerned with self-assessment of difficulties, of felt capacity to handle their own problems, and of attitudes toward accepting help with their problems. A short questionnaire was included to permit the girls to rate how they felt, whether they felt better "now" than in the recent past, how well they were getting along with friends, schoolmates, and family, whether they felt they were bothered by many problems, and whether they felt that they would be able to take care of these problems in the future.

In addition to the objective criteria and the more clinical criteria that have just been described, another behavioral measure was sought that might possibly have some relationship to changes induced by treatment and hence become available as an interpretable criterion of successful perventive treatment. This was a general *sociometric questionnaire* asking the student to list classmates who are "friends of yours, whom you pal around with." Several alternative hypotheses bearing on succesful treatment experience might be investigated with such sociometric data. First, it might be hypothesized that casework treatment might reduce perception of social isolation at school or increase gregariousness. Second, it might be hypothesized that the healthier girls would be more often chosen than those with more manifest problems. Third, the hypothesis might be proposed that composition of the friendship circle might change for successfully treated girls toward greater association with those showing positive rather than negative characteristics. Thus successfully influenced clients might be expected to have fewer "bad associates." In particular, changes through the years in the type of choices made and received might reflect trends in positive or negative directions that could be indicative of beneficial influence from YCS.

In the most general terms, the program tried to help adolescent girls who face crises "to add significantly to their repertoire of reality-based problem-solving techniques and thus improve their crisis-coping capacity for the future." It is hoped that this intervention helped them emerge relatively undamaged from the critical period of adolescence.

Effects of Social Work Service

Experimental and control cases were, as intended, essentially alike at the beginning of the experimental project. This was to be expected from the random procedure of assigning potential problem cases to experimental and control groups.

The potential problem group itself (including both experimental and control cases) differed from the remaining girls in their school classes (residual cases) in the "negative" ways one would expect from the deliberate selection of potential problem girls to constitute the pool from which experimental and control cases were chosen. For example, a significantly smaller proportion of potential problem than of residual cases remained throughout the three high school years. We may be reasonably confident therefore, that the therapeutic program for experimental cases among the potential problem group was offered to girls who were less promising, girls who were, for the most part, "in need of treatment," as the social workers saw them.

Almost all of the girls (95 per cent) received some treatment services, and that half of these had 17 or more treatment contacts with social workers.

Indeed, only 16 per cent of the 189 girls in the experimental group had fewer than five such contacts, whereas 44 per cent of them had more than 20 treatment contacts. Therefore, the experimental cases as a group were clearly well-exposed to the therapeutic program. In short, the experimental cases consisted of high school girls more likely to get into trouble, recognized by social workers as needing treatment, and actually receiving treatment.

Measures of effect are provided by the periodic testing procedures at the end of each school year and by the collection of terminal data about each potential problem case three years after entrance into high school or as of a cut-off date in the summer of 1960. Four cohorts were subject to the experimental program, beginning with the cohort entering in September, 1955. Therefore, the normal three-year period of the high school had elapsed for the first three of the cohorts by the terminal date in 1960. For the fourth cohort, only two years had elapsed. In the analysis of effects, where criteria are appropriately applied only to cases with the longer time span (for example, graduation from high school), the first three cohorts taken together will be examined. This group of cases had the longest exposure to the therapeutic program. Where lapse of time is less relevant (school grades or behavior ratings), the fourth cohort will be included and the total potential problem sample examined. For all cohorts the random selection procedure resulted in equivalent duration of time for experimental and control cases when measures of effect were taken.

The samples used in the analysis may be summarized as follows:

Elapsed time from school entrance to terminal date:	Experimental cases	Control cases	Total cases
Cohorts with three years elapsed time	129	132	261
Cohort with two years elapsed time	60	60	120
All cohorts	189	192	381

Completion of School

School Status at the End of the Project

Identical proportions of all experimental and control cases had graduated from high school by the termination of the project: 29 per cent of each. Equal proportions had left school without graduation or were in school, either in their normal grades or below normal grade. Success in the sense of graduation or achieving normally expected grade was the school status of 53 per cent of both experimental and control cases and lack of success in the sense of dropping out of school or being behind normal grade in school was the school status of 47 per cent.

When only those girls are considered who could be observed over three full school years, 48 per cent of both the experimental and the control cases had graduated or were in normal grade. By way of contrast, 65 per cent of the residual cases who could have graduated actually did finish high school.

Clearly the treatment program had no discernible impact with respect to the criterion of graduation from high school.

Highest School Grade Completed

Gradaution is the formal symbol of completion of high school. Neverthe-les, girls who complete their senior year of high school, whether they formally graduate or not, represent a higher level of success when compared to those who do not remain in school as long. Each successive grade completed is that much more education. Proportionately more of the experimental cases than of the control cases completed higher grades of school, although the differ-ences between the two groups are not statistically significant. Among experi-mental cases, 49 per cent compared to 42 per cent among control cases com-pleted the senior year whether they graduated or not. Completing at least the junior year were 73 per cent of the experimental cases and 64 per cent of the control cases. None of the experimental cases compared to 4 per cent of the control cases failed to complete at least the freshman year of high school.

Concerning the number of years attended by those girls who might have attended any high school at least four years by the terminal date of the project, 56 per cent of the experimental cases and 49 per cent of the control cases at-tended four or more years of high school, and 83 per cent compared to 75 per cent attended at least three years. The distribution for residual cases, pre-sented for comparison, shows that significantly more of them than either experimental or control cases attended high school four or more years.

A smaller percentage of experimental cases (52 per cent) than of control cases (56 per cent) were suspended or discharged from school during the period of the project but, again, the difference is not statistically significant. When the reasons for suspension and discharge are classified into nonpunitive and punitive, slightly more of the control than the experimental cases were removed from school for nonpunitive reasons, such as poor health, employ-ment, transfer, or other circumstances not reflecting misbehavior or poor academic performance. This difference hints at the possibility that the ser-vices given to girls by the social agency helped those with circumstantial problems somewhat more than it helped those with behavior problems. This is only the barest of speculations, of course, in view of the minimal difference observed, but it may be worth noting when considering benefits of service pro-grams to high school girls with potential problems.

Taken together, the findings with respect to completion of school can be said to support only an extremely cautious suggestion that the treatment pro-gram had any effect. At most, it can be said that extremely small differences in staying in school favor the experimental cases. Since the differences are not statistically significant, only their consistency permits even this cautious conclusion.

Academic Performance

Grades Earned in Vocational and Academic Subjects

The number of failures can be taken as one indication of academic performance. If the treatment program had any effect, it should be most evident after it had been in operation some time, either because of cumulative influences or because selectively students who perform better stay in school. We know that similar proportions of experimental and control cases drop out. Therefore, unless some factor is operating to differentiate them, similar proportions ought to show failures.

The trend of failures for both vocational and academic subjects are essentially similar. Decreasing proportions of both experimental and control cases are found to have failures between their first and third years, but the decrease is greater for experimental cases. Thus for vocational subjects 40 per cent of the experimental cases had one or more failures their first year but only 16 per cent their third year, and this difference is statistically significant. On the other hand, for control cases there were 31 per cent with one or more failures the first year and 20 per cent the third year, a substantial decrease to be sure but the difference does not reach statistical significance. The corresponding trend for academic subjects is to be noted: a statistically significant decrease from 39 per cent to 24 per cent for experimental cases compared to a smaller decrease, not statistically significant, from 31 per cent to 20 per cent for control cases. It is further to be noted that the record of experimental cases is not as good as that of control cases in the initial year (although the difference is not statistically significant), whereas it is better or equal to that of the control cases in the third year.

The finding is not so clear when academic performance is measured by the number of A and B grades recorded.

Such high grades are about equally found for experimental and control cases at each year with slight tendencies for proportionately fewer A's and B's in the later years, except for a minor counter trend among experimental cases in vocational subjects. None of the differences is statistically significant.

If one is to interpret these findings as evidence of an effect of the treatment program, it must be seen as an effect mediated through the selection process. Rather than conclude that academic performance as reflected in grades is directly improved by the program available to experimental cases, it is more exact to say that girls who would earn better grades (especially fail fewer subjects) were helped to remain in school. Such a positive selective effect is nevertheless a constructive, if modest, achievement to be attributed to the treatment program.

Advancement with Class and Assignment to Cooperative Work-Study Program

Associated with performance in subjects but dependent as well on additional evaluations by the teachers, the promotion or detention of a student at the end of each school year and the decision to assign at the normal time to the cooperative work-study program are further indications of general academic performance.

A slightly greater proportion of experimental cases than of control cases advanced normally with their classes. Thus 74 per cent of all the experimental compared to 70 per cent of the control cases remained in their normal class, whereas 24 per cent of the former and 28 per cent of the latter were held back or reclassified to lower standing vocational programs and the same proportion of both groups (2 per cent) were advanced above the normal levels for their classes. None of these differences is statistically significant and can only be taken as a possible suggestion of better performance by experimental cases.

At this high school, students are placed in work-study jobs in the industry for which they are trained when their work is adequate and they are deemed responsible by teachers of vocational subjects and by the guidance counselors. This is a prized assignment since it provides on-the-job experience, apprentice wages, and potential access to the job market after graduation. Assignments are normally made for the second semester of the junior year and continued throughout the last year of high school. Occasionally, students will be assigned for the first time at the beginning of their senior year if they have shown improvement deemed to warrant it, and occasionally they will be dropped from the work-study program if they do not perform adequately in it.

No differences of significance are found between experimental and control cases in the pattern of assignment. For both groups, 48 per cent were never selected. Slightly more of the control than the experimental cases (48 per cent and 45 per cent, respectively) were assigned in their junior year but a few more of the latter were assigned later, so that altogether half of each group (51 per cent of the experimental and 49 per cent of the control cases) participated in the "co-op" training program.

Honors and Awards, and Service Ratings

Slightly greater percentages of control cases than experimental cases had entries in their records of awards and honors, but in both groups the numbers were few. Only 14 per cent of the former and 9 per cent of the latter were so recognized. Similarly, more of the control cases (65 per cent) than the experimental cases (59 per cent) had at least one service rating, but this difference also is not statistically significant.

In recapitulation of the findings with respect to the several measures of academic performance, we note the positive selective effect of the treatment program in reducing failing grades in academic subjects.

School-Related Behavior

A number of aspects of behavior are related to school but not so directly to academic performance as the aspects previously considered. In this section we examine such measures of effect as attendance and truancy, conduct marks and officially noted teacher ratings for "character traits," as well as special ratings obtained from those responsible for guidance and discipline.

Attendance

No consistent or significant differences were found between the attendance records of experimental and control cases. Calculation of the unexcused-absence rate shows that slightly more than one-third of both groups were absent on the average one day a month or less in their initial year; nearly half the cases in school three years later had this low rate of absences. Experimental cases show a slightly better rate for the latter year (49 per cent compared to 43 per cent with less than ten days, not a statistically significant difference). The decrease in unexcused absences in excess of this rate was more substantial for experimental cases than for control cases, falling from 40 per cent in the first year to 23 per cent in the third year, a statistically significant difference for those with 18 or more days of unexcused absences. This decrease occurs primarily between the second and third years when a lesser decrease for control cases is also apparent.

As pointed out in the discussion of academic performance, differences through time for such measures as attendance may be taken as a positive selective effect of the treatment program provided for experimental cases, but since these cases do not differ significantly from the control cases on these measures one must make no claim for direct effects.

Truancy

There were 107 problem-potential cases who were "truant" during the project; 62, or 58 per cent of these cases, were control cases and 45, or 42 per cent were experimental cases. The difference between experimental and control cases shows the former to have the better record and is substantial enough to take note of, although it does not quite reach the criterion of statistical significance adopted in this analysis. Instances of truancy occur for experimental cases disproportionately in the year of cohort entry when 42 per cent of them are reported. Truancies in later years are disproportionately greater for control cases: being 74 per cent compared to 58 per cent for experimental cases, but with such small numbers of truancies reported this noticeable difference is not quite statistically significant.

We are probably justified in a cautious conclusion that experimental cases were less truant than control cases as an effect of the social work program. This is an effect that might be expected in view of the weekly schedule of interviews or group sessions, attendance at which was of immediate and constant concern to the social workers. Since these scheduled contacts with the social workers took place during the school day, encouragement to meet the appointment with the caseworker or group leader was tantamount to encouragement to come to school. It is perhaps surprising that more favorable truancy and school attendance records were not found for the experimental cases. Nevertheless, the effect that does appear must be accepted as a positive achievement of the treatment program.

Conduct Marks

Each student's official school record includes, for each term, a teacher's rating on "conduct," that is, on appropriate behavior or misbehavior that may or may not subject the student to some form of discipline. We might expect such behavior to be affected favorably as a result of the therapeutic attention to which the experimental cases were subjected.

In each year, the difference between experimental and control cases was minimal and there were no consistent trends that changed the relationship between the distributions of conduct marks for two groups of cases. Significant decreases occurred between the first and third years in the proportions of both experimental and control cases that received unsatisfactory marks for conduct. The selective process apparently operated with equal effect whether the girls did or did not participate in the therapeutic program. It is to be noted, however, that the major decrease for experimental cases with unsatisfactory conduct marks occurred between the initial and the second years, whereas for the control cases the decrease between each year was more even.

Using conduct marks as a criterion, no interpretable effect from the treatment program was found for the experimental cases.

Teacher Ratings for Character Traits and Work Traits

For each term the student's homeroom teacher, on the basis of reports from all the student's teachers, rated the student on a number of "character traits" and "work traits" and these ratings became part of the official record of the student. Ratings were on a scale from 1 (very poor) to 5 (excellent). The "character traits" rated were: interest, industry, initiative, courtesy, cooperation, self-control, appearance, dependability, and health habits. The "work traits" were: care of tools and equipment, "follows instructions," neatness, speed, attitude, use of English, safety, and workmanship. The records were not entirely consistent in the extent to which all traits were rated but there were usually four or five of each list that were rated. So far as we were able to determine from discussing the ratings with school staff, the teachers varied not only in the meanings and standards they applied but also in the extent to which students were known well enough for judgments to be made. This accounts in part for incomplete ratings for some students and full ratings for others. It is likely that behavior that was noticeably deviant—either negatively or positively—would call the student sufficiently to the teacher's attention so that traits would be rated for her.

With these reservations, the utility of such ratings is obviously limited. Nevertheless, one may assume that students who made up the experimental and control cases had equal opportunities to be rated in the same manner and hence any differences that they exhibited had equal chances of being reflected in the ratings. We have averaged the ratings for each year and/or the comparison of experimental and control cases.

Essentially, the findings for teacher ratings parallel those for conduct marks: no significant differences appear between experimental and control cases, but the latter tend to have slightly higher ratings. Average ratings for both experimental and control cases shift significantly upward between the first and third years, but the shift is approximately the same for both groups of cases. There is no evidence, therefore, of an effect of the treatment program so far as this measure is concerned.

We may summarize the findings on all the measures that have been grouped together as school-related behavior by noting that none of them supplies conclusive evidence of an effect by the therapeutic program. However, the relatively better showing of experimental cases with respect to truancy suggests that the surveillance that accompanies the rendering of treatment services tends to have some effect, and this possibility is by no means a trivial achievement if further research were to show that it does indeed occur. Other deviant forms of behavior have often been observed to be concomitants of truancy. An additional conclusion is suggested by the findings with respect to trends on the measures here examined through the three years observed: that there is some tendency for a favorable differential to develop for experimental cases through the selective process. It would appear that if girls remain in school, those with the benefit of the treatment program exhibit somewhat less negative school-related behavior. From the point of view of the school a less deviant population remains and, possibly, educational objectives might more readily be achieved for them. Likewise, a student body resulting from such favorable selective processes might constitute a more favorable context for students who are not deviant in the ways exhibited by the problem-potential segment of the school population.

Out-of-School Behavior

In the design of the research, no interviews out of the school setting with potential problem cases were planned, since we did not wish to vitiate the experiment by giving special attention to the control cases. School behavior and performance were considered appropriate criteria within the scope of the research. Some information could be obtained, however, that bears on out-of-school behavior.

Entries on Health Record

Matters of health arising from acute circumstances, as well as the results of periodic health examinations by the school nurse and physicians serving the school, are recorded for each student on a health record. Such information covers a broad range of observations, including overweight and underweight, allergies, psychosomatic complaints, and emotional or psychological difficulties. It was considered possible that a treatment program addressed in major part to more positive mental health attitudes and self-understanding might be reflected in such school health records. Believing that the records were not sufficiently detailed for refined diagnostic categories, we have taken the frequency of all entries as a rough index of health status. Experimental and control cases are compared on this basis.

Somewhat fewer entries on the health records are found to be made for experimental cases but the difference from control cases is not statistically significant. There are significant decreases for both groups of cases between the year of cohort entry and the last year observed. It is likely that, in addition to the effects of selection, the older ages of the girls constituting the latter cases would affect this measure. The school health personnel might be less likely to make note of minor health problems for sixteen- to eighteen-year-old than for thirteen- to fifteen-year-old girls, and the girls themselves might be less likely to bring such problems to the attention of school personnel.

Attention of Authorities and Agencies

To see whether experimental and control cases might differ in the extent to which they had come to the attention of the police, courts, and other agencies of community control, the potential problem cases were cleared through the Social Service Exchange at the terminal date of the project. However, the appearance of any entries, especially those with explicit reference to the girls themselves, was so infrequent that it is meaningless to compare experimental and control cases on this measure.

When a girl became involved in court proceedings for some offense, and it was known to the school, a notation was kept and this was taken as a further indication of deviant out-of-school behavior. We cannot accept the information as accurate under the more or less informal manner it was recorded, but the data available do not differentiate experimental and control cases in any event. Thirteen of the former (7 per cent) and nine of the latter (5 per cent) were noted to have been involved in court cases.

Out-of-Wedlock Pregnancy

Because premarital pregnancy is cause for suspension from school, and a rule made it mandatory that resumption of schooling for unmarried mothers must be in a different school, somewhat more reliable information was available about out-of-wedlock pregnancy than other forms of nonschool deviant behavior. To be sure, some such pregnancies were probably undetected, especially those that occurred so late in the school year that they did not become obvious, and it is quite likely that some girls who did not return after the summer recess dropped out of school for this reason. Some pregnancies probably remained undetected because of abortions. It is also likely that some girls gave birth during the summer and returned to school without the pregnancy ever coming to the schools' attention. On the other hand, sex and pregnancy, being sensitive areas of concern for adolescents of high school age, and symptoms of pregnancy, being fairly obvious, the school's effort to identify instances of out-of-wedlock pregnancy was persistent. For all the potential problem cases (except five where data were not available), out-of-wedlock pregnancy was reported for 41 girls, or 11 percent. Of these 41 girls, 23 (56 per cent) were control cases and 18 (44 per cent) were experimental cases, a difference that favors the latter but is not statistically significant.

On the very limited measures of out-of-school behavior available, we may note, in summary, that only the slightest advantage was found for experimental cases. We find very little evidence, therefore, of effect on these measures of the therapeutic program.

Personality Tests

The Junior Personality Quiz was the personality test used throughout the series of test periods in the research.

On only two factors was there the suggestion that experimental and control cases differed significantly or meaningfully.

Compared to control cases, scores on the factor designated as Will Control vs. Relaxed Casualness change toward the higher pole of the dimension for experimental cases. Thus we may conclude that the treatment program promoted personality test responses indicating greater self-control, orderly and persistent behavior. These traits did not increase for the comparable control cases.

Although not statistically significant, slight numerical trends with respect to the factor, Adventurous Cyclothymia vs. Withdrawn Schizothymia, occur in opposite directions for experimental and control cases. The former increase in boldness, whereas the latter increase in shyness, aloofness, lack of confidence. This is a suggestive difference in keeping with the objectives of the treatment program to which the experimental cases were exposed.

On the other ten factors that make up this personality test no interpretable differences appear between experimental and control cases. We must conclude therefore, that the treatment program had only the barest effect on personality changes insofar as this instrument detects them.

The Make A Sentence Test—a projective sentence-completion test with standardized scoring developed in part for purposes of this research failed to reveal interpretable differences and therefore the data will not be presented.

Thus with the use of two standardized measures of personality—one "objective" and the other "projective"—only the barest evidence of an experimental effect of the treatment program can be found.

Sociometric Data

Sociometric choices were analyzed for those students who remained in school throughout the four testing periods and these data will be considered here.

Between the first and fourth test periods, the percentages of control and residual cases naming one or more "serious problem" students decreases, whereas a greater proportion of experimental cases named one or more "serious problem" students. Even so, the differences between the three groups of cases is not large enough to be statistically significant.

When the sociometric data are considered with respect to "outstanding" students named by and choosing experimental control, and residual cases, the trends are similar for both of the potential problem samples (experimental and control cases); no significant differences appear between them. Whether naming or chosen by "outstanding" students, increased proportions of such students are found at the fourth test period when compared to the first period, and these differences are statistically significant. This is merely evidence, of course, that all students become better known as they remain in school and this phenomenon does not appear differentially to any meaningful degree for experimental and control cases. The same trend, however, is sufficiently greater for residual cases than for either of the potential problem samples that the differences found between the residual and the experimental and control cases taken together at the fourth test period are statistically significant. Although not differentiated from one another, both the experimental and the control cases are found to be less likely to name or be named by "outstanding" students than the residual cases. Slightly fewer of the experimental than the control cases at the fourth testing period are found to name or be chosen by "outstanding" students, but the differences are small and cannot constitute evidence of a negative result of the treatment program.

With respect to sociometric volume—that is, the total number of students named by or choosing girls in the several samples of the research population—there are no important differences between experimental, control, and residual cases. The trend is for each of the three groups of cases to name more students at the fourth than at the first test period. Likewise, they are chosen by more at the later period, with the residual cases somewhat more likely to be chosen, but not to a statistically significant degree.

The sociometric data do not show evidence of effect from the treatment program. Insofar as the hypothesis that the program would reduce the undesirable associations of the experimental cases is concerned, there is no evidence to support such a conclusion. Nor has there been an evident effect on the level of general popularity of experimental as compared to control cases.

Conclusion

The attitude, personality test, and sociometric data presented have failed to detect in any important respect an effect of the experimental treatment program. The findings are not entirely negative, since some of the patterns of responses show slight indications that experimental cases appear somewhat less unfavorable in a number of parallel instances. It is clear, however, that response and self-report measures are not more sensitive criteria of effects of the treatment program than the objective behaviors examined in the previous chapter.

We must conclude that, with respect to all of the measures we have used to examine effects of the treatment program, only a minimal effect can be found.